PLACE-BASED SPACES FOR NETWORKED LEARNING

With the boundaries of place softened and extended by digital communications technologies, learning in a networked society necessitates new distributions of activity across time, space, media, and people; and this development is no longer exclusive to formally designated spaces such as school classrooms, lecture halls, or research laboratories. *Place-Based Spaces for Networked Learning* explores how the qualities of physical places make both formal and informal education in a networked society possible. Through a series of investigations and case studies, it illuminates the structural composition and functioning of complex learning environments.

This book offers a wealth of key design elements and attributes for productive learning that educational designers can reuse in multiple contexts. The chapters examine how places are modified, expanded, or supplemented by networking technologies and practices in order to create spaces in which learners can collaboratively develop new understandings, connections, and capabilities. Utilizing a range of diverse but complementary perspectives from anthropology, archaeology, architecture, geography, psychology, sociology, and urban studies, *Place-Based Spaces for Networked Learning* addresses how material places and digital spaces are understood; how sense can be made of new assemblages and configurations of tasks, tools, and people; how the real-time analysis of new flows of data can inform and entertain users of a space; and how access to the digital realm changes our experiences with both places and other people.

Lucila Carvalho is a Research Fellow in the Centre for Research on Learning and Innovation at the University of Sydney, Australia. Her Ph.D. combined research in design, learning technology, and the sociology of knowledge. She has studied and carried out research in Australia, New Zealand, the UK, and Brazil. She has published and presented her work at various international conferences in the fields of education, sociology, systemic functional linguistics, design, and software engineering.

Peter Goodyear is Professor of Education and Co-Director of the Centre for Research on Learning and Innovation at the University of Sydney, Australia. He has been carrying out research in the field of learning and technology since the early 1980s, working in the UK, Europe, and Australia. He has published nine books and over 100 journal articles and book chapters.

Maarten de Laat is Professor of Professional Development in Social Networks at the Welten Institute of the Open University of the Netherlands. His research concentrates on exploring social learning strategies and networked relationships that facilitate learning and professional development. He has published and presented his research extensively in international research journals, books, and conferences. He is Co-Chair of the biannual International Networked Learning Conference.

The land around us is a reflection, not only of our practical and technological capacities, but also of our culture and society—our very needs, our hopes, our preoccupations and dreams. ... The way in which human identity might be tied to place is thus merely indicative of the fundamental character of our engagement with the world—of all our encounters with persons and things—as always 'taking place' in place.

(Malpas 1999, pp. 1–22)

Malpas, J., 1999. *Place and Experience: A Philosophical Topography*. Cambridge: Cambridge University Press.

In having a body, we are spatially located creatures: we must always be facing some direction, have only certain objects in view, be within reach of certain others. How we manage the space around us, then, is not an afterthought; it is an integral part of the way we think, plan and behave, a central element in the way we shape the very world that constrains and guides our behavior.

(Kirsh 1995, p. 31)

Kirsh, D., 1995. The intelligent use of space. *Artificial Intelligence*, 73, 31–68.

Culture furnishes the forms, nature the materials; in the superimposition of the one upon the other human beings create the artefacts with which, to an ever increasing extent, they surround themselves.

(Ingold 2013, p. 38)

Ingold, T., 2013. *Making: Anthropology, Archaeology, Art and Architecture.* New York: Routledge.

[T]he fibres of culture and nature compose one continuous fabric. Interwoven thus, these fibres are inseparable in experience even if they are distinguishable upon analysis or reflection.

(Casey 1993, p. 256)

Casey, E., 1993. *Getting Back into Place: Toward a Renewed Understanding of the Place-World.* Bloomington: Indiana University Press.

Architectural order is created when the organization of parts makes visible their relationships to each other and the structure as a whole. When these relationships are perceived as mutually reinforcing and contributing to the singular nature of the whole, then a conceptual order exists.

(Ching 2007, p. x)

Ching, F., 2007. *Architecture: Form, Space, and Order.* Hoboken, NJ: John Wiley & Sons.

What makes a building learn is its physical connection to the people within.

(Brand 1994, p. 209)

Brand, S., 1994. *How Buildings Learn. What Happens after They're Built.* London: Phoenix Illustrated.

Because humans rely on things that have to be maintained so that they can be relied on, humans are caught in the lives and temporalities of things, their uncertain vicissitudes and their insatiable needs.

(Hodder 2012, p. 208)

Hodder, I., 2012. *Entangled: An Archaeology of the Relationships between Humans and Things.* Chichester: Wiley-Blackwell.

[F]or pedagogy to put us in relation to thinking—it must create places in which to think without already knowing what we should think.

(Ellsworth 2005, p. 54)

Ellsworth, E., 2005. *Places of Learning: Media, Architecture, Pedagogy.* New York: Routledge.

Ubiquitous devices tease the fine line between familiarity and unfamiliarity. As such they work the thresholds of the urban environment and assist the tuning of place.

(Coyne 2010, p. 169)

Coyne, R., 2010. *The Tuning of Place: Sociable Spaces and Pervasive Digital Media.* Cambridge, MA: MIT Press.

We never educate directly, but indirectly by means of the environment. Whether we permit chance environments to do the work, or whether we design environments for the purpose makes a great difference.

(Dewey 1916/1938, p. 17)

Dewey, J., 1916/1938. *Democracy and Education.* Whitefish, MT: Kessinger.

PLACE-BASED SPACES FOR NETWORKED LEARNING

*Edited by Lucila Carvalho, Peter Goodyear,
and Maarten de Laat*

Routledge
Taylor & Francis Group

NEW YORK AND LONDON

First published 2017
by Routledge
711 Third Avenue, New York, NY 10017

and by Routledge
2 Park Square, Milton Park, Abingdon, Oxon OX14 4RN

Routledge is an imprint of the Taylor & Francis Group, an informa business

Library of Congress Cataloging-in-Publication Data
Names: Carvalho, Lucila, 1966- editor. | Goodyear, Peter, 1952- editor. | Laat, Maarten
de, editor.
Title: Place-based spaces for networked learning / edited by Lucila Carvalho,
Peter Goodyear and Maarten de Laat.
Description: New York, NY : Routledge, 2016. | Includes bibliographical references
and index.
Identifiers: LCCN 2016001716 | ISBN 9781138850866 (hardback) |
ISBN 9781138850880 (pbk.) | ISBN 9781315724485 (ebook)
Subjects: LCSH: Self-managed learning—Computer networks. |
Mobile communication systems in education.
Classification: LCC LC33 .P53 2016 | DDC 371.39/430785—dc23
LC record available at http://lccn.loc.gov/2016001716

ISBN: 978-1-138-85086-6 (hbk)
ISBN: 978-1-138-85088-0 (pbk)
ISBN: 978-1-315-72448-5 (ebk)

Typeset in Bembo
by Keystroke, Station Road, Codsall, Wolverhampton

Printed and bound in the United States of America by Sheridan

We dedicate this book, with love, to our partners and children:
Mark and Bruno; Sonia, Emily, and Michael; Britta, Jasper, and Leni.

CONTENTS

PREFACE

In 1989, I led a team of educational innovators who created an unusual master's degree program. It made extensive use of computer-mediated communications (CMC)—email and online discussion boards—to promote interaction between students and staff. The students came to our campus at Lancaster University for an intensive one-week induction to the course, and in that precious period we also helped them learn how to use a computer and how to make a direct dial-up connection to the university's mainframe. Connection speeds were very slow, the dial-up service unreliable, and social practices for CMC in their infancy. But CMC was the only way for the staff and students to interact during the long periods between on-campus residential sessions, and the need for communication and community overcame the limitations of educational technology that was not yet fit for purpose. The program ran for many years. It went through several cycles of pedagogical, organizational, and technological evolution and became the world's longest continually running master's degree by "e-learning." By the late 1990s we were referring to educational approaches like this as instances of "networked learning"—our improvised practices ran ahead of terminology—and not long after we found ourselves working in an organized field, with conferences, journals, and books reporting various blends of research and development, theory, and experience.

Place-Based Spaces for Networked Learning (PBSNL) evokes a different century. In 1989, the university had to provide all the kit and instruction that the students needed: computers, printers, modems, software, etc. Our design decisions were tightly constrained by the limited range of usable products. Now, students expect to be able to use their own devices, apps, and service providers, and their activity moves almost seamlessly between social, educational, and work-related spaces. Many young city dwellers depend upon 24/7 ubiquitous connectivity and enjoy (but complain about) data rates that are 30,000 times faster than our master's students' modems allowed. Yet strangely, this always-on mobility is making *place* more important. When you can connect from anywhere, other attributes of physical location become more salient, and opportunities for face-to-face interaction take on a different character and value.

In this book, we try to unravel some of the relationships between place, space, and learning. The authors we have invited to write with us explore a variety of approaches to making sense of the subtle connections between the physical, the digital, and the multiple methods that people use, every day, in coming to understand the world and act capably within it. We have not aimed for consensus, but we hope you will find some interesting lines of correspondence.

Like its sister book—*The Architecture of Productive Learning Networks (APLN)*—PBSNL originates in a large-scale research project on "Learning, Technology and Design" that it has been my great good fortune to lead for the last five years. It has been delightful to collaborate with a convivial team, whose diverse contributions to this work are mentioned in the Acknowledgments. As with *APLN*, Lucila Carvalho has been the real boss—transforming the virtual into the actual with inimitable patience, grace, and wisdom. Lucila and I credit each other with the brilliant idea of inviting Maarten de Laat to help us assemble this collection. His reminders of what is important in networked learning are pure gold.

My thanks to them both, to all the members of the "Laureate team," and to the authors whose rich ideas and experiences we have woven together.

Peter Goodyear
Sydney, November 30, 2015

ACKNOWLEDGMENTS

The idea for this book first arose whilst Lucila Carvalho and Peter Goodyear were putting the finishing touches to *The Architecture of Productive Learning Networks*, which was published by Routledge in 2014. The concept for the new book began to take on a more solid form once Maarten de Laat agreed to join in and we began to build a team of prospective authors.

It gives us great pleasure to acknowledge the invaluable support, feedback, and insightful contributions of the ARC Laureate Project team: Ana Pinto, David Ashe, Dewa Wardak, Kate Thompson, Martin Parisio, Pippa Yeoman, and Roberto Martinez Maldonado. We are also grateful for the encouragement we received from our many colleagues in the Centre for Research on Computer Supported Learning and Cognition (CoCo) at the University of Sydney, the Learning and Teaching Unit at the University of South Australia, and the Welten Institute at the Open University of the Netherlands.

We particularly acknowledge the assistance provided by Patricia Thibaut and Dewa Wardak, who both worked on reviewing references and images, helping in the final stages of the book's production. Pippa Yeoman provided three of the images for the book cover and Mark King worked on photography composition and cover design.

An edited volume cannot materialize without the care and dedication of a network of talented co-authors, and so we would like to specially thank: Ana Pinto, David Ashe, David Parsons, James Lamb, Jos Boys, Juliet Sprake, Kate Booth, Kenn Fisher, Leslie Ashor, Lesley Gourlay, Louise Ravelli, Marcus Foth, Maree Stenglin, Mark Bilandzic, Martin Oliver, Michael Sean Gallagher, Nigel Linge, Nina Bonderup Dohn, Peter Rogers, Philip Poronnik, Pippa Yeoman, Robert Ellis, Robert McMurtrie, Sian Bayne, Shane Dawson, Tina Hinton, and Vivien Hodgson.

It would be hard to imagine some of the places and spaces in this volume, without the striking visual representations that accompany the text. We thank the many people who shared their images and granted us permission to use them in this book. In particular, we thank curators Nicole Durling and Delia Nicholls at the Museum of Old and New Art, Hobart, and Hubert Duprat for allowing one of his art works to be reproduced in this volume.

Our analytical thinking is shaped by many discussions with our academic colleagues in the design, education, and networked learning fields. Special thanks then to Andy Dong, Rob Saunders, Cristina Garduño Freeman, Lina Markauskaite, Peter Reimann, Thomas Ryberg, Peter Sloep, Chris Jones, Shane Dawson, George Siemens, Simon Buckingham Shum, Caroline Haythornthwaite, and David McConnell.

Thanks also to Alex Masulis and Daniel Schwartz at Routledge who have, yet again, provided great help during the development of this book, from idea to artifact.

Last but not least, we acknowledge the financial support provided by the Australian Research Council through an Australian Laureate Fellowship grant to Peter Goodyear: FL100100203 Learning, technology and design: architectures for productive networked learning (2010–2015).

1

PLACE, SPACE, AND NETWORKED LEARNING

Lucila Carvalho, Peter Goodyear, and Maarten de Laat

Learning in a networked society involves new distributions of activity across time, space, media, organizations, and people. Learning is not restricted to specific places. It spills across the boundaries of formally designated sites for learning—like classrooms and lecture halls. It can occur anywhere. Indeed, the growing scale and variety of uses of mobile, personal, connected technologies raise questions about the nature of place. "Where?" is no longer a simple question.

Learning is not coterminous with education. It is much more pervasive than that. People sharpen their skills, have new insights, and achieve deeper understandings of themselves and the world—people *learn*—whether or not they are in the role of "student." People help others learn, without having to be called "teacher." Learning can be intentional or it can be incidental—a by-product of some other activity. Complex learning is often a mixture of the intentional and incidental. Some kinds of learning benefit from conscious self-management, using processes like self-monitoring, repetition, and reflection. But learning can also go unnoticed—human beings have evolved to be very good at learning through observing and copying others, for example, and can do this without being aware of the fact. Learning is woven through the fabric of our daily lives.

This sense of learning being almost ubiquitous has parallels in how people use and experience space (Relph 1976; Tuan 1977; Urry 2002; Massey 2005; Boys 2011, 2015;). Imagination and memory have long allowed us to live in ways that are not completely bound to the here and now. Personal, mobile, digital devices are being used in ways that further soften the boundaries of place. They provide access to much wider sets of resources and people. Their use creates and modulates connections: between people, things, ideas, and experiences. One way to think about, analyze, and understand these connections is in terms of networks—whether networks of people, or more heterogeneous networks of people and things (Hodgson et al. 2014; Jones 2015). Such networks can have many functions. We are particularly interested in relations between networks and learning, broadly defined. Networks are assembled in learning, and learning is shaped by existing networks. So the properties of networks are consequential with respect to learning, and are worth researching, even though they also change. We use the term "learning networks" to denote networks in which learning is a significant activity. It is a large, well-populated category, given what we said earlier about the ubiquity of learning.

In a recent book—*The Architecture of Productive Learning Networks* (*APLN*) (Carvalho and Goodyear 2014)—we presented a method for analyzing the key components of learning networks, illustrated with a dozen case studies. A distinguishing feature of the *APLN* book was that many of the case studies traced participants' learning experiences outwards, from the (digital) network into the material world—into the everyday contexts of life and work. This book—*Place-Based Spaces for Networked Learning* (PBSNL)—examines the flip side: it starts with *places* and traces activity outwards into the digital networks that extend each place. In so doing, we look at how spaces are created for networked learning, and we also challenge the assumption that the "digital" and the "material"—or the "virtual" and the "actual"—are easy to separate, or in fact need to be.

Places Extended by Networked Technologies

The phenomena in which we are interested include the use of networked digital devices to extend the experience of visitors to museums, art galleries, and historical sites (Giaccardi 2012; Jewitt 2012). These uses can be quite simple—the addition of audio information about a painting, or its painter, for instance. They can be more complex—allowing museum visitors to record their own thoughts and feelings and share them with unknown future visitors. Technology use can be formally organized—as when gallery or museum staff create and maintain the network infrastructure and its informational resources. Or it may emerge from the spontaneous activity of visitors to, or inhabitants of, a place—for example, when they make and share images and comments over social media.

Places for formal education, like schools and university campuses, are also being extended with network technologies—both institutionally provided and personally owned (Boys 2011, 2015). Many educational institutions have introduced a "Bring Your Own Device" (BYOD) policy, for example: encouraging students to take responsibility for their own learning tools, and transferring costs to them at the same time. As a consequence, student-owned, networked digital devices are now commonplace in many classrooms and lecture halls—bringing with them almost infinite opportunities for enrichment and distraction. Educational architectures are changing to accommodate the use of new technologies (Taylor 2009; Boys 2011, 2015). At a micro level, this may be as simple as providing more power points for charging batteries. At a meso level, we see new kinds of buildings emerging: new "learning commons," "learning hubs," and reconfigured libraries.

The contributions to this book take *place* as their starting point. In various ways, they examine places as modified (extended, expanded, supplemented, colored) by network technologies and networking practices. They help us see how places, thus extended, contribute to the creation of spaces in which people can collaboratively come to new understandings and/or develop new capabilities.

The technologies involved in networked activity are changing very fast. New consumer devices, media habits, and social networking practices are emerging. As these become more mainstream, they can also become less visible—more taken-for-granted than scrutinized. So the chapters in this volume offer a timely opportunity to examine how the material and the digital, places and spaces are understood; how sense can be made of new assemblages and configurations of tasks, tools, and people; how the real-time analysis of new flows of data can inform and entertain users of a space; how the opening-up of access to the digital realm, anywhere and everywhere, 24/7, changes the experience of being in a place, of a place's constraints and affordances, and of being with other people.

Some of the chapters in the book are rooted in the authors' analyses of specific places. Others show how theoretical ideas from a range of disciplines can be integrated to shed new light on place, space, networks, learning, and other human activities. The relations between human activity, thought, experience, and emotion (on the one hand) and place and technology (on the other) have been objects of attention for many disciplines. Fields such as anthropology, archeology, psychology, sociology, semiotics, geography, architecture, and urban studies have, over the years, had something to say about people's experiences of place, the uses of space, and the mutual shaping of human thought and technology, within them. In *Place-Based Spaces for Networked Learning* we bring some of these diverse but complementary perspectives together, as a way of understanding the structural composition of complex environments in which people learn. In so doing, we hope to contribute to a more comprehensive picture of *architectures* for networked learning.

Analysis to Inform Design

Our main concern is to explore ideas that can be reused. We think of this quite concretely. For ideas to be candidates for reuse, there have to be real people and real work processes in which they can be useful. "Actionable knowledge"—knowledge that can play a significant role in guiding action in the world—only has this status by virtue of a relationship between the knowledge and the needs, actions, and capabilities of its users. We employ the general term "designers" for the users we have in mind: people who work together to elucidate complex problems and propose actions—people whose work results in suggestions for what it might be good to do, to make, to build, or to reconfigure and whose suggestions are usually informed by experience, trial and error, and a relentless testing of assumptions about what is really needed. Design often progresses through reframing the apparent problem, not by advancing neat solutions to the problem as posed.

Thus, when we search for the influence of the qualities of place on activity, we do so with a view to extracting and conceptualizing the role of key design elements in networks. We search for elements that work in a particular context, and seek to understand and explain how they might also be useful in other learning settings. We are interested in identifying key attributes and studying their role in characterizing productive learning in physically situated networks, exploring what connects people in certain locations, and which tools and technologies they use when thus connected.

We also reach out to incorporate understandings from fields that have, for a number of years, been dealing with people's perceptions and experiences of places, as a way of enriching the pool of ideas that may be of use to designers who are working to help other people learn. We are convinced that designers have much to gain from drawing on ideas that explore the material and the digital, intentional and incidental, learning places and networks, in formally defined and informal learning places—schools, universities, research labs, museums, galleries, city streets, parks, and hiking trails, to name a few.

The ACAD Framework

In *The Architecture of Productive Learning Networks* (Carvalho and Goodyear 2014) we described an architecturally inspired framework for design and analysis: for explaining how various structural elements come together in complex learning situations. We call this the Activity-Centred Analysis and Design (ACAD) framework. The key principles motivating ACAD are that in order to understand learning (and in order to successfully design for learning) we must: (i) pay close attention to human activity: to what people actually do—mentally, physically, emotionally, perceptually; and (ii) examine the relations between this activity and the structures within which it emerges. The ACAD framework draws attention to three main kinds of structures—physical, social, and epistemic/intentional. Design work—undertaken prior to the times in which people are acting and learning—can focus on physical, social, and epistemic/intentional design components. In *APLN*, to be concise, we labeled these *set design, social design*, and *epistemic design*. The fourth element in the framework is not designable—this is the actual activity in which people engage: activity in and through which they *co-create* knowledge and *co-configure* their learning environment and their working relationships (divisions of labor, etc.). This insistence on separating what designers can actually design from what people actually do in their subsequent (learning) activity allows conceptual space for these people's agency—in reshaping and reconfiguring what has been designed.

Take an example from design in university education. When analyzing or designing for learning, educational designers will usually consider digital and material elements that come to hand, such as the tools and resources students will access, the arrangement of furniture in a classroom, or the layout of an online learning platform. These types of elements are referred to as components in the "set design" for a particular learning situation. The second designable component concerns social arrangements. It relates to social structures, roles, divisions of labor, etc. It concerns such things as whether educational designers have plans for how learners will be organized: in pairs, groups, the use of scripted roles, etc. In the ACAD framework such structures form part of the "social design." Last but not least, there will normally also be some planning of the tasks students will be asked to undertake. Task design is normally informed by ideas about the nature, form, and structure of knowledge, appropriate sequencing and pacing, relations between different kinds of knowledge and different ways of learning, etc. So we refer to this—in formal educational situations, or more broadly where intentional learning is expected—as "epistemic design."

In the actual flux of real-world activity—in what people are *actually* doing—the epistemic, social, and set become entangled. This is partly because what is designed does not determine activity. For example, students' interpretive work, their improvisation, and their exercise of agency soften and problematize the connections between designers' intentions, student activity, and outcomes. The affordances of the tools they select, or the place in which they choose to work, can reshape the relations between the designers' epistemic goals for a task and what the students actually do, and therefore what they end up learning. This is what we mean by the fourth element: the actual activity in which people engage.

In the case of "informal" or "incidental" learning, these relations between the epistemic, set, and social design components (on the one hand) and what people actually do and learn (on the other) can become even more tenuous. For example, consider the case of a museum which is being visited by small family groups who have no wish to be trammeled by any kind of prescribed educational activity. Does this rule out any legitimate role for "epistemic" and "social" design? We think not. It can still be perfectly appropriate for museum design staff to think in terms of more and less valuable activities, to think about how physical design may be used to "nudge" activity one way rather than another, and to take into account the different modes in which younger and older family members may engage with the spaces and resources of the museum. It is still valuable to think in terms of *tasks*, as invitations to engage in more rather than less valued activities, even if the invitations are offered through the physical configuration of exhibits and even if the invitations may be missed or rejected.

In summary, ACAD helps focus on what designers can do to nudge activity in directions that they believe will be useful to the actors. In analyzing what is happening in the studies reported in the chapters below, we think it can be a valuable discipline to keep these distinctions in mind: What is designable? What has been designed? What then occurs? How is this valued? What can be claimed about the relationships between the designed and what occurs? What can this tell us about how to do things better when it is time to redesign, modify, or augment what has already been set in place?

Additional Sources of Theoretical Ideas

There is now a substantial literature in the field of networked learning and learning networks. Good summaries can be found in Hodgson et al. (2014), Jandric and Boras (2015), Jones (2015), and Bayne et al. (2016). Within this literature, there is a strong focus on pedagogical and design approaches that favor participation, social inclusion, equality of opportunity, empowerment of learners, self-organization, community-building, networking, and collective action. This is not to say that networked learning researchers and practitioners are naive about the difficulties and tensions involved in trying to act on these intentions—particularly when this has to be done within the constraints and power relationships that exist in formal educational institutions. But it is important to stress the distinctive social and educational values that color this field. They distinguish it from the adjacent fields of e-learning/online learning and computer-supported collaborative learning (CSCL), which are more concerned with technical efficiency—serving the expressed needs of the labor market and formal schooling.[1]

This distinctive social orientation within networked learning means that certain kinds of theoretical ideas come to the fore, including ideas associated with the nature of self-directed and adult learning (heutagogy and andragogy), emancipatory and liberationist pedagogies, human agency, and the relations between agency and various kinds of social and material structures.

Each of these has a role to play in understanding the concerns explored in this book. However, we would like to single out a loose program of theoretical work that is proving particularly useful in framing relations between human activity, place, and technology. This sits under the broad title of studies of sociomateriality and is, in part, concerned with repositioning *things* within social life—rediscovering the importance of the material world, attending to the qualities of materials, looking more closely at the nature and functioning of tools and infrastructure, understanding how places come to be as they are, etc.

The theoretical ideas come from a range of disciplines, which—unusually—are in active discussion with each other. Anthropology and archeology have long been the prime disciplines for studies of material culture; ideas from these sources are now being used to make sense of the digital, as well as the material and their hybrids, and to trace links between world, mind, brain, and body (de Marrais, Gosden, and Renfrew 2004; Malafouris and Renfrew 2010; Hodder 2012; Malafouris 2013). Geography provides a source for thinking about how people experience place, the nature of space, mobilities, and flows (Relph 1976; Tuan 1977; Urry 2002; Massey 2005; Boys 2011, 2015). Architecture and urban studies have lately become interested in what the digital means for the material environment, and in ways of understanding how people use, change, and experience increasingly hybrid forms of built space (Mitchell 1995, 2003; McCullough 2004, 2013; Coyne 2010; Shepard 2011). Semiotic research into texts, displays, places, and spaces also contributes to our sense of how people, things, and meanings are interrelated. As Bill Mitchell (2008) so sharply observed, human beings have to be understood as simultaneously making things and making meanings (Kress and Van Leeuwen 2006; O'Toole 2011). In addition, people shape things, and things shape people: there is no room here for technological, social, or geographical determinism (Orlikowski 2010; Shove, Pantzar, and Watson 2012).

A number of core theoretical terms and ideas are used and refined in the chapters below. For now, we think it useful to point out that:

- We are using both "place" and "space" deliberately. Although there are times when these can be used as simple synonyms, and sometimes one is more mellifluous than the other, it is important to note some critical distinctions. Of these, the most common is to interpret "place" as concrete, singular, realized, and experienced and "space" as abstract, generalized, conceptual, and managed.
- We refer to "digital," "physical," "material," and "virtual." These and related terms suffuse the literature on technology and learning. In the ACAD framework, we take the "physical" to include the material and the digital/virtual as well as other kinds of phenomena whose materiality is questionable, yet which have physical effects (e.g. cold weather). Human bodies—and brains—aren't immaterial, of course, but from a design perspective, ACAD mainly treats other people as socially rather than materially related. (For an exception, see our analysis of the training of paramedics in mountain rescue situations—Goodyear and Carvalho 2013.) Some analysts get tangled in their attempts to distinguish cleanly between the digital and the

material (Faulkner and Runde 2011; Hafermalz and Riemer 2015). In our view, two aspects of this distinction matter—the properties and capabilities of the objects concerned (e.g. how they travel, what is needed to make them persist) and the ways in which human beings sense and interact with them (e.g. through vision or touch).

Overview of Chapters

The core of the book consists of a set of empirical research studies, together with some more conceptually oriented pieces. Each chapter contains a description of the place and context in which the research is situated, complemented with an analysis of how material and digital enhancements interact with the activities in that place. The examples are taken from schools, universities, research labs, museums, community-led initiatives, and open spaces. The more conceptually driven chapters introduce analytic perspectives from a range of disciplines, including from philosophy, anthropology, ergonomics, and semiotics. The book concludes with a synthesis chapter that draws out implications for practice, theory, and further research.

Each of the chapters offers a different vantage point from which to view and make sense of selected relations between place, space, activity, experience, and learning. Each offers a good position from which to map some of the ideas that constitute the conceptual landscape.

The first set of chapters revolves around notions of individual experience and activity in a variety of contexts (Chapters 2, 3, and 4). After that comes a set of chapters that arise from research in higher education contexts—currently a fertile area for consideration of relations between place, space, and learning (Chapters 5–9). After these higher education chapters we have grouped some studies based in galleries, museums, outdoor spaces, and grassroots learning spaces (Chapters 10–14). Then, in Chapters 15 and 16 we return to higher education contexts, but the focus moves up a level, to explore how places/spaces come to be designed and managed.

Each of the chapters in this volume provides a unique combination of theoretical ideas, enabling the authors to frame and interpret key phenomena and relationships. In Chapter 2, David Ashe and Nina Bonderup Dohn theorize about relationships between the physical layouts of the "place of learning" in networked learning and the "bodily being" of the learner. Through illustrative examples, the authors discuss how focus is placed and how a physical layout—in combination with what goes on in a learning activity, and the bodily history of the participant—all interact to determine what appears to be "focal" and what is perceived as "the background." In Chapter 3, Ana Pinto discusses the importance of *secondary design elements*—designed features that once in a while "materialize," but which nevertheless play a significant role in sustaining the wider network. Pinto draws on the work of Alexander (2002) to explore relationships between the digital *and* physical "buildings" that support networked learning, arguing that secondary elements nurture deep connections between learners' feelings and aspirations, beyond the more immediate objectives of a network. These ideas are illustrated through the discussion of a hybrid network, run by the Irish National Adult Literacy Agency (NALA), and the analysis of the "Dublin Student Day," an event that takes place once a year. In Chapter 4, Pippa Yeoman speaks of learning as the refining of skill and the development of agency in the learner, within a primary school context. Drawing on Ingold (2011, 2012) and the ACAD framework (Goodyear and Carvalho 2014), Yeoman explores the concept of *improvisation,* arguing that the emergent activity of learners and teachers can be seen as a measured response to the task, the tools, and the people present. Yeoman's reflections on educational design speak of orchestrated moves, and the importance of going beyond notions of bounded spaces within which the learning of others is expected to eventuate. In Chapter 5, Jos Boys discusses the impact of delegating some aspects of learning to non-human components (e.g. studio tutorial, online blog) and the effects of specific breaching intentions on learning. Boys draws on theorists such as Garfinkel (1967), Latour (2005), and others to conceptualize learning as an everyday social and spatial practice, where different levels of membership, and repertoires of learning, exist in higher education—including its spaces, technologies, "rules of the game," and educational frameworks. Boys uses the case of undergraduate interior design students and tutors, with a nuanced and rich analysis of the relationships between physical space and the activity that goes on in it, arguing that improving learning is not just a case of "better" technologies or "innovative" spaces, but something that exists in the spaces in-between the students, their tutors, their setting, and facilities. Lesley Gourlay and Martin Oliver, in Chapter 6, draw on sociomaterial perspectives (e.g. Fenwick, Edwards, and Sawchuk 2011) and theories of space as a social phenomenon (e.g. Massey 2005) to show how spaces are not simply "found," nor are they just "containers" for social practice, but instead, they are constantly generated by students. Gourlay and Oliver argue that the complexity of university students' day-to-day practices, in their courses, relies on heterogeneous networks of people and things. With examples of activity using images and textual data, the authors discuss students' sites of study, showing how even when places seemed to be provided by their institution—for example, the library—some of the students went to great lengths to personalize or adapt them, or to find ways of dealing with their shortcomings. In Chapter 7, Michael Sean Gallagher, James Lamb, and Sian Bayne combine aural, textual, and visual data to analyze online distance learners' representations of learning spaces. Their research project investigates notions of place and institution for distance students enrolled in a master's course in the School of Education (University of Edinburgh, Scotland). The authors reflect on what counts as "place" for these students' digital imaginaries of "the campus." Gallagher, Lamb, and Bayne draw on Mol and Law's (1994; Law and Mol 2001) work on social topology, and on the "spatial turn" in social science research (Fenwick et al. 2011), also questioning the view that space functions as a "static container" for people's actions. Rather, the authors refer to space as a dynamic entity produced by social and material interactions. In the following chapter, Maarten de Laat and Shane Dawson discuss the place-based networked learning potential of the new learning center at the University of South Australia (UNISA) (Chapter 8). This multi-storey building offers an open learning space that students can access 24/7 to conduct their studies, work collaboratively, and establish "learning friendships." The chapter explores the use of a mobile, place-based awareness tool to visualize people's expertise and learning interest as well as their current location, and the support this tool may provide in developing networks and finding people who are working on similar topics. In Chapter 9, Louise Ravelli and Robert McMurtrie outline a social-semiotic model of analysis, where physical and virtual "texts" are questioned in regard to their communicative potential. Ravelli and McMurtrie speak of networked spaces as places that "make meaning" in terms of potential uses, the kinds of relationships that can be enabled by participation in a networked place, and the different ways the component elements are integrated into a meaningful whole. Drawing on Kress and Van Leeuwen (2006) and Halliday (1978), and extending recent work by the authors on Spatial Discourse Analysis (SpDA) (Ravelli and McMurtrie 2015), the chapter discusses the analysis of the reconfiguration of the Menzies Library at the University of New South Wales (Australia). In Chapter 10, Maree Stenglin explores the importance of emotion and space to learning in a museum context. Drawing on analytical tools from social semiotics, namely the concepts of Binding and Bonding (Stenglin 2004), and Macken-Horarik's domains of learning (1996), Stenglin discusses connections between design, emotion, and museum learning, including the nature of the human interaction, the importance of object selection and sequencing, and implications of Binding and Bonding for networked learning. In Chapter 11, Lucila Carvalho addresses museums as spaces for networked learning, discussing the influence of technology on people's experiences of cultural heritage, and emerging co-created, museum-visitor activities. Carvalho combines theoretical ideas from the architectural framework of Goodyear and Carvalho (2014) and Ian Hodder's theory of "entanglement" (2012) to distinguish different kinds of relationships between people and things, within a museum scenario. The Museum of Old and New Art (MONA) provides the backdrop for the discussion of the incorporation of a novel mobile device (the "O") in people's visits to MONA. The analysis reveals nuanced structural relations between people and things, highlighting how one element allows other elements to function in relation to an end—networked learning—and importantly, how key elements come together to contribute to the functioning of the whole, in a cohesive way. In Chapter 12, Nigel Linge, Kate Booth, and David Parsons discuss practicalities of developing and deploying a handheld multimedia guide for museum visitors. The authors use their experience gained in developing and deploying the mi-Guide multimedia visitor guide within the Connecting Manchester telecommunications gallery at the Museum of Science and Industry in Manchester (UK) to highlight an often hidden (but important) side of transforming a museum environment into a learning space. In particular, the authors explore issues associated with presentation style and interface design, technology life span, how network coverage can be maintained through a space, and how the space itself must also offer a worthwhile engagement for those who do not have access to, or wish to engage with, the enhancing technology. In "Citizen Cartographer" (Chapter 13), Juliet Sprake and Peter Rogers introduce the concept of *vantage points,* used professionally in urban and landscape planning, archeology, and the military to survey areas of land that are in the line of sight. Sprake and Rogers argue that, in everyday contexts, tourists and city dwellers use vantage points as places of meeting and reflection. Viewing the urban landscape by looking down or across a distance affects how one feels about space, and offers opportunities for exploring the surrounding area. The Citizen Cartographer project investigates notions associated with how height affects situated awareness of the city. It explores the possibilities of creating a user generated map that shares accessible vantage points so that people can playfully move from one point to another to see many alternate views of the city. The chapter discusses the ideas behind the project and investigates the significance of altitude in contributing to situated learning. It presents a set of perspectives from the service in use as a smartphone app in a range of locations. Mark Bilandzic and Marcus Foth introduce *connected learning* as a design approach in Chapter 14. They argue that learning is not restricted to a particular space, but instead can be seen as an aggregation of individual experiences made through intrinsically motivated, active participation in and across various socio-cultural environments (school, university, cooking class, sports clubs, etc.) as well as online spaces (YouTube, Flickr, Blogs, Facebook, Twitter, etc.). Bilandzic and Foth discuss design aspects that may contribute to successful place-based spaces for connected learning, drawing on observations and interviews with users and managers of three different types of local, community-led learning environments. The chapter reveals how social, spatial, and technological interventions were applied in these spaces to nourish a culture of learning, sharing, and peer interaction. In Chapter 15, Tina Hinton, Pippa Yeoman, Leslie Ashor, and Philip Poronnik discuss research conducted in an innovative space—the X-lab—which is part of the Charles Perkins Centre (CPC) hub, recently built at the University of Sydney (Australia). The CPC facilities were designed to foster new, campus-wide patterns of trans-disciplinary research and teaching, and closer integration between research and teaching. This chapter looks at the functioning of a large, innovative, laboratory learning space, incorporating virtual and physical elements. The chapter describes the use of these facilities exploring the influence of spatial elements in the activities of students, academics, and technical and administrative staff. Robert Ellis and Kenn Fisher discuss a translational research agenda for place-based spaces for networked learning in Chapter 16. The chapter addresses methods of designing and managing learning places/spaces in higher education. It looks to the health sector for examples of how translational research is being used to connect research evidence to space design. In Chapter 17, Peter Goodyear, Lucila Carvalho, Vivien Hodgson, and Maarten de Laat conclude the book, drawing out implications for practice, theory, and further research in relation to place-based spaces for networked learning.

Endnote

1. In passing, we should also mention research and development work in the area known as "connected learning" (Ito et al. 2013) which has some similarities with networked learning. Much of the research and development in this area is concerned with socially oriented, interest-driven learning activities engaged in by teenage children, outside of formal education settings. "Connected learning" is characterized by the linking of informal learning experiences and interests to academic achievement, career success, and/or civic engagement. It does not necessarily involve digital technology, though the emergence and use of new media is noted as promoting the development of environments that support connected learning. Use of new media is seen as fostering opportunities for self-expression, social support, inclusion, and capacity-building. As Jones (2015) remarks, connected learning can be seen as complementary to networked learning, but with a focus on younger learners and serving a narrower, and perhaps a more conservative, set of values.

References

Alexander, C., 2002. *The nature of order: An essay on the art of building and the nature of the universe.* New York: Oxford University Press.

Bayne, S., De Laat, M., Ryberg, T., and Sinclair, C., eds., 2016. *Research, boundaries and policy in networked learning.* New York: Springer.

Boys, J., 2011. *Towards creative learning spaces: Re-thinking the architecture of post-compulsory education.* New York: Routledge.

Boys, J., 2015. *Building better universities: Strategies, spaces, technologies.* New York: Routledge.

Carvalho, L. and Goodyear, P., eds., 2014. *The architecture of productive learning networks.* New York: Routledge.

Coyne, R., 2010. *The tuning of place: Sociable spaces and pervasive digital media.* Cambridge, MA: MIT Press.

de Marrais, E., Gosden, C., and Renfrew, C., eds., 2004. *Rethinking materiality: The engagement of mind with the material world* (McDonald Institute Monographs). Cambridge: McDonald Institute for Archaeological Research.

Faulkner, P. and Runde, J., 2011. *The social, the material, and the ontology of non-material technological objects.* Paper presented at the 27th EGOS (European Group for Organizational Studies) Colloquium, July 6–9, 2011, Gothenburg. [online]. Available from: www.researchgate.net/profile/Jochen_Runde/publication/228849865_The_Social_the_material_and_the_ontology_of_non-material_technological_objects/links/0deec523553f4a861c000000.pdf [Accessed October 27, 2015].

Fenwick, T., Edwards, R., and Sawchuk, P., 2011. *Emerging approaches to educational research: Tracing the sociomaterial.* London: Routledge.

Garfinkel, H., 1967. *Studies in ethnomethodology.* Englewood Cliffs, NJ: Prentice Hall.

Giaccardi, E., ed., 2012. *Heritage and social media. Understanding heritage in a participatory culture.* New York: Routledge.

Goodyear, P. and Carvalho, L., 2013. The analysis of complex learning environments. In: H. Beetham and R. Sharpe, eds., *Rethinking pedagogy for a digital age: Designing and delivering e-learning* (pp. 49–63). New York: Routledge.

Goodyear, P. and Carvalho, L., 2014. Framing the analysis of learning network architectures. In: L. Carvalho and P. Goodyear, eds., *The architecture of productive learning networks* (pp. 48–70). New York: Routledge.

Hafermalz, E. and Riemer, K., 2015. The question of materiality: Mattering in the network society. *ECIS 2015 Completed Research Papers.* Paper 66. [online]. Available from: http://aisel.aisnet.org/ecis2015_cr/66 [Accessed February 23, 2016].

Halliday, M. A. K., 1978. *Language as social semiotic.* London: Edward Arnold.

Hodder, I., 2012. *Entangled: An archaeology of the relationships between humans and things.* Chichester: Wiley-Blackwell.

Hodgson, V., De Laat, M. F., McConnell, D., and Ryberg, T., eds., 2014. *The design, experience and practice of networked learning.* Dordrecht: Springer.

Ingold, T., 2011. *Being alive: Essays on movement, knowledge and description.* Oxford: Routledge.

Ingold, T., 2012. Toward an ecology of materials. *Annual Review of Anthropology*, 41(1), 427–442.

Ito, M., Gutiérrez, K., Livingstone, S., Penuel, B., Rhodes, J., Salen, K., Schor, J., Sefton-Green, J., and Watkins, C., 2013. *Connected learning: An agenda for research and design.* Irvine, CA: Digital Media and Learning Research Hub.

Jandric, P. and Boras, D., eds., 2015. *Critical learning in digital networks.* Dordrecht: Springer.

Jewitt, C., 2012. Digital technologies in museums: New routes to engagement and participation. *Designs for Learning,* 5(1–2), 74–93.

Jones, C., 2015. *Networked learning: An educational paradigm for the age of digital networks.* Dordrecht: Springer.

Kress, G. and Van Leeuwen, T., 2006. *Reading images: The grammar of visual design.* London: Routledge.

Latour, B., 2005. *Reassembling the social: An introduction to Actor-Network-Theory.* Oxford: Oxford University Press.

Law, J. and Mol, A., 2001. Situating technoscience: An inquiry into spatialities. *Environment & Planning D: Society and Space,* 19, 609–612.

Macken-Horarik, M., 1996. *Construing the invisible: Specialized literacy practices in junior secondary English.* Thesis (Ph.D.). University of Sydney.

Malafouris, L., 2013. *How things shape the mind: A theory of material engagement.* Cambridge, MA: MIT Press.

Malafouris, L. and Renfrew, C., eds., 2010. *The cognitive life of things: Recasting the boundaries of the mind.* Cambridge: McDonald Institute for Archaeological Research, University of Cambridge.

Massey, D., 2005. *For space.* London: Sage.

McCullough, M., 2004. *Digital ground: Architecture, pervasive computing, and environmental knowing.* Cambridge, MA: MIT Press.

McCullough, M., 2013. *Ambient commons: Attention in the age of embodied information.* Cambridge, MA: MIT Press.

Mitchell, W. J., 1995. *City of bits: Space, place, and the infobahn.* Cambridge, MA: MIT Press.

Mitchell, W. J., 2003. *Me++: The cyborg self and the networked city.* Cambridge, MA: MIT Press.

Mitchell, W. J., 2008. *World's greatest architect: Making, meaning, and network culture.* Cambridge, MA: MIT Press.

Mol, A. and Law, J., 1994. Regions, networks and fluids: Anaemia and social topology. *Social Studies of Science,* 24(4), 641–671.

O'Toole, M., 2011. *The language of displayed art.* London: Leicester University Press.

Orlikowski, W. J., 2010. The sociomateriality of organisational life: Considering technology in management research. *Cambridge Journal of Economics,* 34, 125–141.

Ravelli, L. J. and McMurtrie, R. J., 2015. *Multimodality in the built environment: Spatial discourse analysis.* London: Routledge.

Relph, E., 1976. *Place and placelessness.* London: Pion Ltd.

Shepard, M., ed., 2011. *Sentient city: Ubiquitous computing, architecture, and the future of urban space.* Cambridge, MA: MIT Press.

Shove, E., Pantzar, M., and Watson, M., 2012. *The dynamics of social practice: Everyday life and how it changes.* London: Sage.

Stenglin, M., 2004. *Packaging curiosities: Towards a grammar of three-dimensional space.* Thesis (Ph.D.). University of Sydney.

Taylor, A., 2009. *Linking architecture and education: Sustainable design for learning environments.* Albuquerque: University of New Mexico Press.

Tuan, Y.-F., 1977. *Space and place: The perspective of experience.* Minneapolis: University of Minnesota Press.

Urry, J., 2002. Mobility and proximity. *Sociology,* 36(2), 255–274.

2

PLACING FOCUS IN THE PLACE-BASED SPACES FOR NETWORKED LEARNING

David Ashe and Nina Bonderup Dohn

This chapter concerns the question of how focus is placed when a learner is in a given learning situation. We look at how the various elements of an environment interact with individuals and how those interactions bring about shifts in participants' focus. These shifts depend on which environmental elements are available and also on how particular individuals interact with the environment. It is tempting to consider a learning environment in terms of a pre-existing "place"—that which is designed by a designer, teacher, or educationalist, and which is separate from the learner who then enters the place. This may come from our feeling that products are designed for a purpose and then individuals, as users, come along and use the designed object for the designed purpose. In many cases this is appropriate; a hammer is designed to knock nails into wood and this is often how an individual uses a hammer. Similarly, classrooms, equipped with furniture and educational artifacts, seemingly await their teachers and students who then enter and make use of the equipment. However, it is not difficult to imagine scenarios when a hammer is used for other purposes. Educational artifacts certainly often are, e.g. when a ruler is tapped on the desk to command silence instead of being used for measuring, or a whiteboard pen is held up to illustrate a color instead of being used for writing. Individuals use objects in ways that were not expected, or even considered, by the object's designer. We will look at that which is designed, and external to the learner, alongside the learner as a bodily being and hope to highlight how the complex relationship between individuals, the environment, and what is actually going on plays out to decide what is currently "in focus."

Learning takes place throughout life and is not limited to academy settings. Many examples in this volume consider learning in places such as art galleries and museums. On the face of it, museums seem obvious examples of pre-existing places established precisely for visitors to be able to enter and experience them "as they are." It seems natural to consider the physical space, along with exhibited artifacts and designed information systems (both analog and digital), as separate from the visitor as he or she traverses, either alone or in a social group, the space. On the other hand, museums are increasingly installing artifacts which rely on interactions with a visitor to become an "exhibit." Concrete examples from MONA in Hobart are given in Carvalho (Chapter 11); other examples include several sculptures at the annual Sculpture by the Sea, Sydney,[1] the 150-meter long art work *Your Rainbow Panorama* at Aros, Aarhus, Denmark, by Olafur Eliasson,[2] as well as many other works by this artist. Museums, like formal learning institutions, are thus moving in the direction of involving the user/learner in creating their learning experience. This increases complexity and makes it even more essential to ask what is involved in "placing the focus" for the learner.

To gain a better understanding of designed, pre-existing places, we briefly investigate how the concept of "context" has been discussed in the literature. In "Understanding context before using it" (Bazire and Brézillon 2005) more than 150 different definitions of context were collected from a variety of disciplines (such as computer science, philosophy, and business). In their paper, Bazire and Brézillon pose a number of questions: "Which context is relevant for our study? The context of the person? The context of the task? The context of the interaction? The context of the situation? When does a context begin and where does it stop?" (p. 29). McCarthy (1993) discusses "context" as an external object and attempts to define it in abstract mathematical terms. This view, as he acknowledges, is difficult as individuals interact on an epistemological level with the context: "human intelligence involves an ability that no-one has yet undertaken to put in computer programs—namely the ability to transcend the context of one's beliefs" (p. 8). Gero and Smith (2009) understand "context" as external to the individual but refer to individuals "situating" themselves within the external context. They therefore use "context" to refer to those elements that are external to an individual, and "situation" to refer to the individual's "internal" sense making. According to them, people use their prior experience to situate themselves within an external context.

Placing the Focus: Background and Figure

In our terminology, prior experiences help people to find or place focus. However, we feel that separating the external context from an internal situation is unhelpful as it tempts one to reduce the current experience (in the sense of the German *Erlebnis*) to a mathematical formula, of the form $E = f(c,s)$, where experience (*Erlebnis*) is a function of the external context and an individual's situation, made up of past experience (in the sense of the German *Erfahrung*). Put differently, the problem is that when engaging in the world, past experience is not only a subjective notion inside the learner to be added to objective phenomena in the outside world, it is also there in the world as the significance presented to an individual in the situation. In the words of Dreyfus:

> When we are at home in the world, the meaningful objects embedded in their context of references among which we live are not a model of the world stored in our mind or brain; they are the world itself . . . My personal plans and my memories are inscribed in the things around me just as are the public goals of men in general.
>
> (1992, pp. 265–266)

Rather than considering experience as a mathematical function, we think that it depends, complexly and subtly, not only on prior experiences, but also on how persons, as bodily beings, interact with the environment and how these interactions change their focus. To illustrate the complexity involved when placing focus, we provide a series of examples. These examples highlight the significance that our bodily being as well as our socio-cultural upbringing have when trying to determine what is "background" and what is "figure"– and, therefore, how focus is placed. The examples have been chosen to progressively point out further aspects involved in the process. For this reason, we present them under the heading of the aspect they illustrate. For the sake of clarity we should stress, however, that the aspects demonstrated in the first, simpler examples persist into the more complex ones. Thus, the headings should not be misunderstood as indicating that the aspects in the subsection are limited to the kind of examples presented.

The Significance of the Background

In books on phenomenology, Rubin's Peter-Paul Goblet (Figure 2.1) is often used to explain the dependency of what we experience on a more or less indeterminate background to which we do not attend. There are a variety of ways in which this image can be viewed. If one is well acquainted with foreground/background switching images, one may immediately recognize it as such an image and see the image (in its entirety) as foreground on the background of the printed page. Without prior acquaintance with this type of image, and/or if one "looks into" the image to see what it depicts, one may view it as two silhouetted faces in conversation on a white background or as a white vase on a black background. It is not possible to view both figures as figures at once: when one focuses on the background of the figure, it itself transforms into a figure which lets the first figure recede into unattended background. The background, however, is as necessary as the figure itself for determining what the figure is a figure of. The background lets the figure stand out; moreover it lets the figure stand out in a certain way with a certain meaning (as a vase or talking faces). The phenomenological point is that experience is always like this; that which becomes salient for us does so on a background of which we are not focally aware, but which is essential in determining the meaning of that which is salient. A foreground relies on a background; the background is essential in determining our experience.

This picture is, however, special. As a pedagogical illustration of the significance of background, it is apposite, but what makes it illustrative—that there is no preferred figure for the viewer and that he or she can switch back and forth between seeing the two possible figures—may, at the same time, be very misleading. Of course, Rubin's vase is not the only image that can be viewed in multiple ways—a number of them exist—but notably these are intriguing, and have been purposefully designed to be fun, precisely because the possibility of switching foregrounds (or choosing "which figure to see now") is atypical. A further example of an artifact of this type is one of the sculptures at the 2013 Sculpture by the Sea exhibition (Figure 2.2) which has been designed specifically

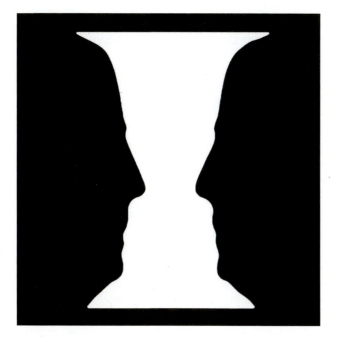

FIGURE 2.1 Rubin's Peter–Paul Goblet

FIGURE 2.2 The Foreground and Background Can Switch, Bringing Different Aspects into Focus

Source: "Horizon" by Lucy Humphrey (artist). Photograph © William Patino

to make us reflect on the figure-ground structure itself and on how background contributes to determining what is in (what is the meaning of) the figure. Again, such an artwork is eye-catching precisely because the switching it prompts us to undertake is not typical of perception.

Immediacy of Figure-Ground Structure, Given Our Bodily, Socio-Cultural Being

In general, our focus is neither arbitrary nor a matter of choice; rather, some aspects of a situation immediately and seemingly naturally present themselves as in focus. Consider the situation where you are walking along a street lined with trees. The trees are here experienced as the figure on the background of the air (understood as "the transparent space between the trees," not in the physics sense of "a mixture of gases"). It is very hard to perceive it the other way around. However, the reason that we do not focus on the air, making that the figure, is not because the air is unobservable, nor that the air is "nothing," it is that the trees are naturally presenting themselves as the current focus. But if, whilst walking down the street, you pass a wall with a large hole in it, you will see the space (the hole) as the figure on the background of the wall. Visually, the space may present itself as a dark shadow on the wall or even with whatever is behind the wall (which we can now see through the hole). Still, we experience seeing the hole, i.e. the lack of material, the space, as figure. Artists sometimes refer to this phenomenon (that holes or lack of material may be perceived as figures) as "negative space." The work of Tang Yau Hoong gives elegant illustrations of the way in which space (or negative space) can be a figure.[3] The point we wish to make is not that "objectively given," the trees and the hole, respectively, have salience—at least not if "objectively given" is taken to mean "with no reference to a human point of view." The point is, rather, that given the kind of beings we are (humans) and the lives we live (human lives), trees and holes, respectively, have significance for us and therefore immediately, "naturally," stand out for us as figures.

Unpacking this a little, "the kind of being we humans are" is a bodily being, brought up in specific, historically developed, socio-cultural ways of inhabiting and making sense of the environment around us. Trees and holes are significant for us because we can (respectively) bump into them, climb them, enjoy their beauty or despair at their weakling growth, utilize them for furniture or warmth, crawl through them, utilize them for a shortcut or an escape, ventilate or freeze because of the air let through, etc. That is, they are significant, given the kind of body we have and the ways in which we have learned to use this body in the socio-cultural settings in which we partake. The immediacy and naturalness of the figure-ground structuring is a result of "the kind of being we are." Not in the sense that we are born with an ability to see trees as figures—we have to learn to focus just as we have to learn to walk—but in the sense that the way we learn to go about the world as bodily beings establishes this as the way the world presents itself to us without a deliberate act of choice on our part. As indicated, we wish to stress both the significance of the fact that we act bodily in the world (we are not free-floating minds) and of the socio-cultural practices we are born into and in which we engage.

As to the first, it is reasonable to suppose that trees and holes are figures because whatever we do with trees and holes will be framed, enabled, and constrained by facts about our body and the interactions we can take on with trees and holes. For example, we are unable to move a tree (once past its seedling stage) with our bare hands, and we can close a hole (if it's not too big) with our bodies.

As to the second, consider again the Sculpture by the Sea exhibition. On one interpretation, the sculptures at the exhibition (with a few exceptions such as the sphere—Figure 2.2) are the obvious figures and the ocean/cityscape is the background. This is the immediate and natural "reading" of the situation as one stands facing each of them. However, the immediacy is fundamentally dependent on practices such as designing an artwork, visiting an exhibition, going for a leisurely stroll by the sea, i.e. on culturally developed ways that we as bodily beings can move ourselves around in

FIGURE 2.3 A Sculpture in the Foreground with the Sydney Cityscape in the Background

Source: "Diminish and Ascend" by David McCracken (artist). Photograph © William Patino a landscape and thereby actively engage ourselves in having experiences. The specific sculpture shown in Figure 2.3 is immediately seen as a stairway (indeed, perhaps even a "stairway to heaven") on the background of the city, which again, of course, depends for its meaning (and for the immediacy with which this meaning is given) on socio-cultural practices of, for example, stairs building, stairs traversing, and urban organization of human dwellings (see Sprake and Rogers, Chapter 13).

In general, these two aspects—our bodily being and our socio-culturally developed expectations and practices—are not factors working independently of one another to determine focus. Rather, in most instances, they act in integration so that what stands out for us as the "naturally" given figure does so on the basis of our bodily being with all its socio-culturally acquired skills and understandings. An interesting example is the fact that the Aboriginal people of Australia, when observing the night sky, not only observe the points of lights (as observed by European astronomers), but also observe "the very dark patches between or besides the points and blurs of light" (Johnson 2014, p. 126). Thus, in contrast to the Europeans, for the Aboriginal people of Australia, the space between the lights in the sky (if not the space between trees on the ground) "naturally" presents itself as figure.

The complex integration of bodily and socio-culturally given aspects in determining what "naturally" is the focus can also be seen in the Sculpture by the Sea example. Once one faces a sculpture, then that sculpture is likely to be the immediate and obvious focus. However, the process of coming to face a sculpture—and the focus shifts involved therein—should not be neglected. The exhibition does not just incidentally happen to be arranged on the cliff plateaus and along the path between them. Rather, as visitors walk along the path, different phenomena in their surroundings come into, and disappear out of, view. Their focus will shift between the sculptures and the surroundings of rocks, cliffs, sea, and beach (and, perhaps, the other visitors that they walk, and maybe even collide, with). Some sculptures are "hidden" in the cliffs and have to be searched for—their figures have to be detected or uncovered from their background. Other sculptures are integrated with the rocks or sand so that they incorporate part of the natural surroundings in the making of their figure. A significant part of the experience of visiting Sculpture by the Sea is precisely this process—that of making out the sculptures, of enjoying the city and seascapes as figures in between facing sculptures, of being intrigued by the new figures one can spot as one turns a corner, and of shifting one's focus constantly between figures. All of this depends on the immediacy of focus given through bodily movements in integration with socio-cultural expectations and practices connected to visiting an exhibition (e.g. that turning a corner will bring new pieces of artwork into sight).

Place-Based ICT: Physical Surroundings, Dynamicity, and Interaction with Others

As we explained at the beginning of this section, we have chosen examples to progressively show the complexity of aspects involved in determining the figure-ground structure and in placing the focus in any given situation. Therefore we have started with examples which do not employ ICT, and do not concern networked learning. Our next example adds complexity by looking at a place-based software application. It underscores the significance of the physical surroundings themselves, of dynamicity, and of interaction with other people. It concerns a new app for mobile devices, called "Place-AR."[4] We provide a brief overview of Place-AR as, at the time of writing, the app is in its infancy. By the time this volume is published Place-AR, or other similar networking tools, may be well established and little clarification may be necessary.

Place-AR is a mobile application that enables messages and comments to be left at physical locations. These messages can only be read, and interactions can only take place, when the user of the application is at an appointed geographical location as specified by the message. Private messages

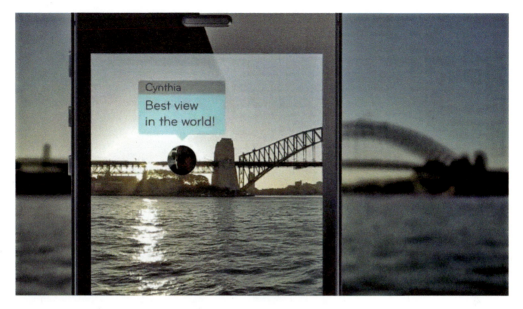

FIGURE 2.4 The Mobile Application Place-AR Displaying a Message Fixed to a Geographical Location

Source: Image © Place-AR

may be left for known contacts, or open messages left for anyone to view and respond. In this way individuals can interact across time with others, sharing thoughts and experiences.

Individual messages can be left at locations, or "trails" left for others to follow. Messages left in trails can be added to, and so a conversation about a physical location can be created; others can join the conversation and take part. In this way, a conversation can take place with people who may never have met and may not be known to each other.

When looking at Figure 2.4 and considering what is involved in figure-ground structuring and in placing the focus when users interact with the mobile app, the face circle and the text naturally appear as figures on the background of whatever picture the mobile phone is rendering of its surroundings. It is not unusual to be presented with extra information when observing a scene through a digital device; cameras often present information such as focus, aperture, and shutter speed. However, the information presented in Place-AR naturally appears as figures as, after all, the point of looking at the device is to see if there are any messages. For this reason, the face circles will not be ignored in the same way that people can ignore data supplied to the photographer. Interestingly, however, because the text comments on the geographical location, it directs focus to what is in the picture, thereby recommending a shift away from itself to an aspect of the picture. We say "recommending" instead of "initiating" because the text and circle do not recede into the background. If one were only interested in the scenery, corresponding to a full backgrounding of the text and circle, one would not be looking at the device at all, but directly at the scenery. As it is, whilst using the app the focus will dynamically shift between text and circle, on the one hand, and the scenery displayed behind them, on the other. The text and circle will always, to some extent, be foregrounded if only in the sense that it is somewhat "in the way of" and distracting from the scenery on the phone. Here we encounter a paradox; the message is obstructing the scene but the scene is brought into focus because of the message. This switch of focus from the message to the background can be seen in Place-AR's marketing material, shown in Figure 2.5 (Place-AR 2014).

This issue becomes more salient as more "place markers" are added (see Figure 2.6). Again, the intentions of the designer may not be realized in what actually happens; a complex interplay

FIGURE 2.5 Place-AR Marketing
Material

Source: Image © Place-AR

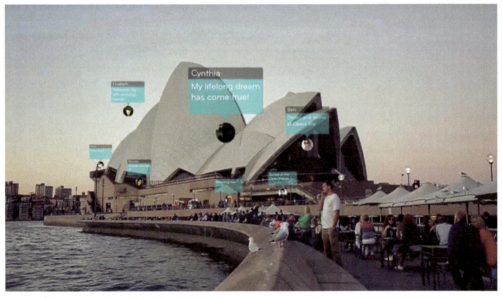

FIGURE 2.6 The App Place-AR Displaying Several Messages Fixed to the Same Geographical Location

Source: Image © Place-AR

between the app use and the wider activity is to be expected. One extreme would be that the user
becomes so engrossed in the comments on the app that he or she never looks out but only experiences the location through the window of the mobile phone. The other extreme would be that
the user merely glances at the interface to see, for example, where there is a high concentration of
circles (as an indication of something interesting), but does not read, or interact with, the comments.

This latter scenario is illustrative of the significance that the physical surroundings (socio-
culturally interpreted) can have in deciding what it is that the circles point out; that is, how the

physical surroundings determine the role that the circles play in placing focus in each specific case. Looking closely at Figure 2.6, two of the circles are seen to be somewhat up in the air and displaced in relation to the Opera House. However, given the building's physical magnitude and socio-cultural importance, this fact is not what initially "meets the eye." Rather, our immediate bodily reading of the picture is that the circles, all in conjunction, point out the Opera House as the place for focus. It requires an effort to see the top-left circle as indicating the air or cityscape behind the Opera House. Were we standing with the app in front of the Opera House, this immediate reading would be even stronger: the circles would point us to directing our body toward the building (which is not to say that we would conform to being so directed).

As for the role of dynamicity in placing focus, in all cases, the user's movements around the physical location will effect changes in what is displayed on the app, but these movements may themselves be instantiated or influenced by what was previously displayed. Events occurring in the geographical location may divert attention and cause the user to swing round, thus changing the display and leading to the neglect of comments. On the other hand, a comment on the interface may cause the user to miss out on something happening in the user's immediate vicinity. Placing focus with Place-AR will be a complex interaction of the physical surroundings, their socio-cultural significance, the events occurring there, the physical movements of the user, the circles and text on the app, the interactions with others through the app and on location, along with other prior intentions the user may have had of what to do in the geographical location. Using Place-AR at Sculpture by the Sea may thus lead to a complex series of shifts between what is the figure and what is the background. As individuals leave messages, and interact with messages, the sculptures in the foreground become background and the digital device and the message content take over as the foreground. However, they take over in a somewhat different way than is the case for Rubin's vase. In the Rubin's vase case, the background frames the foreground, allowing the figure to stand out. In contrast, adding messages in Place-AR amounts to doing work in the foreground on the background. This adds complexity to the placing of focus as well as to the interrelation between foreground and background. The determining factor of what is in focus is not solely what is there (physically and virtually), but rather is based on a complex interaction of designed environment, messages on the app, personal experiences, deliberation about where to find and how to interpret sculptures in their physical surroundings, and bodily actions (such as changing location, searching for "hidden" sculptures, and adding new messages). The ease of shifting focus from the landscape to the sculpture, and from the sculpture to the digital device, and from the digital device to a message, and from one message to a thread of messages, and back to the environment, will itself be determined in an interaction between the person and the available objects.

Placing the Focus: Summary

What we have sought to establish with our examples is that "placing the focus" is a complex interplay between: (a) what we, as bodily beings brought up in and familiar with specific socio-cultural settings, naturally and immediately foreground; (b) what is (physically and culturally) perceptually obvious in the situation (in the sense of "clearly to be noticed here" as, for example, in Figure 2.6 the Opera House is the immediately noticed object rather than the "air" in which the face–circle is actually located); (c) our interaction with others (present in person or through digital mediation); (d) our interests, experience, and possible prior intentions; and (e) our actual actions in the situation. Our bodily being and the understanding we have incorporated of the world through our interaction with it, and with other people in the course of our lives, here act to fore-structure the situation into background and figure (and to enable dynamic shifts in background and figure) in response to the designed and natural, material and human aspects we meet there, and are influenced by what we are interested in, care about, and intend. The problem for designers is that only aspects (a) and (b) can be designed for directly—and not even easily so, because what will actually be "naturally foregrounded" and "perceptually obvious" may differ from that which the designer believes to be the case. The other aspects will vary between individuals and, for (c) and (e), between the situations in which encounters play out. Designers can design for people to undertake certain actions and inter-actions, but people may still act differently, out of deliberate choice, prior experience and interests, or habit. In short, though awareness of aspects (a) to (e) may guide designers in thinking about the complexity of the encounters and activities they design for, the placing of focus is not predictable. Aspects (a) to (e) may, nonetheless, act as a framework for explaining, after the fact as it were, how focus has been placed in specific situations. In the next section, we illustrate this with an example.

An Example: Analyzing the Placing of Focus

The next example concerns the utilization of a handheld digital device running a mathematics-learning application in two very different school settings, one in Malawi where up to 250 students share a single teacher and one in the UK where class sizes rarely exceed 30. We have argued that placing the focus is a complex interaction between five aspects (see (a) to (e) above). We now illustrate how these five aspects may work as a framework for explaining how focus is placed in specific mathematics learning situations.

Networked learning takes on many guises; one that is perhaps more unusual than most, is the use of digital tools to teach mathematics at a Malawian primary school. What makes this place,

FIGURE 2.7 Learners at a Malawian Primary School Engaged in a Mathematics Lesson

Source: Photograph © onebillion.org

FIGURE 2.8 Standard 2 Girls Helping Each Other to Trace Numbers

Source: Photograph © onebillion.org

for digitally mediated learning, surprising is that the school has almost no electrical/electronic infrastructure. Whilst it does have an electricity supply—there is one outlet, located in the head teacher's office—it only works intermittently. Contrast this with a well-equipped, award-winning, UK primary school with not only electricity but also IT equipment, small class sizes, and well-trained and well-resourced teachers. Clearly, these are two very different contexts in which learning is expected to take place. In both of these places, researchers from Nottingham University have studied groups of children undertaking mathematics lessons using a handheld digital device (Kelly 2014; Pitchford 2014, 2015). Despite the very different learning places, the externally designed learning environment is surprisingly similar. In both places students sit in groups of up to 30 children, students sit on mats on the floor to work, and students predominately work on their own with their own digital computing device. In Malawi, this is achieved by splitting the large student group into smaller groups. Each of the groups spends 40 minutes, three times a week, in a separate classroom using the digital devices. The devices are powered using solar panels and the students' work is recorded and uploaded to a central server running on a Raspberry Pi (an inexpensive, low-cost, single-board computer). The students, for the most part, interact with the learning material on their own (see Figure 2.7). However, there are times when individual learners interact with each other (see Figure 2.8).

The results of the studies in both the Malawi and the UK locations showed an increase in the students' learning outcomes compared to local control groups. Pitchford (2015) documented that the method is "significantly more effective at improving mathematical attainment than current instructional practice" (p. 10). Despite similar results in both locations, the physical and digital artifacts surrounding the students had very different effects. For example, in Malawi where the students had no previous experience of using digital technology, the students had to recognize that digital representations could be manipulated (dragged across a touch screen) in a similar way to their non-virtual counterparts. This process appeared not to present a problem for the students, who typically grasped the idea within a matter of seconds: "the first time, they [the students] are a bit nervous, but they only have to do it once and then they just do it" (Stuart 2014). One difference between the two locations was the students' focus on the headphones that were used for audio feedback. Students in the UK, familiar with using headphones, treated them as a tool (as the designers' intended) to receive feedback. However, students in Malawi, having never seen or heard of headphones, were amazed to be spoken to in their own language—"the child will say 'eeee' when they hear Chichewa coming out of the headphones" (Stuart 2014). As these Malawian, early-primary school students had been in very large class groups, this may have been the first time a "teacher" had spoken to them directly. When completing a task, the audio feedback may be the first personal, verbal congratulation they have heard in school:

> because of the big classes, the teachers often don't even know their names, no one has ever said to them "well done," you see these children break out into a smile—they even give themselves a little clap, it's a wonderful moment.
>
> (Stuart 2014)

As each learner progresses through the material, they are able to "pass" assessments, which mark learning milestones. When a child reaches one of these milestones, the server recognizes the achievement and a small thermal (till roll) printer, at the front of the class, automatically prints out an individual certificate. The teacher presents this certificate and a spontaneous round of applause erupts from the other learners. "We feel that this is a very important moment, connecting what they are doing on the machine to something in the real-world" (Stuart 2014). These events change the focus of the students from a solo activity to that of recognizing that they are part of a learning group. The printer starting up and the presentation of the certificate have an effect not only on the receiver of the certificate, but also on the entire cohort.

In both the Malawi and the UK settings, focus for the students is clearly placed in such a way that the app becomes conducive to their learning. However, the differences between the children's reactions indicate that focus may not be placed in entirely the same way in the two locations. In the Malawi case, and utilizing the framework of aspects (a) to (e) above, the novelty of the experience (technologically, physically, socially, and psychologically) is a large part of what acts to make the digital device and its tasks, the printer, and the certificates, the figures on which the children alternatingly focus. Thus, these artifacts are new, not just to the children but also, to a large extent, to their community—indeed, given the lack of other learning resources, they appear to constitute most of the artifacts present in the classroom. This makes them stand out, both physically and culturally, in their own right (aspect (b)). The actions required of the children to bring about the learning situation with the digital device (aspect (e)) add to the placing of focus on the device and its tasks. So does the presence of the researcher and, in general, the articulation of and emphasis on the special learning situation as "a project" (aspects (b) and (c))—the so-called Hawthorne effect. The occasional help given, one to another (see Figure 2.8), the praise sounding from the earphones, and the social interaction that develops around the certificates also direct focus (aspect (c)). As described by Stuart, the latter two phenomena further motivate the students to engage with the tasks, leading to a yet stronger focus on the tasks and the printer in alternation (aspect (d)). Because of the novelty of the artifacts and the whole learning situation, phenomena relating to aspect (a) will not contribute directly to placing focus on the device or its tasks, though there may be aspect (a) focusing involved in, for example, foregrounding trees as students pass them on their way to the classroom. Indirectly, foregrounding the floor as something to sit on once they are there may also contribute to allowing the learning activities to proceed. In contrast, in the UK case, students may be so familiar with handheld digital devices and earphones that these are "naturally" foregrounded (aspect (a))—in interaction of course, and competition perhaps, with phenomena relating to aspects (b) to (e). As Kelly (2014) notes, after 30 minutes most children have had enough and want to go outside to play.

This is, of course, a very generalized description of how focus is placed with the mathematics learning application. It does not do justice to the individual differences between students and their varying interest and skill in mathematics. Presumably, for some students (both Malawian and English), the focus is placed more consistently on the mathematics tasks whereas others are distracted more easily—by noises outside the classroom, by their classmates" movements, and by the expectation that the printer will soon start up to produce a certificate for someone else. To some degree, our description is an idealized reconstruction. Still, the positive effect on learning outcomes, as compared to control groups (documented in Pitchford's study), warrants postulating such a reconstruction.

Implications for Designers of Place-Based Spaces for Networked Learning

We began by pointing out that viewing "context" as a pre-existing place which learners move into and out of does not do justice to the contribution of the learner in determining what the context is. Neither, we argued, can one easily separate contributions from "external context" and "internal situation" because what the external context is will not be objectively or neutrally given, but will come into being in the interaction between the learner, the artifacts, and the other learners. We developed this point through an explication of the figure-ground structure to perception (and, more generally, to experience), stressing that the question of where focus is placed is determined by a complex interplay between what is physically and culturally obvious; what the learner as a bodily, socio-cultural being immediately foregrounds; the interests and possible prior intentions of the learner; and his or her actual actions and interactions with others in the situation.

By way of conclusion we want to touch on the question of where these points leave the designer of place-based spaces for networked learning. To answer this question, it may be helpful to consider Gibson's notion of affordances. Gibson (1977) suggests that the environment (and items in it) has meaning for us in terms of what it offers us—"what it provides or furnishes, either for good or ill" as he puts it (p. 127). He terms this meaning the environment's affordances. Further, he claims that we can perceive such affordances directly, including the possibilities of action which they pose to us. However, given the differences (personally, socio-culturally, and bodily) in the skills we have each developed, an object's affordance will vary between individuals and across cultures. Therefore, the affordance of an object is not held within the object alone, but is a relationship between object and individual. In addition, even if an object poses an affordance for action for a person, there is no guarantee that the individual will act on it. Greeno (1994) states: "the presence in a situation of a system that provides an affordance for some activity does not imply that the activity will occur, although it contributes to the possibility of that activity" (p. 340).

In the same way, designed elements in spaces for networked learning do not, of themselves, ensure certain activities will (or will not) occur; rather, designed elements can contribute to the likelihood of a particular activity taking place. The activity is not determined by the designed objects or by the learners, but becomes a relationship between both.

So what designers can do is design for the complexity and dynamicity of the way focus is placed, taking into account the way context develops in interaction between learners and artifacts, whilst accepting that whatever features they design may be taken up in different ways by the learners—or not taken up at all. For example, in the Malawian case, the design of the learning concerns not only the mathematics-learning application (as the Pitchford quotation above might lead one to believe), but also the social and physical classroom space into which the app comes into use.

Endnotes

1. See www.sculpturebythesea.com
2. See http://en.aros.dk/visit-aros/the-collection/your-rainbow-panorama
3. Cf. http://tangyauhoong.com. His Land Rover illustrations are particularly apt as exemplifications of the way holes stand out as figures, cf. http://tangyauhoong.com/portfolio/land-rover
4. www.placear.com

References

Bazire, M. and Brézillon, P., 2005. Understanding context before using it. In: A. Dey, B. Kokinov, D. Leake, and R. Turner, eds., *Proceedings of the 5th International Conference on Modeling and Using Context* (pp. 29–40), July 5–8, 2005, Paris. Chicago: Springer-Verlag.

Dreyfus, H., 1992. *What computers still can't do: A critique of artificial reason.* Cambridge, MA: MIT Press.

Gero, J. S. and Smith, G. J., 2009. Context, situations, and design agents. *Knowledge-Based Systems*, 22(8), 600–609.

Gibson, J., 1977. The theory of affordances. In: R. Shaw and J. Bransford, eds., *Perceiving, acting, and knowing: Toward an ecological psychology* (pp. 67–82). Hillsdale, NJ: Lawrence Erlbaum.

Greeno, J. G., 1994. Gibson's affordances. *Psychological Review*, 101(2), 336–342.

Johnson, D., 2014. *Night skies of Aboriginal Australia: A noctuary.* Sydney: Sydney University Press.

Kelly, S., 2014. *BBC News—Malawi app "teaches UK pupils 18 months of maths in six weeks."* [online]. Available from: www.bbc.com/news/technology-29063614 [Accessed October 30, 2015].

McCarthy, J., 1993. *Notes on formalizing context.* Stanford, CA: Stanford University. [online]. Available from: http://cogprints.org/418 [Accessed October 30, 2015].

Pitchford, N., 2014. *Unlocking talent: Evaluation of a tablet-based Masamu intervention in a Malawian primary school.* Nottingham: Nottingham University. [online]. Available from: https://onebillion.org.uk/downloads/unlocking-talent-final-report.pdf [Accessed October 30, 2015].

Pitchford, N., 2015. Development of early mathematical skills with a tablet intervention: A randomized control trial in Malawi. *Frontiers in Psychology*, 6 (485). [online]. Available from: http://journal.frontiersin.org/article/10.3389/fpsyg.2015.00485/full [Accessed July 22, 2015].

Place-AR, 2014. *Location based messaging.* [online]. Available from: https://vimeo.com/139248884 [Accessed October 30, 2015].

Stuart, J., 2014. Telephone interview, September 21, 2014.

3

EDUCATIONAL DESIGN AND BIRDS ON TREES

Ana Pinto

Introduction

In times of continuous and rapid change, in technologies and in patterns of human–human inter-action, educational design researchers and practitioners have been striving to find effective ways to deal with increasing complexity in designing for learning. Design patterns and pattern languages (Alexander et al. 1977; Alexander 1979) have been proving useful for representing and sharing design knowledge for reuse. However, major concepts underpinning pattern language theory, such as the "quality without a name" and "wholeness," have proved too elusive to formalize. Yet, being able to systematically draw on ideas involving qualities is essential, otherwise *any* pattern can potentially qualify for abstraction and sharing. Alexander's most recent theory, explained in *The Nature of Order* (2002a, 2002b, 2004, 2005), offers new conceptual and methodological tools that complement and expand his original ideas on developing pattern languages to support and facilitate designs imbued with life-improving qualities. This chapter explores some of these tools: especially the concept of "centers." At the core of Alexander's general design theory is a deep concern with the effects of natural and man-made "things" on people's general wellbeing and the harmonious life of communities.

In exploring the usefulness of the concept of centers within the context of networked learning, the study presented in this chapter "stretches" current thinking and approaches in educational design. The chapter suggests that the combination of Alexander's "older" and more recent ideas about design can help educational designers understand how designs for networked learning *materialize* in the world. In line with this argument, the analytic work presented in the chapter aims to illustrate how concepts such as *wholeness* and *centers* can be used to support decisions about which design patterns are worth abstracting and sharing. Through the means of a case study, the chapter examines how a secondary design element—an event that takes place only once a year—helps to sustain and expand a wider learning network. The chapter starts with an introduction to theoretical considera-tions from Christopher Alexander's work and the conceptual framework for this research. Next, the chapter presents the case study of a learning network (NALA 2015) and a place-based component of this learning network: the NALA 2014 Dublin Student Day. This is followed by a preliminary analysis of this place-based component, which is then supplemented with theoretical ideas from *The Nature of Order* (Alexander 2002a, 2002b, 2004, 2005). Overall, the chapter illustrates how a more holistic approach to analysis and design can be useful for revealing otherwise elusive, yet important, design patterns. "Secondary" design elements—those less prominent designed features that only occasionally and/or *ephemerally* "materialize" around a main network—nevertheless show intricate connections amongst the core activities taking place. The chapter argues that unless such relations are unveiled and understood, the essential core of a learning network cannot be entirely grasped.

Theoretical Considerations

Designing for learning is a very complex endeavor; it involves merging technological, pedagogical, and content knowledge domains. Educational design researchers and practitioners have been making great efforts to capture design patterns that can be reused to facilitate design processes and practices. A learning design pattern is a piece of knowledge, a proven solution to a pedagogical problem; it presents the core of the solution to a recurring teaching problem as well as guidance on when and in which context the solution is applicable (Goodyear, De Laat, and Lally 2006; Conole and Jones 2010; Goodyear and Retalis 2010; Mor et al. 2014). Once successful learning experiences have been captured in design patterns, these can be interrelated and assembled into pattern languages to tackle complex problems.

The idea of capturing and sharing good design solutions using patterns originated in the work of architect Christopher Alexander and his team in the late 1970s. The 253 individual architectural patterns presented in the book *A Pattern Language: Towns, Buildings, Construction* (Alexander et al. 1977) are meant to guide ordinary people in the reshaping of the environment for improved and more pleasant conditions of life. Alexander argues that poor design disrupts both the environment and people's wellbeing. Whilst the idea of using design patterns to encapsulate and render design knowledge for reuse has been largely embraced (Goodyear and Retalis 2010), subtleties concerning life-improving patterns remain underexplored within the educational design context (for exceptions see Pinto 2014b, forthcoming; Goodyear et al. 2015). Particularly elusive is the idea that "things" which are well designed imbue a quality that fosters good experiences and a deep sense of connectedness with surrounding life.

For Alexander, spaces and structures acquire their characters according to certain patterns of events that happen in combination. These patterns of events involve both human and non-human phenomena. For instance, natural phenomena such as "the sunshine shining on the windowsill, the wind blowing in the grass" affect people just as much as social events do (1979, p. 64). A "quality without a name" manifests itself when the patterns of events happening in a space allow a person to feel most alive and whole (1979, p. 41). In this sense, pattern language theory involves much more than the application of objective scientific design principles. This is illustrated in the passage below, where Alexander critiques the way software design patterns have been written:

> I understand that the software patterns . . . can make a program better. That isn't the same thing, because in that sentence "better" could mean merely technically efficient, not actually "good" . . . I would ask that the use of pattern language in software has the tendency to make the program or the thing that is being created morally profound—actually has the capacity to play a more significant role in human life.
>
> (Alexander 1999, p. 74)

Thus, pattern languages do not simply involve identification of problems and solutions. It is essential to identify and/or produce design patterns that are both infused with life-enhancing quality and "alive." Alexander's concept of "life" means far more than is usually entailed in conventional scientific understanding—it is not limited to self-replicating systems (see also Bauer and Baumgartner 2010; Goodyear et al. 2015). This is a major topic addressed in *The Nature of Order*

(Alexander 2002a). Whilst a full account of the conceptual ideas in this theory is beyond the scope of this chapter, basic concepts that provide the rationale for the analytic work that follows will be introduced here. In the remainder of this section, all discussions and references are based on the book *The Phenomenon of Life* (Alexander 2002a), which is one of the four volumes comprising *The Nature of Order*. A key idea in this theory is that *all* things in the environment have life: stones, grass, rivers, bricks, cities, paintings, etc. (p. 77). Life is an emergent property of structure; structures present discernible degrees of life, degrees of wholeness (p. 110). That is, life participates in a greater whole; it is *in* and it is a part of space—in varying degrees.

According to Alexander, the phenomenon of life varies in different parts of space because of entities he calls "the wholeness" and "centers" (p. 80). Neutral wholeness, or life, exists everywhere, in all things. *Centers* are coherent configurations that have existence as a local center of activity within living structures. A center is made of other centers—that is the basic definition Alexander provides (p. 116). The *wholeness* of a thing or place depends on the extent to which, at a certain point in time and according to a fluid configuration, centers reinforce one another and/or create new ones. It is the strength of centers (how they overlap and are nested) that determines the *wholeness* of something, its degree of life. That is, centers are the building blocks of wholeness. The fact that wholeness is made of parts and the parts are created by the wholeness is only apparently paradoxical: for Alexander, "parts" and "wholes" *always* work in a holistic way (p. 84). This is fundamentally different from pervasive Cartesian understandings of parts creating wholes. Instead, the relationship described by Alexander is akin to the recursiveness observed in natural systems. For example, the wholeness of a rose is a global structure that manifests itself through the configurations of its petals (centers). The shape and size of the petals depend upon their relationship to the rose plant as a whole and the time when they appear on it (pp. 87–88). The wholeness of the rose comes first, as does a fetus; like everything in nature, human beings grow as a whole (e.g. not the head or legs first and then the arms and torso). One should say that the tree makes its leaves, rather than a tree is made of leaves. A whole is not a sum of parts—it is much greater.

Alexander suggests the replacement of the notion of "a whole" with the conception of "centers." He argues that when designers think in terms of "centers" they are more likely to be aware of the impact of things they design, both on people and on the wider environment. In the case of a fishpond, for instance, seeing it as "a whole" automatically implies mathematical boundaries—what exactly constitutes it, where it begins and ends (p. 84). Conversely, if conceived as "centers," even the shade provided by a tree or fallen leaves in its water, for example, can be seen as part and parcel of the designed fishpond. In this case, the relationships between different elements are always in the forefront of the design conception, helping to highlight the fact that they exist both physically (the actual physical system of the fishpond) and mentally (people's perception of the pond).

> The same is true of all the entities which appear in the world. When I think of them as wholes, or entities, I focus on their boundedness, their separation. When I think of them as centers, I become more aware of their relatedness; I see them as focal points in a larger unbroken whole and I see the world as whole.
>
> (p. 85)

A broader (yet simplistic) example may be helpful for considering the potential of the concept of centers to designers. If one imagines a country road, the details that come to mind may all be potentially contributing centers: the road with possible crossing paths, trees, some types of flower, kangaroos or sheep, a fence, a sign by the road, hills in the background, etc. Additionally, there may be a farmer and his dog, droving the herd, children playing (perhaps just the sound of their voices or laughter), birds singing, a passing cyclist, etc. These are all centers and their combination creates the wholeness of the place. The degree of life conveyed through this example could be compared with a different country spot, plagued with drought and deserted. In this scenario, a lack of contributing centers indicates a lesser degree of life, less wholeness. The phenomenon of a center occurs when various entities work together in a way that creates a field effect.

For Alexander, observation of degrees of life is not purely a cognitive matter, as the entities seen in any configuration are actually real physical features of the space itself. For him, cognitive aspects of perception fall short of explaining the way the world *works* and therefore cannot account for important *subtleties* between humans and the larger environment (pp. 64–66). He argues that evolution has equipped human beings to appreciate subtle qualities in the environment, and people intuitively assign degrees of wholeness to both designed and natural worlds. Accordingly, people intuitively recognize that a place, a city, a building, a painting, a little artifact, etc. manifests life. Likewise, we intuitively realize if a river, a mountain, a beach, or even a person is more, or less, alive. If this is so, then there is a need to account for how people experience life in their surroundings. However, Alexander posits that mainstream science needs to move beyond machine-like views of the universe, which cannot entirely account for how people perceive and interact with a world that encompasses subtle spatial structures not describable using prevalent mechanistic conceptions of order.

Thus, Alexander argues that the gradations of life of different things and places and events are well defined, exist objectively, and are measurable. That is, degrees of life have "an existence" beyond what an individual feels (p. 77). Furthermore, he distinguishes personal opinion and idiosyncrasy from what may be called "shared subjective values."

> We feel that a certain tree, or a certain rock, or a certain clearing, has great power or spirit— or at least we acknowledge that we feel awe in that place, or we feel an intensity or life. Furthermore, this experience is shared and common. It is not idiosyncratic. Many people feel the same way about . . . *this* garden gate, *this* room, *this* bridge, *this* stream, *this* beach.
>
> (p. 72, emphasis in the original)

Alexander has developed a range of methodologies for assessing judgments about the degree of value or relative coherence inherent in a complex system. His methods for measuring the wholeness and life of a "thing" are not purely external—they involve objective observations about the inner reality of feelings. One such method for investigating quality and life in artifacts and places involves simply asking someone to "feel" which of two objects, A or B, is experienced as provoking a good feeling, generating greater wholeness. Based on his extensive empirical research studies, Alexander asserts that he has proved *the fact* that people consistently agree that certain places, artifacts, or events have more or less life when compared to others. "Instinct," he says, partly explains how people sense life in a place or a thing. Most importantly, Alexander claims that "shared subjectivity" (as opposed to idiosyncrasies) must be taken into consideration if science is to be able to completely account for contemporary, increasingly complex systems.

In the next section, I present the conceptual framework of this research, followed by an introduction to NALA—the learning network in this study—and one of its place-based components, which is the focus of this chapter. The analysis of this place-based component encompasses its key structural elements as well as their connections to Alexander's ideas, described above.

Approach to the Case Study

The analytic work presented in this chapter draws on an activity-centered approach (Goodyear and Carvalho 2014). The Activity-Centred Analysis and Design (ACAD) framework focuses on how designed elements and their relationships to pedagogy and context influence what learners do and the quality of their learning outcomes. Central to this framing is the assumption that it is essential to distinguish what has been (and can be) designed and what emerges during learntime, as well as to examine how learners' activities reshape and reorganize learning settings. Designers can only indirectly influence learning and the influence of designed elements on participants' activity cannot be determined in advance. Accordingly, the analytic work explores the three basic components of the problem space of educational design: (i) digital and material spaces, both local and remote; (ii) epistemic tasks considered in relation to nested structures of sub-tasks and supra-tasks, as well as broader conceptualizations of knowledge and ways of knowing; and (iii) interpersonal relationships and divisions of labor, and then inferences on how they combine to influence activity.

In line with the activity-centered framework, the discussions involving selected design elements of the case study presented in this chapter focus on exploring how tools and resources and social interactions become bound up in human activity. In addition to this comprehensive analytic work, some ideas and methods derived from Alexander's design theory are also explored. The aim of this extended analysis is to investigate whether concepts such as wholeness and centers could be useful to supplement analysis for design for learning. In an attempt to explore Alexander's propositions about intuitive assessment of life and shared subjective values, a simple study was devised. The experiment involved using Alexander's A versus B comparison method, as explained in the previous section. The result of this study, which involved only ten students, is in no way presented as being generalizable. It is hoped, however, that it may provide insights to educational design researchers and practitioners following similar lines of inquiry.

The data stems from participant observation in a day-long, place-based learning situation (the NALA 2014 Dublin Student Day), informal conversations with students, unstructured interviews with NALA staff members, analyses of web-based environments, and the small experiment mentioned above. Whilst the research consisted of rigorous data collection in the form of participant observation and field notes, and close analysis of websites and screenshots, I acknowledge that my interpretations may well be influenced by my long involvement in the field of adult literacy as an educator in the slums of Rio de Janeiro, Brazil.

The Case Study: NALA as a Learning Network

Introduction to NALA

The National Adult Literacy Agency (NALA) is an Irish, independent, member-based organization committed to providing learning opportunities for adults with unmet, new, or changing literacy needs in their personal, social, or working life. For over 30 years, NALA has been supporting adult learners, tutors, and literacy providers, and developing policy and research. Initially using the media of television and radio, and more recently the Internet, NALA has been striving to bring learning opportunities closer to adult literacy learners.

From NALA's homepage, adult learners can access a myriad of resources and environments concerned with a "multiplicity" of literacies. These digital resources involve knowledge related to family literacy, health literacy, financial literacy, workplace literacy, and so on. On the homepage, people can also check recent posts featuring in NALA's social media sites such as Facebook and Twitter. From NALA's dedicated YouTube page, learners can access a range of interesting archived materials that include television series especially produced for adult literacy learners. Also accessible from NALA's homepage is a learning environment called Write On. In the www.writeon.ie site, adult literacy learners have a *rare* opportunity to work on traditional literacy (reading and writing) whilst at the same time developing familiarity with digital literacies. (For another example of a network in this domain, see www.alphaplus.ca.) Write On has been redesigned in accordance with the

National Framework of Qualifications of Ireland. It enables Irish learners to work independently, from home, and then apply for official accreditation, if they so choose. Yet, any learner anywhere in the world can get a password and log in to the network. Write On can be used independently, in blended learning contexts (e.g. adult literacy centers), or with the help of NALA's free telephone tutoring. In the latter case, local tutors make use of a complementary sophisticated system that has been designed to allow detailed recording of each learning interaction.

Whilst the World Wide Web affords numerous new channels and modes for reaching and attending to the diverse needs and interests of adult literacy learners, simply by making resources and environments available online, it does not automatically attract adult literacy learners. In many cases, people are not aware that such learning opportunities exist or may be unsure of whether they are relevant to them. Moreover, adults with substantial literacy needs may require some convincing before they feel willing to engage in organized learning tasks. This is due to a range of factors. In many cases, adult literacy learners have been let down by inefficient (or nonexistent) educational systems, which may lead them to believe they are not capable of learning. Furthermore, a pervasive stigma prevents some being willing to admit publicly that they have literacy difficulties. In other cases, people may not have the reading and writing proficiency and/or lack confidence to actively engage in productive networked learning. In the case of Write On, for example, whilst it has been designed for independent work, it may be the case that people lack basic operational skills to engage with the platform. In order to tackle issues such as these, NALA occasionally organizes and promotes special co-presence events, such as Student Days.

Student Days take place once a year, usually in two locations around Ireland, but they seem to have lasting implications for both the organization and its members. Recruitment for the event takes place through the NALA membership, information on its main website, and support from local adult literacy practitioners who encourage their students to attend the event. Registration is open to adults who are improving their literacy and numeracy in an adult education center and/or using www.writeon.ie, and to people who are taking courses to improve their English proficiency. That is, Student Days bring together those who are already members of a "loose" community or network of students and others who have never engaged with NALA. Student Days have three major aims: (i) to heighten awareness, identification, and articulation of adult literacy student issues; (ii) to increase confidence and involvement in events, local services, and beyond; and (iii) to attract new members and/or to facilitate engagement of existing members with other students and NALA.

Rather than being primarily designed by staff, a Student Day is to a great extent designed by NALA's Student Subcommittee (Figure 3.1), which is linked to the NALA Executive Committee. The role of the members in the subcommittee is to focus on adult literacy student needs and report back to the Executive Committee. Such a democratic approach to design is far removed from the historical stereotypes that construct adult literacy in welfarist, deficit, and therapeutic terms (Freire 1970, 1972; Wickert 1992; Hamilton 2011).

The inclusive character of the design of a Student Day is consistent with an important strand of networked learning that upholds democratic and dialogical values. This critical-humanistic strand of work aligns networked learning with issues of power, voice, access, and inclusion (Hodgson, McConnell, and Dirckinck-Holmfeld 2011; McConnell, Hodgson, and Dirckinck-Holmfeld 2011). Networked learning in this sense can be seen as a contemporary literacy practice that involves formal and/or informal learning (Jones 2008). A singular aspect that distinguishes networked learning from similar pedagogies (e.g. computer supported collaborative learning) is its emphasis on connectedness (Goodyear et al. 2004). The inherent, socially situated character of networked learning parallels it with contemporary views of literacy, going beyond the mechanics of reading and writing skills. That is, a significant role of literacy (and networked learning) is to facilitate connections between members of the community so they can learn together and from each other (Barton and Hamilton

FIGURE 3.1 Members of NALA's Student Subcommittee

1998). Initiatives that champion productive networked learning opportunities for adult literacy learners can potentially help to address severe gaps in current educational provision in this domain.

NALA 2014 Dublin Student Day: A Place-based Component

The NALA 2014 Dublin Student Day took place in a local hotel on Saturday April 12. It is estimated that at least 120 people attended the event, which encompassed about six meeting hours. The day started at 10:30 a.m. with registration and morning tea in a reserved area of the hotel. Then the whole group assembled in a large conference room where the chair of the Student Subcommittee officially opened the day by reading a poem before detailing how the day-long event would unfold. Workshops constituted the main items on the agenda. These ran simultaneously between 11 a.m. and 1 p.m. The offerings for 2014 were: (i) "Introduction to Write On"; (ii) "Storytelling"; (iii) "Fun with Numbers"; and (iv) "Moving Debate." Following workshops, lunch was served in an open area of the hotel. Before departing, the whole group joined together again in the main conference room to hear updates and plans for NALA and participate in plenary discussions and evaluations.

The place-based component comprising the Student Day used a range of physical spaces of the hotel allocated for the event. Pleasant, open areas of the hotel were reserved for food breaks. One of these spaces is illustrated in the image on the top of Figure 3.2. Surrounded by natural plants on walls and in pots, it provided a pleasant atmosphere for social interactions during food breaks. A spacious, well-lit conference room, with large windows overlooking Dublin city, had been beautifully set up with 22 round tables surrounded by six chairs each (Figure 3.2). The conference room, temporarily split into two by a moving wall, provided the physical space for two of the workshops. Other than the large conference room and the open areas of the hotel used for food breaks, physical spaces included two additional separate rooms for the two other workshops. Other physical tools

FIGURE 3.2 Physical, Human, and Digital Resources

and resources included a folder containing a range of information flyers about NALA's services and other local organizations working with adult literacy, paper notebooks, and a CD-ROM disk, as well as paper, pencils, crayons, etc. used in workshops.

The digital/electronic set-up involved laptop computers, projectors, Internet access, and software (e.g. Write On, PowerPoint), as well as microphones used during whole-group sessions. The bottom image in Figure 3.2 shows a slide on display as people entered the conference room for the Welcome Session. The message on the projected slide conveys NALA's aim of attracting new people to systematically engage with the network. Every year, a high number of first-time participants sign up to become NALA members, during or following the event. The event seems to inspire newcomers, as suggested in the following remark by a first-time participant about the achievements of students in the subcommittee: "I struggle to believe (name omitted) only learned how to read and write recently. Isn't this amazing?" (46-year-old first-time participant). Observation notes reveal that there were various similar comments where people often highlighted that Student Days offer them valuable chances to network with other adults like themselves and to understand that they are not alone in facing their literacy difficulties. Feedback provided by participants is compiled by NALA and used to inform ongoing design and redesign of the network.

Social, Epistemic, and Set Design, and the Enactment of Multiple Literacies

Except for "Introduction to Write On," all other workshops and sessions were run solely by members of the Student Subcommittee. The success of the whole event demonstrates their professionalism and commitment. By performing organizational, administrative, and teaching roles during the event, the students in the subcommittee create value for themselves and for the whole network (Wenger, Trayner, and De Laat 2011). In fact, the overall participatory design character of the Student Day is consistent with the philosophical underpinning of the original architectural pattern language (Alexander et al. 1977) in that it seeks to empower lay people to take on active roles as designers. The warmth all participants showed toward me, as an overseas researcher, was very impressive.

The incentive for active participation was evident in all workshops and in the case of the "Moving Debate" helped create a productive atmosphere for discussions. The task specification for this workshop was "Share your opinions on a fun topic, then change sides if you change your mind!" Photos of everyday life situations were projected using PowerPoint to trigger initial discussions. Dynamic debates resulted from participants engaging in meaningful and open discussions of their ideas within the friendly environment. By valuing vernacular literacies (Barton and Hamilton 1998), the design of this workshop intended to support interactions that would promote a sense of belonging to a community of learners. Bonds developed during the workshop can potentially lead to, or strengthen, ongoing collaborative learning (e.g. through the Forum and Chat facilities within the Write On platform, which tend to remain underused).

As is the case with well thought-out design for learning, NALA's designers tried to ensure relevant literacy pedagogy was aligned with the desired learning goals and objectives. Teaching and learning practices in all workshops were consistent with approaches to literacy being multimodal and socially situated (Cope and Kalantzis 2000; Gee 2008). The image on the left of Figure 3.3 shows one of the material resources produced during the "Fun with Math" workshop, which did not involve any digital technology. The students facilitating this workshop deployed a variety of semiotic systems (Kress 2000). These included graphical images, colors, as well as gestures (e.g. showing how results for the "9-times table" can be calculated with the use of one hand for "tens" and the other for "ones").

Similar to "Fun with Math", the "Storytelling" workshop did not involve digital technology. Some useful insights can be derived from the way pedagogy and a major element of set design—the "grid" shown on the right side of Figure 3.3—combined to influence activity. The designed grid, provided to each participant, is consistent with a multimodal, socially situated approach to literacy. The designers' decision to use just one single line in each square (as distinct from a full lined page), and to leave blank space for drawing, conveys a message that writing and reading are not prerequisites for sharing meaningful stories. That is, the design afforded activity, irrespective of writing skills, by relaying a message that a meaningful story can also be told through drawings. Further, the artifact afforded the creation of authentic stories, allowing participants to produce their own meanings, according to their interests and life-worlds. This is distinct from learning situations in which all learners are provided with a preselected sequence of images to "create" a story. In such cases, the artifact is likely to constrain personal meaning making when the learner finds the preprinted images uninspiring; a common issue in adult literacy learning contexts. Furthermore, the numbering of each square can function as scaffolding for the sequence of the story (e.g. introduction, body, and

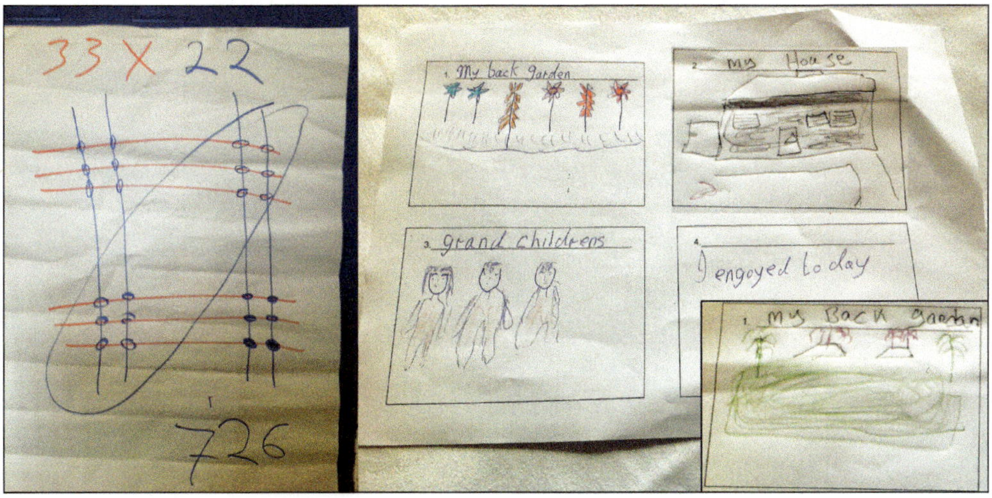

FIGURE 3.3 Physical Resources

end). Thus, despite its simplicity (or because of it) the "story grid" designed in the way shown in Figure 3.3 afforded active participation, irrespective of literacy proficiency. The grid depicted is a composite of two stories (to preserve anonymity) that were particularly captivating. The two ladies, as I personally witnessed in the telling part of this workshop, engaged everyone in listening to their passionate stories, which in both cases started with their *gardens* placed in the number one spot.

The "Introduction to Write On" workshop was the most popular of the day. The design of this workshop was primarily concerned with providing people with basic operational skills (and motivation and confidence) so they could engage in new literacy practices. Whilst the Write On platform is designed for independent work, in many cases people lack basic operational skills to engage with it. By teaching basic navigation skills and providing time for scaffolded experience and peer-to-peer interactions, the workshop helped to bridge gaps, which may prevent people from benefiting from the digitally networked learning opportunities NALA offers. Accordingly, the workshop was specially designed to address issues such as getting a password, logging in, and becoming familiar with basic navigation functionalities. Despite the availability of a video resource (Figure 3.4) to support these procedures, those unfamiliar with computers may easily miss it. This lack of familiarity can cause people to be unable to complete the initial task of entering the system and then missing out working on literacy and numeracy with the support of designed-in scaffolding. This workshop was the only one not solely run by members of the Student Subcommittee; the two NALA staff members present on the day played major roles.

The "Introduction to Write On" workshop had a special physical and digital set-up (Figure 3.4). The physical setting was purposefully arranged to leave space between the chairs and walls so

FIGURE 3.4 Write On Workshop: Digital and Physical Set-Up

as to allow less confident learners (e.g. those who had never used a computer before) to observe peers "over the shoulder." The strategy seemed to work as a senior participant, who initially did not want to try, eventually said: "I think I'll end up missing lunch but I feel like giving it a go." The workshop facilitators also reminded people they should use the telephone tutoring service when experiencing difficulties during independent work. NALA's tutors have a flexible schedule; they work from home and some are available outside regular working hours. This is another important aspect as adult learners are likely to prioritize job and family duties and consequently have limited time for studying during working hours on weekdays.

Traversing and Connecting Digital and Material Spaces

Whilst a Student Day takes place in the material world, its design also concerns activity in the digital world, in a number of important ways. The tangling between the physical and the digital occurs through increased "visibility" and expansion of the network. Two interrelated aspects in particular bring this relationship between digital and material worlds into focus: (i) one of the main aims of the co-presence event is to sustain and expand the community of learners; and (ii) learning interactions are more productive when learners are able to engage with the network's web-based environments (e.g. Write On). The proximal function of the place-based component is to provide people with motivation, tools, and skills that will enable them to engage in online networked learning at a later date. The more socially distal function is to enable the literacy learners to feel better-prepared to fulfill ordinary everyday activities, such as engaging with children in the family whose homework activities are likely to involve multiple literacies. To this end, a small amount of time during the "Introduction to Write On" workshop was dedicated to showcasing NALA's family literacy site: www.helpmykidlearn.ie. In this sense, beneficial effects are extended to others who are not direct participants in the event, or in NALA's learning network.

Visual Clues and Their Influence on Learners' Activity

The complexity of socio-technical ensembles requires deep understandings of the intricate relationships between physical and digital tools and spaces and human activity. The "history" of the learning path, a major element within the Write On online platform, tells us that there are no simple and definitive solutions (Dimitriadis and Goodyear 2013). For example, the learning path (Figure 3.5) was designed after results of usability tests conducted by NALA indicated that the original design—a long list with the sequencing of activities—proved too hard for most learners to *read* and understand. The solution was to replace text with the graphic representation reproduced in Figure 3.5, top. The learning path serves manifold purposes, including the provision of an easy way to navigate through the learning materials that allows learners to keep track of their progress (e.g. learners' activities become reified in the setting).

The arrows in each version of the learning path indicate a collapsible menu. On the top image, the partial vertical rectangle on the far left side failed to afford navigation. Unless "moused over," the vital navigation menu would remain collapsed. Because legibility of the visual clue was weak, learners remained unable to visit many parts of the environment. The bottom image shows the redesigned version in which the word "Options" replaces the partially collapsed rectangle. In this case, legibility was improved through using text—the elimination of which had, paradoxically, generated the design of the original path. The simple text (in this case the word "Options") functions as "an object" (see Carvalho and Goodyear 2014); people may identify it as a clickable anchor due to its bluish color and hyperlink-like character. The text, its shape, and color "tells" them: "click on me."

FIGURE 3.5
Learning Path and
the Redesigned
Learning Path

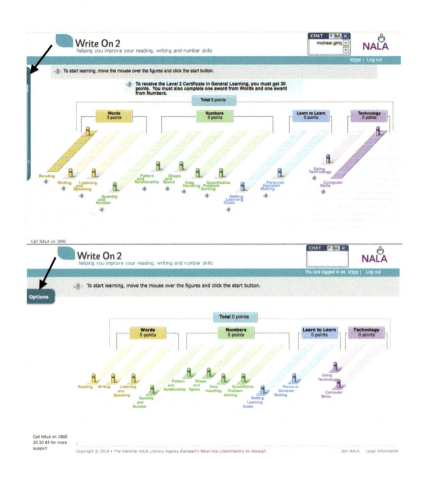

Stretching the Analysis: A Centers-Based Approach

Taking an Alexandrian perspective, the Student Day can be seen as composed of thousands (if not millions) of centers rather than as a "whole" (e.g. the designed tasks, roles, tools, and resources). In this "centered view," the music playing in the background, the natural plants covering walls in common areas of the venue, the plants and flowers in pots and jars and the ways these are arranged in the space (Figure 3.2), the smell of coffee from the open bar, art works, the sun shining through the windows of the hotel, the nearby ships being loaded or unloaded in the Dublin port, the tram that stops by the hotel's entrance, etc. would all be part and parcel of the "design." Further, each participant, the hotel guests and their luggage, the hotel staff, the two NALA staff, the visiting researcher, the meals, and so forth, would also be seen as potential contributing centers. All tools and resources, including those inside the take-home folder distributed to Student Day participants (e.g. CD-ROM disk), are also centers. In turn, each of these centers is recursively constituted of numerous other centers. For example, Figure 3.6 shows a screen shot of one of six "Stories with Me in It" recorded in the CD-ROM. In each story, a different, famous, professional writer works with a different adult literacy learner.

A "*centered approach lens*" helps not only to bring the CD-ROM disk "out of the folder," but also reveals how this "secondary" design element (a take-home resource) entails significant contributing centers in relation to the wholeness of the Student Day. The two people seen strolling in the astonishing natural scenario (a center) are an adult literacy learner (a center) and a best-selling professional writer (a center). Whilst the learning task "simply" requires the learner to write a story

FIGURE 3.6 Image from CD-ROM

for an authentic audience, the unfolding activities show the two "peers" engaging in inspirational mutual-learning interactions, discussing life experiences, and making collaborative decisions about processes, tools, and spaces. It seems fair to say that there is a powerful "*pedagogy of wholeness*" (Pinto forthcoming) imbued in this design, which reflects Alexander's ideas about life-improving patterns. The message conveyed by the "whole" design of the Student Day is one that is likely to resonate with *shared values*, as proposed by Alexander. In the next subsection, a brief practical illustration of these ideas in relation to the conception of centers is presented, using aspects of the design of the Write On platform.

Wholeness and Subjective Shared Values

In early findings of this research (Pinto 2014a), the paired images shown in Figure 3.7 generated some interesting comments. Regarding the top image, an observer declared: "The woman looks more like a zombie . . . it all looks very clinical!" In contrast, the bottom image was described as "creating a nice feeling due to the big windows and connections to nature."

These early observations generated the basis for a pilot study conducted with some of the participants in the Student Day. The aim of this study was to devise analytical tools that could potentially support the exploration of Alexander's ideas about wholeness and subjective shared values, and ways of exploring people's varied perceptions. Alexander's method involved a comparison of two objects. In the pilot study, Artifact A (Figure 3.7, top) was a print out of the Write On Log in page, and Artifact B was a printout of the Welcome page (Figure 3.7, bottom). The researcher showed the two printed colored copies to ten participants individually (four male, six female) and asked the question: "To you, which one of these two *feels* more alive, and provides you with a personal sense of life?" (Alexander 2002a, p. 76). Two people did not make an explicit choice and both concentrated on functional aspects of the software instead (e.g. challenges associated with navigation). Eight out of ten participants referred to the plants seen through the windows and inside the room in Artifact B as determining factors in their reasons for preferring this option over the other. Out of these, four also mentioned the painting on the wall. The more lifelike appearance of the three people in Artifact B seemed also to be appreciated. The higher degree of life "felt" in Artifact B can be traced to Alexander's proposition in relation to how centers overlap to reinforce and/or create new ones, in ways that induce "life" in structures.

FIGURE 3.7 Write On Log In Page (top); Write On Welcome Page (bottom)

Main centers within the central part of the image shown as Artifact B include: each of the three people, the spaces between their bodies, their gentle smiles, the friendliness of what they are saying, the speech bubbles, the vivid colors of their clothes, the work of art on the wall, each brick that forms the wall and the spaces between them, the window, the window sill, the mountains in the background, the trees, the houses, the sky, and so on and so forth. Meanwhile, the main centers in the central part of the Log in page (Artifact A) are: the woman, the balloon with her speech, the boxes to enter the password, and the audio icons and their accompanying texts. It is not, however, simply the presence or absence of centers that indicates the degree of life in structure. It depends on how configurations become coherent and whether the centers form *living* structures. Artifact A not only has fewer centers than B but its centers do not seem to help one another. For example, the body language of the "zombie"-like image of the woman is poor when compared to Sean's (the person to the left in Artifact B). Whilst the position of Sean's arms induces "an action" center through its movement, her arms fail to produce a contributing center.

Whilst not suggesting that such a modest study can be generalized, it does reinforce and illustrate two of Alexander's main claims: (i) the degree of life discerned in a structure is objective, that is, it resides *in* the structure itself and has a real existence in space; (ii) there tends to be a high level of agreement in people's observations of structures. Moreover, it seems to support his claim that we, being centers ourselves, tend to feel our inner life intensified by the presence of living centers.

Concluding Remarks

One of the aims of this chapter was to suggest that analysis for design for learning needs to look for patterns that embrace both complexities and subtleties. As Alexander sensitively posits, good design involves "a state of mind and a control over process and adaptation, which allows things to be made so they genuinely support you, me, the cat next door, the birds in the garden" (1999, p. 5). Following Alexander, I have suggested we should pay more attention to the wholeness of the world, including subjective shared values, and degrees of life in the artifacts we design or assign to infrastructures for learning. Therefore, the point I have tried to make goes beyond what mainstream cognitive psychology, human computer interaction, interface design, etc. already cover. I have suggested that designers could benefit from exploring sensibilities that stretch "conventional" approaches used in educational design.

It seems as though an explicit language to talk about the effects of natural and designed elements on people's physical, mental, emotional, and even spiritual wellbeing should be part of an educational designer's repertoire. For example, platforms such as Facebook and Twitter have been providing users with prime space to customize their pages; personal profiles in such platforms, as well as blogs, wikis, etc., invariably illustrate a high incidence of shared values (e.g. photos of people in "special" places such as in natural settings). All of this concurs with Alexander's general design theory. Thus, Alexander's *The Nature of Order* seems a good starting point for research in this area, which remains undertheorized within educational design contexts. Concepts such as *wholeness* and *centers* seem to provide a useful basis for a new metalanguage which could be helpful not only for more informed design decisions in general (e.g. interdisciplinary design processes and practices), but also for unveiling life-improving design patterns and pattern languages. As a result, we may become more aware of how our designs are designing the world. In this sense, it is hoped that the case study presented in this chapter provides inspiration on how citizens' commitment to inclusive, democratic, and participatory design can help build a better world for all.

Acknowledgments

The author gratefully acknowledges the contributions to this study by NALA's Student Subcommittee members and all other participants in the Student Day, as well as the whole NALA staff.

References

Alexander, C., 1979. *The timeless way of building.* New York: Oxford University Press.

Alexander, C., 1999. The origins of pattern theory: The future of the theory, and the generation of a living world. *IEEE Software,* 16(5), 71–82.

Alexander, C., 2002a. *The nature of order—an essay on the art of building and the nature of the universe, Book One: The phenomenon of life.* Berkeley, CA: The Center for Environmental Structure.

Alexander, C., 2002b. *The nature of order—an essay on the art of building and the nature of the universe, Book Two: The process of creating life.* Berkeley, CA: The Center for Environmental Structure.

Alexander, C., 2004. *The nature of order—an essay on the art of building and the nature of the universe, Book Four: The luminous ground.* Berkeley, CA: The Center for Environmental Structure.

Alexander, C., 2005. *The nature of order—an essay on the art of building and the nature of the universe, Book Three: A vision of a living world.* Berkeley, CA: The Center for Environmental Structure.

Alexander, C., Ishikawa, S., Silverstein, M., Jacobson, M., Fiksdahl-King, I., and Angel, S., 1977. *A pattern language: Towns, buildings, construction.* New York: Oxford University Press.

Barton, D. and Hamilton, M., 1998. *Local literacies: Reading and writing in one community.* New York: Routledge.

Bauer, R. and Baumgartner, P., 2010. A first glimpse at the whole: Christopher Alexander's fifteen fundamental properties of living centers and their implications for education. In: C. Kohls and J. Wedekind, eds., *Investigations of e-learning patterns: Context factors, problems and solutions* (pp. 272–284). Hershey, PA: IGI Global.

Carvalho, L. and Goodyear, P., eds., 2014. *The architecture of productive learning networks.* New York: Routledge.

Conole, G. and Jones, C., 2010. Sharing practice, problems and solutions for institutional change: Comparing different forms of representation. In: P. Goodyear and S. Retalis, eds., *Technology-enhanced learning: Design patterns and pattern languages* (pp. 87–112). Rotterdam: Sense Publishers.

Cope, B. and Kalantzis, M., eds., 2000. *Multiliteracies: Literacy learning and the design of social futures*. London: Psychology Press.

Dimitriadis, Y. and Goodyear, P., 2013. Forward-oriented design for learning: Illustrating the approach. *Research in Learning Technology,* 21, 1–13. [online]. Available from: http://www.researchinlearningtechnology.net/index.php/rlt/article/view/20290/pdf_1 [Accessed July 18, 2015].

Freire, P., 1970. The adult literacy process as cultural action for freedom. *Harvard Educational Review*, 40(2), 205–225.

Freire, P., 1972. *Pedagogy of the oppressed*. Harmondsworth, UK: Penguin.

Gee, J. P., 2008. Learning and games. In: K. Salen, ed., *The ecology of games: Connecting youth, games, and learning* (pp. 21–40). Cambridge, MA: MIT Press.

Goodyear, P. and Carvalho, L., 2014. Framing the analysis of learning network architectures. In: L. Carvalho and P. Goodyear., eds., *The architecture of productive learning networks* (pp. 48–70). New York: Routledge.

Goodyear, P. and Retalis, S., eds., 2010. Learning, technology and design. In: P. Goodyear and S. Retalis, eds., *Technology-enhanced learning: Design patterns and pattern languages* (pp. 1–27). Rotterdam: Sense Publishers.

Goodyear, P., Banks, S., Hodgson, V., and McConnell, D., 2004. Research on networked learning: An overview. In: P. Goodyear, S. Banks, V. Hodgson, and D. McConnell., eds., *Advances in research on networked learning* (pp.1–9). Dordrecht, The Netherlands: Kluwer Academic.

Goodyear, P., De Laat, M., and Lally, V., 2006. Using pattern languages to mediate theory-praxis conversations in design for networked learning. *ALT-J: Research in Learning Technology*, 14(3), 211–223.

Goodyear, P., Thompson, K., Ashe, D., Pinto, A., Carvalho, L., Parisio, M., Parker, P., Schwendimann, B., Wardak, D., and Yeoman, P., 2015. Analysing the structural properties of learning networks: Architectural insights into buildable forms. In: B. Craft, Y. Mor, and M. Maina, *The art and science of learning design* (pp. 15–30). Rotterdam: Sense Publishers.

Hamilton, M., 2011. Unruly practices: What a sociology of translations can offer to educational policy analysis. *Educational Philosophy and Theory*, 43(1), 55–75.

Hodgson, V., McConnell, D., and Dirckinck-Holmfeld, L., 2011. The theory, practice and pedagogy of networked learning. In: L. Dirckinck-Holmfeld, V, Hodgson, and D. McConnell, eds., *Exploring the theory, pedagogy and practice of networked learning* (pp. 291–305). New York: Springer.

Jones, C., 2008. Networked learning: A social practice perspective. In: V. Hodgson, C. Jones, T. Kargidis, D. McConnell, S. Retalis, D. Stamatis, and M. Zenios, eds., *Proceedings of the 6th International Conference on Networked Learning* (pp. 616–623), May 5–6, Halkidiki, Greece. Available from: http://www.networked learningconference.org.uk/past/nlc2008/abstracts/PDFs/Jones_616–623.pdf [Accessed March 1, 2016].

Kress, G., 2000. Design and transformation: New theories of meaning. In: B. Cope and M. Kalantzis, eds., *Multiliteracies: Literacy learning and the design of social futures* (pp.153–161). New York: Routledge.

McConnell, D., Hodgson, V., and Dirckinck-Holmfeld, L., 2011. Networked learning: A brief history and new trends. In: L. Dirckinck-Holmfeld, V. Hodgson, and D. McConnell, eds., *Exploring the theory, pedagogy and practice of networked learning* (pp. 3–24). New York: Springer.

Mor, Y., Mellar, H., Warburton, S., and Winters, N., 2014. *Practical design patterns for teaching and learning with technology*. Dordrecht, The Netherlands: Springer.

NALA, 2015. The national agency for adult literacy. [online]. Available from: www.nala.ie [Accessed July 18, 2015].

Pinto, A., 2014a. Networked learning: Designing for adult literacy education. *Literacy and Numeracy Studies*, 22(1), 21–38.

Pinto, A., 2014b. Design and the functioning of a productive learning network. In: S. Bayne, C. Jones, M. de Laat, T. Ryberg, and C. Sinclair, eds., *Proceedings of the Ninth Networked Learning Conference,* April 7–9, Edinburgh. Edinburgh: Networked Learning Conference Organiser.

Pinto, A., (forthcoming). *Pedagogy of wholeness*. Thesis (Ph.D.). University of Sydney.

Wenger, E., Trayner, B., and De Laat, M., 2011. *Promoting and assessing value creation in communities and networks: A conceptual framework*. Heerlen, The Netherlands: Ruud de Moor Centrum.

Wickert, R., 1992. Constructing adult illiteracy: Mythologies and identities, *Discourse*, 12(2), 29–38.

4

A STUDY OF CORRESPONDENCE, DISSONANCE, AND IMPROVISATION IN THE DESIGN AND USE OF A SCHOOL-BASED NETWORKED LEARNING ENVIRONMENT

Pippa Yeoman

In a collection about learning networks with an emphasis on place it is both appropriate and necessary to examine our thoughts about *things*, and in turning to the literature one finds that one has opened a veritable Pandora's box. For if we are to give things their due, we find that a meaningful engagement with the material requires more than the reintroduction of things into an existing worldview. The absence of things, in all their forms, is more than an oversight—it is an expression of a deeply held view of the world with man at its center, and in questioning this view Karen Barad asks:

> What compels the belief that we have a direct access to cultural representations and their content that we lack toward the things represented? How did language come to be more trustworthy than matter? Why are language and culture granted their own agency and historicity while matter is figured as passive and immutable, or at best inherits a potential for change derivatively from language and culture? How does one even go about inquiring after the material conditions that have led us to such a brute reversal of naturalist beliefs when materiality itself is always already figured within a linguistic domain as its condition of possibility?
>
> (2003, p. 801)

How does one begin to address the consequences of this framing? Bill Brown, toying with the notion of theory and the work that it accomplishes, considers the merits of a "Thing Theory" (Brown 2001). Whilst Tim Ingold suggests that we need nothing less than a theory of life itself in which matter is no longer cast as inanimate, raw material, awaiting animation but as we find it in processes of flow and transformation. Where things are perceived as gatherings of materials in movement, as distinct from objects, "completed forms that stand over and against the perceiver" (Ingold 2012, p. 439) blocking movement; and the body "a dynamic center of unfolding activity, rather than a sink into which practices are sedimented" (Ingold 2012, p. 439). Where one makes one's way in the world—not in successional moves, with each action predetermined by its place in a sequence of steps—but processionally, with each action a measured response to the last (Ingold 2011, p. 62). And knowledge is understood as an increased sensitivity to cues in the environment, rendering the skillful those who learn to match their movements to perturbations in the environment without interrupting the flow of their actions. Where it is not so much what you know, but how well you know it that is valued (Ingold 2011, p. 94) and the distance of interaction gives way to entwined correspondence, which offers us the possibility of joining with, and answering to, a world perpetually unfolding.

Dominated by humanistic approaches that start with people and their needs, educational research has barely begun to consider a world in which materials are anything more than "instruments for educational practice" (Sørensen 2009, p. 2). In describing how this perspective has led to conclusions that attribute success or failure with little regard for observable changes that deviate from expectations, Estrid Sørensen (2009) makes a case for a post-humanist perspective. Invoking "a minimal methodology" in which she articulates two central questions—namely *How do materials participate in practice?* and *How do we account for their participation?*—she moves the debate from one in which materials are described as either meeting or failing to meet expectations, to one in which materials both new and old are described—in activity, irrespective of expectations.

On the fringes of metropolitan Sydney, Australia, is a school that has worked very hard to integrate its physical, virtual, and pedagogic spaces (Harris 2010). At Northern Beaches Christian School (NBCS) they carefully consider how things and people shape both learning and the learning environment. In 2005 they initiated a ten-year plan that started with the creation of an online learning space for every physical learning space in the school, from Kindergarten to Year 12. As these spaces were incorporated into teaching and learning practices staff reported that the physical spaces, as they were, worked against their best efforts to effect change. With alterations made to the built environment, online spaces assumed critical structural and administrative functions and both the shape and role of space and time in teaching were renegotiated. Environments that had been designed to replicate the same for all concurrently gave way to open, agile, and activity-based spaces, and time more generously apportioned facilitated deeper engagement over a longer arc. The substance of this chapter draws on 549 hours of participant observation in one particular learning environment at NBCS, called the Zone; home to 180 Year 5 and Year 6 students (aged between 10 and 12) and their team of seven teachers. The Zone was born out of the success of an earlier project, designed to deliver a flexible online curriculum to Years 7 and 8, using one-to-one desktop technology. The Zone differed from this project in one critical respect. From the outset it was conceived of as a digitally enabled space, rather than a digitally enabled curriculum, and all design decisions were made assuming a mobile one-to-one network of learners, resources, and teachers. In the absence of 180 copies of every textbook, workbook, and reference book the requirements of the physical space were radically altered, setting in motion a cascade of change in both teaching and learning.

One might ask if a digitally connected physical learning space can be described as a learning network? If so, how would this develop our understanding of the role of materials in learning? Early descriptions of networked learning focused on how computing technologies promoted connections between learners, tutors, learning communities, and learning resources (Goodyear, Hodgson, and Steeples 1998). More recently Goodyear and Carvalho (2014) have described the movement of people, objects, or messages as fundamental to networking. As such a learning network can be described as one in which learners are connected to one another, to their teachers, and to learning resources via technology which facilitates needs- or activity-based connections over time and space. These connections tend to be less durable over the long term but provide moments of rich exchange during periods of mutually aligned focus and are characterized by the movement of people and things, where things are described as "gatherings of materials in movement" as distinct from objects: "completed forms that stand over and against the perceiver and block further movement" (Ingold 2012, p. 439). As such, where the digital and physical merge—in learning—activity is strongly anchored in a particular place, yet travels out of, into, and through this permeable space in ways that are only possible via networked technologies. One may conclude that it is indeed a locus of networked learning activity. Moreover, it is crucial to understand the degree to which the physicality of this learning space is born out of the mobility and openness inherent in its digital elements.

In examining how elements come together in ways that influence learning in networks Goodyear and Carvalho (2013) have identified three central components, namely the structures of place (set design), task (epistemic design), and social organization (social design). Their framework has been applied in the analysis of several online learning networks (Carvalho and Goodyear 2014) and in preliminary work exploring place-based learning activity (Yeoman and Carvalho 2014) and multimedia project work (Thibaut et al. 2015) in the Zone. Research examining the relationships between learning activity and purely physical learning environments is scarce (Woolner et al. 2007) and where it can be found it is often "inconclusive, contradictory or incomplete" (Woolner and Hall 2010, p. 3255). There is arguably more research into learning activity in online environments (Spector et al. 2013); however, this research seldom accounts for the physically situated nature of digital learning. This may be attributed to the complexity of these environments and the fact that until recently researchers have considered teaching and learning in isolation, or have limited their focus to the effects of the built environment, or teaching practice alone (Gislason 2010). Where the built environment has been shown to influence learning (Barrett et al. 2013; Woolner et al. 2012) these relationships are multifactorial, vary considerably according to context, and are often unidirectional. That is, physical spaces have been shown to entrench practice. However, changed physical spaces do not always change practice (Woolner et al. 2012). What distinguishes Goodyear and Carvalho's framework is its focus on the quality of emergent learning activity and how it is broadly supported by those elements of the environment, social organization, and task that are open to alteration, and the role of teachers and learners in the co-construction and co-configuration of these elements at learntime.

There is a tension between design conceived of as prescription in advance and design that flows out of the embodied perception of action within the environment. The former, an activity based on representations in the mind of the designer—planned and strategic. The latter, an activity based on the perceptual response of the designer to perturbations in the environment—more organic and improvisatory in nature. In this chapter, I focus on the things that make a space a learning place. I consider what can be gained from a view of the world in which design is understood, not only as "finding the grain of the world's becoming—the way it wants to go—but also in bending it to an evolving purpose . . . giving direction rather than specifying end points" (Gatt and Ingold 2013, p. 144). I will argue that both the planned for and the organic have their place when it comes to the design and use of complex learning environments and that it is the ability to hold this tension, in the doing, that sets the conditions within which the coupling of perception and action in learning activity give rise to moments of deep learning.

In what follows, I briefly describe the epistemic, social, and set design of the Zone before presenting a rich description of one particular moment of learning activity. After which I explore how the coherence and/or dissonance between the three dimensions influences learning activity, in the hopes of deepening our understanding of the role of improvisation in both the design and practice of teaching and learning in complex networked learning environments. For, in so doing, I hope to explore how thinking about things illuminates a world-already-in-motion and how this should alter our thinking about design for learning.

Epistemic Design of the Zone

From its inception the Zone was designed to facilitate the delivery of a mobile digital curriculum geared toward independent learning, in a purpose-built environment for 180 Year 5 and Year 6 students. The first team of teachers to work in the Zone moved in prior to the commencement of building works. During this year they were active participants in shaping a new style of digitally-enabled team teaching and the space that would accommodate it. Whilst this opportunity was unusual, it was offered within a context in which all teachers were encouraged to reflect on their current teaching practice, participate in research-based innovation, and contribute to personal learning networks, both physical and digital. It was an environment in which time itself had not escaped examination, resulting in the adoption of term-based units of time, supported by four 75-minute learning sessions per day, rather than smaller discrete units of lesson-based learning. The flexibility this arrangement afforded resulted in a qualitatively different engagement with tasks. Not to mention the freedom it gave teachers to alter pace, depth, and content depending on either an individual student's or group's progress. Days in the Zone were loosely shaped, with literacy and numeracy in the first two learning sessions and matrix (project-based work) in the last. The third learning session accommodated sports, music, languages, and assemblies, or additional literacy, numeracy, or project work, as needed. Moreover, housed within thematic units, what was learnt in numeracy often filtered into literacy and appeared in practice in the completion of project work. Within this structure students were flexibly streamed across the two-year stage and were allocated to teachers based on learning style or interests, and performance.

Social Design of the Zone

The community of 180 students in the Zone was divided into three home classes, for Years 5 and 6 respectively. Each group of approximately 30 students was allocated to a home class teacher and the seventh member of staff was tasked with oversight of the whole. Home classes gathered at the beginning and end of every day and did both project work and sports together. At all other times it was hard to identify particular groups of working students either by their location or their proximity to a particular member of staff. Literacy and numeracy were taught in groups of varying sizes (10, 50, and 120 or 15, 45, 85, and 35) before students dispersed to work independently or in small groups. Most students had at least one other principal teacher for numeracy or literacy and this fostered the development of supportive learning relationships between the staff and students who spent two years together in the Zone. Work was often collaborative by design and where it was not officially referred to as such, varying degrees of collaboration were frequently evident. Teachers offered direct instruction and role modeling of effective strategies for working in teams, in person, and in moderating online class environments. Discussion threads were largely administrative or organizational in nature, connecting work at school with work at home and vice versa. Homework often included posting an original response to a task in addition to a constructive response to the post of another, online. Parents were encouraged to access a customized view of their child's Edmodo dashboard, which provided information about work set, submitted, and assessed, and a view of their child's contributions to online discussions. As a faith-based school the teachers and many of the students shared a common point of reference, valuing relationships, community, and the individual's place within it. Learning from past mistakes and "having a go" were encouraged and when pressed for "the general rules of the Zone," one teacher described them to me as follows: "Respect the learning, respect the people, respect the space."

Set Design of the Zone

The Zone was a refurbishment of what had been the primary school library and a number of smaller classrooms that had formed the base of an adjacent school block. Connected by a series of broad carpeted stairs it spread out over two levels in one uninterrupted volume with the exception of a small glass–walled staff room, a soundproof recording room, and an art supply cupboard. The lower rectangular section was fitted with two sets of retractable glass doors, which when drawn created two smaller spaces on either side of the central section that was continuous with the stairs and the upper section. At the start of each year, the students in Year 5 were allocated home classes in the lower section as it offered slightly less unbounded physical space in which they could learn the skills necessary to work in a flexible digitally extended learning environment. After six months

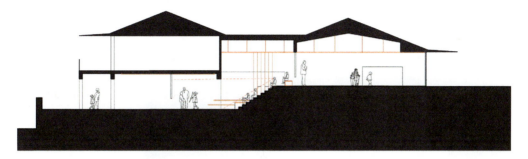

FIGURE 4.1 Cross Section of the Zone

Source: BVN Architecture, Sydney, 2010

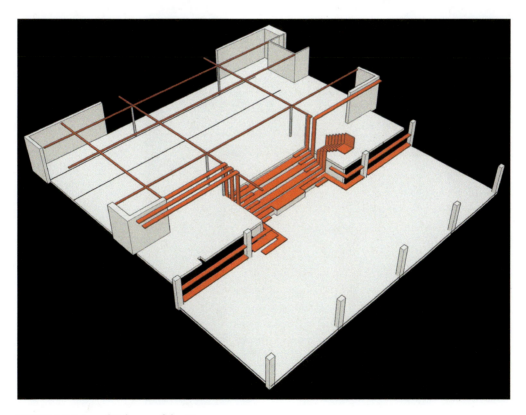

FIGURE 4.2 Internal Volume of the Zone

Source: BVN Architecture, Sydney, 2010

they switched home bases with the students in Year 6. The rationale behind this was twofold: it gave the students in Year 5 a chance to practice their newly established independent learning skills; and it prevented the staff responsible for the Year 5 classes from "reverting back to four-walled-teaching." For even in this refurbished space the pull toward separate, less mobile groups of students oriented toward the teacher "at the front"—was stronger downstairs.

In furnishing the Zone, careful attention was given to providing sufficient appropriate work-stations for all without this translating into the same for all, concurrently. This meant that each of the six internal centers was furnished with different types of activity in mind and whilst each functioned as the home base for one of the six classes, this did not confer ownership or exclusive rights of use on this particular group. Use of space was determined by the size of the learning whole (1, 2, 10, 15, 30, 90, or 180) and activity type.

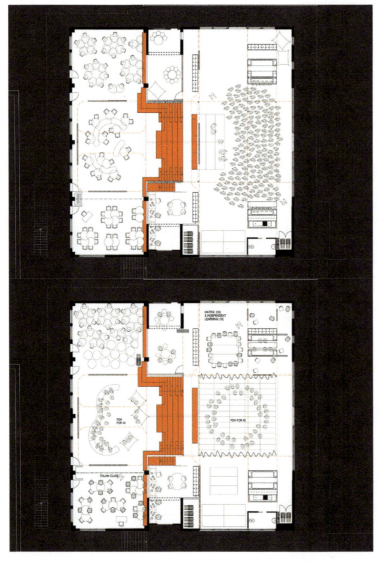

FIGURE 4.3 Two Possible Activity-Centered Configurations of the Zone

Source: BVN Architecture, Sydney, 2010

TABLE 4.1 Physical Tools (Materials) in the Zone

	Surface	Seating	Storage	Other
Tables (standard)	X		X	
Tables (high)	X		X	
Tables (low)	X	X	X	X
Concrete floor	X	X		
Carpeted floor	X	X		X
Stairs	X	X		X
Laptop supports	X			X
Writable walls	X		X	X
Writable glass windows	X		X	X
Writable glass doors	X		X	X
Large whiteboards	X		X	X
A5 whiteboards	X		X	X
Storage cupboards	X		X	X
Desk chairs	X	X		X
Studio chairs	X	X		X
Upholstered sofas		X		X
Bean bags		X		
Ottomans	X	X	X	X
Laptop cages			X	X
Boxed shelving			X	X
Art supply cupboard			X	
Teacher's caddies	X		X	
Bag hooks outside			X	
Shared printer				X
Digital cameras			X	X
Large screen TVs	X			X
Paper recycling			X	
General waste				X
Whiteboard markers	X			

The Zone's digital learning environment was housed in PETE (Primary Education Through eLearning), a Moodle based learning management system. Accessed via a unique login, students navigated by stage (year group), subject (numeracy, literacy, and project work), and school term to choose from a large selection of independent and collaborative tasks. Each task was described on a "task card," which included the aim, steps, and resources required, and additional hyperlinks to websites, templates, and tools. All students were required to provide their own personal digital device. Whilst the school took responsibility for providing schoolwide WiFi for up to three

TABLE 4.2 Digital (Mobile) Tools Used in the Zone

Function	Application
Internet browser	Safari, Explorer, and Firefox
Text editor	MS Word, Excel, and PowerPoint
	Pages, Numbers, and Keynote
	Google documents
Design	GoogleSketchup and Minecraft
Video recording	iMovie
Camera	Photobooth
Voice recording	Assorted applications
Image processing	iMovie, Photoshop, and Pixilmator
Reference apps	Google Maps, Google Earth, and Google Body
Content curating	Weebly, WordPress, glog, PowerPoint, Prezi, Woordle, Storify, and Bamboo Paper
Content distribution	YouTube, Vimeo, and Edmodo
Organization	Google calendar, iCal, Google documents, Evernote, and Edmodo
Video communication	Skype and FaceTime
Text communication	Google mail and documents, Skype, and Edmodo
Mirror	Photobooth and FaceTime
Light box	Image in Preview on backlit screen of laptop
Calculator	Assorted applications and Excel
Compass	Assorted applications

digital devices per student, multiple online environments, and shared printing capabilities, maintenance and the basic skills associated with using the devices were the responsibility of the students and their parents. A list of various self-selected software applications in use during 2012 can be found in Table 4.2.

The Zone in Action

In exploring this unusual environment it was never my intention to reduce what I had seen to a list of necessary objects and candidate moves, the faithful duplication of which would replicate its success. Rather, through rich description of learning activity as it occurred in the Zone, I hope to broaden our perspective of what a productive, placed-based learning network looks like and, in so doing, refocus our attention on those things which are open to alteration: elements across all three dimensions, at multiple scales—as evidenced in learning activity.

October 31, 2012: Edward and Isobel Develop a Method

Part of the way through a learning session dedicated to numeracy my attention is drawn to the far upper corner of the Zone where I can see Edward sitting on the floor, whilst Isobel jumps around him. I make my way over to the edge of the central carpeted space and pause, not wanting to disturb them. As I get closer I can see that Edward is doing his best to hold two 30-cm rulers, one on top of the other, in order to measure the height of Isobel's jumps. His attempts to do this mid-air fail repeatedly and it is not long before Mr. Osborne has also taken note of their activity, although he does not move toward them. They continue jumping until finally, from a heap on the floor, they both look to where I am sitting. I smile, remain seated at a distance, and hope that they will persevere. They laugh and collapse animatedly on the floor, for my benefit. Torn between doing nothing and having them abandon their work—and interfering, I ever so slightly nod at the wall behind them. Interpreting my action in an instant, they quickly locate an appropriate marker and set to work recording height jumped against the semi-permanent writing surface of the white wall. The task they have selected involves calculating the height of their jumps, on the moon—without actually going to the moon.

Scanning the space I see that Mr. Osborne is slowly making his way toward them, stopping to check in with others along the way. He approaches and, withholding judgment, questions them about the rationale behind their method. Satisfied, he goes on to ask about the relationship between the weight of the jumper and the height of their jump. This leads to predictions about the height of his jump on the moon, considering his weight on the earth. Predictions made, he seamlessly moves from interested observer to participant. Jumping, adding his data to the wall, and—after a brief discussion—withdrawing from the group.

The wall had initially been used to mark and measure the height of each jump but having done this, Edward, with pen in hand, begins to record these measurements at standing height in a list to the left of where they had been working. As a small group gathers they refine their method: jump; mark, measure, and call it out; calculate and call out the conversion; echo and add the converted height to the list; calculate the moon-weight of the jumper and tabulate it against the moon-height of their jump. The table had been a natural outworking of their predictions about the effect of weight on the height of their jumps on the moon and as it began to fill up with data it provided an effective aid in explaining their method to others who joined in. During this process Edward's laptop, safely placed on a nearby workbench, was consulted many times to clarify the structure of the task and locate resources to illustrate and then calculate the conversions.

As the learning session drew to a close it dawned on them that the only record of their work was on the wall. Undeterred they recruited me to photograph both their list and their table. Marveling at their resourcefulness—I capture their work but my reverie is short lived for without the correct cable to transfer the images in a useable format, I think I am powerless to help. Mumbling an apology and trying to assess the capabilities of their laptops before suggesting alternatives, I am stopped by Edward—who simply asks where to find the SD card in my camera. Rolling my camera around in my hands I locate the correct door in the housing and try to open it. Edward helps to remove the card and dashes off to find a friend with a computer that will accommodate it. Laptop sourced and access negotiated he downloads the correct files, emails them to himself, returns the card to me, and uploads their work in a PowerPoint presentation to Ms. Bailey, well satisfied. I am left wondering what Ms. Bailey will make of their submission, for she was tasked with the responsibility of seeing that they make adequate progress—according to the curriculum, but how could she possibly account for all that had transpired during these 17 minutes, not having watched as it played out?

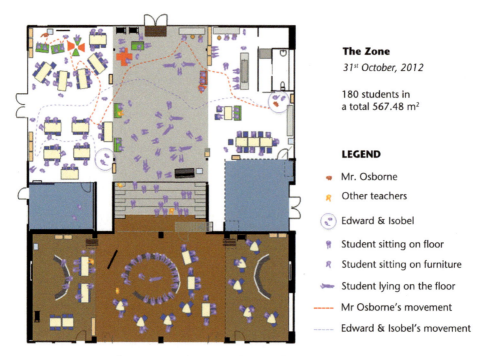

The Zone

31st October, 2012

180 students in
a total 567.48 m²

LEGEND

🦐 Mr. Osborne

ᴿ Other teachers

ⓒ Edward & Isobel

🧍 Student sitting on floor

ᴿ Student sitting on furniture

🏊 Student lying on the floor

----- Mr Osborne's movement

----- Edward & Isobel's movement

FIGURE 4.4 Overview of Activity in the Zone during This Learning Session (Illustrated Using a Diagraming Tool Created by Mie Guldbæk Brøns of LOOP.bz, Denmark)

11.14 am: Method 1: rulers Method 2: wall and markers Edward initiates the list

Online instructions and calculator 11.26 am: Isobel initates the table 11.26 am: Mr Osborne approaches

11.28 am: They explain their method He challenges them Predictions made, he jumps

11.28 am: Others join in The final list – evidence of work complete The final table – evidence of work complete

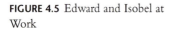

FIGURE 4.5 Edward and Isobel at Work

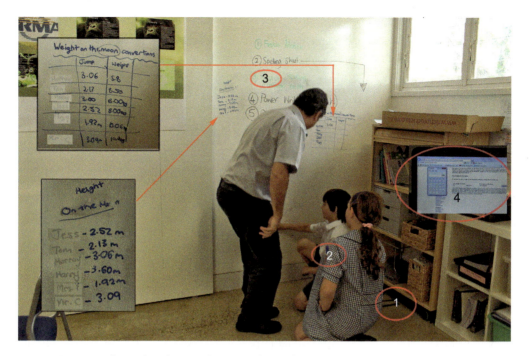

FIGURE 4.6 Materials Used in the Development of a Method

Note: Figure 4.6 illustrates the location, choice and order in which things were employed in the doing of this task. Working independently these students selected a corner with room to jump. When their attempts to use their rulers (1) failed, they used markers (2) on the white wall (3) to indicate height jumped. Following their success they used the wall (3) to record and tabulate data, while referring to (4) the task card housed in the primary LMS, additional online resources, and a calculator application on Edward's laptop.

Tracing Correspondence, Dissonance, and Improvisation in Learning Activity

Following things caught up in learning activity, with reference to the elements of the framework, I explore how correspondence, dissonance, and the improvisational skill involved in navigating the tension between the two shed light on how we might re-imagine both the roles of the instructional designer and the teacher. In doing so I draw on Tim Ingold's use of correspondence, where "To correspond with the world . . . is not to describe it, or to represent it, but to answer to it" (Gatt and Ingold 2013, p. 144). However, in examining emergent learning activity I use Ingold's conceptualizations to describe the ways in which learning is a correspondence, or response in the learner, to the task, the tool, and/or the people present. Furthermore, by introducing the notion of dissonance I distinguish between moments in which correspondence, so defined, leads to a continuation of activity, and moments in which correspondence calls for an alteration in course, due to temporary dissonance, in which one sees the emergence of improvisatory skills in the learner. For in a world-already-in-motion, the skilled are those who can match their movements to the perturbations in the environment without interrupting the flow of their actions. So defined, skill is not an attribute to be acquired once, but something that grows in the doer as he or she develops through active engagement with his or her environment (Ingold 2011). And within this framing, the role of things becomes increasingly important to understand—in learning, as in life.

In creating the turn-by-turn list of actions from the thick description as seen in Table 4.3, I was careful to follow materials in use, looking always for the underlying rhythm of learning activity with reference to changes in the materials and the quality of the activity that precipitated or followed these changes. In this way I identified five phases, noting moments of correspondence, dissonance, and improvisation across all three dimensions of the framework. A detailed description of each of the five phases is listed below.

TABLE 4.3 Phases of Learning Activity Highlighting (C) Correspondence, (D) Dissonance, and (I) Improvisational Skill

Phase	ID	Activity	Epistemic	Social	Set
1	Isobel	Selects partner	C	C	C
	Edward & Isobel	Select task	C	C	C
	Edward & Isobel	Select location	C	C	C
	Edward	Selects tools	C	C	C
2	Edward	Holds rulers	C	C	D
	Isobel	Jumps	C	C	C
	Edward	Tries to measure	C	C	D
	Isobel	Repeatedly jumps	C	D	D
	Edward	Fails to accurately measure	D	D	D
	Researcher	Notes activity and moves closer	C	C	C
	Mr. Osborne	Notes movement	C	C	C
	Isobel	Jumps	D	D	D
	Edward	Rejects Method 1	D	C	D
3	Edward, Isobel & researcher	Select alternate tool (wall)	I	I	I
	Isobel	Jumps	C	C	C
	Edward	Marks height	C	C	C
	Edward & Isobel	Measure height	C	C	C
	Isobel	Creates list on wall	C	I	I
	Edward	Consults task card	C	C	C
	Edward	Selects calculator app	C	C	C
	Edward	Completes calculation	C	C	C
	Edward	Calls out calculation	C	C	C
	Isobel	Echoes calculation	C	C	C
	Isobel	Initiates table	I	I	C
	Edward & Isobel	Method 2 defined	C	C	C
4	Mr. Osborne	Observes and questions	C	C	C
	Edward & Isobel	Contemplate & respond	C	C	C
	Mr. Osborne	Teacher jumps	C	C	C
	Edward & Isobel	Repeat Method 2	C	C	C
	Students	Watch	C	C	C
	Student	Joins the group	C	C	C
	Mr. Osborne	Leaves the group	C	C	C
	Edward & Isobel	Explain method to others	C	C	C
	Edward & Isobel	Repeat cycle with others	C	C	C
	Mr. Osborne	End of lesson	C	C	C
5	Edward	Work on the wall not transferable	D	D	D
	Edward & Isobel	Request photographs	I	I	I
	Researcher	Takes photographs	C	C	C
	Edward	Removes SD card	C	C	C
	Edward	Copies files	C	C	C
	Edward & Isobel	Submit work	C	C	C

Phase 1: Getting Ready

Movement and discussion characterize Phase 1, as 120 students either resume work on an existing task or select a new one. This group works upstairs with the help of three teachers who offer direction and assistance as they move through the settling students. Edward and Isobel agree to work together, select a task and the tools and location in which they will work. The last of these choices is of particular interest. For having chosen a task, which to their way of thinking involves jumping, they are free to make their way across the upper section to a corner that is largely unfurnished and seldom occupied. At this point there is a high degree of correspondence across the dimensions of the framework. The teachers had carefully structured a unit of independent online tasks of varying degrees of complexity (epistemic), for students who were loosely streamed according to ability and independence (social), and free to choose both the tools and location in which to work (set). At this point, having designed what they could in advance and with the freedom that came from knowing that each student had access to the complete unit of work from wherever they chose to sit, the teachers were relieved of general organizational and administrative oversight. Moving amongst the students they gave timely and appropriate assistance, guided by their observations of the group as a whole. Whilst this particular example illustrates a high degree of correspondence, its importance was highlighted by its absence on other occasions. For controlling this phase too tightly, by limiting choice or enforcing uniformity in the hopes of curtailing the commotion associated with getting ready, often had the perverse effect of extending this phase unduly. Furthermore, where students were not left to make their own way, their engagement often remained superficial and their dependence on their teachers high.

Phase 2: Experimentation

Phase 2 is characterized by experimentation. Edward, sitting on the floor, struggles to hold two 30-cm rulers together to measure the height of Isobel's jumps. He uses one hand to create a single 60-cm ruler because he wants to use the other to mark the height of her jump—as she jumps. He is unable to hold the rulers together, mark height jumped, and read the measurement with any accuracy. It is their combined movement that catches my eye from across the room; it is qualitatively different against a dynamic landscape. Edward eventually rejects their method, and scanning their environment for help or inspiration the pair note my interest and attempt to draw me in, to source an alternate solution. A nod is all I reluctantly offer and they quickly interpret and implement the suggestion without further assistance. Had I not been there they would have looked to their peers; or a teacher, cued by their activity, would have helped refocus their efforts. It is worth noting the role of visibility within this space and how it supports independent learning activity and an openness to people and things, both of which were often actively recruited in the service of learning. Limiting choice, freedom to move, and visibility in this space would result in lost opportunities for learning and a decrease in autonomy. Truncating time for experimentation, by intervening too quickly or with too much direction, would at times undermine resilience and the ability to solve problems. Edward and Isobel's inability to measure height jumped with two rulers is the first moment of dissonance; the challenge is open-ended (epistemic), they have successfully allocated roles (social) but the rulers (set) are not fit for purpose. In retrospect this moment of dissonance can be characterized as positive for it precedes a moment of improvisation, followed by an increase in confidence and improvisational skill as they develop a working method.

Phase 3: Developing a Working Method

Phase 3 starts with their interpretation of my suggestion (nodding toward the white wall) and their improvisatory use of the marker and white wall to record height jumped. In this phase there are two slightly less obvious moments of improvisation using the wall. The first when Edward, having marked and measured the height of Isobel's jump, reports it verbally and amidst Isobel's mild mannered questioning of its veracity turns and writes it, as reported, on the wall. Without further debate they move to where Edward's computer sits and access the online task card, which leads them to a hyperlinked resource detailing the calculations necessary to convert this measurement to moon height. Using a calculator application Edward completes the step and returns to the wall, replacing the original earth height with the newly calculated moon height. Standing at the wall, pen in hand and contemplating the next step, he gives the measurement a number 1, labels it as Isobel's, and gives the newly established list a heading "moon height." The second moment of improvisation using the wall occurs as Isobel, finding she has insufficient room to list weight next to height, relocates their data to a newly created table to the right of some unrelated administrative information. This progression from list, to two lists, to the compound table was a fluid response of the learners to the tools and task on that day. If their use of the two rulers resulted in dissonance, their use of the wall promoted a cascade of correspondence, which can be described as skillful improvisation. Hidden within this account is a second layer of correspondence—between the materials (or elements of the set dimension) themselves. For the laptop provided access, structure, and guidance as perceived in advance and the wall afforded—in the moment—a surface fit for function, jointly owned, and visible to all. This responsive correspondence establishes the preconditions in which these students skillfully improvise a method leveraging the affordance of one medium to compensate for a lack in another. Moreover, had they not been at liberty to seek out help from others or to write on the white wall, or if they had been accustomed to seeking out the single correct method or answer, they would have been less likely to engage in this type of improvisatory problem-solving activity in the first place.

Phase 4: Expanding Collaborative Activity

Phase 4 starts with the arrival of Mr. Osborne who measures his words, noting the student's responses with care before making a judgment about the productivity of their actions. He questions both Edward and Isobel in turn. Looking them in the eye to gauge their grasp of the problem. Having explored their understanding "on the fly" he increases the complexity of the problem by adding (his) weight as a factor in their predictions. The convivial nature of his questioning draws the attention of a few students sitting nearby. Predictions made, he jumps and they measure, do the calculations, and discuss the results in relation to their predictions as they write them into their table. At no point does Mr. Osborn take control of this activity. His questions are designed to challenge and he lets the activity speak for itself, before quietly slipping away. As a small group gathers, the list and table are used to explain their method to the new participants. The externalization of their thinking—first an aid to their work—now scaffolds others' engagement with what is not even their task of choice. This expanding shared activity is not censured by anyone. The correspondence evident in Edward and Isobel's activity flows from the improvisatory use of the wall (set), through to their skillful explanation of their method (epistemic), and their willingness to allow others to participate in the task (social). At any moment this "fluid conversation" between the task, tools, and people present could have been disrupted. Mr. Osborne or one of the other teachers could have deemed their initial activity inappropriate (social) and insisted that they remain seated with their numeracy group where there was little room (set) to jump, or the task could have been less open-ended (epistemic), stipulating fictitious earth heights. The skill evident in weaving multiple elements across all three dimensions together in productive learning activity, at multiple levels, belies the complexity of the doing of this task collaboratively in this space. Moreover, this degree of social and epistemic maneuvring would be hard, if not impossible, to accommodate in a more traditional, unconnected learning space.

Phase 5: End and Submission

Phase 5 is precipitated by the dissonance created at the end of the learning session when they realize that their work is not in a transferable form. The writing surface (tool) that had initially served to support their learning activity, now worked against the requirement to asynchronously demonstrate their learning (task). This task-tool dissonance could so easily have led to the perception of failure. However, it quickly gave rise to an improvisatory move in which they recruit me as a resource, to photograph their work. The quality of this second moment in which I am recruited is markedly different from the first. They act with autonomy and I am the one trying to navigate the tools, task, and social niceties of an adequate solution. Accustomed to transferring images from my camera via USB cable I anticipate problems transferring the images before the end of the learning session. However, working with dexterity and skill the students quietly and confidently resolve the issue by questioning me on the functionality of my camera. And after removing the SD card they locate and negotiate the use of a laptop that will accept it. Before downloading the correct images, emailing them to themselves, inserting them into a PowerPoint presentation, and submitting the completed task. This online submission was sent to their numeracy teacher, Ms. Bailey, who had not witnessed the turn-by-turn details of their activity. Knowing her, I am certain that she will have taken note of their movement and seen first my move toward them and then Mr. Osborne's but at no point was I aware of her presence. This speaks to her confidence in the online structure, her teaching peers, and her students' growing ability to navigate their learning landscape with skill.

Phases 1 through 5: Continuity and Growth

There are two notable aspects of tool use that build in complexity across the five phases of learning activity and pertain to the material qualities of the tools to hand (set), the rules of social engagement (social), and the structure of the task (epistemic). The first is the improvisatory enrollment of the wall in learning activity to: (i) mark height jumped, (ii) fix or formalize the vaguely contested height of this jump; (iii) list the height of a number of subsequent jumps; and (iv) organize their collaborative activity resulting in the table, which is then used as (v) a teaching resource, and later (vi) photographed as evidence of work completed. Each of these moments of set-enrollment mitigates a dissonance between elements (tools, task, or students) of the three dimensions, in the active doing of the task. And, as such, highlights the previously unrecognized importance of place (set), in productive networked learning. The second is the gap between the intended use of the computer and its actual employment in practice. The presence of the laptop in this learning environment afforded these students an unusual degree of independence; however, due to its material qualities it was placed out of harm's way, which meant that the instructions were a little removed from where the students worked. Thus despite design intentions, the mobile digital device became decoupled from the working students and it was the presence of the white wall and the social norms governing its use that filled this gap in orchestrating learning activity. Furthermore, the need for "something else" to scaffold this place-based learning activity was increased by the limitations of the single small screen of the laptop on which multiple applications were running, through which the students had to toggle, one at a time, mentally "carrying" what was necessary between views. Arguably it was the unencumbered digital access offered by the laptop coupled with its physical working constraints,

TABLE 4.4 Summary of the Phases of Activity across the Dimensions of the Framework

	EPISTEMIC	*SOCIAL*	*SET*
	Constructivist	*Collaborative*	*Variety and visibility*
ACTIVITY			
Phase 1: Getting Ready	Independent	Choice and movement	Enables and supports
Phase 2: Experimentation	Challenge	Role differentiation	Not fit for purpose (D)
Phase 3: Developing a Working Method	Develop	Seeking help	Recognizes potential (I)
Phase 4: Expanding Collaborative Activity	Elaborate	Collaborate	Supports
Phase 5: End and Submission	Assessment/ accountability	Recruit assistance, negotiate access (I)	Does not support transfer (D)

in the presence of the white wall and the freedom to use it, that facilitated this fluid activity—or correspondence between the task, the tools, and the people present.

Conclusion

Initially I traced Edward and Isobel's learning activity in this manner (see Table 4.3) to illustrate that with each turn there were multiple considerations at play, each arising out of a different element of the design. I was curious to see if some activity could be attributed to elements in only one of the three dimensions, or if there were moments in which a single element had primacy over the others. However, as I considered each in turn it became clear that for every action there was an underlying influence that could be traced to all three design dimensions: the social, the epistemic, and the set—at multiple scales (see Figure 4.5). Starting with Edward and Isobel's choice of location, working together (social) they selected a task (epistemic), which required space (set) in which to move. Moving up a level we see a constructivist commitment (epistemic) by the teachers, to collaborative (social) group work, carried out in a flexible, digitally enabled learning environment (set). Up a third level and we see a school leadership committed to innovative, research-based practice (epistemic), in which teachers are encouraged to work in teams (social), in a flexible, adaptive, physical, and digital environment (set). In each of these examples there is both correspondence within the elements of each dimension and across all three dimensions, which belies the complexity of these relationships. Dissonance, too, is experienced at all three levels. However, a distinction can be drawn between positive dissonance as experienced in learning activity within a coherent whole; and negative dissonance that arises from a misalignment of, say, epistemic design intentions and either the current social norms or the existing setting.

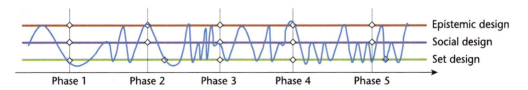

FIGURE 4.7 Tracing Learning Activity over Time through the Elements of the Framework

If we are to take things seriously we need to reconsider how our notions of design, learning, and teaching should shift in response. The framework for the analysis of complex learning environments gives us a good place to start: drawing our attention to those aspects of the epistemic, social, and set design that are open to design-in-advance. However, supported by digital technologies, there are aspects of complex learning environments that are open to design-in-the-doing, where improvisational correspondence is a skill to be learned in dialogue with the tools, the task, and the people present. Interestingly, where design-in-advance bleeds into learning activity one is unlikely to see place-based learning networks reach their full potential. That is, when teachers or instructional designers focus on controlling phases in which students are active they are likely to experience resistance from learners, or find that the degree of improvisational correspondence required of them is unsustainable. Furthermore, they are unlikely to witness the emergence of improvisational skill in learners as they navigate their environs leveraging both humans and things in the doing of the task.

If designers are to lead the way into uncharted territory and, turning back, place markers within ongoing practice to suggest pathways through a learning landscape for learners to follow (Gatt and Ingold 2013), what then can we learn from this rich description? First, that close scripting, design-in-advance is crucial in forming the necessary conditions for both learning and teaching. That is, those things that to the trained eye are likely to nudge a learner in a desired direction should be carefully laid out in advance: broad access to a variety of tasks; training in the social norms that support and encourage independent, collaborative, and collegial work; and the provision of spaces, both physical and digital, variously equipped to support and encourage a number of productive pathways through a rich and diverse learning landscape. And second, that improvisation or design-in-the-doing should be valued and supported, for it is this skillful coupling of perception and action in unfolding activity that lies at the heart of productive place-based learning networks where learning activity is characterized by the nuanced interplay of the tools, the task, and the people present.

References

Barad, K., 2003. Posthumanist performativity: Toward an understanding of how matter comes to matter. *Signs: Journal of Women in Culture and Society*, 28(3), 801–831.

Barrett, P., Zhang, Y., Moffat, J., and Kobbacy, K., 2013. A holistic, multi-level analysis identifying the impact of classroom design on pupils' learning. *Building and Environment*, 59, 678–689.

Brown, B., 2001. Thing theory. *Critical Inquiry*, 28(1), 1–22.

Carvalho, L. and Goodyear, P., eds., 2014. *The architecture of productive learning networks*. New York: Routledge.

Gatt, C. and Ingold, T., 2013. From description to correspondence: Anthropology in real time. In: W. Gunn, T. Otto, and R. C. Smith, eds., *Design anthropology* (pp. 139–158). London: Bloomsbury.

Gislason, N., 2010. Architectural design and the learning environment: A framework for school design research. *Learning Environments Research*, 13(2), 127–145.

Goodyear, P. and Carvalho, L., 2013. The analysis of complex learning environments. In: H. Beetham and E. Sharpe, eds., *Rethinking pedagogy for the digital age: Designing and delivering e-learning* (pp. 49–63). New York: Routledge.

Goodyear, P. and Carvalho, L., 2014. Framing the analysis of learning network architectures. In: L. Carvalho and P. Goodyear, eds., *The architecture of productive learning networks* (pp. 48–70). New York: Routledge.

Goodyear, P., Hodgson, V., and Steeples, C., 1998. *Student experiences of networked learning in higher education*. Lancaster, UK: Lancaster University. Research proposal to the UK JISC, October 1998.

Harris, S., 2010. *The place of virtual, pedagogic and physical space in the 21st century classroom*. Sydney: Sydney Centre for Innovation in Learning. [online]. Available from: http://static1.squarespace.com/static/510b86cce4b0f6b4fb690106/t/51998ebce4b00c954c5fd2f0/1369018044049/stephen-harris_virtual-pedagogical-physical-space-21st-century.pdf [Accessed October 30, 2015].

Ingold, T., 2011. *Being alive: Essays on movement, knowledge and description*. Abingdon, UK: Routledge.

Ingold, T., 2012. Toward an ecology of materials. *Annual Review of Anthropology*, 41(1), 427–442.

Sørensen, E., 2009. *The materiality of learning: Technology and knowledge in educational practice.* Cambridge: Cambridge University Press.

Spector, J. M., Merrill, M. D., Elen, J., and Bishop, M. J., eds., 2013. *Handbook of research on educational communications and technology,* 4th edition. New York: Springer.

Thibaut, P., Curwood, J. S., Carvalho, L., and Simpson, A., 2015. Moving across physical and online spaces: A case study in a blended primary classroom. *Learning, Media and Technology*, 40(4), 458–479.

Woolner, P. and Hall, E., 2010. Noise in schools: A holistic approach to the issue. *International Journal of Environmental Research and Public Health*, 7(8), 3255–3269.

Woolner, P., Hall, E., Higgins, S., McCaughey, C., and Wall, K., 2007. A sound foundation? What we know about the impact of environments on learning and the implications for building schools for the future. *Oxford Review of Education*, 33(1), 47–70.

Woolner, P., McCarter, S., Wall, K., and Higgins, S., 2012. Changed learning through changed space: When can a participatory approach to the learning environment challenge preconceptions and alter practice? *Improving Schools*, 15(1), 45–60.

Yeoman, P. and Carvalho, L., 2014. Material entanglement in a primary school learning network. In: S. Bayne, C. Jones, M. de Laat, T. Ryberg, and C. Sinclair, eds., *Proceedings of the Ninth Networked Learning Conference* (pp. 331–338). 7–9 April, Edinburgh. Available from: http://www.lancaster.ac.uk/fss/organisations/netlc/past/nlc2014/abstracts/pdf/yeoman.pdf [Accessed March 11, 2016].

5

FINDING THE SPACES IN-BETWEEN

Learning as a Social Material Practice

Jos Boys

Learning spaces is an emerging field; one intertwined with educational design services and developing across and between many subject disciplines, from estates management to human-computer interaction, by way of geography, environmental psychology, and architecture. It thus brings together many shared concerns, but also varied perspectives, conceptual frameworks, and methodologies (Boddington and Boys 2011). At the same time, with what has been called the "spatial turn," many theorists are rethinking relationships between space—taken in its widest sense—and the activities that go on in it; using terms such as entanglements and meshworks (Latour 2005, 2009; Ingold 2011). Here I will focus on what these more recent conceptual frameworks can offer to our understandings of learning spaces in higher education, by opening up learning as a messy, complex, and—most crucially—completely interconnected process, where space, objects, humans, and events are inherently inseparable. This approach, with many variations, has mainly developed across science and technology studies, Actor-Network Theory, ethnomethodology, phenomenology, anthropology, and geography (Garfinkel 1967; Sacks 1984; Callon 1987; Law and Hassard 1999; Thrift 2008; Ingold 2011, 2013). First, it challenges the basic assumption that space and occupants exist as pre-existing entities that then have "relationships" with each other. This means refusing to accept the assumed "logic" of, say, behavioral cause/effect, function, or meaning. Rather, spaces, objects, our bodies, and our encounters are utterly intermeshed, and need to be analyzed instead as *dynamic practices*. Second, this approach suggests that we make sense of, and survive in, the world through the continuous accumulation and negotiation of our embodied enactments with the most "ordinary" of everyday social and material activities. It is the very mundanity of such activity that allows it to go unnoticed and unremarked upon, when in fact it is actually *work*—what has been called "problematic accomplishments" (Ryave and Schenkein 1974, pp. 65–274). It takes time and effort to *perform* everyday routines as obvious and natural and to readapt or "breach" them (Garfinkel 1967, pp. 37–38).

Third, and just as importantly, these everyday practices are completely entangled between humans and non-humans (Latour 1988). In higher education, for example, the curriculum, teaching methods and equipment, patterns of assessment, and timetabling are all part of a seemingly obvious and "normal" interweaving of spaces, artifacts, and people that continually enacts teaching and learning in one particular shape rather than another. Both the physical places and technologies of learning are key ways (amongst others such as body language, discourse, rules and regulations, etc.), through which such ongoing practices are both contested and become routinized and concrete. Fourth, then, this approach argues that people, spaces, technologies, *and* objects all have the potential to be "actants" that have an effect in perpetuating, adapting, or challenging particular social and material practices. As Latour puts it, an actant is anything that "modif[ies] other actors through a series of . . . actions" (2009, p. 75).

Fifth, learning practices are always situated. For example, they will vary across what Latour calls *assemblages* (2005, p. 75)—similar to what Wenger calls "repertoires" (1998, pp. 58–59)—the particular courses, programs, faculties, or institutions that become routinized through the endless repetition and accumulation of enactments in different settings. Sixth and finally, then, whilst current research of this type aims to offer the detailed unraveling of "normal" social and material practices, it does not expect these to be congruent or complete, or to form neatly aligned coherent, comprehensive, and stable frameworks. This is understood as multiplicity—not merely multiple perspectives on the same "object" but different co-existing *worlds* (Mol 2002; Law 2004). Any patterns that can be discerned are what Geertz (1973) famously called a "thick description"; that is, it is a rich and layered account that accepts inconsistencies, and does not result in a "solution" or conclusion:

> This means suspending a need for explanation and resisting desires to seek clear patterns, solutions, singularities or other closure in the research. It is instead about noticing the strains, the uncanny, the difficult and the ill-fitting, allowing the messes of difference and tension to emerge alongside each other, rather than smoothing them into some kind of relation.
> (Fenwick and Edwards 2010, p. 156)

This approach therefore affects how the physical and virtual spaces of learning in higher education are initially conceptualized. Importantly, they are not differentiated. Instead the focus is on the *social and material practices* of learning—including, for example, specific subject knowledges and expertise, instructional design theories and methods, student and teacher perceptions and experiences. Space, whether physical, virtual, or hybrid, is one of the modes through which these practices are enacted, (re)imagined, and negotiated. Space is *not* some kind of "map" that can—through intended relationships between its material and pedagogic design—be more or less aligned, more or less effective in enabling learning. Spaces, and technologies and artifacts and thus assemblages more generally, are in fact inherently sites of struggle and contestation over what are or should be the "proper" and "ordinary" social and material practices of learning and teaching. In current debates, for example, around "next generation" learning spaces (Joint Information Systems Committee (JISC) 2006; Oblinger 2006; Scottish Funding Council 2006; Tertiary Education Facilities Management Association (TEFMA) 2006; Boys 2010; Harrison and Hutton 2013; Temple 2014) we can begin to unravel how various participant-worlds are being constructed and contested, and how this is entangled with the roles that spaces and technologies are expected to enact. Rather than aiming to assess lesser or greater student satisfaction with, or "successful" performance in, specific learning environments, the research I am arguing for here is much more interested in the *collisions* between, and endlessly unfinished negotiations across, the multiple and embodied worlds of higher education's various actants. What effects are these processes having on how learning in universities and colleges is conceptualized and realized? Such an approach does not provide us with any simple answers about how to improve learning. What it does is illuminate (Parlett and Hamilton 1972) the "spaces in-between," that is, the complex intersections between co-existing worlds; so as to analyze the enabling and disabling effects for various participants in specific learning situations, in order to inform future actions. To explore this further, I will first consider in more detail how we can unravel learning and teaching in higher education as a multiplicity of social and material practices, focusing in on two aspects—*delegation* and *breaching*. I will then go on to consider, through a case study, how specific elements of a course—in this example, the studio tutorial and the online blog—can be analyzed as sites of collision and negotiation, as the various participants involved both co-constructed and contested some of the specific "ordinary" practices of learning in higher education.

Unraveling the Entanglements of Learning

As already outlined, it is through the ongoing reproduction of a whole assemblage or meshwork of spaces, objects, and people that particular social and material practices come to be "normal," so obvious as to go unnoticed and unremarked upon. In analyzing how learning takes place, Wenger calls such a process "reification"—where "aspects of human experience and practice are congealed into fixed form and given the status of an object" (1998, p. 60). For Wenger reification is a useful and constructive mechanism that helps glue together particular communities as stable entities, precisely through repetition and normalization of their specific practices. But for many other authors it is a problematic and potentially inequitable process. This is for two reasons. First, the accomplishment—the work involved—in making and remaking everyday life and its communities in one way rather than another becomes invisible, making it harder to challenge. Second, the "ordinary" that becomes congealed tends to act for particular interests and against others. Theorists such as Foucault (1970, 1977/1995), Bourdieu (1987), and Bhabha (1994) have all explored these issues.[1] Reification here becomes the attempt to make transparent and obvious—by locating it externally in the "concrete" world—that which is actually a specific enunciation of ideas and practices; and a particular translation of these ideas and practices into things and spaces. Assemblages, in coming in one form rather than other, enact particular patterns of power and inequity, of exclusion and inclusion and, precisely for this reason, are inherently unstable and contested. Thus in investigating, for example, particular patternings of higher education learning and of subject knowledges, we also need to see what (and who) is being left out, and what is unstable, inconsistent, contested, and multiple.

Thus, at the same time as working to unravel the mechanisms through which specific social and material practices come to seem "normal," we need to open up what different participants bring to the process—conceptually, emotionally, experientially—and how their perceptions and enactments intersect *differentially* with those practices. Here individual actions are completely entangled with what is "storyable" (Sacks 1995, p. 218) in an institution or society more generally, that is, both with what can be "thought" and what it is permissible to say. All universities and colleges, as well as disciplines and sub-groups, have beliefs, assumptions, and practices that are woven into their own preferred narratives about themselves, and that act both explicitly and implicitly to define who is included or excluded from "membership." Gatekeeping procedures can be both explicit (achieving certain entry qualifications) and implicit (having the "right attitude").

Of course, learning in higher education is centrally about inculcating new members into an existing, usually discipline-based, knowledge community. Students come into universities as newbies and may then work their way through to "old-timers" (Lave and Wenger 1991) either within the academy or beyond it. This may center on learning to become part of an existing academic and/or professional entity (by reproducing normal social and material practices) or by developing, challenging, and transforming knowledge and practices (including their current inclusions and exclusions). Ryave and Schenkein use the active sense of "doing" to underscore "the concerted accomplishment of members of the community involved as a matter of course in (their) production and recognition" (1974, p. 265). In universities and colleges, "doing" learning is the process through which students become first introduced to, and then embedded in, both the appropriate practices of their discipline and of higher education itself; just as "doing" teaching and research is the process through which academics come to find their position within a discipline, course, and institution. How, then, can we better understand the effects of making explicit attempts at *changing* this "doing"? This might be around subject content knowledge and/or educational design and/or the "normal" social and material practices of learning in higher education. How do new kinds of rearticulation become interwoven with, so as to challenge, existing assemblages and different participant-worlds? How can they or should they affect current patternings of inclusion and exclusion? And how can we examine the enabling and disabling effects of specific interventions? What are the resonances, discomforts, gaps, and unintended consequences, both for individual participant-worlds, for disciplinary fields, and for learning practices more generally? In this chapter I will explore two particular concepts using the approach outlined above—*delegation* and *breaching*—to see whether and how these might illuminate a specific attempt at educational change. The first concept allows us to investigate what happens when, through the redesigning process, we allocate different roles to non-humans such as spaces and technology. The second explicitly engages with the disruptive effects of challenging an existing set of social and material learning practices.

Delegation

Latour introduces the concept of delegation as a means of seeing how and when humans and non-humans can act interchangeably. For example, writing under the pseudonym of Jim Johnson, he examines the simple automatic door closer. The material door and its (usually working) closer are seen as being *delegated* the work of differentiating between a particular inside and a more ambiguous outside, because—in the specific situation being explored—

> the reversible door is the only way to irreversibly trap inside a differential accumulation of warm sociologists, knowledge, papers and also, alas, paperwork; the hinged door allows a selection of what gets in and what gets out so as to locally increase order or information.
>
> (1988, p. 299)

This, then, is a way of understanding the intersections of human and non-human actants—the latter perform a role as a substitute for what would otherwise be a much more complicated human activity, for example by rebuilding the wall every time you want to go in or out; closing the door properly on each occasion; or employing a doorman. Such a delegation can be to any space, object, or process. Unfortunately, though, Latour only tends to see this delegation back and forth expressed as a kind of balance sheet, weighing up shifts in effectiveness, based on relative degrees of effort-saving and robustness "from a provisional less reliable one to a longer-lasting more faithful one" (p. 306). Like many other critics, I would argue that acts of delegation (say from physical places to online networks) are not only about effectiveness, but also concern existing patterns of power and differentiation, already inscribed with assumptions about what is *normal* or *should be normal*. Human and non-human assemblages, then, are not just exchanges of agency evaluated against some abstract concept of durability, but include a tendency to delegate *toward* or *away from* particular bodies, technologies, spaces, functions, etc. What, then, is "storyable" in these different types of delegation? What can we unravel about the impact of delegating certain aspects of learning to non-human components, such as a studio tutorial and an online blog, within the existing social and material practices of learning? This becomes the first question addressed in the case study.

Breaching

The second concept explored is breaching. When Garfinkel developed the idea of breaching, its main aim was to expose how deeply embedded are our ordinary material practices, as well as the banality and everydayness of the mechanisms through which these are perpetuated:

Procedurally it is my preference to start with familiar scenes and ask what can be done to make trouble. The operations that one would have to perform in order to multiply the senseless features of perceived environments, to produce and sustain bewilderment, consternation and confusion; to produce the socially constructed affects of anxiety, shame, guilt and indignation and to produce disorganised interaction should tell us something about how the structures of everyday activities are ordinarily and routinely produced and maintained.

(Garfinkel 1967, pp. 37–38)

Here, though, I want to suggest that breaching is both interesting in its own right and more complex than Garfinkel implies. This is because it can be either an involuntary or conscious individual *response to* a particular existing situation; and also be either an implicit or explicit *action on* that situation. Thus, on the one hand, involuntary breaching (for example by not knowing the "rules" of the education game as a new student) can be distinctly uncomfortable; whilst another "newbie" may deliberately refuse to conform and be—at least temporarily—empowered by this action. On the other hand, an institution, faculty, tutor, course, or session may aim to breach the conventional social and material practices of higher education for clearly specified reasons, or might experiment with changing functionality (for example, in online and hybrid modes of delivery) without necessarily properly examining the effects on the "normal" practices of learning and teaching. In the case study examined below, there was a deliberate attempt to "cause trouble"—to breach—the everyday knowledge practices of architecture and interior design. Thus, the second question for this case study is, "What were the effects of such a breaching on the participants' learning?"

Causing Trouble? Challenging the "Normal" in Architectural and Interiors Education

The study examined here was an Arts Council England (ACE) funded, studio-based design project that aimed to challenge how disability is located within architecture and interior design; and to explore alternative ways of introducing students to disability, and occupancy more generally, in their design processes. I have written elsewhere about the problems with the location of disability within built environment education (Boys 2014). In this study—called *Making Discursive Spaces*—seven Deaf and disabled[2] artists collaborated with a group of ten second-year undergraduate interior architecture students at the University of Brighton, UK, on a design project for creating artists' studios in a large dilapidated London warehouse. The project explicitly refused to frame disabled people in the "standard" way within architectural education, for example, by designing a special school, or care home, but instead aimed to provide integrated facilities for disabled and non-disabled creative people. Second, disabled people were engaged as tutors rather than users. That is, they were involved as professional and artistic individuals with important insights to offer, integral to the building design process. They were there to develop speculative discussions about how the experiences of disabled people might be articulated more resonantly within architectural and interior design education. This was a very conscious breaching. By having a sizeable number of (very different) disabled tutors relative to students, we wanted to move beyond each "standing for" a particular disability; and by working with artists—all with considerable experience in both education and practice—we made central the creativity of disabled perceptions and experiences, rather than seeing disability as a "lack," which is much more often the case.

The other additional components to teaching-as-usual were a blog, where students and tutors were asked to share resources, comment on design work, and to open discussions beyond the design process about underlying issues and problems (http://discursivespaces.blogspot.com—see Figure 5.1); and an evaluation of student and tutor experiences (www.discursivespaces.co.uk—

FIGURE 5.1 Screenshot from Blog   **FIGURE 5.2** Screenshot from Website

see Figure 5.2). Whilst the students had "normal" learning outcomes for a design project—the same as other second year undergraduates doing parallel design projects in other studios—they were also aware of the wider intentions to learn from the experiences of Deaf and disabled people themselves.

Next, then, I will outline some of the things that were learnt from this project, initially focusing on the studio-based design tutorial and networked space of the blog; before going on to consider the enabling and disabling experiences of these specific delegations, and then the overall consequences, both intentional and unintentional, of our breaching activities. Finally, I will explore the relative value of the conceptual framework used here, and the implications for educational design services more generally.

Enacting the Studio Tutorial

Historically the "doing being ordinary" (Sacks 1984) of design education has centered on the studio. For the students and tutors in this study, the physical studio was a place inseparably entangled with the everyday routines of art, design, architectural, and interior design education, at the center of its project-based and dialogue-centered pedagogic practices. Usually open plan, the studio provides space for every student to work on their own creative project, and to engage in tutorials with teachers, who are often expert practitioners. Whilst the amount of space, the degree of "hot-desking," and the repertoire of equipment—from paper to computer for example—has changed; and whilst student numbers have increased to an extent where studio tutorials, whether individually or in small groups, have become harder to manage, the studio and its assumed culture remain foundational. In this project we deliberately worked within the "normal" framework of the studio tutorial and crit.[3] This was in order to legitimize firmly the role of disabled artists as tutors, working in the "usual" way. All the artists gave presentations of their work as an introduction to students, again reflecting conventional procedures (Figure 5.3). At the same time we wanted to open up such conventional places to the positive disruptions of disability. Sign language interpretation, thinking about making visual presentations meaningful for partially sighted artists, and studio and crit-rooms rearranged for the different kinds of spatiality of wheelchair users, all momentarily disrupted the typical educational spaces of architecture and interiors education.

Within this place ("the second year studio") tutorials also have an "ordinary" shape. Studio tutorials are usually concerned with co-developing design work through both dialogue and non-verbal interactions—using sketching and modeling to analyze problems and test out propositions. Through time, this process is generally understood as less about telling students what to do, and more about building their capacity to generate a design in response to a particular situation, through experimentation and then increasingly detailed and realistic development. Implicitly there is inculcation toward a shared and increasingly sophisticated tacit knowledge about what design is, and the activities through which it is undertaken. This interweaves—often in confusing and poorly articulated ways—with other unspoken interactions, about the "rules of the game" of both learning in higher education and of architecture and interior design (Morrow, Parnell, and Torrington 2004; Austerlitz 2008). At the undergraduate levels, teaching tends to focus on increasing fluency in creating three-dimensional entities that work constructionally, materially, organizationally, and as pleasing compositions; already a very complex task to learn. Many studies have shown that in these processes, concepts of occupation, diversity, and difference are not well developed, with students at this level often relying on their own experiences, or on stereotypes (Morrow 2000; Morrow et al. 2004; Heylighen 2008; De Cauwer et al. 2009). Not surprisingly, the students in our study were at different levels in their overall understanding of design, which affected how much they could absorb from the artist-tutors. As second-year undergraduates, they were, after all, only just beginning to explore how to interpret relationships between personal, social, and cultural activities and material space and to respond creatively and appropriately with designed interventions. They could recognize the artists' different insights but particularly lacked many "translation" tools to take these forward into a design method or realization:

FIGURE 5.3 A Studio Tutorial in Progress

Some students coped with the set of circumstances and some were just busy coping with [the] whole premise of the project and the course.

Some dived right in and some just dipped their toes in and some shuffled around like moles . . .

Some of the students seemed to be avoiding access issues or maybe it was fear of not knowing.

(Artists' feedback May 11, 2007)

Nonetheless, because the studio tutorial is most commonly enacted as a relatively wide-ranging "chat" that need not make strong demands on students to perform or produce immediate results, it is not surprising that they reported feeling most comfortable in this context. When surveyed, both students and artists found the tutorials most fruitful, particularly in working through issues in relation to a specific design:

For me the 1:1 contact, particularly when Rachel gave me such a good reference to an artist who I could go and explore—it was a perfect reference for me.

A breakthrough for me was when both Naomi and Rubbena actually talked about how they use their artist studio/space or any space when they are making work . . . so learning about, for example, the light and materials that were good to have around them.

I just got so much exploring the lift as a separate and more meaningful fun inclusive experience alongside the obvious logic of lifts re: access.

(Students' feedback May 11, 2007)

Studio days therefore flourished as known, unremarked-upon conventions of informal discussions of work in progress, using simultaneous sketching and talk, exploring design analysis, precedents, appropriate materials and technologies, and alternative design ideas. However, in reviewing both the project process, and the resulting work, it became increasingly clear that it was precisely these "congealed" understandings within the design tutorial about what the interior design process is, and how it is taught, that in fact limited how tutors and students enacted an alternative disability sensibility. In delegating key aspects of disability discourse and design development to the studio tutorial, we failed to effectively challenge its everyday embedded educational practices. As a device it invisibly shaped what was *sayable* about design as a process, both in general and in relationship to this specific design project. Yet, at the same time, it was precisely this failure that enabled us to afterwards *really see* those previously unnoticed practices, a key point to which I will return.

Blogging Online

If at one extreme the studio tutorial was thick with congealed practices about *how to learn* to design, the blog came with almost no preconceptions for this group of students and tutors—who had not used networked learning in this way before. Perhaps naively it was assumed that such a space could enable different registers to operate simultaneously—project updates, information and resources, informal chat, sharing of work-in-progress, as well as explorations of wider issues. In fact, using the blog was much more problematic for both artist-tutors and students than their place-based learning. In part this was due more to problems with access to the Internet, and using the blog itself, than had been expected:

I couldn't get on it.

Sometimes I posted stuff up and it never appeared.

I spent some time putting my stuff up and then received no comments so I felt a bit disheartened.

I actually found the 1:1 more immediate and valuable.

(Students' feedback May 11, 2007)

But it was also because all participants were anxious about how and what to communicate with each other. This included issues of language and tone. Some, across both students and artist-tutors, found it too academic. Others felt unsure about how considered or immediate their posts or responses were meant to be, and wondered what others would think of their comments, or that these might be found offensive or at the "wrong" level:

The language in the blog was quite academic and intensive, I found it quite alienating and it was hard to connect with it.

I was concerned about how I came across. I didn't express how I felt because I wanted to be sensitive, so I didn't say half of what I would have liked to have said.

I am not an academic and I would have to sit and think about what was being said and sometimes I would have to get my dictionary out.

(Artists' feedback May 11, 2007)

Finally, as with the project more broadly, participants were unsure about the status or authority of the networked space; about whether it was assessed and how its content would intersect with their studio-based work. Students were most confident using it to post simple descriptions of their work, or to give positive feedback to the artists. Tutors were most comfortable using it to share information about, for example, useful web resources. The lack of success of the blog was partly about differences in participants' experiences and aims for the *Making Discursive Spaces* project—the tensions and potentially contradictory intersections of its academic, artistic, and political threads. But it was also generally perceived as an "unsafe" space. It did not become a "normal" part of learning practices. If the studio tutorials so congealed the educational and subject-specific rules of the game into common sense that alternative knowledge content and processes became easy to avoid, then the blog did the opposite. It made all the participants too ill at ease to participate in the ways hoped. In this context, the blog became predominantly used only as an *extension* of the place-based learning—of the known and "normal," of the studio tutorial, with students posting descriptions and images of their work in progress, and tutors noting down resources as a follow-on to face-to-face discussions.

What We Learnt: The Power of Embedded Practices

As the project progressed, the most immediately powerful impact on students' learning was in shifting their perceptions of the role of the senses in designing. The students all reported feeling themselves much more intensely *in* the material spaces around them; expanding their awareness of their own bodily sensations and taking notice of barriers in the built environment they had previously ignored. As one student commented: "I felt my space, because the disabled artists have helped put *me* in my space" (Student feedback May 11, 2007).

For the artist-tutors, though, this increasing awareness of tactility, movement, and gesture was only a first step; these were seen as only the most immediate, intuitive, and "common sense" responses to their presence. Instead the artists were interested in how this beginning understanding and willingness might be enabled to impact on the students' detailed design work—and, as the project progressed, they expressed frustration about how difficult such a "leap" seemed to be to engender.

For them, working within the *Making Discursive Spaces* project increasingly focused on the problems of transition (in concepts) and translation (from concept to action) for students. How could they take these new embodied feelings about space into a more general understanding of what a disabled-led creative perspective might entail, and then be enabled to begin to translate this idea *into* their design project, so as to be able to creatively adapt an existing place for a diversity of users?

Here, the underlying shape of the studio tutorial, as a device for mediating the design process, was criticized—both for what happened in these sessions, and for what was left out. Crucially the disabled artist-tutors argued that an inherent difficulty in incorporating disability issues into the student design process was the unspoken assumption about "how design works." And this was staunchly, if invisibly, delegated to the studio tutorial. The repeated enactments of the tutorial made concrete the ordinary and unnoticed belief that "normal" design progresses from a general conceptual idea (about form, materiality, or construction, for example) through increasing building detail to a realized design. For the artist-tutors, the conclusion from the project was that designing needs to work in reverse to this; beginning instead from a detailed study of occupational practicalities, so as to generate creative ideas out of an attentiveness to the details of how different bodies intersect with built space. This was not just about noticing functional differences in space usage or heightened sensual awareness of our physical surroundings, but also about how "normal" assumptions about what constitute disability *and ability* are literally built into social and material practices and environments.

In addition, the artist-tutors queried the extent to which tutorial dialogue was framed as a relatively unstructured conversation. This was partly exacerbated by their different uncertainties about their roles, and the extent to which they could or should breach the "normal" demands of a design project. But it was also because they wanted to more explicitly offer students designing techniques or tools that could help translate ideas into material propositions.[4] Ultimately though—whatever the tutors said or did—the students' engagement with disability returned, by the end of the project, to its "normal" framing within building design education and practice. That is to say, they defaulted to the usual process where "accessibility" is tacked on as a minor problem to be resolved in the final stages of a conventional idea-to-detail development. Thus the unspoken strength (and appearance of certainty) of already inculcated design practices—made concrete, obvious, and natural through the studio tutorial and crit—won out over the troublesome concepts we were offering.

It should also be noted that this tendency to fall back on—rather than have the confidence to challenge—"congealed understandings" was exacerbated by the context in which our participants were operating. In the case of *Making Discursive Spaces*, the recognition by all the students involved of the project's outsider status meant that they also looked to what *other* tutors in the school thought, as a means of informing their design choices. In addition, students were all too aware that the disability-led aspect of the project was not officially assessed and that other tutors were not all supportive of incorporating disability issues into the design studio. This was because some tutors were made uncomfortable, in different ways, about how such a project fitted into the wider curriculum; or in some cases, they colluded in the predominant but unspoken discourse—the very assumption we were trying to challenge—that learning about disability is only about accessibility, which remains conventionally and implicitly understood as simultaneously politically correct, marginal, boring, and technical in design education (Boys 2014). In addition, other tutors were worried that introducing disability as a design issue was a potentially "unfair" critique if applied to the other design studio projects running in parallel:

> It felt hard to battle what was obviously the academic agenda and the way things are organized for the students.

> (Artists' feedback May 11, 2007)

We would need to know that going through this and learning from it and feeling differently should be endorsed by all the staff, so they encourage us to build this thinking into all our assignments.

I just don't think I will not think these issues through the next time. The problem is when some tutors actually actively stop you from thinking about these issues.

I just hope the tutors will [be] taking this on board and not say things like "are you putting a lift in because you think you have to . . . ?"

(Students' feedback May 11, 2007)

As these feedback comments show, our artist-tutors and students found themselves negotiating between and across their own perceptions and experiences, the normal everyday and embodied practices of both the subject discipline and its learning and teaching methods, and the unexpected consequences of this particular attempt at instructional design and delivery. For the students, under-pinned by the everyday culture of the design studio and their own personal experiences, what must have felt like unresolvable tensions in our educational design and delivery had, if anything, made them more anxious to stay *within* the "normal" social and material practices of learning their subject.

Toward Critical Learning Practices?

It is relatively easy to make criticisms of this project from the position of educational design as a discipline. We had, after all, failed to recognize the importance of properly scaffolding the online activities, or of exploiting possible networks beyond the course, such as existing disability and design sites. We had not effectively introduced or supported the alternative premise of the design project by building in more explicit disability awareness and other discussion seminars. We could have better engaged with the artist-tutors, co-creating protocols in advance to inform their role. We also missed opportunities to adjust the tutorial and crit mechanism to include much more explicit and structured engagements with disability issues and design concepts and processes. All such comments would be fair.[5] Here though, I want to end by exploring what other kinds of lessons can be learnt—lessons that also look to challenge and expand the "normal" boundaries of educational design practices. First, what can we unravel from the two central questions of this case study—the impacts of delegating certain aspects of learning to non-human components and the effects of particular breaching intentions on the participants' learning? And second, what does the conceptual approach outlined above offer to educational designers?

Educational Design as Delegation

Educational design is centrally about delegating backwards and forwards across humans, objects, technologies, and spaces (both physical and virtual). Interestingly, that delegation is often treated as neutral and straightforward. The arguments behind moving toward active learning—or blended, or flipped, or any other of the terms currently in use—are offered up as straightforward and inevitable; as a new "normality" for the twenty-first century university. Of course, these alternative interven-tions are actually contested, part of a contemporary process where newer approaches are colliding with—and through that entanglement are altering—the "doing being ordinary" of learning practices in higher education: the lecture, the seminar, the lab, and the studio. It is the very everydayness of such previous assemblages that have allowed them to go unnoticed and unremarked upon, and to be non-human actants in the reproduction of higher education in particular forms rather than others. This, though, is not about the "obvious" need to replace one patterning with another. Delegation to non-human spaces and/or technologies is not just about functionality and effectiveness but also about the specific social and material practices *already bound up in* those spaces and technologies. It is about struggles over the "normal" that have their own effects—in both the intended and unintended consequences of delegation—in reinforcing or undermining existing social and material practices. In our project this has led to two conclusions about the forms of delegation that we used; first, that we needed to take much more into account the extent to which assumptions about interior design as a method are inseparably intertwined with the studio tutorial as a delegated mechanism; and second, that challenging assumptions about disability within architecture and interior design requires a rethinking of both that design method and its modes of delivery.

The Consequences of "Breaching" on Learning

New forms of delegation across humans and non-humans, then, collide with congealed under-standings (or not) of previous patterns of human, object, and spatial entanglements in particular contexts. How this collision—this breaching—is perceived and experienced through the life-worlds of different participants will affect their abilities to respond. In our project there were varying degrees of fearfulness and anxiety about moving outside normal social and material edu-cational design practices, most of which had disabling influences on risk-taking, and therefore on being able to constructively and creatively challenge existing assumptions about disability. This anxiety could be seen amongst the students, concerned about their assessments and wanting to "fit-in" with studio culture more generally; amongst the artist-tutors, who wanted to challenge more, but were too aware of the risks for students and of their uncertain status in the school; and amongst the regular tutors, who felt more generally threatened by the potential undermining of their current design teaching practices. Equally crucially, although our potential breaching was around subject knowledge content, it has its greatest and most troubling effects in the "normal" social and material practices of *education*.

Both of these questions have wider relevance for educational designers, opening up some of the spaces-in-between—often invisible—across specific subject knowledges and expertise, instruc-tional design practices, and student and teacher perceptions and experiences. At the same time, the approach outlined here can also open up educational design itself as a subject discipline, particularly in reflecting on its own assumed practices and boundaries. For example, as Kanuka (2006) notes, educational design has tended to frame itself as separate from disciplinary knowledge; developing a general set of pedagogic and technological practices that are assumed to be applicable to any learning situation. The case study here suggests that educational design in architecture and interior design is intimately intermeshed with its subject's practices, raising wider issues about either the accuracy or the "normality" of maintaining a separation. Similar questions can be raised about the extent to which "doing being ordinary" as an educational designer intersects with the contesta-tions inherent in subject disciplines. To what extent is or should educational design be implicated in "taking sides" across different subject debates? How much should it also be engaging explicitly with social equity or with critical or inclusive pedagogies?

Finally, to what extent have the conceptual ideas outlined at the beginning of this chapter thrown new light on the intersections of physical spaces, virtual networks, objects, and practices? A key aim, underpinning such work, is to move beyond simplistic understandings about how to improve learning as just a case of implementing better technologies or innovative learning spaces. By getting under the surface of the multiple spaces of different participants (both human and non-human) as they enact the everyday social and material practices of learning and subject, I suggest that we can produce much more detailed and sophisticated understandings of how we learn, and that we can take better account of the complexities of our everyday entanglements across both conceptual spaces and actual—situated—places. For educational designers, this chapter has aimed to illustrate the value of unraveling existing social and material practices of learning, and to develop forms of research that can better open up the collisions, contestations, and unintended consequences in what we do. It argues for a more complex engagement with the varieties of possible delegation across human and non-human actants. And it highlights the importance of understanding the potential disabling, as well as enabling, effects of various kinds of breaching on students'—and tutors'—perceptions and experiences. Working in this way can help educational designers to be more aware of their own assumptions and ordinary, unnoticed practices; and even more crucially, to be able to better analyze, and therefore engage effectively with, the everyday *practices-in-place* of learning.

Endnotes

1. Although this chapter owes a lot to the work of Bruno Latour, and to developments within Actor-Network Theory and science and technology studies more generally, there are many problems with these approaches, which have not been dealt with here. See Boys (2014), especially Chapter 9, for a more detailed critique.
2. Many Deaf people, particularly those who use sign language, argue that they are a linguistic minority with their own language and culture, and therefore do not define themselves as disabled. For this reason, in some disability writing the term Deaf and disabled people is used. The use of a capital D for Deaf recognizes this differentiation; acknowledging that many people who use sign language have a strongly developed sense of their own cultural identity.
3. The "crit" in architectural, art, and design education is a key assessment process whereby learners present their work to a panel of tutors, and often students, and are quizzed on it.
4. The learning from this project about the deep problems with current design methods based on concept-to-detail are forming the background to an ongoing research project about how to better engage with diverse occupation within architectural education and practice.
5. As is often the case, the circumstances for the development of this action research project were not ideal; with artist-tutors only involved at a late stage in development and implementation.

References

Austerlitz, N., ed., 2008. *Unspoken interactions: Exploring the unspoken dimension of learning and teaching in creative subjects.* London: The Centre for Learning and Teaching in Art and Design.

Bhabha, H. K., 1994. *The Location of Culture.* New York: Routledge.

Boddington, A. and Boys, J., eds., 2011. *Reshaping learning: A critical reader. The future of learning spaces in post-compulsory education.* Rotterdam: Sense Publishers.

Bourdieu, P., 1987. *Distinction: A social critique of the judgment of taste.* Cambridge, MA: Harvard University Press.

Boys, J., 2010. *Towards creative learning spaces: Re-thinking the architecture of post-compulsory education.* New York: Routledge.

Boys, J., 2014. *Doing disability differently: An alternative handbook on architecture, dis/ability, and designing for everyday life.* New York: Routledge.

Callon, M., 1987. Society in the making: The study of technology as a tool for sociological analysis. In: W. Bijker, T. Hughes, and T. Pinch, *The social construction of technological systems: New directions in the sociology and history of technology* (pp. 83–103). London: MIT Press.

De Cauwer, P., Clement, M., Buelens, H., and Heylighen, A., 2009. Four reasons not to teach inclusive design. In: *Proceedings of the International Conference Include*, April 5–8, 2009, Helen Hamlyn Centre, London. London: Royal College of Art.

Fenwick, T. and Edwards, R., 2010. *Actor-network theory in education.* London: Routledge.

Foucault, M., 1970. *The order of things: An archaeology of the human sciences.* New York: Pantheon Books.

Foucault, M., 1995 (1977). *Discipline and punish: The birth of the prison.* New York: Vintage Books.

Garfinkel, H., 1967. *Studies in ethnomethodology.* Prentice Hall, NJ: Englewood Cliffs.

Geertz, C., 1973. Thick description: Towards an interpretative theory of culture. In: C. Geertz, ed., *The interpretation of culture: Selected essays* (pp. 3–30). New York: Basic Books.

Harrison, A. and Hutton, L., 2013. *Learning environments: Space, place and the future of learning.* London: Routledge.

Heylighen, A., 2008. Sustainable and inclusive design: A matter of knowledge? *Local Environment: The International Journal of Justice and Sustainability*, 13(6), 531–540.

Ingold, T., 2011. *Being alive: Essays on movement, knowledge and description.* New York: Routledge.

Ingold, T., 2013. *Making: Anthropology, archaeology, art and architecture.* New York: Routledge.

Joint Information Systems Committee (JISC), 2006. *Designing spaces for effective learning.* [online]. Available from: www.jisc.ac.uk/eli_learningspaces.html [Accessed February 1, 2015].

Kanuka, H., 2006. Instructional design and eLearning: A discussion of pedagogical content knowledge as a missing construct. *e-Journal of Instructional Science and Technology (e-JIST)*, 9(2) September. [online]. Available from: http://ascilite.org/archived-journals/e-jist/docs/vol9_no2/papers/full_papers/kanuka.htm [Accessed July 17, 2015].

Latour, B., 2005. *Reassembling the social: An introduction to Actor-Network-Theory.* Oxford: Oxford University Press.

Latour, B., 2009. *On the modern cult of the factish gods.* Oxford: Duke University Press.

Latour, B. (Johnson, J.), 1988. Mixing humans and non-humans together: The sociology of a door-closer. *Social Problems*, 35(3), 298–310.

Lave, J. and Wenger, E., 1991. *Situated learning: Legitimate peripheral participation.* Cambridge: Cambridge University Press.

Law, J., 2004. *After method. Mess in social science research.* Abingdon, UK: Routledge.

Law, J. and Hassard, J., eds., 1999. *Actor network theory and after.* Oxford: Blackwell and The Sociological Review.

Mol, A., 2002. *The body multiple: Ontology in medical practice.* London: Duke University Press.

Morrow, R., 2000. Architectural assumptions and environmental discrimination: The case for more inclusive design in schools of architecture. In: D. Nicol and S. Pilling, eds., *Changing architectural education towards a new professionalism* (pp. 43–48). London: Taylor & Francis.

Morrow, R., Parnell, R., and Torrington, J., 2004. Reality versus creativity? *CEBE Transactions*, 1(2), 91–99.

Oblinger, D. G., ed., 2006. *Learning spaces.* Educause [online]. Available from: www.educause.edu/LearningSpaces/10569 [Accessed January 1, 2015].

Parlett, M. and Hamilton, D., 1972. *Evaluation as illumination: A new approach to the study of innovative programs.* Edinburgh University Centre for Research in the Educational Sciences/Nuffield Foundation [online]. Available from: www.eric.ed.gov:80/ERICWebPortal/custom/portlets/recordDetails/detailmini.jsp?_nfpb=true&_&ERICExtSearch_SearchValue_0=ED167634&ERICExtSearch_SearchType_0=no&accno=ED167634 [Accessed October 30, 2015].

Ryave, A. L. and Schenkein, J. N., 1974. *Notes on the art of walking.* In: R. Turner, ed., *Ethnomethodology* (pp. 265–274). New York: Penguin.

Sacks, H., 1984. On doing "being ordinary." In: J. M. Atkinson and J. Heritage, eds., *Structures of social action. Studies in conversation analysis* (pp. 413–440). Cambridge, MA: Cambridge University Press.

Sacks, H., 1995. *Lectures on Conversation, Volumes 1 and 2,* Malden, MA: Wiley-Blackwell.

Scottish Funding Council, 2006. *Spaces for learning: A review of learning spaces in further and higher education.* [online]. Available from: http://aleximarmot.com/research [Accessed February 7, 2009].

Temple, P., ed., 2014. *The physical university: Contours of space and place in higher education.* New York: Routledge.

Tertiary Education Facilities Management Association (TEFMA), 2006. *Learning environments in tertiary education.* [online]. Available from: www.tefma.com/infoservices/publications/learning.jsp [Accessed February 7, 2009].

Thrift, N., 2008. *Non-representational theory: Space/politics/effect.* New York: Routledge.

Wenger, E., 1998. *Communities of practice: Learning, meaning and identity.* Cambridge, MA: Cambridge University Press.

6

STUDENTS' PHYSICAL AND DIGITAL SITES OF STUDY

Making, Marking, and Breaking Boundaries

Lesley Gourlay and Martin Oliver

Introduction

Students' day-to-day study practices are complex, relying on heterogeneous networks of people and things. In this chapter, we will argue that studying draws in a wide array of technologies, takes place in both institutional and personal settings, and involves the consumption and production of a variety of digital and print texts.

Drawing on sociomaterial perspectives (e.g. Fenwick, Edwards, and Sawchuk 2011) and theories of space as a social phenomenon (e.g. Massey 2005), we will analyze evidence from a JISC-funded study exploring students' accounts of learning with technology. This analysis shows how spaces are not simply found, nor are they just "containers" for social practice, but they are constantly generated by students.

First, the theoretical framing for this work will be outlined. Then, the study will be described. Examples will be provided that demonstrate the ways in which students manage sites of study, creating and breaking boundaries between these sites. The chapter will conclude by identifying implications for research and practice.

Background

The Apparent Problem of Places and Spaces

Early writing about online study characterized it using phrases such as "any time, any place" learning (e.g. Hiltz and Wellman 1997), often idealizing the virtuality of educational experiences (e.g. Hamilton and Zimmerman 2002). Rhetorically, these experiences were set against the traditional classroom, creating an either/or binary between online and traditional forms of education, and were framed in terms of liberation and freedom. However, studies of fully or partially online courses have since shown that assumptions such as this can be jarringly different from what students actually experience (Holley 2002). One explanation of why this happens is that such idealistic writing frequently relies on what Land (2005) has described as the "incorporeal fallacy": the idea that in online learning, the bodies of learners somehow disappear, or at the least, are rendered irrelevant, and that the spaces and places they inhabit somehow dissolve or dissipate.

This idea of the dissolution of spaces can be seen as a powerful fantasy for education, one that—if it were only true—might solve some of the challenges of providing sufficient high-quality education for the millions worldwide who want to participate in education (Laurillard 2008). As a result, the persistence of this discourse is easy to understand, as are the very negative connotations that it carries about the role of "space" in education. In the literature on educational flexibility, for example, which seeks to improve access to educational opportunities, "space" is framed in terms of an obstacle to be overcome. Technology is then framed as a way of overcoming this limitation—it becomes the means of liberation. Considerable work has been done to understand the different ways in which education could be made more flexible—Nikolova and Collis (1998), for example, outline 19 different kinds of flexibility, clustered around the time of participation, course content, entry requirements, instructional approaches, and course delivery. However, the primary orientation for this work has been to support distance learning, and so the idea of space as a problem to be overcome persists. In Nikolova and Collis's framework, for example, the only times location is mentioned are in "places for study and course participation" and "times and places for support," neither of which substantially develops the idea of space or place. These issues persist. For example, a report sponsored by the Higher Education Academy in the UK framed the situation in a way that is linguistically revealing.

> Technology offers a number of opportunities and challenges for higher education, both enhancing existing provision and opening up new potential. . . . Technology naturally enables the provision and delivery of flexible learning and pedagogy. Flexible learning is concerned with the pace, place and mode of learning: . . . [where] place is concerned with the physical location, which may be work based or at home, on public transport while commuting, or abroad when travelling. . . . Thinking of the three variables above, namely pace, place and mode, then a pedagogical approach can be positioned within the three degrees of freedom, i.e. a three-dimensional space of flexible learning. In the following diagram, the bottom, front-left point being no flexibility in any axis, and increasing levels of flexibility, i.e. choice, as the space is traversed from left to right, front to back and bottom to top.
>
> (Gordon 2014)

In this framing, "place" is a constraint. To be fair, mathematically speaking, the term, "degrees of freedom" is not value-laden; however, in this case, the association of this term with "increasing levels of flexibility, i.e. choice," is. Technology under this formulation is something that cannot help but liberate us: it "naturally" enables flexibility.

This highly deterministic framing fits a particular pattern of talking about education, and specifically, about how it can be "opened." Knox (2013), exploring educational discourses about openness, challenged the negative way in which discussions of technology framed the idea of liberty. Openness, Knox argues, is typically described in terms of shedding "unfreedoms," such as the constraints and bottlenecks of institutional spaces and places, which become associated with exclusion and closure. There are echoes of this, for example, in the kinds of disaggregated future for higher education discussed by Weller (2011); his functional account of higher education makes the point that existing forms have arisen in part due to the economics of physical provision, and the networked alternatives he envisages, being digital, are described without any reference to their physical instantiation. The problem with this framing of the situation is that, "as a result of this focus, there is a distinct lack of consideration for how learning might take place once these obstacles are overcome" (Knox 2013, p. 824). Simply stripping away infrastructure does not necessarily offer anything in terms of new, positive liberties for learners. In order to explore this concern further, it is useful to consider what it is that such infrastructures provide for learners.

The Materiality of Study

Perspectives such as sociomateriality can help to move beyond this kind of idealized, simplistic account. This perspective draws attention precisely to the ways in which successful practices are instantiated physically and socially through networks of people and things.

> Humans, and what they take to be their learning and social process, do not float, distinct, in container-like contexts of education, such a classrooms or community sites, that can be conceptualized and dismissed as simply a wash of material stuff and spaces.
>
> (Fenwick et al. 2011, p. vii)

Such a sociomaterial perspective shifts the emphasis away from projecting what technology might enable (or even necessitate) and toward understanding how existing things have been achieved—a reframing that both opens a possibility for critique, and supports the pragmatic aim of achieving change. As Latour argues, "to explain is not a mysterious cognitive feat, but a very practical world-building enterprise that consists in connecting entities with other entities, that is, in tracing a network" (2005, p. 103). In pursuing such explanations, research can respond to Selwyn's challenge (2008) that research on educational technology should turn away from speculation about what might be possible and instead ground itself in the "state of the actual," in order to connect to contemporary debates within the field of education and beyond. From this perspective, Weller's comments (2011) about the economics of physical provision look less like a problem, and more like a success story of heterogeneous engineering.

> The campus is best thought of not simply as a constraint but, to borrow Brown and Duguid's phrase, as a "resourceful constraint" (Brown and Duguid 2000, p. 246), one it would be premature to write off and which those developing distributed learning need to take seriously. ...The campus—or more generally, the co–location of learners, teachers, labs, class-rooms, lecture theatres, libraries and so on—refuses to lie down and die.... Those seeking to develop distributed education should understand the support a campus setting gives the educational process and should be prepared for the necessity to find new ways of providing that support in a distributed education context.
>
> (Cornford and Pollock 2005, pp. 18 and 170)

Understanding how the campus enables education through the provision of established socio-material networks requires close attention to contemporary teaching and learning practices. This is not simply some romantic nostalgia for some ideal, monastic past, but a more profound reshaping of our being-with technology (Cousin 2005). It demands a close look at the "state of the actual," something that challenges many of the claims popular in educational technology, which draw their rhetorical power from dismissing current teaching as outmoded, obsolete, or, at the least, under threat from new approaches. Clark (2010), for example, lambasts lectures as a "hopeless pedagogic technique," damned through the "tyranny of location." However, his account portrays lectures purely as a means of transmitting information (ideally in an entertaining manner); it assumes that the lecture simply consists of talking at an audience, and is therefore ready to be replaced by more efficient means of broadcasting that information. However, as Fuller (2009) has argued, viewing the lecture in such an instrumental way ignores various important aspects of its purpose—such as, that it is also an argument that is being exposed to critical scrutiny in a public setting, and that it forms part of a wider array of socially framed knowledge work.

This richer understanding of educational practice undermines the idea that lectures (and other educational moments) are tightly bound by time and space, allowing it to be replaced by an analysis that shows the ways in which it connects and relates to other social practices. For example, within contemporary lecturing practice, it has been argued that the extensive use of digital media, such as automated capture or student recordings, extends the lecture beyond the immediate performance and, through networks of technologies and practices, connects it to other, wider, conversations and debates.

> "The classroom" or lecture hall has perhaps remained the most iconic symbol of what is seen as the "traditional" university, and is often placed in opposition to "elearning" as somehow representing the essence of what is "face-to-face" and non-digital. . . . [but] the VLE also causes the epistemological nature of the lecture and the ontological status of the lecturer and students to be destabilised. The claims of the lecturer may be more easily called into question, and may be simultaneously checked, challenged or undermined in class with recourse to external online authorities. . . . The biological body of the lecturer has been displaced, shifted to the side or dwarfed by the screen. The lecturer's voice has become a voiceover to an increasingly visual spectacle. The point at which new knowledge is made available has become radically dispersed.
>
> (Gourlay 2012)

The post-human, sociomaterial perspective Gourlay uses highlights another important principle: the idea that things such as technology also need to be treated as actors in social processes. As Hayles explains:

> The more one works with digital technologies, the more one comes to appreciate the capacity of networked and programmable machines to carry out sophisticated cognitive tasks, and the more the keyboard comes to seem an extension of one's thoughts rather than an external device on which one types. Embodiment then takes the form of extended cognition, in which human agency and thought are enmeshed within larger networks that extend beyond the desktop computer into the environment.
>
> (2012, p. 3)

Once technologies are identified as potential actors, it also becomes possible to reconsider educational practices in distinctive and interesting new ways. A well-established principle of ethnographic work informed by Actor-Network Theory is that it is important to "follow the actors themselves" (Latour 2005, p. 12), whether those actors are people or things. This has enabled careful accounts to be developed both of how technologies are entangled in practices, such as Thompson's exploration (2012) of how the delete button forms an important part of learning, "acting as a line of defence against information overload, arbitrating relevance, serving to presence and absence other actors, safeguarding against intrusion, and both opening and enclosing spaces" (p. 106). By studying these entanglements it becomes possible to explain how technologies become "fluid," acting in different ways depending on the network of relations in which they are embedded (e.g. Enriquez 2009); in this way, technologies enable different configurations of mobility, resulting in new arrangements of "moorings" that tie practices to specific configurations of space (Enriquez 2011). These new arrangements have been described as "cyberspaces . . . the complex webs of material practices through which technologically mediated education is enacted" (Edwards, Tracy, and Jordan 2011).

Rethinking education in this way emphasizes the relational framing of educational spaces. Rather than understanding a space such as a lecture theater in terms of measurements or classification, it is seen as a place in which certain social practices are enacted, so that it is understood in terms of "a simultaneous multiplicity of spaces: cross-cutting, intersecting, aligning with one-another, or existing in relations of paradox or antagonism" (Massey 1994, p. 3). Rather than seeing space as a container or backcloth, a mobilities analysis examines the ways in which such spaces are enacted and become sedimented across time (Edwards et al. 2011). Such an analysis therefore requires research to focus on the enactment of educational practices—and the way that they change and develop it over time—in order to understand how these constitute something as a recognizable space, rather than relying on the free-floating, ungrounded designation of some location as (say) a lecture theater.

> We recognise space as the product of interrelations; as constituted through interactions, from the immensity of the global to the intimately tiny. . . . We recognise space as always under construction. Precisely because space on this reading is a product of relations-between, relations which are necessarily embedded in material practices which have to be carried out, it is always in the process of being made. It is never finished; never closed. Perhaps we could imagine space as a simultaneity of stories-so-far.
>
> (Massey 2005, p. 9)

This theorization of space—as something achieved through social practices, constituted materially, related to other spaces, people, and things—formed the basis for the research described here. Rather than focusing on "unfreedoms," and how the "tyranny" of institutional infrastructures can be overcome, this approach explored the sociomaterial enactment of educational practices over time, and the ways in which specific places were entangled in this. Instead of starting out by assuming that what was required was a study of classrooms or libraries, it began from the assumptions that students are embodied actors, are already studying, and that in order to understand this studying, it is necessary to explain how it draws in complex networks of people, things, and places.

Methodology

Building on the theoretical foundations outlined above, a project was undertaken that sought to explore students' study practices, with a focus on understanding how these were achieved. Drawing on a sociomaterial perspective and the idea of space as relational, this involved investigating where, when, and with what students studied. The project was funded as part of the UK JISC's digital literacies program (Payton 2012).

The study was undertaken at a large postgraduate institution specializing in educational research. The student body is predominantly mature, mainly female, and many students combine study with work and family responsibilities. Students are from diverse countries of origin and a broad range of education cultures. Most have been out of formal education for several years. Consequently, they may never have used the kinds of digital technologies that are regarded as mainstream in higher education, although they are likely to have well-established repertoires of digital practices derived from personal or professional settings.

The study received institutional ethical clearance and followed British Education Research Association (BERA) guidelines about informed consent, including guarantees of anonymity and confidentiality, and the right to opt out at any point (BERA 2011). As a pilot, focus groups were held with four groups of students—initial teacher education (PGCE) students, students on taught master's programs, students on master's programs that are taught entirely at a distance, and doctoral students. Participants were recruited to ensure diversity of gender, age, home/EU or international and full-time/part-time status. The focus groups opened by asking participants to draw maps of where they studied, and what with.

TABLE 6.1 Overview of the Journaling Participants

Category	Pseudonym	Details
MA	Nahid	M, 26 Bangladeshi
MA	Juan	M, 30s British
MA	Yuki	F, 42 Japanese
Ph.D.	Django	F, 39 British
Ph.D.	Sally	F, 41 British
Ph.D.	Frederick	M, 25 German
PGCE	Louise	F, 22 British
PGCE	Faith	F, 30 Taiwanese
PGCE	Polly	F, 40 British
Distance	Bokeh	M, 30s British
Distance	Darren	M, 40s American
Distance	Lara	F, 40s Chilean

This pilot was followed by a longitudinal, multimodal journaling study. For this, three students were invited from each of the focus groups; again, these were selected to reflect the diversity of the student body, as shown in Table 6.1.

Each participant took part in 3–4 interviews over a period of 6–12 months. In the first interview, participants were asked to draw a new, more detailed version of their map of study spaces, and to explain what they were drawing as they did so. Subsequently, they were each provided with an iPod Touch, and shown how to use this to produce images, videos, and textual notes. They were then asked to use the iPod Touches to generate data by documenting their study practices, and were encouraged to focus on "messy," micro-level, day-to-day lived activities, including the material, spatial, and temporal elements of their practices.

Students took a month or more to create these first "journals" of their practice, consisting of a collection of multimodal data. They curated the data they had created, and brought this back for the second interview. In this interview, they reported on their experiences by presenting the journaling data to the interviewer and discussing them. This process of data generation and presentation through interview was then repeated two or three times; in each iteration, the participant was encouraged to narrow their focus (e.g. to the use of the library, or to the production of a piece of assessed work) and to take greater responsibility for the curation, presentation, and interpretation of their journaling data. Some students created presentations using PowerPoint or Prezi, but many also brought along printed papers, books, folders, notebooks, post-it notes, pens, and other print literacy resources. The data were analyzed thematically, coding both sections of interview transcript and also images (digital photos and drawn maps), presentation slides, and video clips. The subset of themes relating to students' use of space are reported here.

Findings

Nowhere and Everywhere

Several students discussed ways in which they felt that technology liberated them from having to study in specific places. Mostly, this was discussed in terms of ubiquity and connectivity, of studying "everywhere"; in more extreme cases it was suggested that they could almost be "nowhere."

> That's really interesting how much I use the iPad for a start everywhere and anywhere . . . And I have the information there all the time constantly, and I just feel as though I don't have to be anywhere physical at all anymore . . .
>
> (Django, Interview 3)

However, such comments were very general, and closer analysis showed two kinds of inconsistency. First, it became clear from more detailed discussion of specific examples that "studying" was too broad a category to work with; instead, spaces and technologies became associated with specific study practices, such as searching, reading, or writing.

> For me the most important thing is portability, because I use technologies, ICT, everywhere I go, anywhere I go. For example of course I use some technologies, PCs and laptops and my iPad in the [institutional] building, and in the [institutional] building I use PC, I use them in PC room, in library, and for searching some data or journals. In the lecture room I record my, record the lectures and taking memos by that.
>
> (Yuki, Interview 1)

Second, when details were requested during the interviews about the materiality of studying, the discussions moved quickly to lists of the multiplicity of spaces in which studying happened. Whilst this suggested a sense of happening "everywhere," it was a very particular kind of "everywhere" that was achieved by bringing together specific combinations of space and technology. Space was able to vary (enabling study to happen "everywhere") when technologies were stable and consistent (such as the same book being carried around, or a laptop with work files that could be taken to different places, or an iPad that could access remotely stored files).

From a mobilities perspective, then, spaces were constituted in part by the devices that were taken from location to location, and which were used to support study across these times and places. Analytically, within Actor-Network Theory, the idea of "following the actor" is important as a way of exploring the series of entanglements that constitute practice. In this study, it was possible (for example) to follow Yuki's iPad and create an account of the kinds of study practices and spaces that it was involved with. She used this to curate digitized resources, hold the audio recordings of lectures, make notes, browse online materials, email others, and so on. It thus provided continuity between lecture spaces, the library, and private, personal spaces. Digital technologies were not the only kinds of resource that enabled this; Yuki also discussed a photo of reading a book on a bench in the park, for example.

The more general point, however, is that although students talked about studying "everywhere," or even being "nowhere" when they studied, the sociomaterial grounding in these interviews showed that neither of these general terms adequately captures the way in which technology is taken up to support studying. Instead, technology allows different kinds of "moorings," enabling more spaces to be connected together so that study can take place in a greater variety of places than would be possible without it. In this sense, to use Yuki's description, technology allowed her to become "less bound by place," but it also served to constitute the spaces where studying happened.

Somewhere

Many of the students' accounts emphasized the importance of specific places for their studies. As noted above, students described a range of specific places where studying took place. Formal educational settings such as classrooms or lecture rooms were mentioned, but were only one site amongst many: the library featured strongly in students' accounts, as did homes, workplaces (schools, in the case of PGCE students), and public spaces such as buses, trains, parks, and cafes. What also became apparent was the way in which movement between these spaces formed part of the rhythm of studying: certain spaces were strung together in sequences (e.g. reading on the bus, accessing files on a computer in the library, searching for books on the library shelves, etc.), and these were often associated with specific phases of studying (e.g. working in the library when looking for resources at an early stage of writing an essay, visiting a field site when undertaking empirical studies, etc.).

Some of the descriptions of these sites were very emotive: successful study was not only a socio-technical achievement, a matter of engineering human and non-human actors, but was also about how studying felt.

> I enjoy . . . the image of being, sort of, in a dusty, you know, sort of, wooden shelved, kind of, old library, where it's, sort of, cosy and warm, that's, you know, I like that and that's a part of the experience of studying that I enjoy.
>
> (Juan, Interview 1)

Part of what enabled an "academic" atmosphere were characteristics such as quietness, or having sufficient space to bring resources together. (This point about marshaling resources to enable study will be returned to, below.) However, equally, what created this sense of atmosphere was understood relationally: these places were associated with particular histories, individuals, or kinds of work.

Juan, for example, described how his journey to the institutional library formed an important part of his preparation to study.

> Where I live it could be, you could be in a town sort of anywhere and you wouldn't really necessarily notice. Whereas you come in here and you come over the Waterloo Bridge and you see St Paul's and the Houses of Parliament, you know, you're in London, you're doing something again. You know, this is where people do important things and that, kind of, thing and it gives it a reality. . . . It focuses me a little bit on that.
>
> (Juan, Interview 3)

Others also spoke about the presence of international students and scholars making them feel that they were part of something important. Studying could be achieved in a range of places, and all students described studying (for example, reading) in "dead time," wherever that arose. However, the places students actively chose to spend time studying were frequently the ones that carried connotations of studiousness, scholarly work, and concentration.

Whilst study took place in a range of settings, it was striking that some of these were intensely personal and private—even intimate. For example, Yuki shared an image that she titled, "The Bathroom is a Good Place to Read" (Figure 6.1).

FIGURE 6.1 Yuki's Bath

In her account of this image, Yuki described how digitized books, recorded lectures, personal notes, web links, and so on were curated using her iPad, which she placed into a clear zip-lock plastic bag so that she could study whilst bathing, an environment that provided her with the peace and space to focus on the work.

Yuki's accounts of places where she studied did include specific technical requirements ("sometimes I need to get good Wi-Fi access," for example), but more were emotive.

> When I get tired, or need fresh air, I go to the park. This is my friend, squirrel, in Tavistock Square. And also, sometimes I read in the bathroom. This place is very good to concentrate to my reading.
>
> (Yuki, Interview 3)

Creating Study Spaces

A recurrent theme across all participants' accounts was the way in which spaces for study were made, not just found. An obvious example of this was the way in which public transport was used as a site of study. Many of the maps that participants drew included buses and trains, for example Figure 6.2, and, as noted above, many participants discussed the way in which they sought to make "dead time" whilst traveling more productive.

Reading was by far the most common activity whilst on public transport, either using books or iPads, or (if reading emails) smartphones.

Similar experiences were reported for working in public spaces such as cafes and parks. Figure 6.3, for example, is an image that Django brought to an interview, showing how a book, pen, and smartphone were used in a cafe by a river when planning work.

Most examples of creating study spaces were relatively simple, usually involving reading from a single resource or device, writing into a single book or on one device, or annotating a printed text. These examples also included using laptops or tablet computers on a sofa or in bed at home—environments that were not set up for study, but which were easily adapted. In these examples, studying was "moored" (Edwards et al. 2011) within these improvised spaces through the way that the same technologies were incorporated consistently within them.

FIGURE 6.2 A Map Showing Sites of Study

A few examples, however, were more complex. Juan described how he browsed and collected texts at an early stage of the writing process. In order to do this, he worked in the institutional library. He moved between book stacks and a desk with a computer, on which he browsed electronic holdings. He skim-read articles on screen to assess their relevance, but wanted to reread these in a more measured way later, annotating a print-based version of the material. However, the printers in the library only supported single-sided printing: in order to save money, he walked a short distance to another institution's library, where he used his girlfriend's login and password to access their network, and then printed the articles he wanted from a memory stick on a double-sided printer. His sense of the library as a successful study space, therefore, involved connecting it to another library, another institution's computer networks and printers, and his girlfriend.

FIGURE 6.3 Studying in a Cafe

Not all attempts to create spaces for study were successful. Faith, for example, brought along a picture of a printer on a desk, and explained how this had resulted in problems for her when on a placement in a school as part of her course. Whilst the space was, notionally, open to her, the politics of the staffroom prevented her from using it successfully.

> Our staff room was equipped . . . one, two, three, four, five, six, seven . . . seven computers now we can use and only one of them attached with a printer. So, . . . everybody wants to get to that computer where you can use the printer. . . . So, six student teachers tried to use other computer. So, it, kind of, sometimes feels a bit crowded. And when the school staff want to use it, well, okay, it seems like we are the invaders, intruders?
>
> (Faith, Interview 2)

Again, the emotional aspects of Faith's experience are notable; she was hesitant even when describing the situation, and had found it difficult to be excluded in this way. Faith was unable to resolve how to get reliable access to this device, but eventually managed to find another space she could go to where there was a computer with a printer, and so she used that instead. Unlike Yuki, who described how she was able to set up a range of highly idiosyncratic spaces that suited the way she studied, Faith could not enroll these institutional technologies successfully—however, in some ways she was, like Yuki, "less bound by space" than might be expected, simply by virtue of being able to opt out of the problematic space she found herself in, and by moving to a new space where there was less competition for the resources she needed.

Breaking, Making, and Marking Boundaries

All the previous examples highlight the ways in which study spilled across what might normally be considered discrete spaces; the boundaries between them were constantly traversed, and sites of study had to be enacted (and were therefore bounded) by bringing together a range of people, devices, and print resources.

This analysis draws very different boundaries around spaces than might be expected. Juan's library, for example, was not neatly circumscribed by the institution's walls; it spilt over into another building. Yuki's bath was connected to the institutional library, as she could use her iPad and WiFi network to access e-journals and other digital library resources. Louise used a series of technologies to bring theater performances into her classroom (Figure 6.4).

> When I took some photos at the Globe I couldn't believe how easy it was to transfer into the computer. It was just as easy as a digital camera and the quality pretty impressive as well. So and then I can just copy them into my Interactive Whiteboard.
>
> (Louise, Interview 3)

This illustrates the ways in which individuals made and remade boundaries, where "boundary marking is not about putting a fence around a field, but about marking the relations that can be made in specific enactments" (Edwards et al. 2011, p. 231).

This experience was markedly different from the supposed "tyranny of location" described in earlier research (Clark 2010). Indeed, some of the participants found studying to be *too* mobile; they described an active struggle to limit such movement, and to reinscribe boundaries between studying and their private life, for example.

Juan's map illustrates this well. He drew his home as far away from university as possible on the paper he used, and emphasized the separation of these spaces by drawing a dashed line between them. The line was dashed rather than solid, he explained, because these two sets of spaces simply could not be kept separate in practice; however, he tried to minimize the extent to which university work crept into his home life.

> I like having a break between things and that kind of thing. And the same very much I think between home and university. . . . When you're in one thing then you're there and you're in that moment for a while and then you might change to sort of another one. . . . Without too much work, I could do all of this [at home], you know, but I choose not to because I like the change. And I like the movement maybe as well, so it is, yes, it's an important thing I suppose for there to be these sort of, these areas of not necessarily nothing, but of distinction, clear distinction between them.
>
> (Juan, Interview 1)

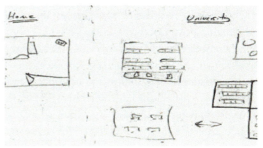

FIGURE 6.4 Louise's Images of a Play at the Globe Being Prepared for Classroom Use

FIGURE 6.5 Juan's Map

FIGURE 6.6 Sally's Portable Hotspot

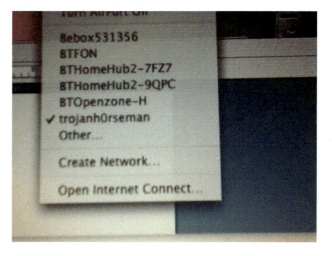

This was echoed elsewhere in the interviews, for example in the ways in which people used multiple email addresses to keep private, professional, and study activities separate.

Boundaries were also marked to keep others out, as well as to keep personal activities in. Sally, for example, shared an image that illustrated one way in which she worked to keep out others that she saw as a threat (Figure 6.6).

Sally drew on conventions of hacker culture and "leetspeak" to try to persuade others not to enter the spaces created by her phone.

> This is my portable hotspot on my phone, and I'm using it to connect my internet, and I can't use the encryption on it because the computer was too old to use the encryption, so in other words, I then had to come up with a scary name so that nobody in my local area would, like, use my connection, so I called it trojanh0rseman because that's, like, I'm some kind of scary hacker or something, so I thought, if that's an example of me . . . and I put a 0 in so it looked, do you know what I mean, that looks really dodgy, you wouldn't click on that would you?
>
> (Sally, Interview)

Conclusions

Although much attention has been given to the idea of overcoming the limitations of study spaces, close analysis of students' day-to-day study practices provides an insight into what spaces are, and what they mean to learners. Space cannot be understood simply as a kind of container, a backcloth, or something that just forms a neutral, given context in which studying happens. Instead, it is contingent, emergent, and endlessly constituted through the networked unfolding of sociomaterial, post-human, and textual practices—practices that cannot be neatly bundled together as "studying," but instead consist of countless acts of reading, writing, noting, curating, speaking, and so on. Space is constantly enacted through, and entangled in, these complex day-to-day practices that make up students' studying. "A space, then, . . . is neither a container for always-already constituted identities nor a completed closure of holism. This is a space of loose ends and missing links. For the future to be open, space must by open too" (Massey 2005, p. 12).

Rather than being bound within educational institutions, studying spills out across many public and private spaces, moored as part of a consistent practice of education by the consistent uses of print and digital technologies. Within this, institutionally provided spaces remain important, not least because they allow connections to other people, times, and places that carry connotations of studiousness and academic-ness. Such spaces cannot "bind," because of the way learners, technologies, and practices move into, through, and out of them: however, they do form an important resource for learners seeking to create boundaries between areas of their life, and mark the points at which their educational practices can stop.

References

British Educational Research Association (BERA), 2011. *Ethical guidelines for educational research*. London: British Educational Research Association.

Clark, D., 2010. *Don't lecture me*. Transcript of a keynote presentation. ALT-C 2010, Nottingham. [online]. Available from: http://repository.alt.ac.uk/841 [Accessed October 5, 2014].

Cornford, J. and Pollock, N., 2005. The university campus as a "resourceful constraint": Process and practice in the construction of the virtual university. In: M. Lea and K. Nicoll, eds., *Distributed learning: Social and cultural approaches to practice* (pp. 170–181). London: RoutledgeFalmer.

Cousin, G., 2005. Learning from cyberspace. In: R. Land and S. Bayne, eds., *Education in cyberspace* (pp. 117–145). London: Routledge.

Edwards, R., Tracy, F., and Jordan, K., 2011. Mobilities, moorings and boundary marking in developing semantic technologies in educational practices. *Research in Learning Technology*, 19(3), 219–232.

Enriquez, J., 2009. From bush pump to blackboard: The fluid workings of a virtual environment. *E-Learning and Digital Media*, 6(4), 385–399.

Enriquez, J., 2011. Tug-o-where: Situating mobilities of learning (t)here. *Learning, Media and Technology*, 36(1), 39–53.

Fenwick, T., Edwards, R., and Sawchuk, P., 2011. *Emerging approaches to educational research: Tracing the sociomaterial*. London: Routledge.

Fuller, S., 2009. *The sociology of intellectual life: The career of the mind in and around academy*. London: Sage.

Gordon, N., 2014. *Flexible pedagogies: Technology-enhanced learning*. York: Higher Education Academy. [online]. Available from: https://www.heacademy.ac.uk/flexible-pedagogies-technology-enhanced-learning [Accessed March 17, 2015].

Gourlay, L., 2012. Cyborg ontologies and the lecturer's voice: A posthuman reading of the "face-to-face." *Learning, Media and Technology*, 37(2), 198–211.

Hamilton, S. and Zimmerman, J., 2002. Breaking through zero-sum academics: Two students' perspectives on computer-mediated learning environments. In: K. Rudestram and J. Schoenholtz-Read, eds., *The handbook of online learning innovations in higher education and corporate training* (pp. 257–276). London: Sage.

Hayles, K., 2012. *How we think: Digital media contemporary technogenesis*. Chicago: University of Chicago Press.

Hiltz, S. R. and Wellman, B., 1997. Asynchronous learning networks as a virtual classroom. *Communications of the ACM*, 40(9), 44–49.

Holley, D., 2002. Which room is the virtual seminar in please? *Education & Training*, 44(3), 112–121.

Knox, J., 2013. Five critiques of the open educational resources movement. *Teaching in Higher Education*, 18(8), 821–832.

Land, R., 2005. Embodiment and risk in cyberspace education. In: R. Land and S. Bayne, eds., *Education in cyberspace* (pp. 149–164). London: Routledge.

Latour, B., 2005. *Reassembling the social: An introduction to actor-network-theory*. Oxford: Oxford University Press.

Laurillard, D., 2008. Open teaching: The key to sustainable and effective open education. In: T. Iiyoshi and M. V. Kumar, eds., *Opening up education: The collective advancement of education through open technology, open content, and open knowledge* (pp. 319–336). Cambridge, MA: MIT Press.

Massey, D., 1994. *Space, place and gender*. Cambridge: Polity Press.

Massey, D., 2005. *For space*. London: Sage.

Nikolova, I. and Collis, B., 1998. Flexible learning and the design of instruction. *British Journal of Educational Technology*, 29(1), 59–72.

Payton, S., 2012. Developing digital literacies. Bristol: JISC. [online]. Available from: www.jisc.ac.uk/media/documents/publications/briefingpaper/2012/Developing_Digital_Literacies.pdf [Accessed March 3, 2015].

Selwyn, N., 2008. From state-of-the-art to state-of-the-actual? Introduction to a special issue. *Technology, Pedagogy and Education*, 17(2), 83–87.

Thompson, T. L., 2012. I'm deleting as fast as I can: Negotiating learning practices in cyberspace. In: T. Fenwick and P. Landri, eds., *Materialities, textures and pedagogies* (pp. 93–112). Abingdon, UK: Routledge.

Weller, M., 2011. *The digital scholar: How technology is transforming scholarly practice*. London: Bloomsbury Academic. [online]. Available from: www.bloomsbury.com/uk/the-digital-scholar-9781849666268 [Accessed March 1, 2015].

7

THE SONIC SPACES OF ONLINE DISTANCE LEARNERS

Michael Sean Gallagher, James Lamb, and Sian Bayne

Introduction

The growing influence of the digital within higher education prompts us to rethink conventional understandings of how and where learning takes place. Traditional understandings of the university, with its lecture theaters, seminar rooms, and social areas, are problematized by the varied and fluid learning spaces of online students who may never cross the threshold of the physical campus. Much has been written about the digital environments where online learning takes place; however, up to this point relatively little attention has been paid to the material spaces that online distance students occupy whilst learning.

There are some notable exceptions to this. Kirkwood (2000), for example, explores the complexity and diversity of the domestic context for online students—a complexity which in turn impacts the use of technology and the educational process itself—whilst Kahu et al. (2014) interrogate the role of space and time in shaping the study practices of mature online students. Of particular interest to the research presented in this chapter is Kahu et al.'s presentation of student engagement in online education as a complex aggregation of factors, of which access to and control over domestic space is one. Additionally, Moss's (2004) concepts of time and space as qualitative entities and their role in creating space for learning has resonance for the work described here.

In this chapter we describe and discuss how we used a combination of aural, textual, and visual data to gain insights into the learning spaces of online distance students. In particular, we were interested in the sonic and material components of student study spaces. Our focus on "space" is influenced by Mol and Law's (1994; Law and Mol 2001) work on social topology, and on the "spatial turn" in social science research identified by Fenwick, Edwards, and Sawchuk, which draws into question the assumption that space functions as a "static container" (2011, p. 129) within which individuals act. Rather, space is seen as a dynamic entity which is produced by the social and material interactions which take place "within" it.

Our work here builds on earlier research where we explored the social topologies of distance students (Bayne, Gallagher, and Lamb 2013) and the construction of "nearness" for distance students to their affiliated university (Ross, Gallagher, and Macleod 2013). Using data generated from our earlier research, this chapter suggests that the construction of student study space often has to be negotiated from within domestic space, and doing so involves the deliberate use of manufactured silence or sound in order to establish territories for personal learning.

Our research found that for every considered and composed construction of visual study space (neatly arranged laptop, notebook, and pens), we saw contested aural space (streets, cars, and horns; children and TV playing cartoons in the background). It also suggests that the practices that these distance students developed to create study space all involved varying degrees of territorialism (Fluegge 2011). From a methodological perspective, therefore, we highlight the value of a multimodal approach, arguing in particular for greater attention to the use of aural data in helping us to understand the construction of space, including its interaction with the visual. Aurality is currently neglected within the educational literature, an absence that we have started to address here.

Methods and Context: Listening to Data

The chapter draws on research undertaken with students from the M.Sc. in Digital Education (formerly the M.Sc. in E-Learning) at the University of Edinburgh. This is a taught postgraduate program that has been delivered entirely online since 2006. The program has a strong global reach with a cohort typically comprising students from around 40 countries at any one time, many of whom will never venture onto the physical campus of their university. This is a class that works within the uncertain boundaries of a highly technologized educational space with a complex, shifting relation to its material, institutional "base." We set out to investigate what it meant to be a student *at* Edinburgh, but not *in* Edinburgh, and what insights this gave us into learning design for online distance programs.

Over the period of a year we generated data with 28 students and recent graduates of the program. Our earlier published research (Bayne et al. 2013; Ross et al. 2013) drew on 20 in-depth, online, narrative interviews that elicited stories about students' experiences of place, space, and institution. A further stage of data collection invited these and other students from the same program to capture and submit a "digital postcard" depicting a place from where they commonly conducted their studies. We requested that each postcard should comprise a photograph, a short audio "field recording," and an explanatory message.[1] Using the data from the 21 digital postcards that were submitted, we created short videos, viewable at http://edinspace.weebly.com/postcards. html. For the purposes of this chapter, we have merged the images and text provided into a composite image, and attempted to convey something of the soundscape submitted by describing it below each image, with a link to the audio recording.

In what follows we attend primarily to the visual and aural data generated by these digital postcards. In doing this we have worked to avoid the tendency amongst Internet scholars to privilege image over sound (Sterne 2006), favoring a multimodal approach where aural, visual, and (to an extent) textual data were considered as interdependent. A helpful explanation of modes and multimodality can be found in the work of Kress and Van Leeuwen (2001), and of Jewitt (2009). These authors propose that meaning is conveyed through a wide range of semiotic material. Within this range it is the particular configuration of different modes—for instance sound, image, and text—and how they interact, that influences the creation of meaning.

We thus developed a model that allowed us to analyze image, audio, and text interdependently, by discussing, whenever possible, the coherence between them. Our transcription model borrowed from methodologies concerned with visual data (Kress and Van Leeuwen 1996; Rose 2012), sound (Fluegge 2011), and also methods of coherence (Van Leeuwen 2004; Monaco 2009). From Fluegge's work on personal sound space (2011), we adapted the notions of territorialism, sonic trespass, and spatial-acoustic self-determination in order to suit the specific context of spatial construction for students, as well as our interest in the combined aural, visual, and text data of each digital postcard. We used what Fluegge describes as the "individual's auditory experience" as a way of thinking more broadly about the different components of the participant's learning space. Using Fluegge's description of territoriality, we looked for evidence within the sound, image, and text that participants had attempted to create a place for learning within a wider social space. This included searching within the sound, image, and text of each postcard submission for the use of sound reproduction or repression devices (speakers or headphones, for instance) that reflected attempts at spatial-acoustic self-determination. We were interested to see whether participants set out to use sound or silence as a way of accompanying or enhancing their scholarly activity.

This approach was augmented by specific attention to what was seen in the submitted images. The visual data was transcribed using an adaptation of Rose (2012), particularly making reference to sites of the image and audiencing. An additional attribute—coherence—was drawn from Monaco (2009) and the positioning of sound as parallel or contrapuntal to the visual and textual data. We similarly borrowed from Van Leeuwen's (2004) concepts of information linking, or how temporal or causal links are established between elements in multimodal texts.

This approach provided a mechanism for considering how the semiotic resources presented in the audio, visual, and text data were integrated, or "spoke" to one another. It should be noted again at this point that the postcards seen below represent our attempt to share the data as clearly as possible: participants submitted image, audio, and text within a single submission form, but not as a combined artifact as they are represented in this chapter.

From our transcription of 15 postcards we noted the following emergent and often interrelated themes:

- the prevalence of informal, homely, and domestic spaces from which online students participated in learning activity
- apparent attempts to mark out a material and/or aural territory, with the purpose of establishing a corner or haven for personal study: a space that would be free from disruption
- creation of a learning space within a wider shared space (in contrast to attempts to carve out a distinct personal territory)
- sonic trespass, where the participant's learning space was penetrated from outside by the intrusion of sound and its material agents
- a contrast between manufactured silence and sound (including the use of music in apparent attempts at spatial-acoustic self-determination).

In what follows we use the above themes to discuss specific examples of student study spaces, with a particular focus on the aural dimensions of these. First, however, we will briefly consider aurality as a neglected mode within social science research, and attempt to make a case for a greater consideration of sound as a factor in the construction of study space.

Aurality: A Neglected Mode

The literature on multimodal analysis often prioritizes the image and moving image over the aural (Burn and Parker 2003; Kress and Van Leeuwen 2006). Within the aural mode itself, there is a tendency to place the emphasis on voice acts (Neumark, Gibson, and Van Leeuwen 2011) and, to a lesser extent, music (McKee 2006; Monaco 2009). When sound is considered in the multimodal literature (for example, Neumark et al. 2011), it is often as a composed, discrete piece of "intentional" sound manipulation, rather than the aural documentation of a particular space. The kind of ambient audio discussed in this research remains undertheorized and unrepresented.

For this reason, we reiterate a case for a sounded anthropology (Samuels et al. 2010), or a means of identifying and articulating the role of sound in our spatial constructions, and—in this case—our study spaces. Research (outlined in Samuels et al. 2010) is beginning to reveal the role of sound in spatial, or material, constructions of space, suggesting that sonic performance is shaped by ideologies of aural and listening practices. As such, there are spaces explicitly designed or adapted for "sonorous" purposes (churches, cathedrals, Paleolithic caves as described by Reznikoff 2006) and "nonsonorous" purposes (the shopping malls as described by Sterne 1997). This distinction between spaces of sonorous and nonsonorous purpose parallels many of the spaces presented in this research, as many were designed for silence, many were adapted to existing sound, and many were immersed in a crafted sounded environment.

Fluegge (2011) provides a structure for analyzing aural data and its effect on the creation and manipulation of space, a structure that has been adapted for this research. Fluegge advances several concepts that have proven useful to us, all of which foreground the idea that aural space is fluid, and the result of evolving relations between the individual and his or her immediate environment. All suggest that sound space is to an extent territorial and subject to contestation. *Personal sound space* is a way of denoting the auditory environment of an individual that emphasizes his or her conscious participation in a dynamic social exchange within that space (Fluegge 2011). It relates to the "individual's auditory experience, which entails not only what a person may be hearing or where they are hearing it, but also the social conditions influencing their apprehension."

Related to this idea of personal sound space are the concepts of territoriality, sonic trespass, and spatial–acoustic self-determination (Fluegge 2011). *Territoriality* adheres to the idea that space is negotiated: the communal space can be made private if the individual has the power to appropriate it as such. Personal sound space suggests a degree of territoriality, or a claim on space for private use. Once personal sound space has been established, there exists the possibility of *sonic trespass*, or an unwelcome intrusion across the permeable boundaries of the personal sound space. *Spatial-acoustic self-determination* refers to the methods or capacity for combating sonic trespass; it is the economic and technological capacity for employing technology to manipulate the personal sound space (the headset, for example, is the "sonic equivalent of private property" (Sterne 2003)). As adapted for this research, these concepts all involve the conversion, or construction, of space for study purposes, a process that is heavily rooted in a network of social, economic, and technological relationships.

Analysis: Trespass and Determination

Territorialism and Trespass

As described above, we broadened Fluegge's description of territorialism and sonic trespass to consider the ways that students were seen to carve out, in an aural and material way, a personal learning space within a wider social environment. Whilst this included acts of negotiation or assimilation (multitasking study with childcare; assimilating the sounds of the street into the study place), it also included attempts to act against intrusion, resulting in the occupation and construction of corners for study. Josie provides a particularly clear enactment of this material and aural territorialism.

> Josie's audio recording captures what we might understand as composed silence. We can hear the faint and muffled sound of noise emanating (voices mediated through a television, possibly) from a different space, perhaps seeping through the walls from an adjacent room. The only sound of any note is the click of the recording being terminated.
>
> (Audio available at http://bit.ly/edinspace1)

To begin, Josie presents an intimate, yet communal space. Her sofa, books and bookcase, end table, and lamps could all be categorized as attributes shared with her family. It is from this homely, domestic space that Josie establishes a territory in which to engage in learning. In contrast to

"I tend to study in corners of my house where it's quiet and books are to hand."

FIGURE 7.1 Josie's Learning Space

many of the submitted postcards where there was an apparent alignment or assimilation of the participant within a shared space (we will consider Aggie's example shortly), a kind of barricading is demonstrated in Josie's data. There is a close coherence between the text description and the two sides of the composite image: the "corners of my house" and "books at hand" are simultaneously described and seen. Closer examination of the images draws our attention to the same tower of textbooks within each, positioned "at hand" in each setting. One might reasonably assume that the presence of the same stack of books reflects how, during the period that the images were captured, Josie migrated from sofa to bedroom whilst studying. It is difficult, however, to ignore the possibility that the particular positioning of the books resulted from a conscious attempt on Josie's part to control or mark her space in an active way: this is not a "retreat" from the communal, or a cocooning (Fluegge 2011), but is instead an intentional act of territorialism.

The sense of territorialism demonstrated in Josie's postcard is only fully grasped, however, when we consider the image and text alongside the audio recording. Josie composes an approximation of silence for her personal sound space. This manufactured silence reflects an attempt to mark out her aural territory and to resist the sonic intrusion that might interrupt her work. The nature of the sound—faintly muffled voices seeping through an adjoining wall—suggests the material barrier of closed doors. Josie is present in the recording but takes steps to limit her audible exposure: we become aware of her presence only when she clicks the "stop" button on her recording device. The implication here is that Josie is aware of herself as an audible agent, suggesting a "hyper-awareness of oneself as audible" (2011). Yet, Josie's silence remained a sounded space, or what McKee refers to as "the almost sound of no sound" (2006, p. 337). It also remained one that was highly contested, suggesting the presence of imminent sonic trespass. In this environment, silence is a deliberate effort to prevent sonic intrusion.

> Aggie's audio recording demonstrates complexity, with overlapping layers of sounds, presumably emanating from outside the immediate study space depicted in the image. We hear the sounds of an active urban and domestic environment: children playing, people walking in the foreground and background, traffic, construction work, mechanical noise, animals, brass instruments, conversation, and what might be the sound of vegetables being prepared.
>
> (Audio available at http://bit.ly/edinspace2)

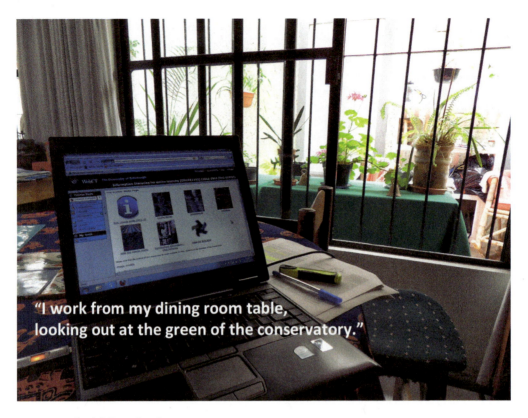

"I work from my dining room table, looking out at the green of the conservatory."

FIGURE 7.2 Aggie's Learning Space

In contrast to the territorialism demonstrated in Josie's data, Aggie's postcard presents an overlapping of personal space with shared space. Rather than attempting to actively mark out aural or material boundaries, Aggie either chooses or is compelled to undertake her scholarly activity within a busy, non-private setting. This is far from the haven of quiet that Josie strives to construct. What both examples have in common, however, is that they demonstrate the value of considering audio within a wider modal assemblage of data. Considered in isolation— or even in conjunction with the text description—Aggie's image depicts what we imagine to be a calm domesticity. However, when considered alongside the audio field recording, the imagined calm is disrupted by a wave of sound that flows over Aggie's learning space. A perpetual din of voices, distant music, conversation, and other domestic sound envelops the study space. This perpetually evolving audio pattern seeps in from outside, down corridors and through walls: there is clear sonic intrusion but not, as far as we can determine, any attempt to repress this aural trespass. It is almost as if Aggie has accepted and then become immune to it, or perhaps draws positively on the ambience or energy of her wider environment whilst studying. Thus, the data encourages us to consider that Aggie has assimilated her varied domestic aural accompaniment into what we might call a "sonic commons," a sound-scape of both private and public layers of sounds (Auinger and Odland 2009).

By drawing on Rose's (2012) site of audiencing it becomes possible to consider not simply the content of the image, but also the particular visual perspective we are given as a viewer. A quick glance at Aggie's image might lead us to conclude that she is foregrounding the presence of her laptop in order to emphasize how this technological device dominates her learning space. Yet when we consider the image in conjunction with the text, which describes, "looking out at the green of the conservatory," we become aware that the photograph has been captured at a particular, significant angle. Using Rose's site of audiencing we appreciate that the photograph has been taken from the side of Aggie's computer, rather than "face-on" as she would sit when using the device. The laptop continues to dominate the image. However, she wants us to recognize the significance of her wider environment to her learning activity. This of course is consistent with our earlier suggestion that, rather than attempting to suppress aspects of her environment as Josie appears to do, Aggie instead draws on it. Therefore, contrary to first impressions, there is in fact clear coherence between the aural and visual material, material that might be considered trespass in other postcards, that Aggie welcomes into her learning space.

Whereas the data submitted by Aggie and Josie all depict domestic spaces, our final example presents us with a formal workplace. Elise was one of only two participants whose postcard depicted a workspace. By this we are referring to a place that exists solely or predominantly as a place of employment (for instance, an office). The dominance of domestic spaces and the underrepresentation of workplaces within the postcards is interesting considering the growing accessibility of mobile technology. It is also surprising in light of our earlier research which pointed to the fluidity and mobility of online learning, where the space of the university was enacted in cafes, in hotel rooms, whilst traveling, in the office, as well as at home.

"This is where I joggle between work and study."

FIGURE 7.3 Elise's Learning Space

There is a clear formality to the sounds we hear in Elise's audio recording. We hear the echoing sound of conversation from an adjacent workspace, the dark thud of a heavy door closing, the sound of a colleague walking from an adjoining corridor. There is an absence, however, of the digital or white noise that we might expect from what we presume to be a place of work.

(Audio available at http://bit.ly/edinspace4)

The nature of the space captured within Elise's postcard also challenges our use of territoriality and sonic trespass as a way of thinking about learning spaces. Whereas Aggie and Josie presented some form of opportunity to influence or control their material and/or aural planes, we cannot be certain that Elise would have the authority to exercise control over her place of work. Although her submitted postcard depicts some limited trappings of a private space in the form of a desk and plant, the dominant impression is one of formality.

There is very limited evidence within the data that Elise is able, or chooses, to mark out the territory of her learning space; indeed her text description of "joggling between work and study" evokes a flickering, rather than any sense of lasting, territorial occupation. Whereas Josie describes and then visually depicts study corners that are free from distraction, we do not have the aural, textual, or visual data to suggest that Elise is similarly empowered. Instead, the data suggests that Elise studies in a communal space that is subject to the everyday intrusion that we would expect of a shared workplace. This is particularly evidenced in the aural data where we hear sonic trespass in the form of nearby conversation, colleagues walking along an adjacent corridor, and a heavy door firmly closing. Yet, identifying this trespass in the data is elusive as we lack an understanding of Elise's contextual perspective on the space. Does Elise inherently welcome these sounds into her learning space, as Aggie did, or does she perceive them as unwanted intrusions, against which Josie might construct silence?

Spatial-Acoustic Self-Determination

The postcards submitted by a small number of participants included a music MP3 rather than the requested audio field recording. These perhaps can be seen as enacting what Fluegge proposes as spatial-acoustic self-determination in that these students' audio submissions suggest a capacity for controlling (or attempting to control) the sound within their respective shared spaces. Although we cannot say with certainty whether their aural space is entirely dominated by music, their pointed submission of a music track (rather than the requested field recording) suggests an intention to manipulate the aural plane of their respective learning spaces. We have already discussed Josie's attempts to construct silent corners for study; however, Reva (discussed below) and her fellow students use music as a way of building their own individual sonic worlds. These contrasting approaches to shaping aural space offer a particularly useful way of applying Fluegge's concept of "noise" within the particular context of the personal spaces of online learners. Fluegge proposes "noise" not simply as any sonic material we might employ in everyday usage, but instead as the intrusion of *unwanted* sound. This view would be in contrast to the existence of other "wanted" sounds or silence, for instance. In the context of a student's learning space our concern is with disruption to the environment that diminishes the individual's ability to engage effectively with study.

The fact that music features strongly within more than a third of all the learning spaces is surprising and significant. Music as a theme did not emerge during the interview discussions that formed the major part of our earlier research. Furthermore, other than in two examples where participants specifically drew attention to accompanying music within their description, the combined visual and text data offers no clue as to the music that features so significantly within these learning spaces. If we study the images submitted by these students we see little clear evidence of the presence of what Fluegge describes as technologies of sound reproduction (such as speakers), or sound repression (such as earphones).

From an analytical perspective, the postcards that feature music offer insights we would not otherwise have had access to, had we focused only on the visual and textual data. If we take Reva's postcard, for example, a reading of her learning space alters dramatically when we draw sound into the multimodal orchestration. What we might otherwise (through a reading of image and text) imagine to be a depiction of cold, snowy, suburban calm is transformed through music into a warm, energetic learning space. Thus we see the benefit of analyzing a range of modal data, with due attention paid to the aural material. Or put it another way, in the postcards submitted by Reva, Aggie, and other participants, our understanding of their learning space is incomplete and inaccurate when the sound is turned down.

Reva presents a full music track as her accompanying sound.

(Audio available at http://bit.ly/edinspace5)

FIGURE 7.4 Reva's Learning Space

Whilst the preferred choice of music-to-study-by evidently varies between the different participants discussed here, they are nevertheless united in their apparent control and freedom to make conscious decisions to reproduce sound in this particular way. The same cannot be said, however, for every participant. We have already discussed the formal, communal place of employment that constitutes Elise's study space. It is difficult to imagine how Elise might realize any meaningful form of spatial-acoustic self-determination, assuming she even wished to do so. We cannot see a set of earphones or headphones within her image, or indeed any device into which they might connect in order to effect sound reduction.

Payton's postcard depicts a space that bears little resemblance to that of her fellow student Elise; however, she might similarly have difficulty employing acts of sound reproduction or repression. To begin, any sound reproduction device would have to compete with the TV that shares the communal space (as clearly captured in the audio recording). Meanwhile, the child that we hear demanding Payton's attention in the sound recording might not have been willing to allow the wearing of headphones, which would otherwise have enabled Payton to shut out the loud, intrusive sound of cartoons emanating from a nearby TV.

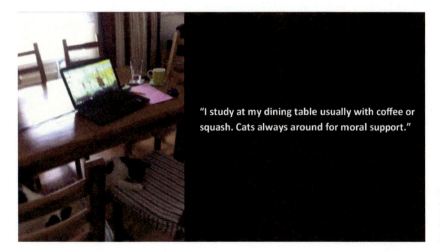

FIGURE 7.5 Payton's Learning Space

The sounds of a TV show in the background, along with a child saying "Watch this" drawing Payton's attention and perhaps accelerating the abrupt end of the recording.

(Audio available at http://bit.ly/edinspace6)

We should therefore be wary of assuming that the online learner necessarily has the ability to exercise spatial-acoustic self-determination. Depending on the particular context, the presence of other individuals, as well as the norms that exist within these shared spaces, might prevent or discourage the use of technologies to reproduce or repress sound. Significantly, this is seen to apply to both the formal environment of the open-plan office, but also the informal, domestic space that is shared with family. Finally, even where spatial-acoustic self-determination would seem appropriate and achievable, it might not be desirable to the learner. If we revisit Aggie's learning space, for instance, where she seems to sit center stage in a theater of noise, it would be easy to imagine that she could easily and willingly don a set of earphones to drown out the noise.

To draw this section to a close, therefore, there would seem to be a tendency amongst some online learners to play music to exercise spatial-acoustic self-determination over their learning spaces. For other online students, however, we have seen that spatial-acoustic self-determination is neither necessarily achievable—dependent on the individual's surroundings—or indeed desirable, based upon how they use their environment to inform or support their study activity.

In Conclusion

A straightforward yet significant theme to have emerged from this research was the dominance of the domestic environment as a space for learning amongst distance students. Contrary to aspects of our earlier research where we identified the mobile and nomadic nature of online learning, this chapter presents distance education—or the selected learning spaces of this group of students, at least—as domestically rooted. The recurring theme of couches, beds, and cushions suggests what we might describe as a body of "comfort learners," rather than the roaming, mobile learner that is often associated with online education. Similarly, the depiction of traditional scholarly materials—textbooks, printed journal articles, pads, and pens—alongside or instead of digital devices, was at odds with what one might have assumed to be the approach of students engaged in a Digital Education program that is delivered entirely online.

We should, however, be wary of assuming that some form of homogenous space is represented in the dining tables, soft furnishings, laptops, and textbooks depicted in the visual data. On the contrary, our analysis provided evidence of the range of spatial constructions that take place within the learning environments of these students. Whilst there was a strong degree of consistency in the sites depicted in the photographs, the aural mode was much more variable. By drawing the sound recording from each postcard into our analysis, we became aware of the different ways that students aligned with, or attempted to control, their respective learning spaces. In the pulled blinds, piled books, closed doors, and relative quiet of some postcards we saw deliberate attempts to build material barriers against disruption. In contrast, other postcards reflected how participants had inhabited learning spaces that were shaped by the relative chaos of street sounds, family, and the white noise of machines. In some cases we saw attempts at spatial-acoustic self-determination (Fluegge 2011) as participants intentionally drew music into their learning spaces. On other occasions, however, we inferred that aural manipulation achieved through devices of sound repression or reproduction might have been neither appropriate nor possible. Thus the postcards tell us about different learning preferences, but they also highlight the varying power of the individual to influence the material and aural make-up of her environment, particularly where her personal learning space exists within a wider shared space.

Just as the different postcards reveal the varying preferences and control of participants, they also suggest differing approaches to what might be seen as disruption or intrusion within their learning spaces. As we have already noted, Fluegge (2011) proposes noise as the intrusion of "unwanted sound," which in turn implies the existence of "wanted sound" or silence. We found significant evidence of wanted sound in the use of music, in personal aural expression (humming, sighing, clicking), and in other domestic activity (stirring coffee, purring cats). Where these sounded actions were deliberate we can understand the student using sound as a means of orienting herself to learning, to the performance of an activity, or to some hybrid of both (multitasking), as in Payton's use of the sound of the television.

For other participants however, the same sonic material would be seen as an unwelcome disruption to the business of studying. The almost-silence of Josie's space, pregnant with the mere possibility of sonic trespass, might prove deafening to Reva, fully immersed in the aural totality of her music. Thus, the varying attitudes toward sonic trespass with the different learning spaces is likely to have itself been informed by differing positions on the type of sonic material that would be understood as noise. This reiterates Moss's (2004) qualitative positioning of space, in this case sonic space, suggesting that each group or individual will attach different values to its composition. As such, it is critical to position the individual, their study place, the overlapping layers of the communal and personal sounds, and the methods employed to manage them, as sets of sociomaterial relationships that, depending on the task at hand, evolve constantly.

Our discussion here does not rigidly propose any hard-and-fast rules that might dictate the design of distance education programs. However, it does draw attention to the different ways that students configure the aural and material components of their environment in order to create learning spaces. It also challenges preconceptions that we might hold about the mobile and highly-technologized character of the spaces from which online education students engage in learning.

Whilst we have been careful to avoid any suggestion that the insights gained from our analysis of the data are necessarily representative of online education in general, we are confident in pointing to the broader applicability of our methodological approach. We have attempted to represent the underconsidered by investigating how sound, and its coherence with other material elements, contributes to the construction and character of learning space. By coming from the position that sound is an under-considered mode (McKee 2006) we have worked to address this lack of critical attention by adapting the work of Fluegge (2011), Rose (2012), and others in a way that has enabled us to analyze study space across multiple modes.

Our data suggests the need for a greater understanding of modal coherence, or how sound, images, and texts work together. Furthermore, there is a pragmatic need for distance educators to understand how territoriality (Fluegge 2011), or the active carving out of space for study purposes, is enacted across the aural and material planes, and how this in turn influences students' engagement with their program and institution. All of this suggests a need for a sounded analytical framework, one that addresses the call for a sounded anthropology for research (Samuels et al. 2010), and one that identifies the spatial arrangements of study and learning space in which sound is most certainly a significant "mode-in-relation" (Kress and Van Leeuwen 2001). The data discussed in this chapter has demonstrated that the construction of study space is a complex negotiation between the private and the shared, the sounded and the silent, the bounded and the fluid (Law and Mol 2001).

In this chapter we have proposed that a methodological approach that considers the significance of aural data, and its relationship with other material, can enable us to gain a clearer picture of what exists on the other side of the screen. Using the example of the M.Sc. in Digital Education at the University of Edinburgh, we have shown how students negotiate or occupy spaces from which to engage with their program of study. This includes varying approaches to the use of sound and material objects to carve out personal learning territories, or to negotiate within a wider shared space. We propose that the learning environments of online students have been underinvestigated, and the significance of aurality in understanding the construction of personal space has been underconsidered. It is our hope that we have opened a discussion in this chapter that will begin to address these gaps.

Endnote

1. Instructions provided to the participants were as follows:

> We would like to invite you to send a postcard of the place (or one of the places) from which you most frequently engage with the M.Sc. in E-Learning. Consistent with the nature of the program, however, we're looking for you to submit a multimodal, digital e-postcard comprising image, sound, and text. Our intention is to turn the data from each postcard into a short video clip that can then be added to a "class map" depicting your different study spaces. Don't worry, however, about compiling the video—all we want you to do is submit the following elements:
>
> * a photo of a place from which you engage with the course
> * a short message explaining what's in the photo and something about how or why you study there or what that space means to you
> * the approximate location where the photo was taken
> * a 30-second sound clip recorded at your study space (or something more elaborate if you feel that is more appropriate).

References

Auinger, S. and Odland, B., 2009. Reflections on the sonic commons. *Leonardo Music Journal,* 19, 63–68. [online]. Available from: www.mitpressjournals.org/doi/pdf/10.1162/lmj.2009.19.63 [Accessed July 22, 2015].

Bayne, S., Gallagher, M. S., and Lamb, J., 2013. Being "at" university: The social topologies of distance students. *Higher Education,* 67(5), 569–583.

Burn, A. and Parker, D., 2003. *Analysing media texts.* London: Bloomsbury Publishing.

Fenwick, T., Edwards, R., and Sawchuk, P., 2011. *Emerging approaches to educational research: Tracing the sociomaterial.* London: Routledge.

Fluegge, E., 2011. The consideration of personal sound space. *Journal of Sonic Studies,* 1(1). [online]. Available from: http://journal.sonicstudies.org/vol01/nr01/a09 [Accessed July 18, 2015].

Jewitt, C. ed., 2009. *The Routledge handbook of multimodal analysis.* London: Routledge.

Kahu, E. R., Stephens, C., Zepke, N., and Leach, L., 2014. Space and time to engage: Mature-aged distance students learn to fit study into their lives. *International Journal of Lifelong Education,* 33(4), 523–540.

Kirkwood, A., 2000. Learning at home with information and communication technologies. *Distance Education,* 21(2), 248–259.

Kress, G. and Van Leeuwen, T., 1996, 2006. *Reading images: The grammar of visual design.* London: Routledge.

Kress, G. and Van Leeuwen, T., 2001. *Multimodal discourse: The modes and media of contemporary communication.* London: Arnold.

Law, J. and Mol, A., 2001. Situating technoscience: An inquiry into spatialities. *Environment and Planning D: Society and Space,* 19(5), 609–621.

McKee, H., 2006. Sound matters: Notes towards the analysis and design of sound in multimodal webtexts. *Computers and Composition,* 23(2006), 335–354.

Mol, A. and Law, J., 1994. Regions, networks and fluids: Anaemia and social topology. *Social Studies of Science,* 24(4), 641–671.

Monaco, J., 2009. *How to read a film: Movies, media, multimedia.* London: Oxford University Press.

Moss, D., 2004. Creating space for learning: Conceptualizing women and higher education through space and time. *Gender and Education,* 16(3), 283–302.

Neumark, N., Gibson, R., and Van Leeuwen, T., 2011. *VOICE* (Leonardo Book Series). Cambridge, MA: MIT Press.

Reznikoff, I., 2006. The evidence of the use of sound resonance from Palaeolithic to Medieval times. In: C. Scarre and G. Lawson, eds., *Archaeoacoustics* (pp. 77–84). Cambridge: Cambridge University Press.

Rose, G., 2012. *Visual methodologies: An introduction to researching with visual materials*. London: Sage.

Ross, J., Gallagher, M., and Macleod, H., 2013. Making distance visible: Assembling nearness in an online distance learning programme. *The International Review of Research in Open and Distance Education* (IRRODL), 14(4). [online]. Available from: www.irrodl.org/index.php/irrodl/article/view/1545 [Accessed July 17, 2015].

Samuels, D. W., Meintjes, L., Ochoa, A. M., and Porcello, T., 2010. Soundscapes: Toward a sounded anthropology. *Annual Review of Anthropology*, 39, 329–345.

Sterne, J., 1997. Sounds like the Mall of America: Programmed music and the architectonics of commercial space. *Ethnomusicology*, 41(1), 22–50.

Sterne, J., 2003. *The audible past. Cultural origins of sound reproduction*. Durham, NC: Duke University Press.

Sterne, J., 2006. The historiography of cyberculture. In: D. Silver and A. Massanari, eds., *Critical Cyberculture Studies* (pp. 17–28). New York: New York University Press.

Van Leeuwen, T., 2004. *Introducing social semiotics: An introductory textbook*. London: Routledge.

8

IS THERE ANYBODY OUT THERE? PLACE-BASED NETWORKS FOR LEARNING

NetMap—a Tool for Accessing Hidden Informal Learning Networks

Maarten de Laat and Shane Dawson

Introduction

> If it were possible to define generally the mission of education one could say that its funda-
> mental purpose is to ensure that all students benefit from learning in ways that allow them
> to participate fully in public, community and economic life.
>
> (New London Group 1996, p. 60)

The above statement by the New London Group reflects the ongoing importance of developing education practices that effectively foster the skills and attributes learners require to participate
fully in society. There has long been a connection between higher education and the development
of a nation's workforce skills and capacities (Marginson 2008). The formal schooling processes promoted throughout the twentieth century were largely focused toward the preparation of graduates
for an industrial economy. This form of mass education practice not only established the types of
graduates the workforce required but also provided a strong quality assurance model. Students were
streamed based on academic ability, and disciplines were independently taught and subject to strict
timetables. Although the skills and capacities commonly promoted for productive participation in
the information age have significantly changed, arguably, education practices have failed to keep
pace. Standardized assessments designed to demonstrate an understanding of disciplinary expertise
are not adequately representative of a graduate's future employment requirements and expectations.

Learning Futures and Twenty-First-Century Skills

Learning for the twenty-first century is no longer characterized by the mode of pedagogical instruction received, but more so by the ubiquitous digital presence that covers all aspects of a student's life.
There is a blurring of social, academic, and, increasingly, professional worlds, and entertainment and
education that today's student must be able to navigate, evaluate, and leverage. The information age
requires the basic literacies associated with the industrial age to be merged with the more technical,
visual, and media-related savvy. As Warschauer (2007) points out, "New literacies seldom sweep out
old ones, but instead new and old are woven together in a complex web reflecting evolving social,
economic, and political relationships" (pp. 47–48). It is the commingling of industrial age literacies
with new media and digital literacies that contemporary learners must adopt.

The industrial model of education is no longer fit for purpose in terms of developing the work-force skills and capacities required for the information or digital age. Commentators and researchers such as Robinson (2000) and Griffin and colleagues (2012) argue for the need to develop practices that actively promote twenty-first-century literacies or capacities. The development of literacies such as critical thinking, problem-solving, digital literacy, creativity, and collaborative and communication skills, alongside intercultural aptitudes are essential competencies for the twenty-first-century world of work. Whilst there is much rhetoric clearly espousing the need for such literacies and competencies the pathway for effective development and implementation within education is far less certain (Tan et al. 2014). Numerous frameworks for development and assessment of twenty-first-century literacies have been proposed; however, to date there are few empirical studies that can demonstrate broad-scale impact. The challenge now lies in identifying the types of learning models that can more effectively characterize, measure, monitor, and scaffold the development of twenty-first-century competencies.

Learning in the twenty-first-century context is increasingly seen to be most effective when it is collaborative, social, and connected in networked structures (De Laat 2012; Dawson and Siemens 2014). In social forms of learning, the focus is on the co-construction of knowledge, meaning, and understanding. This takes into consideration how the practical, social situation influences individual and collective outcomes of learning. Learning in a social context is a process of "meaning-making" where this meaning can be based upon prior experiences as well as the more immediate social context in which something is learned. New metaphors framing the social nature of learning have gained currency and are used to develop a language for learning that emphasizes important aspects such as participation, co-construction, and becoming (Packer and Goicoechea 2000; Hager and Hodkinson 2009). Boud and Hager (2012) argue that learning should be seen as an ongoing process. They emphasize terms such as organic growth, evolution, and gradual unfolding and see learning as a process of becoming. In this process people continuously develop their own identity and abilities in response to events in their environment. From a developmental perspective, participation in social practices is needed to promote learning and continuous improvement (Wenger 1998). Participation provides access to a social arena where issues or problems can be introduced and together people construct new solutions and reflect on them. Enabling this perspective of learning involves being in touch with one's peers, building the networked connections required to participate in constructive dialogues in order to learn and solve problems together (De Laat 2012).

For education institutions a transition to social and networked learning can pose significant challenges in establishing broad-scale adoption of the core pedagogical practices that effectively promote and scaffold the development of twenty-first-century literacies. Such practices also need to be sensitive to the highly networked, technology-mediated social and learning contexts of the contemporary student. Such familiarity is not always consistent amongst our academic staff. Here, the concept of digital learning is gaining momentum amongst higher education institutions and schools. For instance, blended learning or the flipped classroom is seen as one approach that can cater to the increasing student demands around mobility and flexibility of access to course materials and activities alongside the promotion of a more social learning agenda. There is now an increasing suite of education technologies available to support this process. These technologies facilitate synchronous and asynchronous learner to learner and learner to teacher interactions.

At the same time education institutions are re-evaluating and altering their physical learning landscapes with a focus on providing open collaborative spaces where students have an opportunity to maximize their learning experience, both in formal and informal contexts. As a "zone of proximal development" these open practices provide students with the means to prepare themselves for successful participation in a networked society. Hence, promoting student capacity and capabilities to develop personal learning networks and transition across networks are much needed twenty-first-century skills that reflect contemporary workforce requirements. Being able to navigate open practices and utilize them successfully commences with engagement and awareness of the potential access to knowledge such open and networked spaces offer. Through the use of an innovative network tool, this chapter aims to explore how the promotion of technologies and practices to develop networked awareness can help students to navigate openness and enable learners to find and develop short and longer-term learning partnerships. In so doing we first discuss the emergence and prominence of open educational practices in association with social learning in networks. Next we unpack the implications for learning and campus design and locations of learning. Based on a reflection of the challenges learners are faced with in open learning environments we propose a location-based tool that can facilitate students' mobility and access to potential social learning practices.

Networking in Open Practices

Public and private sector organizations are increasingly realizing that many opportunities for growth, development, and innovation lie outside their own organizational boundaries. To tap into this productive potential they are looking for new ways to *open up*, and to integrate externally-sourced ideas into their core processes. Examples of current strategies include "crowdsourcing" (seeking ideas from large communities of people over the Web) and open competitions, where people win prizes for submitting usable ideas to organizations for development and product innovation. Strategies for making organizational boundaries more permeable are being complemented by internally focused strategies, such as the creation of more open workplaces to improve interaction between employees, the use of social media and other tools for sharing knowledge and social networking. Traditional organizational boundaries are fading and professional workers (and others) are becoming very actively involved in creating and maintaining networked relationships with their peers, often on a global scale, to tackle work-related challenges.

With this radical change from hierarchical, industrial models to networked, knowledge-based models come complex, and often conflicting, demands on professionals, who are not only held accountable for their actions but are also required to be more autonomous and proactive in relationship-building (Forrester 2000; Chesbrough 2003; Huysman and De Wit 2003; Svetina and Prodan 2008; Phelps, Heidl, and Wadhwa 2012; Windmuller 2012; Berchicci 2013). The growing significance of human and social capital in our society and economy makes it important and urgent to update our understanding of learning and the role educational institutions play in preparing students for productive participation in the digital age (Christakis and Fowler 2009; Price 2013; Pugh and Prusak 2013).

The development and maintenance of relationships obviously plays an important role in any approach to social learning. Networked learning research takes particular interest in how individuals create and maintain the web of social relations they draw upon to enable their learning process (De Laat 2012). Here we adopt Goodyear et al.'s (2004, p. 2) earlier definition of networked learning as "learning in which information and communication technology (ICT) is used to promote connections: between one learner and other learners; between learners and tutors; between a learning community and its learning resources" (Goodyear et al. 2004, p. 2). Whilst there is strong recognition surrounding the use of ICTs in networked learning, the focus lies on the learner and the learning process (Hodgson et al. 2014). Networked learning incorporates learning as an individual as well as the types of learning that occur in social contexts. It is the interactions with materials, tools, and fellow learners that comprise the essential elements of networked learning.

Individual learners bring their own sets of pedagogical beliefs and values that either encourage or impede their capacity to act as co-producers and participants in a collective learning process.

Network structures facilitate collaboration, but eventually it is through the network members'' agency that the design of their learning emerges (Hodgson et al. 2014). Within a network, the learning needs of the members determine the pace, the content, and the overall accessibility and connectivity of the network (Walton 1999). Participants collectively share ownership and responsibility over what happens in their networks. In education learners may therefore take on different roles in the learning context with respect to coordination and regulation. Learners, for example, take on the role of teachers and start to tutor each other during their collaborative task (De Laat et al. 2007a), and vice versa in that teachers take on the role of learners during their participation in group discussions (De Laat et al. 2007b).

Given the rapidly shifting economic and socio-technical landscapes it is important for education institutions to rethink what it means to be an effective and functional learner. Particular consideration needs to be paid to how individuals and groups shape learning in an increasingly open and networked society. For higher education to remain relevant to the social settings in which they exist, Wiley and Hilton III (2009) argue that creating an institutional culture of openness is the most pressing priority. The rapid development and uptake of Massive Open Online Courses (MOOCs) and Open Educational Resources (OERs) are demonstrative of the societal movement toward more openness in the higher education sector. Pedagogical designs are increasingly evolving toward more open access, promoting networked activities, and linking education with professional learning communities and lifelong learning to provide students with opportunities to access a broader pool of social capital.

According to Ehlers (2011), as higher education institutions prepare open educational practices (OEP) they go through several stages of development and awareness. These stages are related to "degrees of freedom to practice open education" and "degrees of involvement of others into the OEP" (see Figure 8.1 for a complete list of stages A through to I).

Figure 8.1 is helpful when thinking about transforming education toward Ehlers' highest level "C stage"—that is OEP that has a high advanced degree of embedding into learning and teaching accompanied by a high degree of collaboration and sharing. At its core the underlying principles are concerned with developing open connected practices to promote social learning and access to social capital (De Laat and Prinsen 2014). Participation in open practices and being connected with what happens outside an organization is becoming fundamental for both students and professionals. However, it raises crucial questions about how to design and utilize open practices within educational institutions. More openness means less control and planning by the formal educational

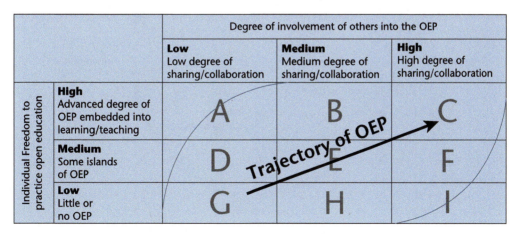

FIGURE 8.1 Trajectory of Open Educational Practice

Source: Ehlers 2011

curriculum and increases student flexibility to regulate their learning informally and engage in networks that contribute to their learning goals.

Numerous universities internationally have been redesigning their physical settings, in part as a response to calls for greater openness, and in recognition of the importance of creating space and opportunity for social learning. These modern open campuses, also referred to as "sticky campuses" (e.g. Lefebvre 2013; Dane 2014), are designed to offer a mixture of formal and informal learning experiences aimed at providing a quality rich environment where students want to be, not only to study but to socialize and learn. As such modern higher education learning landscapes are turning into open learning spaces aimed at becoming vibrant social hubs where people meet and connect 24/7, on and offline (De Laat and Prinsen 2014).

Open practices involve networks that are collections of individuals and teams who come together across organizational, spatial, and disciplinary boundaries to collaborate and share knowledge (Price 2013). The focus of such networks is usually on developing, distributing, and applying knowledge (Pugh and Prusak 2013). Network members come together around a common goal and share social and operational norms. Members typically participate out of common interest and shared purpose rather than a required or enforced contract, quid pro quo, or hierarchy. Such networks exemplify open practices as they are dispersed across geographical and organizational boundaries, informal and self-directed by nature, and disentangled from hierarchy. Open practices have always occurred informally, used by students as well as by professionals, but nowadays technological platforms enable them to connect with their peers with greater ease, on a larger scale, and on a continuing basis.

An interesting question in relation to location is *where* and *when* does learning in open practices take place? And, how do we facilitate productive social connectivity and mobility in these open learning spaces? When learning is designed around social engagement and interaction, there is a

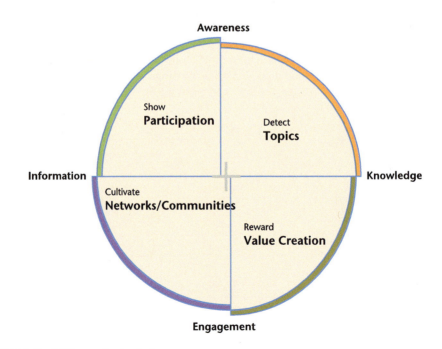

FIGURE 8.2 Social Enterprise Analytics

Source: De Laat 2014

need to develop new ways of understanding and promoting student social mobility. Open practices enable learners to connect with their peers with greater ease, on a larger scale, and on a continuing basis. But with this comes the danger of fragmentation and isolation. Below we discuss a model (see Figure 8.2) in an attempt to frame these social mobility challenges in open practices. This model is a combination of raising awareness about social learning activity as well as leveraging a culture of knowledge and value creation. We think it is important to not only raise awareness about the activities and focus of these learning practices. We need to pay more attention to the cultural aspects that contextualize learning, rather than keeping our focus mainly on learning outcomes and products (De Laat 2012). This will require higher education institutes to review their approach to learning and try to move from an individualistic and formal curriculum-driven educational culture toward a learning culture that comprises a blend of formal and informal, embraces the value of being engaged in social learning processes, and brings forward opportunities for students to find and join in meaningful events that are suited to their personal learning needs.

On the one hand this model can, metaphorically speaking, take "the pulse" of a higher education organization by revealing people's learning activities and movements. The top half of the model deals with making explicit *who* is doing *what* at any given point in time. Based on information concerning the specific activity we can make explicit the level of student participation in learning events in connection with the content of the set task they are working on. Providing this information opens up the possibility for others to join in or simply access information related to the activity. Raising awareness is therefore a first step in making learning more visible, more accessible, and, ultimately, more personalized and relevant. Sharing this knowledge helps learners to find out what is currently going on and who the main "drivers" of these activities are. Essentially, this brings forward and works toward openness and transparency. Finding ways to identify, access, and assess informal emerging activity and topics will be a way to connect people to learning and make informed decisions about participation and develop learning friendships.

Whilst the top half of the model is aimed at increasing the level of organizational awareness in order to link people to content (and vice versa), the lower part is concerned with leveraging a culture of knowledge. Here the focus is on cultivating networks and communities and the promotion of student autonomy and increased responsibility. A greater degree of openness means less control and planning within the formal educational curriculum and increases student flexibility and freedom to informally regulate their learning and engage in (professional) networks that contribute to their learning goals. This aim may be realized by stimulating and encouraging student engagement in active networks and communities associated with their courses, optimizing how students learn in such network structures, and developing new ways to appreciate and reward value creation (Wenger, Trayner, and De Laat 2011). However, at present such endeavors in the higher education space are likely to receive at best a mixed level of enthusiasm. Higher education curriculum structures can form significant barriers to innovation and establishing informal learning opportunities. Modern higher education institutions will need to find ways to develop an open culture and rethink their curriculum to link formal and informal learning events. Providing flexible, transparent, open learning spaces is a good start but more needs to be done to embed this in the organizational culture and address ways of working with students and assess their results. This also requires a reorientation on management and leadership. We believe that the organizational culture and structure needs to change to be able to adopt an open networking style and provide more autonomy to the teacher and the student. Being able to reward both formal and informal learning also comes with new challenges. Instead of contrasting them, we need to develop a hybrid form of informal-formal learning. A form that expands a culture of learning by creating social learning spaces for teaching and learning.

Jeffrey Smart Building

Consistent with contemporary models of architecture in higher education, the University of South Australia recently established a student-centered flexible learning center called the Jeffrey Smart Building (JSB).[1] The seven-storey building opened in mid-2014 and was designed with a strong emphasis on collaboration, juxtaposing formal student learning with informal encounters (Figure 8.3). The building was designed to be pedagogically fluid in terms of classroom configurations and designed teaching practices ranging from small group work sessions to lab instruction to individual learning. The building is technically rich enabling student connectivity and the promotion of student-to-student interactions in both formal and informal settings. The multi-storey building offers a diversity of open learning spaces that students can access 24/7 to conduct their studies, work collaboratively, and establish short- and longer-term "learning friendships." Whilst the establishment of the building has greatly assisted in the uptake of more social and blended learning models of instruction there remain challenges associated with the promotion of learning networks that transcend programs of study and established cohort structures. That is, the building of networks that may comprise students in differing programs of study and year levels. The capacity to assist students in accessing peers that have expertise outside their immediate field of study provides a greater source of social capital that could be leveraged to assist them in their academic pursuits. Hence, the concept of a mobile tool to facilitate the establishment of these broader social connections was formed. In this context, it is envisaged that NetMap (presented below) will become a valuable resource to promote informal learning support networks. In the following section we discuss the development of such a tool, and operationalize the functions of the model.

NetMap and Place-Based Networked Learning

The development of the mobile application NetMap was designed to facilitate social mobility in open practices—such as the JSB—to promote awareness about potential learning ties, and to foster peer-to-peer learning engagements that extend beyond the traditional formal course structure. In essence, NetMap serves as a kind of "dating" or location awareness system for developing learning-based relationships in the physical space. The central idea is to map informal networks to raise awareness of potential collaborations for situated learning (Figure 8.4). Post the login to NetMap, the application provides a visual map of the user's initial location—as displayed in Figure 8.4. In the first instance, this map representation and the capacity to visualize other actors' (learners') locations increases the awareness (see Figure 8.2) and therefore provides users with an initial opportunity to engage in a more transparent, open, and networked learning approach.

FIGURE 8.3 Architect's Representation of One Set of Informal Learning Spaces at the Jeffrey Smart Building, University of South Australia

FIGURE 8.4 Representation of a User's Locality and the Presence of Other Learners in the Area in NetMap—a Mobile Location Awareness Application

FIGURE 8.5 Representation of an Individual NetMap User and Their Physical Location

The mapping feature (location awareness) of the tool shows the proximity of other learners indicated by the colored dots on the map in the surrounding area. Selecting these nodes or the "people" icon provides information on what individual users are working on or areas of expertise (see Figure 8.5). By selecting the "skills" icon, a visualization of the learning topics that other students are currently working on is provided within a given locality. This feature allows users to identify the knowledge topics of interest for further engagement (see Figures 8.6a and 8.6b).

When a user enters the physical space, in this instance the JSB, they can select the topics of interest or areas for which they are seeking support or collaborative work, browse people's profiles using the "people" button, and see where they are located within the open space to spark opportunities for collaboration and support or start a conversation first using the "messages" button. Based on this information, users are able to quickly find peers who are open to sharing and collaboration on a

FIGURE 8.6a Overlay of Knowledge Mapping Concept within NetMap

FIGURE 8.6b Detection of Knowledge Topics

particular topic. For example, an open area in the JSB designed for student work and collaboration could in the first instance be established. This is where students pick a seat to study and indicate a topic of interest they are focused on or with which they may require assistance. Using NetMap, likeminded students simply turn up to the same location to identify the diversity of topics people are working on and where they are located in order to engage with them, provide assistance, or seek support. In terms of the model described above—moving from awareness to value creation and engagement. These dedicated areas could potentially be seeded with tutors, university support services, or faculty to establish a threshold level of users and to demonstrate the learning opportunities and benefits to the student body.

Conclusion

Over the past decade we have witnessed across all sectors the rapid growth and uptake of technologies such as social media, smart phones, and, more recently, cloud computing. These technologies merely reflect a societal trend toward lasting connectivity where access to content knowledge, communities, and peers (known and unknown) are constantly integrated, connected, and expanding. Similar to many other industries, higher education is embracing and preparing to capitalize on the affordances of "being digital" (Siemens, Gasevic, and Dawson 2015). Central to achieving lasting and significant benefits from technology adoption will be an associated change in the model of education and the development of twenty-first-century literacies. This will be a major challenge confronting higher education. In essence, universities will need to address how such models can be embedded by first removing the shackles of a structured and formal learning context to embrace an open, informal, and flexible learning setting. The adoption of various tools and learning and teaching approaches that foster networked learning will help facilitate the necessary cultural shift required.

This chapter outlined the development of a mobile application called NetMap to aid student-to-student formal and informal networked learning based on their location. The chapter highlights the need for merging both physical and technical learning spaces in order to provide students with increased opportunity to expand their formal and informal networks. Networked agility as a twenty-first-century competency requires that students utilize the diversity of tools and applications to establish connections and relationships that will ultimately provide two-way social and academic support. There has been much written on the importance of social interactions in the learning process. However, much of this work has centered on developing relationships within the physical or virtual domains. The aim of NetMap is to provide a bridging function that allows students to form "learning friendships" or learning support through the virtual and physical spaces. As such, NetMap helps make use of the networking qualities of physical spaces and bridges these place-based networks with online social networks. NetMap (in combination with other social networking tools such as the "Network Awareness Tool" (see De Laat and Schreurs 2011)) can be used within learning management systems (LMSs), virtual learning environments (VLEs), and MOOCs to facilitate connections between learners virtually or within physical spaces. Other open practice spaces for using NetMap include: museums, libraries, conferences/networking events, festivals, town squares, as well as formal organizations and flexible office and business spaces. Being able to facilitate student learning in the twenty-first century means being able to deal with uncertainties and to solve complex problems through creativity, communication, and collaboration, combined with finding networked learning opportunities that will help one further, and to be prepared for the next step. In this chapter we combined these principles to develop a tool to promote student learning mobility in open practices crossing both formal and informal learning spaces online and offline.

Endnote

1. www.unisa.edu.au/Enterprise-Magazine-Home/Issue-1-2014/Jeffrey-Smart-Building

References

Berchicci, L., 2013. Towards an open R&D system: Internal R&D investment, external knowledge acquisition and innovative performance. *Research Policy*, 42(1), 117–127.

Boud, D. and Hager, P., 2012. Re-thinking continuing professional development through changing metaphors and location in professional practices. *Studies in Continuing Education*, 34(1), 17–30.

Chesbrough, H., 2003. *Open innovation: The new imperative for creating and profiting from technology*. Boston: Harvard Business School Press.

Christakis, N.A. and Fowler, J. H., 2009. *Connected: How your friends' friends' friends affect everything you feel, think, and do.* New York: Back Bay Books.

Dane, J., 2014. *What will the campus of the future look like?* [web log]. Available from: www.woodsbagot.com/news/what–will–the–campus–of–the–future–look–like [Accessed October 12, 2015].

Dawson, S. and Siemens, G., 2014. Analytics to literacies: The development of a learning analytics framework for multiliteracies assessment. *The International Review of Research in Open and Distributed Learning*, 15(4), 284–305.

De Laat, M., 2012. *Enabling professional development networks: How connected are you?* Heerlen: LOOK, Open Universiteit of the Netherlands.

De Laat, M., 2014. *Social enterprise analytics*. Unpublished manuscript. Available from: www.open.ou.nl/rslmlt/Social_Enterprise_Analytics_DeLaat.pdf [Accessed October 12, 2015].

De Laat, M. and Prinsen, F., 2014. Social learning analytics: Navigating the changing settings of higher education. *Journal of Research & Practice in Assessment*, 9(4), 51–60.

De Laat, M. and Schreurs, B., 2011. *Network Awareness Tool: Social learning analytics dashboard for visualizing, analysing and managing social networks.* Heerlen: Ruud de Moor Centrum—Open Universiteit of the Netherlands.

De Laat, M., Lally, V., Lipponen, L., and Simons, P. R. J., 2007a. Patterns of interaction in a networked learning community: Squaring the circle. *International Journal of Computer-Supported Collaborative Learning*, 2(1), 87–103.

De Laat, M., Lally, V., Lipponen, L., and Simons, P. R. J., 2007b. Online teaching in networked learning communities: A multi-method approach to studying the role of the teacher. *Instructional Science*, 35(3), 257–286.

Ehlers, U-D., 2011. Extending the territory: From open educational resources to open educational practices. *Journal of Open, Flexible, and Distance Learning*, 15(2), 1–10.

Forrester, G., 2000. Professional autonomy versus managerial control: The experience of teachers in an English primary school. *International Studies in Sociology of Education*, 10(2), 133–151.

Goodyear, P., Banks, S., Hodgson, V., and McConnell, D., 2004. Research on networked learning: An overview. In: P. Goodyear, S. Banks, V. Hodgson, and D. McConnell, eds., *Advances in research on networked learning* (pp. 1–9). Dordrecht, The Netherlands: Kluwer.

Griffin, P., Care, E., and McGaw, B., 2012. The changing role of education and schools. In: *Assessment and teaching of 21st century skills* (pp. 1–15). Dordrecht, The Netherlands: Springer.

Hager, P. and Hodkinson, P., 2009. Moving beyond the metaphor of transfer of learning. *British Educational Research Journal*, 35(4), 619–638.

Hodgson, V., De Laat, M., McConnell, D., and Ryberg, T., eds, 2014. *The design, experience and practice of networked learning*. New York: Springer.

Huysman, M. and De Wit, D., 2003. *Knowledge sharing in practice*. Deventer, The Netherlands: Kluwer Academics.

Lefebvre, M., 2013. *The library, the city, and infinite possibilities—Ryerson University's Student Learning Centre Project*. Paper presented at the World Library and Information Congress (IFLA), August 17–23, 2013, Singapore.

Marginson, S., 2008. *The global position of Australian higher education to 2020*. Report for the Review of Higher Education, Australia. Centre for the Study of Higher Education (CSHE), University of Melbourne, Australia. Available from: www.voced.edu.au/content/ngv%3A29692 [Accessed October 12, 2015].

New London Group, 1996. A pedagogy of multiliteracies: Designing social futures. *Harvard Educational Review*, 66, 60–92.

Packer, M. J. and Goicoechea, J., 2000. Sociocultural and constructivist theories of learning: Ontology, not just epistemology. *Educational Psychologist*, 35(4), 227–241.

Phelps, C., Heidl, R., and Wadhwa, A., 2012. Knowledge, networks, and knowledge networks. A review and research agenda. *Journal of Management,* 38(4), 1115–1166.

Price, D., 2013. *Open: How we'll work, live and learn in the future.* London: Crux Publishing.

Pugh, K. and Prusak, L., 2013. *Designing effective knowledge networks.* [online]. Available from: http://sloanreview.mit.edu/article/designing-effective-knowledge-networks [Accessed October 12, 2015].

Robinson, K., 2000. *Out of our minds: Learning to be creative.* Oxford: Capstone.

Siemens, G., Gasevic, D., and Dawson, S., 2015. *Preparing for the digital university: A review of the history and current state of distance, blended, and online learning.* Report for the Gates Foundation. Alberta: Athabasca University.

Svetina, A. C. and Prodan, I., 2008. How internal and external sources of knowledge contribute to firms' innovation performance. *Managing Global Transitions, University of Primorska, Faculty of Management Koper,* 6(3), 277–299.

Tan, P-L. T., Caleon, I. S., Jonathan, C. R., and Koh, E., 2014. A dialogic framework for assessing collective creativity in computer-supported collaborative problem-solving tasks. *Research and Practice in Technology Enhanced Learning,* 9(3), 411–437.

Walton, J., 1999. *Strategic human resource development.* Harlow, UK: Prentice Hall.

Warschauer, M., 2007. The paradoxical future of digital learning. *Learning Inquiry,* 1(1), 41–49.

Wenger, E., 1998. *Communities of practice: Learning, meaning, and identity.* Cambridge: Cambridge University Press.

Wenger, E., Trayner, B., and De Laat, M., 2011. *Promoting and assessing value creation in communities and networks: A conceptual framework.* Heerlen, The Netherlands: Ruud de Moor Centrum—Open Universiteit of the Netherlands.

Wiley, D. and Hilton III, J., 2009. Openness, dynamic specialization, and the disaggregated future of higher education. *The International Review of Research in Open and Distributed Learning,* 10(5), 1–16.

Windmuller, I., 2012. *Versterking van de professionaliteit van de leraar basisonderwijs.* [Enhancement of teacher professionalism in primary education] Thesis (Ph.D.). Heerlen: Ruud de Moor Centrum—Open Universiteit of the Netherlands.

9

NETWORKED PLACES AS COMMUNICATIVE RESOURCES

A Social-Semiotic Analysis of a Redesigned University Library

Louise J. Ravelli and Robert J. McMurtrie

Introduction

Universities are inherently networked places, and have always been so. Whatever the current technology, be it pre- or post-digital, universities bring together the material and human aspects of networks (Carvalho and Goodyear 2014). Conceptually and physically, they are places for productive learning, enabling social actors to engage with each other in multiple ways to understand, interrogate, and create knowledge.

The fact that universities have undergone dramatic change in recent years is well established, in terms of student cohorts, numbers, funding and regulation, and, of course, technology (see, for example, Karmel 2000; King, Hill, and Hemmings 2000; Marginson 2000, 2008; Ellis and Goodyear 2010). Part of this ongoing wave of change is the increased attention to and renovation of learning spaces. This chapter takes one such learning space, the Menzies Library at the UNSW, Sydney, which underwent significant recent renovations, and examines how changes to place have the potential to simultaneously reconfigure the nature and potential of learning in these places, and particularly of networked learning.

The approach used here is that of social semiotics (Halliday 1978; Kress and Van Leeuwen 2001; Van Leeuwen 2005). Social semiotics is an approach to the analysis of meaning which considers communicative resources in their social contexts, studying how a resource "has been, is, and can be used for purposes of communication" (Van Leeuwen 2005, p. 5). It requires explicit identification of the communicative resources, and examines them in relation to their social context. Such a model provides tools for analyzing the material, human, and virtual components of a space, to examine their impact on meaning potential. This approach enables networked places to be seen as spaces that "make meaning" in terms of potential uses, the kinds of relationships that can be enabled by participation in a networked place, and the different ways the component elements are integrated into a meaningful whole. At the same time, however it is that the spaces have been designed, users may reconfigure them for their own purposes, and thus change their communicative potential.

It is important to have models for understanding the communicative aspects of learning design, and a social-semiotic model provides resources for interrogating the material, human, and virtual components of a space, to examine their impact on meaning and meaning potential. The model derives from Kress and Van Leeuwen's (2006) grammar of visual analysis, in turn based on the work of Halliday in relation to language (Halliday 1978; Halliday and Matthiessen 2004), and it extends the work of others, such as O'Toole (2011), Ravelli and McMurtrie (2016), and Stenglin (Chapter 10), in relation to Spatial Discourse Analysis.

In a social-semiotic model, the meanings that are or might be made in such spaces are tripartite and derive from three underlying functions of communication: first, to construe interactional relations, that is, the kinds of relationships that might hold between interactants in a text, such as between users, or between users and the institution; second, to construe representational meanings, that is, what the text is "about"—what activities and roles are enabled by the text; and third, to construe organizational meanings, that is, to bring the multiple components of a text into a meaningful whole, showing how the different parts relate to each other as well as to the whole (Kress and Van Leeuwen 2006). These three sets of meanings, or metafunctions, are always co-present within a text. They contribute different, albeit interrelated, strands of meaning to the whole. A social-semiotic approach to communication assumes that meaning-making is a socially—and culturally—contextualized process, whereby contextual factors motivate communication in non-arbitrary ways. That is, any analysis or interpretation of meaning needs to be based on explicit textual evidence, observing resources deployed in the construal of the text. This chapter will demonstrate how a social-semiotic approach can be applied to the physical dimensions of a learning space, in order to provide a particular understanding of "networked" places.

In terms of interactional meanings, it will be argued that the redesign of the library completely reconfigures the traditional power relations holding between the institution and its users (that is, students in the library), as well as enabling the transfer of meanings from "other" places (such as "home") to the library, thus accommodating behaviors which would otherwise not normally be acceptable. Representationally, the physical design and virtual capacity of the space reconfigures the very notion of who the key social actors are (that is, students/learners), as well as the range of activities that can be seen to be part of, or to support, learning. Organizationally, it will be seen that multiple types of networking are both clearly differentiated and yet fundamentally integrated, giving rise to a notion of "macro" network for the library space as a key hub in a larger learning network. Overall, this chapter proposes that the reconfiguration of the physical space, enabling varying social connections and behaviors, simultaneously facilitates a reconfiguration of networked learning within the University.

The scope of this chapter will be limited to an analysis of what Carvalho and Goodyear (2014) call the *set design* of learning networks. This relates particularly to the physical aspects of the space, such as the nature of the room or rooms, as well as the material objects within it. Set design sits alongside *epistemic* (knowledge) design, and *social* design, as the contributing components of learning networks. We strongly believe that the social-semiotic approach can be applied to all three components of learning networks, seeing the network itself as a complex, socially constituted "text," but limitation to the physical aspects of set design will enable a more focused discussion of the potential of this approach.

The Menzies Library, UNSW

The University of New South Wales' (UNSW) main library, officially called the *Menzies Library*, is central to the identity of the University: physically, as it is visually dominant on the campus; educationally, as it provides learning and research resources for students and staff; socially, as it is an important locus for students to work both on their own and in groups; and virtually, as it connects staff and students to the central networked learning resources of the University.

Originally established in 1949, the library has been extensively redeveloped since 2002, with significant renovations commencing in 2009. The social sense of building community was an explicit objective of the architect responsible for the redesign, lahznimmo. lahznimmo architects state that: "Our design accommodates the varied needs of the modern student and academic within a structured and legible landscape of individual and group study spaces: social/collaborative peer to peer settings; reflective settings and seminar feedback settings" (lahznimmo, n.d.). These multiple types of spaces are particularly evident on Levels 3 and 4 of the library (the entry level is Level 2, so these are the next two levels above), and on which this chapter focuses.

Previously, the design of Levels 3 and 4 in the library focused on storing books and providing quiet, individual study spaces in carrels (small desks with screens to obscure other users, usually placed against a wall), with a small amount of "social" space (a quiet area to read newspapers) and "functional" spaces (an information desk, printing area). As with the redesign of many university and public libraries in recent years, these functions have been completely transformed. Whilst individual study carrels remain, there are now also a wide variety of settings allowing for individual, pair, and collaborative work; settings which suggest study and work; other settings which suggest relaxation; maximum facilitation of personal computing devices (for example, with ready availability of power points), and an effective WiFi network. Interestingly, whilst the settings are more diverse and seem to take up a lot of physical room (with beanbags on the floor, for example), overall seating capacity has more than doubled (Fletcher 2011). During term time, Levels 3 and 4 are usually very busy, full of students making use of all the available spaces.

A number of these spaces are illustrated in use in the various settings depicted in Figure 9.1 (pp. 113–122). It should be noted that the various settings enable a number of configurations of interactants: individually; in pairs; in small, informal groups (in an open space, for example); in small, more formal groups (in a dedicated room, for example). The design does not enable large, formal groups (as in a lecture theater, for instance). Some settings allow for multiple smaller groups to be in the same space at the same time. Many of the settings can be reconfigured at will (by moving chairs, opening or closing a curtain, and so on), and none are completely separated from any other space (even small rooms with doors have a glass panel, enabling visual connection between spaces).

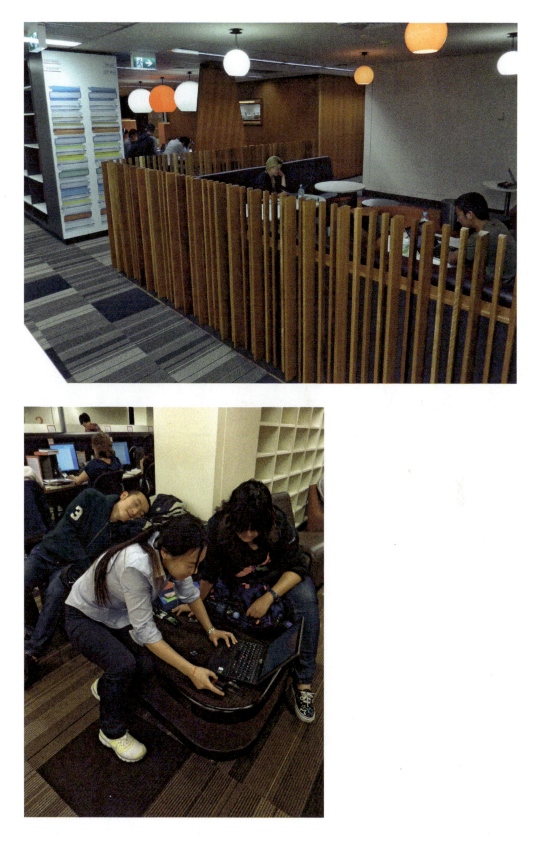

FIGURE 9.1 Various Settings in the Redesigned Menzies Library, UNSW (Photos: Robert McMurtrie)

Interactional Meanings: Reconfiguring Power

Interactional meanings are about fundamental relations between the participants in a text.[1] In the case of the Menzies Library, the key participants (in terms of the current analysis) are the institution itself (that is, the UNSW, as represented by the library and its staff), and the students. The relevant nodes in terms of networked learning also include the learning resources, but the specific focus of this chapter is participant interaction. Specific aspects of the set design can influence how the participants relate to each other, as well as how they are made to feel within the space.

Interactional relations are expressed along four key dimensions: contact, social distance, involvement, and power (Kress and Van Leeuwen 2006). *Contact* refers to whether interactants engage directly with each other, for example, *demanding* attention through direct eye contact, or indirectly, for example, one *observing* another, when interactants are separated but perhaps looking away, or perhaps working next to each other but with a partition between them. Contact between different groupings of students can be limited by physical devices which create separations between groups (walls, curtains), or encouraged when such devices are absent (no walls, glass panels within walls).

Social distance relates to whether interactants are positioned closely, and are therefore in an intimate relation to each other (as with a close-up shot in an image), or distantly, and therefore are in a social or public relation to each other (as with a long shot). In spatial texts, social distance is realized between interactants in terms of whether they can sit close to each other, without barriers, and are therefore positioned in an intimate relation with each other, or whether there is a larger physical distance, or a physical barrier, between them, thus realizing public distance. Thus, for example, two students might be sitting next to each other, but if there is a partition between them, this creates a greater social distance, *as if* they are physically far apart.

Involvement concerns whether interactants are directly *involved* with each other, realized by a frontal angle on the horizontal plane (as when people face each other directly), or *detached*, realized by oblique angles on the horizontal plane (as when we stand on slightly different angles). *Power* is determined by vertical angles: level angles (sitting at the same level, for example) indicate an equal power relation between interactants; high angles (positioned above, looking down) confer power on the participant doing the "looking"; low angles (positioned below, looking above) confer power on the participant being "looked at."

Contact between students and the institution can be thought of in terms of the visibility of the institution: to what extent does the institution make itself visible and explicitly "present?" The provision of a formal information desk with staff behind provides a clear point of contact with the institution; as does the presence of signage which contains rules/instructions for students to follow. Between students and the institution, the realization of social distance is somewhat similar to contact, but subtly different. Contact relates to whether the institution can be "seen" and "accessed"; social distance relates to how *close* the nature of that contact is. Contact may be explicit with a staff member behind a desk, but if they *are* behind a desk, then the social distance is public, not intimate. The absence of a desk or other barrier suggests greater intimacy, such as might hold between friends.

What is notable in the redesign of the Menzies Library is the extent to which the dimensions of contact, social distance, involvement, and power have been left as maximally free as possible. For student-student relations, settings and furniture are provided to enable students to work on their own, in pairs, or in small groups. Some configurations, with fixed seating in parallel, for example, are designed to encourage individual work, where direct *contact* is avoided; *social distance* may appear to be physically close, but is in fact socially maximized by the convention of "uncrossable space" between individuals; *involvement* is detached as students sit side-by-side; and *power* is equal, with students on the same level. Other configurations encourage group work, enabling students to sit together, with direct *contact* and *involvement*, as they face each other, a *personal* social distance (they can be very close to each other), and, again, equal *power*. The multiple configurations in the library demonstrate that these are scalar, not categorical options. It is also notable that students themselves construe the configuration of the space. For example, an individual can isolate him or herself within what is otherwise a group or social setting, by turning their back on others or hunching over their computer. Tables which are set far apart can be brought together. Curtains that close off a space can be opened, and so on. The students very much make these spaces their own.

In terms of student-institution relations, the institution itself is largely invisible. Students need to go downstairs if they want help from a member of staff. Thus, *contact* is offered and *involvement* is detached, rather than direct. Whilst it is the University which sets the rules and provides the facilities, this is only occasionally explicitly signaled (through signage for example, which is kept to a minimum). The liberty given to students to reconfigure many aspects of the setting confers some *power* to them, equalizing otherwise hierarchical relations; at the same time, this liberty decreases the *social distance*: it is as if the students can act as a physical part of the institution, minimizing the social space between the two entities.

There are a number of other dimensions of interactional meaning that are relevant to an analysis of spatial texts, such as the level of *binding* and nature of *bonding* (Stenglin, Chapter 10), as well as the overall *modality* of the space, and levels of *engagement*. Whilst there is not space here to address all of these, it is worth drawing attention to the *bonding* resources in this space. As described by Stenglin (2004), bonding is the creation of affiliation and identification with a space, and may be realized by various resources such as key symbols (flags, logos), rallying cries (national anthems, war cries), as well as by hybridization of spatial functions (putting one space to multiple uses). Hybridization is very evident in the Menzies Library: the multiple configurations enable study, socializing, as well as rest and relaxation. This attracts more people, and encourages them to stay longer, because there is more to do. It redefines the space, away from prior notions fixed on study only, toward a broader range of activities which are legitimated by the set design. In many respects, students are made to feel as if they could be "at home," as comfortable in this space as they would be in their own. Thus, as Ravelli and McMurtrie (2016, pp. 89–90) note: "knowledge management is not understood as a single process that must suit everybody; rather, it consists of multiple processes and various social activities . . . each contributing to a balanced academic life." Part of the learning network of the University, then, as represented by these floors in the Menzies Library, is one of inherent multidimensionality, diverse social relations, and minimal hierarchization.

Representational Meanings: Reconfiguring Action

Through representational meanings, a picture of what is "going on" is constructed: the nature of the activities taking place, who or what undertakes those activities or is affected by them, and the additional circumstances surrounding such activities (Halliday and Matthiessen 2004; Kress and Van Leeuwen 2006). This comes closest to traditional understandings of "meaning," that is, what the text refers to, or what the text is "about." In spatial texts, analysis can begin with a simple identification of what is *denoted* within the space: what is there? Desks, chairs, people, books, carpet, beanbags . . . These can also be considered for their *connotations*: elements of color, style, design, placement, and what they may evoke. In the Menzies Library, the strong orange and brown colors, and often-organic shapes of many of the furniture items, evoke (for some), a kind of retro-nostalgia for the 1970s. And whilst that may not be at the forefront of the mind of the majority of current students—born long after the 1970s—it is nevertheless clear that the colors are neither dull and bland, nor what might be easily identified as "corporate" or "professional."

In addition to connotations, the functions and uses of items placed within the space can also be considered (Ravelli 2006). The inclusion of desks, chairs, and computer terminals is perhaps of no surprise in a library; the inclusion of beanbags and other forms of comfy seating, as well as furniture which can be moved around, and a maximized number of power points, perhaps is. So such choices alone begin to suggest interesting features about this space, and about what the space might be for, or what its users might do here. As Goodyear and Carvalho note (2014, p. 62), activity is shaped by the physical setting in which it unfolds. Evidently, there is considerable overlap here with points already made regarding hybridization, relating to interactional meanings. And indeed, a metafunctional analysis explicitly accounts for the fact that multiple meanings are always co-present in the one text. The same resources function in different ways to contribute to different strands of meaning. Thus, the presence of beanbags tells us that one of the activities people can do in this library is to relax or lounge around. At the same time, this tells us that the functionality of the space has been hybridized, thus increasing its potential to create affiliation, that is, to bond more users to the space. As lahznimmo state, "There is acknowledgement of individual preferences that respond to casual/formal, noisy/quite, private/social, natural light/artificial light, etc. Students will tend to return to the spaces that not only fulfill their functional needs, but also their personal tastes" (lahznimmo, n.d.).

Most important for the analysis of representational meaning, however, is the identification of *processes* and *participants*, as well as associated *circumstances*. This is a complex area of the analysis, and we will only be able to touch on it lightly here. *Processes* refer to the activities that are enabled or suggested by the set design; *participants* are the people or things involved in those actions.[2] In visual and spatial texts, there is a fundamental distinction between narrative processes that are inherently dynamic in some way (they contain vectors, or involve movement), and conceptual processes, which are not dynamic (there are no vectors, and they are inherently still; Kress and Van Leeuwen 2006). When a student is sitting at a traditional carrel reading a book, there is some narrative involved: they are sitting, as realized by the vectors of legs tucked under a chair and back leaning forward a little; and they are reading, as realized by the vector of the gaze upon the book. But the vectors don't go anywhere: the activity of sitting is intransitive, that is, it is not an action extended to anyone or anything else. The actual activities taking place are likely to be behavioral and mental (Halliday and Matthiessen 2004), that is, reading, thinking, and so on. A learning network of this kind is singular in its structure: one node (institution, as represented by a book or a computer) to one node (student). This kind of activity is still enabled in the redesigned Menzies Library; indeed, it is very well supported in a number of different settings, and many students can be seen to be engaged in such processes. Other intransitive processes are also enabled by the redesign: lounging and lying down, for example, which may or may not be accompanied by "reading" (indeed, sleeping is not an uncommon process observed in this space!).

For narrative processes involving multiple [human] participants, processes are extended from one participant to another. This may be uni-directional (where one student helps another, or tells them something), or bi-directional, where each acts upon the other. Such processes characterize the ideal form of pair or group work: where the narrative vectors of talking, telling, pointing, sharing, and so on bounce back and forth around the group, and indeed, this is not only often seen in the new library space, its redesign fully encourages it. Many settings enable such functionality, and if they do not, we have already seen that students will rearrange or make use of furniture to enable this themselves; they actively co-configure the set design (Goodyear and Carvalho 2014, p. 99). Thus the multi-pronged network, web-like in its social relations (De Laat, Schreurs, and Sie 2014, p. 344), is a feature of the redesigned library, and as the participants of that network are engaged in inherently dynamic processes, this says much about the nature of learning encouraged and valued by the institution. Indeed, everywhere in these areas there is a strong hum of activity going on. Voices are generally muted but nevertheless strongly present: lots of people are talking, in distinct contrast to traditional understandings of appropriate behavior in a library.

Whilst narrative processes are one characterizing feature of the redesigned space, conceptual processes also play an important role. Such structures "define the meaning or identity of a participant" (Jewitt and Oyama 2001, p. 144). According to Kress and Van Leeuwen (2006), a key subtype of conceptual processes is the *symbolic* process: where something is represented as carrying symbolic values. This is most commonly in the form of symbolic attributive processes, where the participant is a *Carrier* of the *Attributes* of the symbol ascribed to them. Thus, those who wear the colors of their favorite sporting team are conferred with the Attributes of that team. In the library, we argue that the student studying at a traditional carrel, on their own, is conferred with Attributes such as knowledge, as represented by the books around them. This equates to a "transmission model of knowledge management whereby the authoritative institution passes on knowledge (through books) to the student" (Ravelli and McMurtrie 2016, p. 90). A less obvious but equally important type of symbolic process is the symbolic suggestive process. In this case, the symbolism comes from within. Given that students can be seen to be bonding with the redesigned library space—by taking up the potentiality it offers, and making it their own—then the students and the library together constitute a singular symbolic suggestive process: it is the whole *atmosphere* of the space and how it is used which is symbolic. Thus the library and its users are interdependent in constructing an interactive—and again, inherently dynamic—model of knowledge management (Ravelli and McMurtrie 2016).

Organizational Meanings: Reconfiguring Networks

Organizational meanings are concerned with the way individual parts are organized into a whole, coherent text. *Information values* show whether the parts are equal in value, or have different values. *Framing* shows whether the parts are strongly differentiated one from another, or only barely separated. *Salience* may make one part stand out more than the others, and *reading* or *navigation* paths show how the multiple parts are read or traversed (Kress and Van Leeuwen 2006). In the Menzies Library, the "whole" text for our purposes, is, in physical terms, these two floors of the library; its parts are the various settings within it, where "setting" is both the physical furniture present and the students themselves when using it. But the whole text is not just a physical one; indeed, it is its virtual connections, through web connections, books, and other learning resources, as well as the activities of those using these resources, which make this text come alive. At the same time, within the "whole" text (physical and virtual), each setting can itself be seen as a "whole," which may have its own individual components. So the analysis for organizational meanings addresses these various levels of text (cf. Goodyear and Carvalho 2014, p. 98). The architects, lahznimmo, were again explicitly aware of this, and have their own terminology for it: "The design approach to this project has been to treat the Library as a Community. Within this community there are a series of Precincts that relate to the core functions and facilities of each zone. Within the Precincts are a series of hubs supporting flexible learning centres" (lahznimmo, n.d.).

In terms of information values, many spatial texts have values which are polarized: one component may be central with all others radiating around it, for example; or another may be prioritized as a point of departure that is "Given" or understood, with the status of being "Before" what is next. What comes next is presented as "New," attention-worthy in some way, and is positioned "After" as a point of arrival (Kress and Van Leeuwen 2006; Ravelli 2006). On these two floors in the library, each floor is roughly divided into two distinct areas. There are the student-centered study spaces which are entered first, and the book section itself, positioned in a separate area, to one end of the study spaces. Thus, the study spaces are positioned "Before" the books; they have the value of "Given": an understood point of departure. It is presented as obvious that multiple study spaces of different kinds should be available in the library. The shelved books are positioned "After" and presented as "New," almost surprising, albeit a logical follow-up to the study spaces.

For the area which contains the study spaces, there is no polarization of information values evident. The various settings are widely dispersed; they do not need to be used in any particular order, and no particular setting is prioritized over another. Yet at the same time, particular settings may have a polarized information value themselves. Where there are multiple participants, settings are often provided—or, as we have seen, arranged by the students themselves—in a way that construes Centre/Margin values: students work together around a table, for example, all equal in value around the Margins; the Centre may be literally realized by something physical, such as a book, a screen, or notes being focused upon, but is in fact symbolic: representing the work being undertaken, the process of learning itself. In its idealized form, as noted in relation to representational meaning, if all participants are contributing equally, then no one student takes priority: they are all equal in value, all positioned in relation to the Centre. Thus in terms of the overall space and the particular settings within it, the traditional, hierarchical relations of the classroom or lecture theater, where information values may focus on the teacher, have been elided. Whilst the symbolic focus remains on the activity or learning process, it now only comes to life with students proactively contributing to the life of the network.

Another aspect of organizational meaning is the way in which component parts are *framed*. Framing may be strong or weak (Kress and Van Leeuwen 2006), and in spatial texts is realized by a range of devices such as the presence of walls, changes in color, curtains, and so on (Ravelli and McMurtrie 2016). For the overall library space analyzed here, framing is largely weak, that is, whilst the particular settings have distinct identities, there are few strong borders between them. Participants are free to move between the different settings at will. Many individual settings have weak framing, with no boundaries between settings at all (for example, students can get up from their beanbag and move to a table, or vice versa), indicating that participants have a choice and can move freely between these spaces. Some settings have strong framing (for example, there are closed-off rooms which can only be entered by a door), indicating that the group work in these spaces is important and should not be interrupted, or alternatively, that it creates a certain level of noise that might otherwise disturb others. Yet other settings enable the framing to be changed by choice: a curtain can be pulled across, for example, to give a space a sense of enclosure.

In terms of its implications for an understanding of networked learning, it is notable that where framing is strongest (in a closed-off room), there is still potential to "breach" this frame (a pane of glass beside the door, enabling others to see in; or walls made of glass). That is, no setting is ever completely divorced from the larger space: all the settings make up a seamless whole, giving a strong sense of fluidity between them. At the same time, where framing is weak, participants can choose to increase the strength of framing around a setting themselves, by hunching over their computer, turning their backs to others, using their earbuds. Pairs and small groups can do the same, by bringing tables or chairs closer together, for example, so that they function as one. Again, all this enables maximal diversification of the space on the part of the participants, suggesting that all ways of working are appropriate. This has evident implications for participants' agency, in the sense of enabling more narrative processes on the part of students, as described above.

The largely non-polarized information values, and predominantly weak framing practices, are supported by the absence of any specific salience being given to one setting over another. None stands out in any obvious way, for example, by being larger, differently designed, or highlighted in some regard. Similarly, the weak framing between the different settings facilitates a very open navigational path: there is no particular path through this space; rather, there are many different paths that can be taken. It is a space that can literally be wandered through. Within a pair or group setting, salience would be attributed to the "active" member of the network: the one talking at a specific point, for example. Ideally, this would be something that shifted constantly, but close analysis might show that one member of the network is doing "all the work," and so they would take on greater salience within that setting, and the reading/navigation path would be seen to continually return to them.

The shelved books are somewhat separated from the study spaces by their distinct placement in terms of information values (in the New/After position), and somewhat framed off by the distinctive design of this area (symmetrically arranged bookshelves taking up the majority of floor space in this section, with some individual study carrels available around the perimeter, and no group areas). And yet, framing between this section and the study section is not particularly strong; there is no wall or door to separate the different zones, and some study spaces (even lounges) are still included in this space. Nor is this space marked as being especially salient in any way, and the navigation path enables participants to choose to go there, but does not require them to.

Overall then, the textual patterns on these floors of the library point to great fluidity between different settings, suggesting that any or all of these settings can and should contribute to processes of studying and learning at the University. In addition, the various possible settings (individual, small groups, larger groups) are dispersed throughout the space. It is not the case, for example, that there is just one zone for individual work, or just one zone for group work. The various settings are juxtaposed against each other, and with the generally weak framing between them, this sets up a gentle rhythm throughout, encouraging participants to explore the possibilities. As Martin and Rose (2007) describe, this sets up "waves of periodicity" throughout the text: peaks and troughs of information constantly being recycled. This contrasts with more conventional library designs, which typically establish very staccato-like rhythms: participants enter, do what they need to do (such as find a book, or sit down and read one), and leave. The redesigned library creates a text which suggests a very different kind of usage pattern.

Importantly, the physical aspects of the set design co-articulate with other features to enable productive learning networks. Each setting, when used by a participant, forms its own micro-network. Whilst a network is formally defined as two participants connected by a tie (Carvalho and Goodyear 2014), this does not mean that the two participants need to be physically co-present. So, one student working alone in the library can be part of a network, if their learning resources connect them to other participants in the University (their teacher, other students). Certainly where two or more students *are* working together, we see a very active and localized instantiation of a network, with the great probability that that particular node is itself being connected by learning resources to other parts of the network in, around, and even beyond, the University. Whilst individuals may work alone, and groups may work in isolation from others, all are connected by specific ties to other participants of the University, via all the learning resources of the campus: books, lecture notes and recordings, course materials, and so on. Together, then, the possibilities for networking within these floors of the library mean that they function together as a kind of *macro-network* (cf. Martin and Rose 2007, on macro-genre). The redesigned library becomes a true hub for networked learning at the University.

Conclusion

Goodyear and Carvalho (2014, p. 92) point to the urgent need for greater theorization of complex texts: material, digital, and social. Social semiotics is one theory which can address such complex notions of text, where "text" is understood as a meaningful instance of communication. With its foundations in the study of language (Halliday 1978) and its extension to the analysis of visual texts (Kress and Van Leeuwen 2006), it has already been deployed to explore the built environment (Stenglin Chapter 10, Ravelli and McMurtrie 2016), the discourse and visualization of mathematics (O'Halloran 2005), and hairstyles (McMurtrie 2010), to identify just a few diverse applications. Deep explanations of specific textual resources already exist for some phenomena, such as color and sound (Van Leeuwen 1999, 2011). The model has a fundamentally consistent core, where meaning is identified based on explicit textual resources, where those resources are understood to be embedded within a specific social and cultural context, where meaning is seen to be metafunctional, and with the capacity to isolate the analysis to different levels (ranks) of a text. The model needs to be adapted and extended for each new textual resource, as each brings its own specificities of communication, but it remains robust and seemingly infinitely extendable.

For Levels 3 and 4 of the redesigned Menzies Library at UNSW, the very preliminary analysis presented here begins to explicate some of the ways in which a social-semiotic approach can bring a particular perspective to an understanding of networked learning. Interactionally, the nature of the set design means that the conventional hierarchical relations between the University and its students have been flattened, and students are left largely free to determine how they should relate to each other, if at all. Students are made to feel almost as comfortable as if they were at home. Representationally, the set design continues to enable the intransitive processes of conventional libraries, whilst also enabling many more transitive processes, including those which are bi-directional, that is, bouncing back and forth between participants, with a greater degree of inherent dynamism, with such activity itself becoming symbolic of what the library represents in terms of learning and knowledge. Organizationally, the multiple components of the space contribute to a very coherent "whole," with students again enabled to have considerable autonomy in determining these inter-relations themselves. The overall coherence, combined with internal flexibility, means that the whole space creates a set design which supports a macro-network for learning.

The analysis presented here is no more than a broad sweep across generalized patterns of meaning; there is no close textual analysis as such. Deeper and more explicit analysis is needed to produce something more comprehensive. But it is proposed here as an avenue for future exploration. We have accounted only for physical aspects of the set design, and have not aimed to account for the specific nature of the ties (learning resources) connecting nodes in a network. Nor has there been any attempt to account for epistemic and social design, the other components of learning networks, though we believe that both *can* be accounted for using a social-semiotic approach (see Ravelli and McMurtrie 2016 for some accounting of epistemic design).

The redesign of the library is not perfect, nor without its detractors. For example, the library has been critiqued for downsizing its book collection to accommodate these changes. Also, the considerable liberty afforded to students in terms of how they use the space means that they often leave it in a mess. But the preliminary analysis presented here reveals the *potential* of a built space for explicitly enabling—or not—particular activities (cf. Carvalho and Goodyear 2014, p. 95). Without any specific set design at all, students are more than capable of creating their own "designs for learning": where there are no chairs, they might sit on the floor; where there are no spaces for groups to work, they might just huddle together. But in such cases, the built environment does not explicitly suggest such activities, whereas in the Menzies Library, it does. It not only suggests it; rather, such co-configuration activity is invited, supported, and validated.

Endnotes

1. Note that "participant" here is the human user, as defined by Carvalho and Goodyear (2014). This term will also be used for a more precise grammatical denotation, in the discussion of representational meaning below (cf. Kress and Van Leeuwen 2006).
2. Here, "participant" can include non-human elements.

Acknowledgment

This research was supported by a grant from the School of the Arts and Media, UNSW.

References

Carvalho, L. and Goodyear, P., eds., 2014. *The architecture of productive learning networks.* London: Routledge.

De Laat, M., Schreurs, B., and Sie, R., 2014. Utilizing informal teaching professional development networks using the network awareness tool. In: L. Carvalho and P. Goodyear, eds., *The architecture of productive learning networks* (pp. 239–256). London: Routledge.

Ellis, R. and Goodyear, P., 2010. *Students' experiences of e-learning in higher education: The ecology of sustainable innovation.* New York: RoutledgeFalmer.

Fletcher, J., 2011. Breaking down the barriers—the no desk academic library, UNSW. [online]. Available from: http://handle.unsw.edu.au/1959.4/51368 [Accessed March 9, 2015].

Goodyear, P., and Carvalho, L., 2014. Framing the analysis of learning network architectures. In: L. Carvalho and P. Goodyear, eds., *The architecture of productive learning networks* (pp. 48–70). London: Routledge.

Halliday, M. A. K., 1978. *Language as social semiotic.* London: Edward Arnold.

Halliday, M. A. K. and Matthiessen, C. M. I. M., 2004. *An introduction to functional grammar.* London: Edward Arnold.

Jewitt, C. and Oyama, R., 2001. Visual meaning: A social semiotic approach. In: T. van Leeuwen and C. Jewitt, eds., *Handbook of visual analysis* (pp. 134–156). London: Sage.

Karmel, P., 2000. Reforming higher education. Occasional Paper, Series 2/2000. Academy of the Social Sciences in Australia. [online]. Available from: http://www.assa.edu.au/publications/occasional/2000_No2_Reforming_higher_education.pdf [Accessed March 13, 2016].

King, R. J. R., Hill, D., and Hemmings, B., 2000. *University and diversity: Changing perspectives, policies and practices in Australia.* Wagga Wagga, Australia: Keon Publications.

Kress, G. and Van Leeuwen, T., 2001. *Multimodal discourse: The modes and media of contemporary communication.* London: Arnold.

Kress, G. and Van Leeuwen, T., 2006. *Reading images: The grammar of visual design.* London: Routledge.

lahznimmo. n.d. Main library refurbishment, The University of New South Wales. [online]. Available from: http://lahznimmo.com/wp-content/uploads/2011/12/Project-Sheet-Main-Library-Refurbishment.pdf [Accessed September 29, 2014].

Marginson, S., 2000. *The enterprise university: Power, governance and reinvention in Australia.* Cambridge: Cambridge University Press.

Marginson, S., 2008. *Education, science and public policy: Ideas for an education revolution.* Carlton, Australia: Melbourne University Press.

Martin, J. R. and Rose, D., 2007. *Working with discourse: Meaning beyond the clause.* London: Continuum.

McMurtrie, R. J., 2010. Bobbing for power: An exploration into the modality of hair. *Visual Communication,* 9(4), 399–424.

O'Halloran, K. L., 2005. *Mathematical discourse: Language, symbolism and visual images.* London: Continuum.

O'Toole, M., 2011. *The language of displayed art.* London: Leicester University Press.

Ravelli, L. J., 2006. *Museum texts: Communication frameworks.* London: Routledge.

Ravelli, L. J. and McMurtrie, R. M., 2016. *Multimodality in spatial texts: Spatial discourse analysis.* London: Routledge.

Stenglin, M., 2004. *Packaging curiosities: Towards a grammar of three dimensional space.* Thesis (Ph.D.). The University of Sydney.

Van Leeuwen, T., 1999. *Speech, music, sound.* New York: St. Martin's Press.

Van Leeuwen, T., 2005. *Introducing social semiotics.* New York: Routledge.

Van Leeuwen, T., 2011. *The language of colour: An introduction.* London: Routledge.

10

BUILDING BRIDGES

Design, Emotion, and Museum Learning

Maree Stenglin

We build too many walls and not enough bridges

(Isaac Newton)

This chapter explores the relationship between design, emotion, and museum learning. Like schools and universities, museums are pedagogical sites but they are not only concerned with learning. Like universities, they are involved in research and the production of new knowledge. They are also involved in collection management and the care of material cultural heritage. It is not surprising then that learning in a museum context presents a unique set of challenges. The first challenge is that the starting point for each visitor, in terms of baseline knowledge of an exhibition topic, varies enormously. This means that finding an angle on a topic that is accessible and engaging to as many visitors as possible is a challenge for exhibition design.

Second, learning in a museum context involves many different communicative modes: written texts (text panels and labels), spoken texts (guided tours), 3D objects, visual images, moving images (films and documentaries), databases, music, live performances, and hands-on activities. It also involves information and communication technologies (ICT), including Facebook, Twitter, wikis, blogs, iPhone apps, and so forth. Despite this range, the key communicative mode in most museum exhibitions is the object—the tangible, 3D material object (MacGregor 2010). This object may be whole or fragment, used or preserved, admired or feared; it may include "the humble things of everyday life as well as great works of art" (MacGregor 2010, p. xiii). From a design perspective, deciding which communicative mode(s) will be used to introduce a given concept, and which will further develop visitors' understandings, is a complex undertaking.

Perhaps the greatest challenge for museum design and learning is that most visitors spend very little time in any given exhibition. In a survey of 108 exhibitions, Serrell found that the average time most people spent in an exhibition is less than 20 minutes. She also found that 20 minutes is typical, irrespective of the size of a space or the nature of the topic (1997). So designers have 20 minutes in which to engage visitors, stimulate curiosity, make connections, communicate key concepts, and develop their understandings.

The approach to exploring museum learning, design, and emotion adopted in this chapter is that of a case study. We will focus on an actual story. In our story, a highly motivated museum visitor enters an exhibition space and feels totally overpowered by its design and leaves. Yet two hours later, the same visitor is inside the very same exhibition listening to an audio guide, looking intently at the objects on display, and reading the labels and text panels. The chapter explores what happened to change this experience from fight-or-flight to one of engagement and deep learning. It begins by telling this visitor story in full. It then analyzes how the initial negative relationship between emotion and space in the museum exhibition was overridden by human interaction and a carefully framed tour of the exhibition.

The first analysis of the story will be from the perspective of networked learning. As we know, networked learning is about connections between people, resources, and a learning community, usually having technology as a key component. Carvalho and Goodyear's (2014) architectural framework is applied as we explore connections between the various elements that come together to compose this learning network. The architectural framework is very much activity-centered. It is concerned with what learners actually do—both "mentally and physically" (Carvalho and Goodyear 2014, p. 18). It also explores four components in the design of learning environments: the set design, the social design, the epistemic design, and co-configuration (what learners actually do, which is often not what one imagines). However, emotion plays a key role in this story; and Carvalho and Goodyear's analytical framework does not, as yet, actively explore emotion and the impact of emotion on learning and learning design.

So to analyze the nexus between design, *emotion,* and learning, this chapter will also draw on two social-semiotic tools: Binding and Bonding (Stenglin 2004). Binding is concerned with the emotional relationship of in/security between a person and a space. It sheds light on why the visitor fled from the exhibition. Bonding is also concerned with emotion and space but it focuses on the building of community. In our story, it explores some of the ways learning communities can be built through human mediation and epistemic design. In particular, an education officer played a pivotal role in helping the woman engage with the objects and concepts of the exhibition. The educator did this by using ten carefully selected objects. Many of the objects were taken from the familiar realm of everyday life but the object choices also opened up applied and theoretical understandings of Ancient Egyptian life for the visitor to explore.

In terms of structure, the chapter will begin by retelling the visitor's story. It will then apply key networked learning concepts to analyze the story. Following this, it will introduce Binding and apply it to the visitor's exhibition experience. This will be followed by an exploration of Bonding with a strong focus on how the education officer navigated four Domains of Learning in the guided tour—the everyday, the applied, the theoretical, and the reflexive. These domains were first theorized by Macken-Horarik (1996). The chapter will close with a reflection on the relevance to networked learning of analytical tools drawn from social semiotics such as Binding and Bonding.

The Story

The exhibition that features in our case study is the *Life and Death under the Pharaohs* exhibition from the National Museum of Antiquities in Leiden. It was a blockbuster exhibition that opened in Sydney to an overwhelmingly positive response. Crowds of visitors of all ages queued outside the Australian Museum for hours patiently waiting for their turn to see Ancient Egyptian antiquities. The people of Sydney were so motivated that queues gathered—rain, hail, or shine—winding their way out of the Museum, round the corner into nearby William Street. The waiting period was up to two hours but the visitors still came—day after day, week after week for the entire six-week duration of the exhibition.

One day, a woman joined the queue and waited for several hours. Eventually, the security officer monitoring visitor flow nodded signaling that her long-awaited turn to enter the exhibition had arrived. She moved down the long, black, narrow entrance passageway glancing at the papyrus pages from the *Book of the Dead* along the walls. This entrance passage appears to have been designed to simulate the passageway into a pyramid. With a strong sense of anticipation, she entered the first exhibition space. Objects related to the theme of gods and goddesses were on display inside protective glass cases, but the space was small, dark, and strongly enclosed. Not only did it feel confined, it was crowded to overflowing with people jostling to peer at the objects and read the text panels lining the walls. Within seconds, the woman turned back down the corridor she had just traversed and hastily exited the exhibition.

Concerned, the security guard stopped her and asked why she was leaving. She mumbled something about not feeling up to it today. So he asked if he could arrange for one of the education officers to take her on a short, highlight tour of the exhibition. Before the tour, the woman and the educator agreed to "take in" ten objects. Together they returned inside, walked past the first two rooms and stopped in front of a large display case in the third section of the exhibition, called "Everyday Life." There the educator pointed to one of the objects and asked the woman what she thought it might be. The woman looked at the object carefully and shook her head. She had no idea. The educator asked her to describe her pillow. The woman's jaw dropped. A pillow! How could that be?

The educator explained that the object was a headrest that functioned similarly to a pillow. They then discussed the logistics of sleeping with a headrest and the reasons why it was elevated (to offer the user protection from snakes or scorpions). Tapping into the woman's fascination, the educator continued to draw the visitor's attention to another Ancient Egyptian object that looks very different but is an integral part of contemporary everyday life: a hand mirror made from bronze. The woman was enthralled. The educator then showed her other familiar objects: a comb, a ruler, and a pair of sandals woven from papyrus.

Monitoring their discussion, the educator guided the woman into the fourth room of the exhibition. There they stopped in front of the mummies. The educator briefly explained the process of mummification and they took a close look at some of the Canopic jars, which were used to store the inner organs of a mummified body. The educator then decided to explore abstract concepts related to the afterlife. So she introduced the woman to Egyptian conceptions of the cosmos.

Together, they moved further inside the fourth room and stopped in front of a wooden sarcophagus. There the educator drew the visitor's attention to the inner section of this sarcophagus, in particular the bottom panel, with its image of Nut, goddess of the sky, painted on it. In this particular instance, the goddess has her arms widespread. The two women spent lots of time discussing the significance of this gesture—outstretched arms welcoming the body into the afterlife as they cradle it for all eternity. This gesture also opened up a personal discussion about death and the afterlife; one that drew deeply on their own private beliefs and deep-seated fears.

It was now time for the visitor to engage with the last of the ten objects. So the educator showed her a terracotta sculpture of a man lying in a boat in the fetal position. His hands covered his ears and the two women stood in front of the display case for at least 20 minutes talking about the significance of the piece beginning with the man: Why was he naked? Why was he in a boat? Why was he in the fetal position? Where was he going? Was this his journey into the afterlife? Is this symbolic of the expectation of rebirth after death? And so forth. Significantly, this was the one object in the exhibition that the educator knew nothing about, so both women were speculating and jointly constructing meanings about the object based on the shared knowledge of Ancient Egyptian life and belief systems they had built up together.

After they had finished their exploration of the terracotta sculpture, the woman thanked the educator profusely! She then decided that she wanted to go back into the exhibition and revisit each object again, but this time, on her own. So they parted company. The educator also returned to the exhibition to work with school groups, but kept an eye on the woman. Initially, she noticed the woman re-engaging with each of the objects they had looked at together. An hour later, she noticed her again. Not only was the woman still in the exhibition she now had an audio guide in her hands. Clearly, a whole new world had opened up for this museum visitor—a whole new world that involved a deeper understanding and appreciation of Ancient Egyptian daily life, death, and cosmology. This, thought the educator to herself, is what museum learning is all about!

To understand more fully what happened, we will begin with an analysis of what happened using analytical tools drawn from networked learning. Clearly we will also need to be able to shed light on the importance of emotion and space to learning as well as understanding more about the nature of the human interaction, especially the criteria for object selection and sequencing that lie at the heart of this story. To do this, we will turn to Binding and then Bonding (Stenglin 2004). As explained earlier, Binding can help us understand why the woman fled the space whilst the Bonding analysis will try to illuminate more about how engagement with the exhibition and its content was largely facilitated through carefully sequenced object selection.

Analysis from the Perspective of Networked Learning

This analysis will begin by first exploring what the participant in our story had to "do" on this tour. It will then examine the social design of this learning experience, and then trace some connections between set and epistemic design as well as co-configuration. To explore what the visitor had to do, let's focus on two objects in the tour: the first and the last. The first object was the headrest (pillow) and the dot-points below list each of the visitor's actions (each action is in *italics*):

- *Follow* the guide to the display case
- *Stop* and *look* at the headrest
- *Listen* to the guide's question (What do you think this might be?)
- *Think* about what the object may be
- *Respond*: *shake her head* (to indicate she does not know)
- *Listen* to the answer
- *Respond*: *jaw drop* (to indicate surprise); *ask a question* (How can that be?)
- *Listen* to more information about the function of the headrest
- *Compare* the logistics of sleeping with both headrest and pillow
- *Discuss* reasons why the headrest was elevated.

The sequence is fairly simple and clearly illustrates how the participant moved through a series of actions in order to engage with the object. Once she had made the connection that this object served the same function as her pillow, she had a strong emotional response of incredulity, followed quickly by a rhetorical question (How can that be?), but she was clearly "hooked" and intrigued at this point. So much so that she was open to learning more and engaging much more deeply with the logistics of using a headrest to sleep on as well as its unique design features (e.g. elevation).

The final object on the tour was the terracotta sculpture of the naked man in the boat with his hands on his ears. This time we will use "broader brush-strokes" to try to understand what the two women were *doing* as they attempted to work out the meaning of the sculpture. Initially, through questions and observations, they explored the literal properties of the work—the nakedness of the figure, its location (in a boat), and its position (fetal). Then drawing on the theoretical knowledge shared on the tour about Ancient Egyptian cosmology, they jointly began to tease out the metaphorical meanings associated with the object.

For instance, they first identified the literal meanings—the fetal position of the man; they then moved on to explore what it symbolizes (birth)—and this led them to speculate what realm this adult man might be born into—the afterlife. In this way the initial literal meanings pointed to the symbolic meanings (birth, nakedness, and a journey) and these in turn provided a springboard for speculating about the abstract cosmological meanings of the sculpture. However, it was not all clear-cut: the positioning of the hands over his ears kept them speculating for some time. Overall, the actions the visitor was engaged in were predominantly mental (looking, thinking, comparing, speculating) and verbal (asking questions and giving responses/information).

In terms of *social design*, the museum story clearly involves two participants—a visitor and an education officer involved in a sustained, face-to-face interaction. Significantly, at the end of the tour, the visitor feels comfortable and secure enough in the exhibition space, and with the objects, to adopt a more distance choice of social design: an audio tour. Moving on to *set design*, the case study comprises one "object set" with two clear characteristics. First, the education officer specifically chose each object in the set; second, the only point of negotiation about object choice was agreement on the total number (ten). Furthermore, the *set design* and *epistemic design* in this experience are extremely closely linked. This means that driving the educator's selection of ten objects was a very clear theory of teaching/learning. Known as the Domains of Learning (Macken-Horarik 1996), this theory will be explored more fully later in the section on Bonding.

Configuration, the final component in Carvalho and Goodyear's framework for the analysis of learning networks, is also relevant to our analysis. Despite careful design, participants do indeed behave in unpredictable ways as the beginning of our story shows. In fact, our visitor's behavior is not just unexpected; it also clearly indicates that emotions play a highly significant role in learning. To better understand this role, in particular the relationship between emotions and learning spaces, we now turn to our social-semiotic tools beginning with Binding.

Binding Analysis

Binding and Bonding are tools drawn from social semiotics, which has been strongly inspired by the research of a group of linguists working with *systemic functional* theory (SFT). The key theorists are Halliday (1978, 1985/1994), Halliday and Hasan (1989), Halliday and Matthiessen (1999), Hodge and Kress (1988), Martin (1992), and Matthiessen (1995). In addition to developing a rich theory of language, SFT has also been used to theorize a wide range of communicative modes including 3D space (O'Toole 1994/2004; White 1994; Ravelli 2000; Stenglin 2002, 2004, 2007, 2008a–b, 2009a–c, 2010, 2012, 2013, 2014; Van Leeuwen 2005; Martin and Stenglin 2007; Ravelli and Stenglin 2008; Stenglin and Djonov 2010; Stenglin and Foureur 2013). Of this work, we are most interested in tools designed to explore how spaces make their occupants *feel*, so we turn to Stenglin's work on Binding.

The challenge for Binding is to explain what happened in that initial encounter between the woman and the space that made her run. What was it about the space that made her feel overwhelmed? Being able to answer questions such as these is vital to the work of people involved in learning in all kinds of spaces: exhibitions, schools, universities, and even virtual spaces (Djonov and Stenglin 2010; Stenglin and Djonov 2010). Many museum professionals acknowledge this point. John Falk and Lynne Dierking, for instance, draw attention to the importance of museum architecture and the design of exhibition spaces on the visitor experience (1995, 2000).[1] In particular, they emphasize that a "strong relationship exists between physical context and feelings" (2000, p. 63). Writing about museum spaces, they point out that this is a very complex relationship to articulate: "often their influences are at once the most subconscious and the most powerful, the hardest to verbalize but the easiest to recall" (1995, p. 31).

One tool that can help explain the relationship between emotion and the built environment is Binding. The big question Binding asks is how spaces can be designed to make their occupants feel comfortable and secure. To answer this, Binding is concerned with the way a space closes in on, or opens up around, a user. If a space closes in on a person too tightly, that person is likely to feel smothered, stifled, and want to escape. Spaces that make people feel suffocated can be considered Too Bound. Examples of spaces that are Too Bound are caves, lifts, tunnels, and mines. Most people feel claustrophobic in spaces that feel Too Bound.

At the other extreme of the Binding scale, we find spaces that do not enclose a person tightly enough. Too little spatial enclosure means that a person may feel either vulnerable or overpowered by a space. Examples of such spaces can be found at the edge of cliffs where the ground drops away abruptly evoking a real sense of vulnerability. They can also be found in horizontally "limitless" spaces such as deserts, the Tundra, or the Australian Nullabor. Spaces that do not provide enough spatial enclosure evoke strong feelings of insecurity and are considered to be "Too Unbound." Both examples of insecurity, Too Bound and Too Unbound, are located at the extreme ends of the Binding scale.

Before moving on to explore the other Binding choices, it is important to acknowledge both individual and cultural variation in Binding. Adventurers such as abseilers, for example, delight in scaling cliffs—a choice that would make most people feel too exposed, too vulnerable, and Too Unbound. Similarly, people raised in underground houses such as dugouts, houses recessed deeply into the earth, grow to feel secure in confined, windowless spaces that evoke feelings of claustrophobia for most people. Despite such variation, it is still possible to identify spatial baselines for security.

The Binding scale thus contains two choices for security: Bound and Unbound spaces. Bound spaces evoke feelings of comfort and protection. They do this by enveloping around people, both vertically and horizontally. Vertical enclosure is provided by walls that "wrap around" occupants whilst horizontal enclosure is provided by ceilings that enclose people together with floors that provide security underfoot. The combined effect of these choices is the creation of a cocoon or womb-like space that evokes a strong sense of refuge or shelter. In an Unbound space, on the other hand, security is experienced as partial freedom from enclosure. For example, when a generous amount of space opens up around an occupant, it can evoke a feeling of openness and expansiveness making the user feel unencumbered, free, and Unbound.

Returning to our scenario, on entry to the first exhibition space the woman finds herself in a small, dark, low-lit area that closes in on her, making her feel Too Bound. This small, dark space appears to function as a spatial metaphor designed to evoke a sense of the small, hidden chambers inside the pyramids. Not only is the volume of space small, it is crammed to overflowing with objects, other visitors, as well as text panels and labels that need to be read, understood, and digested. The combined effect is that the woman feels so overwhelmed by the claustrophobic design of the space, the volume of people occupying the space, and the cognitive information load of the objects, text panels, and labels—that she flees.

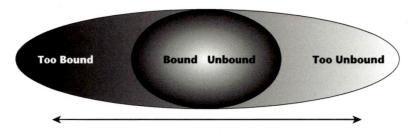

FIGURE 10.1 The Binding Scale

This is obviously not the ideal scenario for museum designers or project teams working on promoting successful blockbuster exhibitions such as *Life and Death under the Pharaohs*. It is much more effective if exhibition spaces can be designed to *establish* and *maintain* a relationship of security with the visitor as they unfold. However, in reality, this is not always the case. So the challenge for museum professionals is whether or not it is possible to rescue the relationship with an overwhelmed, fleeing visitor? If so, how? Or has the visitor been lost irreparably? To shed some light on this challenge, we turn to Bonding.

Bonding Analysis: Inviting the Visitor Back into the Learning Community

The essence of Bonding is human connection. Human connection is one of the most valuable and comforting things there is. The first bridge of connection in our story was laid when the security guard not only noticed the woman leaving but approached her and asked why. He then reached out to her a second time by proactively arranging a short, personalized tour. The third bridge of connectivity was established by the educator, whose offer of ten objects was not overwhelming—it felt "do-able."

Next we need to shed light on the way the educator mediated the interaction between the visitor and the objects in the space. For instance, why did the educator walk past the first two rooms? Was it only because they were crowded? Why didn't she begin by exploring the gods and goddesses of ancient Egypt as well as the role of kings and queens? What was the significance, for instance, in deciding to start with objects such as a pillow, a comb, a ruler, and a mirror? Why did the educator then choose to focus on the more applied dimensions of knowledge such as explaining the processes involved in mummification? Was there any significance in the way she shifted to more theoretical concerns such as explaining the belief systems of another civilization and how they construed the afterlife? Finally, why did she choose to finish with an open-ended discussion about an object that she knew so little about?

To explore these questions, we turn to one particular aspect of Bonding, Macken-Horarik's Domains of Learning (1996). This is an educational theory that does not yet appear to have been applied to museums but is comprehensive enough to offer a unified, inclusive, and cohesive approach to learning in all contexts—museums, schools, universities, and online environments. Grounded in socioculturalism, Macken-Horarik's work includes a theory of knowledge together with a theory of learning. It identifies four domains of knowledge: everyday, applied, theoretical, and reflexive/critical. Let us briefly sketch the characteristics of each.

The *everyday domain* is concerned with the learning that occurs everyday in the lives of each member of a community; for example, tying one's shoelaces. Museum educators sometimes refer to this as informal learning. The *applied domain* is concerned with applied learning. In Australia, this takes place in the technical and further education (TAFE) system (concerned with vocational education and training) and includes subjects such as carpentry, home science, design and technology. It is very much the domain of hands-on learning. The *theoretical domain* refers to the learning that takes place in the institution of schooling K-12 and in the tertiary sphere. Museum educators often refer to this as formal learning. It is concerned with theoretical explanations and abstract concepts. In the final domain, the *reflexive domain*, the boundaries separating the "knower" and the "known" dissolve. Here knowledge is problematized, questioned, and challenged. Some educators refer to this as critical literacy. Others see it as the cutting edges of what is known within a given discipline or field.

In addition to providing us with a theory of learning, Macken-Horarik's four domains give us a powerful analytical tool that can help us explain how the educator in the story was able to engage the visitor so successfully, despite the initial negative response to the space. To do this, we need to add another dimension to Macken-Horarik's theory—one that will allow us to analyze the role of objects in the guided tour. Being able to analyze each object is vital because objects are the nucleus of our *set design*. So we will analyze each object from two complementary angles: their form (shape) and their function (the purpose which they were designed to serve). These two dimensions are vital as they shed light on so many important aspects of the guided tour. Let us now apply the Domains of Learning to the analysis of our story.

First of all, the educator began by "tapping into" the visitor's *everyday knowledge* (represented by the headrest and mirror). These are everyday objects familiar to most people living in Western society. So they represent the ideal starting point for an exploration of a different cultural civilization, as they are recognizable artifacts most people can easily relate to.

In analyzing these objects, let us think about them in terms of both their form (shape) and function (purpose). The function of each object listed above is familiar but they engaged the visitor because their form (or shape) was striking. For instance, the headrest appeared to be unfamiliar but it was not—it is an object that functions in exactly the same way as a pillow. Once this commonality was established—that is, headrest equals pillow—the visitor was intrigued and a multitude of questions flowed from her. Similarly, with the mirror: it is not immediately obvious how an opaque bronze object can function as a mirror. The form is obscure until the capacity of bronze to be polished and offer reflection is pointed out. Then the visitor can "see" how the object functions as a mirror—it suddenly becomes crystal clear. Significantly, it was this *tension* between form and function that first connected the woman with these objects by piquing her interest and curiosity. This form–function tension also provided a "hook" for engagement with the exhibits whilst simultaneously giving the educator a foundation on which to build during the rest of the tour.

Having established a connection between the everyday life of the visitor and the lives of Ancient Egyptian people, the educator's next move was to *consolidate* the visitor's sense of *familiarity* with ancient Egyptian life. This was done by drawing attention to four other objects from the everyday domain: a comb, a ruler, a pair of sandals, and a pair of earrings. Significantly, this time, each object was recognizable in terms of both form and function. Such familiarity served a very important function as it gave the visitor a clear message: everyday life then was not that different to how it is now. This was reassuring.

The educator next moved the visitor into the *applied domain* by explaining the processes involved in mummification. These were represented, in part, by the Canopic jars. Here the interplay between form and function was different again. The form (shape) of the Canopic jars is a familiar one—large rounded jars with a solid lid—but their function is not familiar because the social practices associated with mummification are foreign to most people living in contemporary Western societies. This disjunction is an important one from the perspective of learning because it means the "seemingly familiar" object is actually "unfamiliar" and this opens up the need for new knowledge and understandings. Motivated by the visitor's disposition to learn more, the educator now has the ideal opportunity to "fill in the gaps" for the visitor by explaining the social practices associated with mummification, culminating in the placement of human entrails inside the Canopic jars.

Building on this momentum, the educator next moved into the *theoretical domain* by explaining the belief systems of the afterlife using one of the mummies and the sarcophagus of the goddess Nut as a focal point. Once again, the sarcophagus—a coffin—has a form that is reasonably familiar to the visitor as an object. The unfamiliar dimension is its iconography, which is grounded in the spiritual belief systems of Ancient Egyptian culture. Thus it is the function of the imagery adorning the sarcophagus that is inaccessible to the visitor; creating the opening for the educator to "unpack" this symbolism for the visitor, in particular the layers of cosmological belief associated with the goddess Nut, visually represented in blue to reflect her status as the goddess of the sky as well as the accompanying symbols such as the ankh.

In addition, the gesture of Nut's far-reaching, all encompassing, and embracing arms that cradle the body as they welcome it into eternity provide the educator and visitor with a highly personal entry point for engaging with Ancient Egyptian beliefs of the afterlife bringing them briefly back to the everyday domain and their own value systems. As this analysis shows, the domains are not intended to represent a linear, lock-step progression of learning—but rather a fluid heuristic that can be traversed in various ways as the need arises. Conceivably, for instance, learners often have to move back and forth between theoretical constructs and applied examples as they engage in ongoing activities of learning at school and at university.

The final domain the educator and visitor traversed was the *reflexive domain*. This was their very last stop on the highlights tour and the last object they explored together. Essentially, it involved them interpreting the meaning of a terracotta sculpture, which neither woman knew much about. The form of the object was familiar enough—a terracotta sculpture of a male figure in a boat. Once again, its function was more speculative—he was naked, in a boat, and curled in the fetal position. Having built up considerable knowledge and shared understandings of Ancient Egyptian cosmology, they drew on this to explore themes of a spiritual journey to the afterlife, spiritual rebirth, and eternal life. Significantly, it was at this point that the woman took the lead in terms of analyzing the object and its social significance: an enormous turning point from her initial "flight response" to the exhibition.

Before exploring the implications of the Binding and Bonding analysis, let us stop and take stock of the ten objects in the tour. As we do this, we will try to recap their qualities in terms of form and function as well as the Domain of Learning they were drawn from as summarized in Table 10.1.

One of the striking things about this table is that more than half of the objects on the tour came from the everyday domain. The second striking thing is that there appear to be three very distinct phases in the tour: Phase 1 (unfamiliar form—familiar function), Phase 2 (familiar form—familiar function) and Phase 3 (familiar form—unfamiliar function). In trying to understand the first observation, why the tour was so strongly weighted toward the everyday domain, it appears that it was so because such familiarity was needed to reassure the woman and evoke a strong sense of security. A focus on accessible objects reinforced the message that she could, indeed, relate to the exhibition.

The second observation identifies three different phases of the tour and each of these seems to serve a different but complementary function. For example, Phase 1 moves from "seemingly"

TABLE 10.1 Summary of the Objects on the Highlights Tour

Object	Form	Function	Domain
1. Headrest	Unfamiliar	Familiar	Everyday: arouse curiosity
2. Mirror	Unfamiliar	Familiar	Everyday: arouse curiosity
3. Comb	Familiar	Familiar	Everyday: confirm familiarity
4. Ruler	Familiar	Familiar	Everyday: confirm familiarity
5. Sandals	Familiar	Familiar	Everyday: confirm familiarity
6. Earrings	Familiar	Familiar	Everyday: confirm familiarity
7. Canopic jars	Familiar	Unfamiliar	Applied: open new knowledge
8. Mummy	Familiar	Unfamiliar	Theoretical: open new knowledge
9. Sarcophagus	Familiar	Unfamiliar	Theoretical: open new knowledge
10. Sculpture of man in boat	Familiar	Unfamiliar	Reflexive: explore fluid, abstract, more speculative meanings

unfamiliar forms to familiar functions. It thus appears designed to *engage* the woman, pique her curiosity, and facilitate her emotional and intellectual connection with the exhibition. It is "the hook" for her engagement. Phase 2 explores familiar forms and familiar functions. It builds on this message of familiarity and *reinforces*, with everyday objects, that the material cultural heritage on display is highly accessible. It is "the security blanket." The final phase, which moves from "seemingly" familiar forms to their unfamiliar functions, uses the notion of familiarity as a springboard from which to open up and explore a series of new applied, theoretical, and reflexive understandings. It is "the launch pad" for exploring new knowledge such as cosmology with its heavy symbolism and abstraction.

All three phases, moreover, seem to be integral to the learning experience of this visitor who began by feeling overwhelmed—overwhelmed by the space and overwhelmed by the cognitive load of the objects/information on display. Yet interestingly, only four objects out of the ten were used to move the visitor into the applied, theoretical, and reflexive domains. Clearly this was enough to help the visitor feel able to engage as an independent learner. The first step in her independent learning involved consolidation: revisiting each of the ten objects alone and reconnecting with it in her own time and in her own way. The second step confirmed that she had indeed crossed the bridge to independent learning: she purchased an audio guide and navigated the exhibition again, on her own, for the third time.

Before our analysis draws to a close, let's return to *configuration* and the phenomena of learners surprising us by doing things we did not expect. The purchase of an audio guide was unexpected, as the woman had already spent much longer than the average 20 minutes in this exhibition. This purchase clearly indicates the woman was totally absorbed in Ancient Egyptian cultural heritage by this point—a state Csikszentmihalyi (1997) refers to as the "flow." In our story, it represents a remarkable and inspiring achievement as it signals a notable shift from one extreme of learner autonomy (flight) to another (deep engagement). Importantly, it was facilitated by a combination of human interaction and skilled orchestration of artifacts (set), movement, selection of things to do (epistemic), and emotion, in which subtle reading of how the visitor was reacting was interwoven with suggestions and questions, closely connected to artifacts in the museum.

The Implications of the Binding and Bonding Analysis

One striking thing about the educator's role in making the objects, knowledge, and understandings accessible to the woman is how strongly it impacted on Binding in the space. In particular, it transformed the woman's emotional relationship with the space from one of claustrophobia to one of such comfort and security she remained in the space for another hour. This seems to suggest that aligning people positively around shared knowledge and understandings has the potential to impact not only on their relationship with the space, but, by implication, also on their (inter) personal relationships with the cultural institution (Bonding).

As the Bonding analysis also shows, once visitors are inside exhibition spaces, another important aspect of the visitor experience comes into play: the interactions that mediate the exhibition experience. Clearly, the interaction between the educator and the visitor in the preceding encounter is an important one for museum professionals involved in both the design of exhibitions and the training of museum staff to understand. Such training also appears to be highly relevant to security staff as they were the "first port of call" in our anecdote, but it is particularly relevant to staff giving guided tours and education officers working with school groups. The potential benefit of such training, if well designed and implemented, is visitor engagement that far exceeds the average 20-minute limit in most exhibitions.

Moreover, the expansion of the Domains of Learning in this chapter to include a focus on form and function, in relation to objects, offers a more finely grained set of tools for educators to work with. The newly theorized form/function complementarity provides a guide for informed object choice during the design of a tour or the design of hands-on learning activities (*set* and *epistemic design*). Future research could explore the phases we have identified in this chapter even more. For instance, our tour had three phases: the hook, the security blanket, and the launch pad. It would be interesting to explore whether most tours need all three phases and a security blanket as strong as our visitor did, or whether other phases (yet to be identified) may better suit the needs of different learners.

Furthermore, even though the story was about learning in a museum context, the tools of Binding and Bonding have much broader applicability. For a start, both can be applied to learning in schools and universities. Some university lecturers, for instance, use lighting choices to make lecture theaters feel Bound or Unbound. Dimming the lights makes a space feel Bound. In a lecture theater, this gives salience to PowerPoint slides and focuses student attention on the information—a useful strategy when key theoretical concepts are being introduced, defined, and exemplified (theoretical domain). Increasing lighting levels has the converse effect—it unbinds a space and creates a freer, more open environment. This is strategic when students are required to work in groups or pairs on problem-solving activities (applied domain).

Binding and Bonding are equally applicable to ICT and have already been applied to the analysis of a hypermedia art adventure for young children (Djonov and Stenglin 2010; Stenglin and Djonov 2010). This adventure uses narrative to engage learners but close analysis shows several missed opportunities. First, the Binding analysis showed how the design "trapped" and constrained learners evoking feelings of insecurity and frustration rather than opening up options for exploration. Similarly, the Bonding analysis showed that only *one* of the many task sequences (epistemic design) utilized its full potential. It also showed that the message delivered by the game about the dangers of time travel missed the mark on an important pedagogic opportunity. The benefits of Binding and Bonding to ICT thus appear to be an explicit focus on emotions in learning and the provision of an epistemic framework, which provides accessible learner starting points in relation to knowledge building, and a strong scaffold for principled and engaged knowledge progression.

In closing, Binding and Bonding are powerful tools. They can add a more nuanced perspective to our understing of learning networks; how the complexities of what has been designed (set, epistemic, and social) may influence the activities of learners and how learning takes place in galleries/museums, schools/universities, and ICT. Practically oriented, they help us understand the dialectic between space, learning, and emotion; they also provide us with a framework for starting where learners "are at" by giving them accessible entry points for engaging with the objects and/or key concepts. Bonding through the domains also provides a systematic framework designed to "move learners on" into theoretical, applied, and critical understandings. One of its strengths is that it helps learners move beyond common-sense knowledge and understandings. It also has the potential to rescue learners who are feeling overwhelmed by cognitive load and spatial insecurity. The expanded framework for working with objects through a focus on form and function also opens up many new and exciting possibilities. As a result, the potential for application to learning in real and "virtual spaces," face-to-face or in more distant modes, is enormous and has yet to be fully explored.

Endnote

1. This model was initially known as the Interactive Experience Model (Falk and Dierking 1992).

References

Carvalho, L. and Goodyear, P., eds., 2014. *The architecture of productive learning networks*. New York: Routledge.

Csikszentmihalyi, M., 1997. *Finding flow: The psychology of engagement with everyday life*. New York: Basic Books.

Djonov, E. and Stenglin, M., 2010. Evaluating narrative as a bridge to learning in a hypermedia "artedventure" for children. In: C. Matthiessen, C. Wu, and M. Herke, eds., *Proceedings of ISFC 35: Voices around the world*, July 21–25, 2008 (Vol. 2, pp. 103–108). Sydney: The 35th ISFC Organizing Committee.

Falk, J. and Dierking, L., 1992. *The museum experience*. Washington, DC: Whalesback Books.

Falk, J. and Dierking, L., 1995. Recalling the museum experience. *Journal of Museum Education*, 20(2), 10–13.

Falk, J. and Dierking, L., 2000. *Learning from museums: Visitor experiences and the making of meaning*. New York: AltaMira Press.

Halliday, M. A. K., 1978. *Language as a social semiotic: The social interpretation of language and meaning*. London: Edward Arnold.

Halliday, M. A. K., 1985/1994. *An introduction to functional grammar*. London: Arnold.

Halliday, M. A. K. and Hasan, R., 1989. *Language, context and text: Aspects of language in a social semiotic perspective*, 2nd edition. Oxford: Oxford University Press.

Halliday M. A. K. and Matthiessen C. M. I. M., 1999. *Construing experience through meaning: A language-based approach to cognition*. Open Linguistics Series. London: Continuum International.

Hodge, R. and G. Kress., 1988. *Social semiotics*. Cambridge: Polity.

MacGregor, N., 2010. *A history of the world in 100 objects*. London: Allen Lane.

Macken-Horarik, M., 1996. *Construing the invisible: Specialized literacy practices in junior secondary English*. Thesis (Ph.D.). The University of Sydney.

Martin, J. R., 1992. *English text: System and structure*. Amsterdam: John Benjamins Publishing Company.

Martin, J. R. and Stenglin, M., 2007. Materialising reconciliation: Negotiating difference in a post-colonial exhibition. In: T. Royce and W. Bowcher, eds., *New Directions in the analysis of multimodal discourse* (pp. 215–238). Mahwah, NJ: Lawrence Erlbaum Associates.

Matthiessen, C.M.I.M., 1995. *Lexicogrammatical cartography: English systems*. Tokyo: International Language Sciences Publishers.

O'Toole, M., 1994/2004. *The language of displayed art*. New York: Routledge.

Ravelli, L. R., 2000. Beyond shopping: Constructing the Olympics in three-dimensional text. *Text & Talk*, 20(4), 489–516.

Ravelli, L. R. and Stenglin, M., 2008. Feeling space: Interpersonal communication and spatial semiotics. In: E. Ventola and Gerd Antos, eds., *Handbook of applied linguistics, Volume 2: Interpersonal Communication* (pp. 355–393). Berlin: Mouton de Gruyter.

Serrell, B., 1997. Paying attention: The duration and allocation of visitors' time in museum exhibitions. *Curator: The Museum Journal*, 40(2), 108–125.

Stenglin, M., 2002. Comfort and security: A challenge for exhibition design. In: L. Kelly and J. Barrett, eds., *UNCOVER: Volume 1* (pp. 17–22). Sydney: Australian Museum.

Stenglin, M., 2004. *Packaging curiosities: Towards a grammar of three-dimensional space*. Thesis (Ph.D.). The University of Sydney.

Stenglin, M., 2007. Making art accessible: Opening up a whole new world. *Visual Communication*, special edition. *Immersion*, 6(2), 202–213.

Stenglin, M., 2008a. Binding: A resource for exploring interpersonal meaning in 3D space. *Social Semiotics*, 18(4), 425–447.

Stenglin, M., 2008b. Olympism: How a bonding icon gets its "charge." In: L. Unsworth, ed., *Multimodal semiotics: Functional analysis in the contexts of education* (pp. 50–66). London/New York: Continuum,

Stenglin, M., 2009a. Space odyssey: Towards a social semiotic model of 3D space. *Visual Communication*, 8(1), 35–64.

Stenglin, M., 2009b. Space and communication in exhibitions: Unravelling the nexus. In: C. Jewitt, ed., *Routledge handbook of multimodal analysis* (pp. 272–283). Abingdon, UK/New York: Routledge.

Stenglin, M., 2009c. From musing to amusing: Semogenesis and Western museums. In: E. Ventola and A. J. Moya Guijarro, eds., *The world shown and the world told* (pp. 245–265). New York: Palgrave Macmillan.

Stenglin, M., 2010. Spaced out: An evolving cartography of a visceral semiotic. In: S. Dreyfus, S. Hood and M. Stenglin, eds., *Semiotic margins: Meaning in multimodalities* (pp. 73–100). London: Continuum.

Stenglin, M., 2012. "Glocalisation": Exploring the dialectic between the local and the global. In: W. L. Bowcher, ed., *Multimodal texts from around the world: Cultural and linguistic insights* (pp. 123–145). New York: Palgrave Macmillan.

Stenglin, M., 2013. Interpersonal meaning in 3D space: Binding creates hope for bonding. In: E. Montagna, ed., *Readings in intersemiosis and multimedia* (pp. 319–337). Como/Pavia, Italy: IBIS Editions.

Stenglin, M. 2014. Space and communication in exhibitions: Unraveling the nexus. In: C. Jewitt, ed., *The Routledge handbook of multimodal analysis* (pp. 419–430). New York: Routledge.

Stenglin, M., and Djonov, E., 2010. Unpacking narratives in a hypermedia art adventure for children. In: C. R. Hoffman, ed., *Narrative revisited: Telling a story in the age of new media* (pp. 185–212). Philadelphia, PA: John Benjamins Publishing Company.

Stenglin, M. and Foureur, M., 2013. Designing out the fear cascade to increase the likelihood of normal birth. *Midwifery*, 29(8), 819–825.

Van Leeuwen, T., 2005. *Introducing social semiotics*. New York: Routledge.

White, P., 1994. Images of the shark: Jaws, gold fish or cuddly toy? An analysis of the Australian Museum's 1994 shark exhibition from a communicative perspective. Unpublished manuscript. Department of Linguistics, The University of Sydney.

11

THE O IN MONA

Reshaping Museum Spaces

Lucila Carvalho

In a recent article published in the *New York Times*, Steve Lohr claimed that museums are being redefined as they adapt to the digital age. The transformation, he says, "promises to touch every aspect of what museums do, from how art and objects are presented and experienced to what is defined as art" (Lohr 2014). This chapter takes a socio-spatial networked learning approach to exploring the use of mobile technologies in the digital enhancement of informal learning experiences in museums. The chapter situates museums as spaces for networked learning, delving into the ways technology and social media are influencing people's experiences of cultural heritage, through co-created museum-visitor activities. More specifically, the chapter illustrates the combination of two sets of theoretical ideas that help uncover some important relationships between "people and things." It uses the architectural framework from Goodyear and Carvalho (2014) to distinguish and draw relationships between (i) *designable* and *emergent* phenomena in complex learning situations, and (ii) the design of tasks and the design of the physical and social setting within which activities unfold. These ideas are combined with Ian Hodder's theory of "entanglement," which turns out to be particularly useful for distinguishing different kinds of relationships between people and things and for understanding how networks of entangled people and things adjust to disruption (Hodder 2012, 2013, 2104; Goodyear, Carvalho, and Dohn 2014; Yeoman and Carvalho 2014). Empirical material to illustrate the argument is drawn from a case study of the Museum of Old and New Art (MONA) in Hobart, Tasmania, with special attention being paid to the incorporation of a novel mobile device (the "O") in people's visits to MONA. Experienced practitioners who carry out design and evaluation work in museums *tacitly* understand many of the subtle, structural relations between people and things. One of the aims of this chapter is to render such connections more visible, and thereby more accessible to others.

Museums as Networked Learning Spaces

Museums are significant cultural institutions. They have long been recognized as public spaces for learning, where people can debate and negotiate ideas about the future, and reflect on characteristics and concerns of their community (Falk and Dierking 1992, 2013; Hein 1998; Hooper-Greenhill 2000; Knutson and Crowley 2005). Anderson (2011) points out that at the heart of public spaces are social relationships. Public spaces for learning, such as museums, help shape and reflect the values of our societies, stimulating thinking and generating an awareness about who uses these spaces, and for what reasons they do so, or who controls it and how; and amidst this process, museums also raise fundamental questions about cultural rights and democracy (Anderson 2011). Museums do this by encouraging visitor participation, stimulating creativity and intercultural exchange, creating opportunities for raising awareness of significant events from the past, and showing how these may relate to our present and future. They house artifacts that are of significance for science, arts, culture, and history, which explain our heritage and contribute to community education. Museums promote informal and lifelong learning, welcoming engagement and attracting people from different backgrounds and ages. They offer significant opportunities as out-of-school learning spaces. In sum, museums are important community anchors, and reputable places of trust and expertise.

In recent years, the notion of museums as participatory cultural institutions, where visitors have opportunities to create, share, and connect to others around a given topic of interest, has gained currency (Simon 2010). This phenomenon coincides with the proliferation of digital technologies and social media, whose uses are also opening up new opportunities for museum education (Sharples, Taylor, and Vavoula 2007; Sharples et al. 2009; Giaccardi 2012; Kress and Selander 2012; Lohr 2014). Mobile technologies and social media enable people to engage in activities of collection, preservation, and interpretation of digital artifacts; as a result, there are new forms of heritage practices emerging (Giaccardi 2012). This is apparent in the ways in which people are capturing their life experiences, the nature of the artifacts they are creating, and the ways in which individuals and communities curate and share them. As familiarity with digital technologies increases, so do museum visitors' expectations about the style and quality of exhibitions, options for the integration of innovative technologies, the levels and kinds of information delivered, audience participation, and so on (Linge et al. 2012; Linge, Booth, and Pearson Chapter 12). Digital technologies are challenging museum social practices and the ways our society understands and approaches cultural heritage (Giaccardi 2012; Smith 2013). They are also enabling new forms of in-museum interactive experiences (CATH Projects 2014; CHESS 2014; Jewitt 2012; Smith 2013).

The Museum of Old and New Art (MONA)

The Museum of Old and New Art is situated in Hobart (Australia). MONA houses the private collection of the philanthropist and gambler David Walsh. It includes artworks from different cultures, times, artists, and art forms. Nicole Durling, co-director of exhibitions and collections, and senior curator at MONA, refers to MONA's collection as revolving around the motivations of why humans make art (personal communication, May 16, 2015). The museum's opening in 2011 was an occasion for controversy, with some suggesting it marked a new era for museums, and others fearing that it was the end of art (Flanagan 2013).

Designed by the architect Nonda Katsalidis and his team, MONA won the Sir Zelman Cowen Award for Public Architecture in 2012. The building is set into a sandstone hill, with part of its structure buried underground (Figure 11.1).[1] Its architectural design takes the visual and physical extensions of the landscape into account, in an effort to maintain the building structure in harmony with the surrounding riverbank topography of the Derwent River (Fender Katsalidis Architects 2015).

MONA admits residents of Tasmania and people under the age of eighteen free of charge. MONA has been described as a place that is saying to the world that "art should be accessible to everyone and should not be limited to an elite" (Scott 2011, p.17). In 2012, the Lonely Planet Guide ranked Hobart as one of the top ten cities in the world to visit, justifying the city's nomination by reference to MONA (ABC News 2012a). Lonely Planet's founder compared MONA and Hobart to the Guggenheim in Bilbao. The building of MONA has been cited as "an example of how art and architecture can have an instant impact on the social and cultural reputation of a place" (Butler,

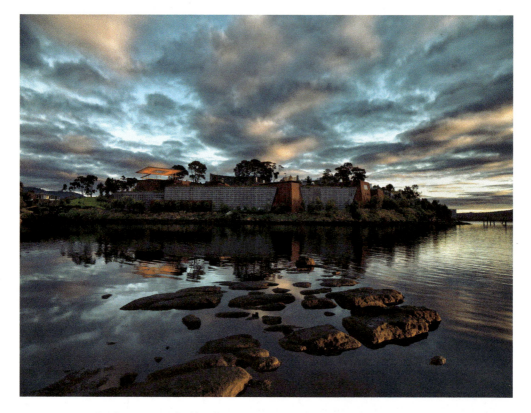

FIGURE 11.1   MONA, Museum of Old and New Art. MONA's Southern Facade Viewed from Little Frying
Pan Island, South of the Museum, and View of Amarna (2015) Skyspace Installation during
Dawn Sequence. Artist: James Turrell (Born 1943, Los Angeles, California). Materials: Steel
Frame, Fiberglass Foam Sandwich Roof Construction, Fiberglass Reinforced Concrete Seating

Source: MONA/Rémi Chauvin. Image courtesy of MONA Museum of Old and New Art, Hobart, Tasmania,
Australia

Hurst, and Smith 2011). MONA is seen as making a radical change to the significance of Hobart
and Tasmania, as places worth the attention of visitors from around the globe.

MONA has over 6,000 square meters of exhibition space, some of which is filled with conventional museum objects, such as cases displaying crafted Roman gold coins on a black background
(Scott 2011). These sit alongside other more unusual features, or what academic Rachel Hurst calls
"a number of corporeal metaphors" that the architectural design suggests (Butler et al. 2011). As
described by Hurst:

> MONA embraces the elemental qualities of water, light, air and smell, with an impressive bal-
> ance between seamless mechanical servicing and raw sensory effect. Reinforcing the tactility
> of much of the art, there are clammy porous tunnels, dazzling crystalline pyramidal passages,
> smooth toxic rooms of lead and glass, and foetid laboratories for gastroenterological art. This
> is multi-sensory architecture of great competence, in terms of both concept and execution.
> (Butler et al. 2011)

On entering the space, visitors are invited to go down three levels, starting their visit from the
bottom up, and away from the light, which is unusual in a museum setting. At MONA, light and

FIGURE 11.2 Untitled, 2008. Artist: Hubert Duprat (born 1957, Nérac, France). Materials: Iceland Spar (Calcite Crystals), Glue

Source: MONA/Rémi Chauvin. Image Courtesy of MONA Museum of Old and New Art, Hobart, Tasmania, Australia

FIGURE 11.3 MONA, Museum of Old and New Art

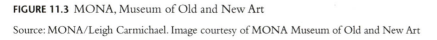

Source: MONA/Leigh Carmichael. Image courtesy of MONA Museum of Old and New Art

darkness are, nevertheless, essential elements of the space (see Figure 11.2 and Figure 11.3). This turns out to be important in a number of ways, not least because low light levels enhance the readability of the screen on the "O."

The O

The O is MONA's tour guide system, developed by Art Processors (2015) and deployed on an iPod Touch (Figure 11.4). Every visitor is offered a pair of headphones and the O at the museum entrance. They carry and interact with the O throughout their visit. The O "senses" the section of the museum in which the visitor is located, displaying pictures of the artworks in that area. The visitor then interacts with the O, selecting which art pieces he or she wants to learn more about. All the information visitors have access to comes solely via the O, and so the walls of the museum space are free of labels and other written messages.

The O is a key element in the design of MONA and in the network of learning experiences the museum offers. There are many different ways in which the device enables people (visitors) to connect to one another and to museum staff and artists, as well as to resources. One of the features of the O is that, as with other audio guides, the device enables visitors to access (learning)[2] resources on request. The way that the platform does that is by sensing where the visitor is physically situated. It then displays a listing of art pieces according to the visitor's proximity, with the closest piece appearing at the top of the list. This list shows title and artist and the visitor then chooses whether to access additional information, by tapping on the image matching the artwork on-screen. At the visitor's request, access is granted to an audio file containing an interview with an artist, more information about a specific piece, a passage specially written by a curator, and so on. However, in contrast

FIGURE 11.4 MONA "O" Device. Created by: Art Processors Pty Ltd.

Source: MONA/Matt Newton. Image Courtesy MONA Museum of Old and New Art, Hobart, Tasmania, Australia

to other museums where audio guides are optional, and often involve extra costs for the visitor, at MONA all visitors receive the O as part of their admission. The design envisages everyone accessing resources via their interactions with the mobile device. Each of the visitors, nevertheless, exercises agency with respect to the objects they want to learn more about. They may also choose not to engage with the device, ignoring any information about the objects or interference in their visit.

In the next few sections, I discuss some examples of the types of networked learning activities afforded by the device (see Linge et al. Chapter 12, for a discussion about the practicalities of implementing guide systems in museums).

Networked Learning: Connecting to Other Visitors and One's Future Self

The O enables the collection of information about what objects a visitor likes or dislikes—through a simple click on a Love or Hate icon. It also allows visitors to see how others voted on a particular object of interest, and, in so doing, visitors become aware of what may please others, or how others in the community see the object in question. Although these icons provide simple factual information, showing percentages of how many others have liked object X, they may also act as a scaffolding element, subtly inviting visitors to ponder more deeply whether they like or dislike something, and why. Moreover, visitors' individual interactions with the O, and the information they get about objects through the prompts they receive, are not always necessarily the same (Art Processors 2015). This is an interesting feature of the O, which aims at encouraging visitors, particularly those visiting the museum in groups, with family or friends, to exchange views about what they learn. The O also allows visitors to communicate their impressions to other visitors, by recording messages for future users of the device they currently hold; for example, commenting on things they liked and would recommend.

When visitors engage in the activity of liking or disliking objects, or as they leave messages to others in their O, they are also enabling museum staff to gather information about visitor activity and preferences. Staff can then potentially learn about what appeals (or not) to people visiting the museum. The O permits collection of data, over time, about visitors' movements and pathways, their engagement levels, and what information they have accessed (Art Processors 2015). It records the individual sights that were seen by each visitor and for how long the visitor engaged with what they were seeing or hearing through the O. Thus, there are many ways and levels of museum learning, not only from a visitors' perspective, in terms of learning about a particular artwork, how it was made, its historical or cultural significance, etc. Visitors also learn about others in the community, as they are given opportunities to check and exchange impressions with other museum visitors. In addition, the network of learners includes the museum staff, through the insights they gain about visitors' activity.

Visitors get access to (learning) resources via their interactions with the O, but there are also activity-based connections happening over time and space. As explained above, the device records the trajectory of visitors in the physical space, the resources they have accessed during the visit, and so on. This information is then made available to each person at the very end of their visit, when visitors are offered opportunities to continue their engagement, by having their trajectory and the objects they saw emailed to them. Visitors who choose to do this can subsequently re-enact their visit, or gain access to objects they missed whilst at the museum.

Physical Space and People's Activities

The connections between the O and the physical qualities of the museum space are plain to see. The device houses all the information available to visitors, and as a consequence no written material is seen in the galleries and exhibition spaces. The absence of written signs on the walls, in turn, affects the activity of people (both visitors and museum staff). For example, curators and designers are left free to experiment with new ways of designing exhibitions and gallery spaces. Moreover, since visitors are no longer required to get close to tags on the walls, in order to read them, their movements and trajectories—the way they walk within the space—are different. Unlike exhibition rooms with entry panels that indicate where an exhibition starts, and which direction is to be followed, MONA visitors are only shown the start of their whole museum visit—as they descend the floors. From then on, they choose their own trajectories, without clues or labels on the walls to direct them.

Earlier in the chapter, I mentioned lighting as one of the salient design aspects of MONA, suggesting how such design connects to the O. I stated that, as with any iPod Touch device, the O requires that the internal physical space of MONA not be too bright. Instead there is generally a dim light, so that visitors can easily see what appears on its small screen. This is not, however, the only way that lighting design influences what visitors see and do in the museum space. In fact, lighting design is strategically configured to reveal aspects of the building and art pieces at various points, through careful balancing between light and darkness (see Figure 11.5 and Figure 11.6). Salisbury (Light Project 2015), one of the designers of MONA, reveals: "For the spiral entry staircase that leads you down into the museum, we used concealed details of light all the way down . . . most of the details within the building are concealed details through gaps and openings in the wall to emphasize the subterranean setting and create a feeling of anticipation moving into and through the exhibition spaces" (Light Project 2015).

The use of light shows that care was taken to illuminate certain points with the intention of helping visitors to notice an art piece or a specific feature of the building, provoking emotions (such

FIGURE 11.5 Corten Stairwell and Surrounding Gallery

Source: Rémi Chauvin. Image Courtesy of MONA Museum of Old and New Art, Hobart, Tasmania, Australia

FIGURE 11.6
Corten Stairwell and
Surrounding Artworks

Source: MONA/Leigh
Carmichael. Image courtesy of
MONA Museum of Old and
New Art, Hobart, Tasmania,
Australia

as feelings of anticipation). This may at first appear as a feature in its architectural design, disconnected from educational design. However, lighting arrangements that evoke visitors' emotions (e.g. anticipation) may potentially affect or nurture curiosity, setting a mood to what can be discovered out there (see Stenglin Chapter 10, for the role of emotions in networked learning).

Theorizing the O in MONA: Architecture and Entanglement

Sharples et al. (2007) speak of learning as "a process of coming to know through conversation across continually re-constructed contexts" (p.10), claiming that it is crucial that we understand the impact of the mobility of learners and how such a phenomenon is augmented by personal and public technology, contributing to ongoing processes of gaining new knowledge, skills, and experience. There are different types of "mobility," which may or may not necessarily be connected to one another; these include mobility in physical space, of technology, in conceptual space, in social space, and learning being dispersed in time (Sharples et al. 2009).

Although many contemporary theories acknowledge the physically and socially situated nature of learning (e.g. Illeris 2009), scholars have only recently been paying more attention to the impact of the "quality of materials" and space, in shaping people's experiences (Ingold 2013; Goodyear et al. 2014). Social materialist approaches argue for the foregrounding of the material alongside the human processes in learning, challenging theories that place social, cultural, and personal as the *only* defining factors for what it means to learn (Fenwick, Edwards, and Sawchuk 2011). Essentially, a social materialist perspective sees the social *and* the material as inextricably related, and so "there is no social that is not also material, and no material that is not also social" (Orlikowski 2007, p. 1437). However, as pointed out by Hodder (2014), relational approaches that see mind and matter, or human and thing, as co-constituting each other, often miss an important aspect in the so-called network of humans and things—the fact that people's relationships with things are often asymmetrical, and that this asymmetry often leads to entrapments in particular pathways, from which it is hard to detach (Hodder 2014). Boddington and Boys (2011) speak of learning as situated and embodied, but in a way that goes beyond the qualities of the physical space itself, to embrace its relationships with individual, social, cultural, and political contexts. Their notion of learning spaces considers not only the material elements displayed in a given scenario, but also the activities of those interacting in that stage, their relationship to the processes of learning, teaching, and researching, and how these are organized and connected. In such a socio-spatial perspective, space is to be understood in *connection* to how it is occupied. This socio-spatial notion, when combined with networked learning, provides an ideal basis for exploring museums as place-based spaces for networked learning. For the analysis of the O in MONA, two sets of theoretical ideas were combined: the Activity-Centered Analysis and Design (ACAD) framework from Goodyear and Carvalho (2014) and Hodder's theory of entanglement (2012).

The Activity-Centered Analysis and Design Framework

Networked learning involves technology-mediated interactions that encourage connections between people, with learning resources and with a learning community (Goodyear, Hodgson, and Steeples 1998). Understanding *connections* between tools, tasks, social organization, and their effects on people's activity is central to networked learning (Goodyear 2005). Network analysis requires paying attention to the movement of people, objects, or messages (Goodyear and Carvalho 2014). Thus, for the analysis of MONA learning network, it is necessary to consider whether/how people (visitors) are connected to one another (and to museum staff, such as exhibition designers, curators, artists, etc.), whether people are able to access (learning) resources via technology, and whether these facilitate activity-based connections over time and space.

The architectural framework of Goodyear and Carvalho (2014) provides the basis for the analysis of the ways digital and material artifacts, as well as people, come together in the museum space. This ACAD framework has been previously used in the analysis of several online networks (Carvalho and Goodyear 2014). The framework distinguishes between elements that can be designed and emergent activity, stressing that what people *do* often reconfigures whatever had been designed. It conceptualizes four analytical dimensions, three of which account for designable components, such as those in: *set design,* that is the tools and materials, in both physical and digital spaces; *epistemic design,* which refers to proposed learning tasks, knowledge, and ways of knowing; and *social design,* which includes suggestions of group arrangements, scripted roles. A fourth dimension—*co-creation and co-configuration activity*—connects what has been designed to what people do. The analysis of MONA learning network discussed in this chapter focuses on elements in *set design,* combining Goodyear and Carvalho's (2014) framing with Hodder's theory of entanglement (2012), which helps unveil nuances in *how* elements in *set design* connect to people's activity, that is, on the ties between space, objects, and people within the networked museum space.

Entanglement and the Dependence and Dependency between Things (T) and Humans (H)

Hodder (2012, 2014) poses that humans rely on tools to evolve as individuals, as society, or to adapt to their environment; and whilst humans rely on things in order to develop their goals, such reliance also requires that things are maintained and cared for, so that they can be relied on. As a result, humans become entrapped in the lives and temporalities of things. Thus, in line with other relational approaches in the social sciences and humanities, Hodder's (2014) theory of entanglement acknowledges that humans and things are relationally produced. However, his focus is on *dependence* rather than relationality, on how humans get caught in dynamic relations with things; or in other words, the ways humans "depend on things that depend on humans" (Hodder 2014, p. 20). Hodder's theory of entanglement conceptualizes the dialectic of *dependence* and *dependency* between humans and things (Hodder 2012, 2014). The concept of *dependence* expresses humans' reliance on things, in a way that is both productive and enabling—that is, *dependence* is about a human use of things that enables humans to eat, to interact with others, to think, to live, and so on (Hodder 2014). In contrast, the concept of *dependency* expresses constraints, which are also existent in the relations between humans and things. *Dependency* is about humans becoming too reliant on things, in a way that limits people's ability to develop as a society or as individuals. Hodder (2012) asserts that a continuous tension exists between *dependence* (reliance) and *dependency* (constraint), and such struggle is due, for example, to finite resources, to the quality of materials, and to social opportunity. Constraints many times generate further dependence—they require investment, and things demand care and engagement. And so, Hodder points out that the affordances of the physical properties of materials and objects for human engagement—or the potentialities that materials provide to humans—are connected to processes of production, use, and disposal, as well as to time and space. Things have temporal rhythms, they change or decay over time, and humans need to account for this temporality of things. Thus, *dependence* and *dependency* express both positive and negative aspects in the relations of humans and things; at the same time that things enable humans "to do more" they also leave humans "entrapped in the needs and demands of things and their limits and instabilities" (2014, p. 21). Hodder explains:

> Our bodies incorporate minerals and energies that we gain from things; the electrochemical activity in our brains depends on food from the world around it; our societies are built on and through things. The environment is not just a backdrop within which we fix problems; rather it is actively involved in our being as a species. And this correspondence . . . leads ineluctably to dependency and more entanglement.
>
> (2014, p. 34)

The various ways that humans depend on things (HT), things depend on other things (TT), things depend on humans (TH), and humans depend on humans (HH) are summed up in Hodder's conceptualization of *entanglement*: as the expression of these four sets of relationships combined. In considering the ways in which HT, TT, TH, and HH dependences produce entanglement, Hodder refers to another key concept: *fittingness*. *Fittingness* has a dual meaning: one relates to the function of the relation—something that adapts to fulfill an end. It is about the "properties" or "qualities" that allow a human or thing to function (Hodder 2012). Any human or thing has many different "qualities," and the usefulness of a given "quality" depends on the context. A "quality" becomes apparent when it allows types of action that achieve an end. The second meaning of *fittingness* is about the "fit"—whether there exists a certain harmony or coherence of the whole. This is about a quality being in harmony with other qualities. *Fittingness*, therefore, involves a "notion that things are 'fitting' in relation to each other and in relation to abstractions and embodied feelings about what is appropriate" (Hodder 2013, p. 584). Accordingly, the three main components of *fittingness* are affordance, abstraction, and resonance (Hodder 2012, 2013). Hodder (2013) speaks of affordance in relation to how elements (in an entanglement) enable other elements to function, in a way that involves adapting to achieve an end. Affordances and functions are often connected to ideas, thoughts, or words (abstraction), and these are reflected within "embodied practices" (resonance). Another of Hodder's concepts, a *conjunctural event* is an occurrence that disturbs the *fittingness* between humans and things, leading to problems that will need fixing and selection of fitting solutions, and which, in turn, lead to changes on the overall entanglement. These relationships and interrelationships enable, rely on, and constrain the human experience, and are expressed in the following (Hodder 2012, p. 217):

E (entanglement) + fittingness + conjunctural event → problem → fixing → selection → E" (total entanglement)

This chapter argues that the introduction of an innovative mobile technology within a museum space can be seen as a conjunctural event, setting out effects in museum practices (and in the *set*, *epistemic*, and *social design* of these environments) and also affecting visitor's activities. The analysis discusses entanglement between humans and things in the MONA learning network, exploring: (i) the ways ubiquitous access to information about the art pieces affects the physical qualities of the museum galleries and exhibition spaces, and, in turn, the activity of visitors and museum staff; and (ii) the ways the quality of the artworks themselves may affect their connections to other objects and people occupying and circulating in this space. These analyses are discussed through examples that illustrate HT, TT, HT, and HH, and *fittingness* between humans and things within the museum context.

Analyzing Connections between Humans (H) and Things (T) around the O and within the Museum Space

The notion of entanglement (Hodder 2012, 2014) offers an interesting way to understand the impact of mobile technologies such as the O in museum spaces and in design for learning more generally. *Entanglement* here involves objects and people, within the museum space, where relationships of *dependence* and *dependency* exist between TH, HT, TT, and HH. For example, visitors depend on the O to learn information about a particular artwork (HT) and such a relationship evokes a cascade of other dependences, also part of this scenario. The O relies on sensors to detect the surrounding art pieces (TT). Dim lights or specific lighting design affects people's interaction with the O, enabling visibility (TH). Each the O is constrained by its life, given through the power of a battery that the device relies on in order to function (TT). Without power visitors will not be able to access any information in the O (HT). The information visitors are exposed to, in their interactions with the technology, involved the work of an exhibition curator, for example, interviewing an artist (HH), thinking about what and how to tell visitors about an art piece in question (HT). The interview with the artist is very likely to have relied on a recorder device so material could be captured and used later (HT). This eventually became an artifact, such as an edited audio file of an interview, and it is now a design component, part of the O (TT).

The O enables access to information about many different art pieces, which also have their own temporalities and care demands. Art pieces rely on walls and ceiling, and rooms with controlled temperatures. They need to be covered and protected from the environment (TT). A Roman gold coin may be placed under a black velvet glass case (TT), and may require the positioning of special lighting and lenses to help visitors see the coin's detailed features (HT). Gloves may be required to protect antique objects (TT) from oils or chemical reactions through the human touch (TH).

The galleries are full of people who wander and wonder around. As MONA visitors navigate the large open physical spaces, they are aware of the presence of other people (HH). Vom Lehn, Heath, and Hindmarsh (2001) have studied the ways people navigate and explore museum spaces to see how individuals (both alone and together) examine exhibits in museums and galleries. They describe how "an encounter with, and experience of, museum exhibits emerges in and through the interaction of those who are in some sense 'together', but also others who just happen to be within the 'same' space" (p. 190). They argue that the "museum experience" arises not only through the actions and activities of visitors with objects and what they do (HT and TH), but it also depends on visitors' awareness of, and sensitivity to, the behavior of others, with whom they happen to share the space at one given time (HH).

Hodder's conceptualizations (2012, 2014) help us see nuances in the ties between things and humans, the way the properties of things connect them to other things (e.g. the O is constrained by batteries, fragile objects rely on the use of gloves, etc.). It becomes possible to see that the various things and humans that compose a learning network have properties that afford certain types of action. These properties or qualities come into play, jointly contributing to an end—museum learning mediated through digital technology. Then, the lighting design, the possibilities generated for the curators' use of the space, the movements of visitors, and so on are all part of the entanglement. Therefore, within MONA learning network we followed the O closely, considering it as a key element of the network, a part that allows other elements to function in relation to some end—in this case museum networked learning. *Fittingness* here is about how well some of the elements of MONA learning network come together, each contributing to the functioning of the whole in a cohesive way. Such understanding of the relationships between various components of a learning network is helpful when considering designing for learning.

Two other detailed examples from MONA's exhibition and gallery spaces, the *Pulse Room* and *Theatre of the World,* also provide vivid illustrations of the ways things and humans connect in these scenarios. The first example illustrates a co-created museum-audience activity, the second how a position of an object in space may emphasize the characteristics of other objects.

Pulse Room: A Co-Created Museum-Audience Activity

Pulse Room is an interactive installation by Rafael Lozano-Hemmer, consisting of 100 light bulbs, hanging in a cable, three meters high. The *Pulse Room* installation was shown at the 2007 Venice Biennale and later acquired as part of MONA's permanent collection. In entering the room where the Rafael Lozano-Hemmer installation is exhibited a visitor is invited to hold a sensor, which detects the person's heart rate, identifying their pulse. A computer then sets the nearest bulb to flash, reflecting the rhythm of the person's heart. Once the interface is released the sequence of flashing bulbs advances by one position in the overall sequence of 100 light bulbs. When the next visitor holds the sensor, the same process of flashing the bulb according to his or her heart rate will take place, and this process will happen again once another visitor holds the sensor. The combination of the various patterns mimicking their hearts is recorded and displayed, and, at any given time, the installation shows the heart beats of recent visitors in this sequence of 100 light bulbs. One representation of a heart rate is followed by another in rows that (symbolically) connect various visitors' hearts. This example is a vivid illustration of entanglement, as both human (H) and thing (T) launch each other into a joint expression and they both depend on each other to keep going.

A visitor relies on the technology to detect his or her pulse, and mimic its rhythm. The technology relies on a person so that it can detect and reproduce a pulse. So the focus is on what is produced within this joint expression, as one element relies on another to create new conditions. Without humans touching the sensor, no pulse is detected and no heart rates reproduced, and vice versa.

Pulse Room can be seen as an example of an artwork that invites the visitor participation through a co-created artist-audience activity. The entanglement, however, continues, when one considers all the other elements that come together: the energy that powers the computer, the walls in the room, the hangers, and so on, including also the work of curators in developing information resources to explain this artwork. As with other exhibits in MONA, visitors can learn more about this object through their interactions with the O.

Theatre of the World: *Finding Connections between Different Artworks*

The second example, *Theatre of the World*, was an exhibition curated by Jean-Hubert Martin, which opened at MONA in June 2012. *Theatre of the World* brought together objects from very different cultures and times, with art pieces curated primarily from the Tasmanian Museum and Art Gallery collection, and from MONA's own collection (ABC News 2012b), but also from other lenders (N. Durling, personal communication, May 16, 2015). At the heart of the exhibition was Martin's sentiment of rejecting the notion that ancient and contemporary artworks are inherently different. The curator and his team strived to find how the artworks related, searching for themes and ways of grouping objects in the collections of these two museums together, to compose a setting where visitors were expected to find order and connections between the art pieces. As a result, striking geometric patterns was the common ground that combined a collection of bark cloths from the Pacific Islands and an Egyptian casket. Similarly, Picasso's painting, *The Weeping Woman*, was placed beside a shield from Papua New Guinea: both art pieces contained representations of eyes and tears.

It is in this juxtaposition—being side by side in the space, in the case of Picasso's painting and the shield, or sharing a room in the case of the bark cloths and the Egyptian casket—that the connection between these objects becomes visible, one art piece (T) makes the details of the adjacent piece (T) more salient to the human sight (H). The symbolic stylized representations of eyes and tears, when co-located in the physical space, made these two different artworks reflect their commonality. In this way, Martin highlights to visitors details of those art pieces that would perhaps pass unnoticed if each piece were seen in isolation. As explained by Martin:

> We found a shield of Papua New Guinea which has got eyes and tears on it, very stylized, but when, once, if you see it separately from the Picasso probably most of the people won't notice that they were eyes, but next to that, they understand it right away . . . We are not only looking at works, but some works, or, many works look at us and some works have even eyes.
> (ABC News 2012b)

In a truly networked spirit, things traveled into other locations to be experienced by different audiences, as the art pieces in the *Theatre of the World* moved temporarily to La Maison Rouge in Paris (France), being exhibited there from October 2013 until January 2014. The network, therefore, expanded with things that travel toward audiences, rather than audiences traveling to see things. They reached people who would perhaps not have had opportunities to learn about the art pieces in the *Theatre of the World*, in Hobart, where the objects were originally housed in the Tasmanian Museum and Art Gallery and MONA.

Re-Shaping Museum Design and Activity

The ways artworks are displayed, and the interrelationships between objects, visitors, and space, can be seen as reflections of entanglement, within a museum scenario. This chapter explored museums as place-based spaces for networked learning, focusing on the entanglement of people and things, and discussing the role of novel devices, such as the O, in reshaping museum spaces and the experiences of those who visit these spaces. The chapter argued that such devices are restructuring the physical qualities of exhibitions and galleries, and, in so doing, are also influencing the work of curators and museum staff, and the experiences of visitors. Digital devices like the O generate opportunities for staff to repurpose spaces in new ways, as well as to unobtrusively collect evaluation data about visitors' activity. These devices also present new ways of engaging museum visitors, promoting participation, encouraging connections to others and to the community, and stimulating interaction with exhibits. They enable new trajectories within the physical space, and offer opportunities for an extended museum visit through online post-visit experiences.

The chapter showed how Hodder's (2012, 2014) conceptualizations of *dependence* and *dependency* help in revealing ways by which objects, people, and space are intrinsically connected to one another, in a web of a never ending entanglement. The suggestion here is that the design of innovative technologies, such as the O within the learning network of MONA, needs to be understood as part of a pool of connected elements. One particular element, and its qualities, when considered *in combination* with others, forms part of an assemblage—where each element allows other elements to function in relation to some end—in this case museum networked learning. As we saw, *fittingness,* in the case of MONA learning network, is about how well the O and other elements came together to contribute to the functioning of the whole in a cohesive way. As museums adapt to the digital age, redefining their practices (Lohr 2014), it is important that educational designers and those involved in museum education understand the complexities of how elements in *set design* influence one another: their *fittingness*, and the various ways these assemblages may, in turn, affect people's activity.

Endnotes

1. Credit for the artwork in the image—AMARNA 2015, James Turrell (born 1943, Los Angeles, California; lives and works in Flagstaff, Arizona), Skyspace series. Dimensions: 7 (H) × 28.3 (W) × 21.15m (D). Museum rooftop plaza. Steel frame, fibreglass foam sandwich roof construction, fibreglass reinforced concrete seating. Copyright James Turrell.
2. I put "learning" in brackets because *all* resources are *potentially* learning resources. They are not learning resources because of some intrinsic pedagogical properties; they *become* learning resources in use. Similarly, all activities within a museum are potentially learning activities.

References

ABC News (Australia), 2012a. MONA helps Hobart make top 10 cities list. [online]. Available from: www.abc.net.au/news/2012-10-22/hobart-makes-top-10-cities-list/4326384 [Accessed January 20, 2015].

ABC News (Australia), 2012b. Inside MONA. [online]. Available from: www.youtube.com/watch?v=2wjT4x0lLlc [Accessed November 4, 2014].

Anderson, D., 2011. Learning beyond the university. In: A. Boddington and J. Boys, eds., *Re-shaping learning: A critical reader. The future of learning spaces in post-compulsory education* (pp. 155–164). Rotterdam, The Netherlands: Sense Publishers.

Art Processors, 2015. News. [online]. Available from: http://artprocessors.net/news [Accessed January 20, 2015].

Boddington, A. and Boys, J., eds., 2011. *Re-shaping learning: A critical reader. The future of learning spaces in post-compulsory education.* Rotterdam, The Netherlands: Sense Publishers.

Butler, K., Hurst, R., and Smith, J., 2011. Museum of Old & New Art (MONA). *Architecture Australia,* 100(5). [online]. Available from: http://architectureau.com/articles/the-museum-of-old-new-art [Accessed December 17, 2014].

Carvalho, L. and Goodyear, P., eds., 2014. *The architecture of productive learning networks.* New York: Routledge.

CATH, 2014. Collaborative art triple helix. [online]. Available from: http://www.cathproject.org.uk [Accessed March 6, 2016].

CHESS, 2014. Cultural heritage experiences through socio-personal interactions and storytelling. [online]. Available from: www.chessexperience.eu/v2/project/concept.html [Accessed November 4, 2014].

Falk, J. and Dierking, L., 1992. *The museum experience.* Washington, DC: Whalesback Books.

Falk, J. and Dierking, L., 2013. *The museum experience revisited.* Walnut Creek, CA: Left Coast Press.

Fender Katsalidis Architects, 2015. MONA Museum. [online]. Available from: www.fkaustralia.com/project/s/name/mona-museum [Accessed January 19, 2014].

Fenwick, T., Edwards, R., and Sawchuk, P., 2011. *Emerging approaches to educational research.* Abingdon, UK: Routledge.

Flanagan, R., 2013. At home with David Walsh, the gambler. [online]. Available from: www.themonthly.com.au/issue/2013/february/1366597433/richard-flanagan/gambler [Accessed December 17, 2014].

Giaccardi, E., ed., 2012. *Heritage and social media.* New York: Routledge.

Goodyear, P., 2005. Educational design and networked learning: Patterns, pattern languages and design practice. *Australasian Journal of Educational Technology,* 21(1), 82–101. [online]. Available from: http://ajet.org.au/index.php/AJET/article/view/1344 [Accessed October 30, 2015].

Goodyear, P. and Carvalho, L., 2014. Framing the analysis of learning network architectures. In: L. Carvalho and P. Goodyear, eds., *The architecture of productive learning networks* (pp. 48–70). New York: Routledge.

Goodyear, P., Carvalho, L., and Dohn, N., 2014. Design for networked learning: Framing relations between participants' activities and the physical setting. In: S. Bayne, C. Jones, M. de Laat, T. Ryberg, and C. Sinclair, eds., *Proceedings of the Ninth International Conference on Networked Learning* (pp. 137–144). April 7–9, 2014, Edinburgh. Edinburgh: Networked Learning Conference Organiser.

Goodyear, P., Hodgson, V., and Steeples, C., 1998. Student experiences of networked learning in higher education. Lancaster, UK: Lancaster University. Research proposal to the UK JISC, October 1998.

Hein, G., 1998. *Learning in the museum.* London: Routledge.

Hodder, I., 2012. *Entangled: An archaeology of the relationships between humans and things.* Chichester, UK: Wiley-Blackwell.

Hodder, I., 2013. Human-thing evolution: The selection and persistence of traits at Çatalhöyük, Turkey. In: S. Bergerbrant and S. Sabatini, eds., *Counterpoint: Essays in archaeology and heritage studies in honour of Professor Kristian Kristiansen* (pp. 583–591). Chichester, UK: Archaeopress.

Hodder, I., 2014. The entanglements of humans and things: A long-term view. *New Literacy History,* 45(1), 19–36.

Hooper-Greenhill, E., 2000. Changing values in the art museum: Rethinking communication and learning. *International Journal of Heritage Studies,* 6(1), 9–3.

Illeris, K., ed., 2009. *Contemporary theories of learning: Learning theorists . . . in their own words.* New York: Routledge.

Ingold, T., 2013. *Making: Anthropology, archaeology, art and architecture.* Abingdon, UK: Routledge.

Jewitt, C., 2012. Digital technologies in museums: New routes to engagement and participation. *Designs for Learning,* 5(1–2), 74–93.

Knutson, K. and Crowley, K., 2005. Museum as learning laboratory: Developing and using a practical theory of informal learning. *Hand to Hand,* 18(4), 4–5.

Kress, G. and Selander, S., 2012. Introduction to the special issue on museum identities, exhibition designs and visitors' meaning-making. *Designs for Learning,* 5(1–2), 6–9.

Light Project, 2015. How light sets MONA apart from other museums. [online]. Available from: http://light-project.com.au/lighting-sets-mona-apart-museums [Accessed January 20, 2015].

Linge, N., Bates, D., Booth, K., Parsons, D., Heatley, L., Webb, P., and Holgate, R., 2012. Realising the potential of multimedia visitor guides—practical experiences of developing mi-Guide. *Museum Management and Curatorship Journal,* 27(1), 67–82.

Lohr, S., 2014. Museums morph digitally. The Met and other museums adapt to the digital age. [online].

Available from: www.nytimes.com/2014/10/26/arts/artsspecial/the-met-and-other-museums-adapt-to-the-digital-age.html?_r=0 [Accessed October 30, 2015].

Orlikowski, W. J., 2007. Socialmaterial practices: Exploring technology at work. *Organization Studies*, 28(9), 1435–1448.

Scott, S., 2011. The MONA Manifesto. *Art Monthly Australia*, 238, April 17–19, 2011. [online]. Available from: http://search.informit.com.au/documentSummary;dn=894085474001828;res=IELLCC ISSN: 1033–4025 [Accessed October 30, 2015].

Sharples, M., Arnedillo-Sánchez, I., Milrad, M., and Vavoula, G., 2009. Mobile learning: Small devices, big issues. In: S. Ludvigsen, N. Balacheff, T. De Jong, A. Lazonder, and S. Barnes, eds., *Technology-enhanced learning: Principles and products* (pp. 233–249). Heidelberg: Springer.

Sharples, M., Taylor, J., and Vavoula, G., 2007. A theory of learning for the mobile age. In: R. Andrews and C. Haythornthwaite, eds., *The Sage handbook of E-learning research* (pp. 221–247). London: Sage.

Simon, N., 2010. *The participatory museum*. Santa Cruz, CA: Museum 2.0.

Smith, R., 2013. Designing heritage for a digital age. In: I. W. Gunn, T. Otto, and R. Smith, eds., *Design anthropology. Theory and practice* (pp. 119–135). London: Bloomsbury.

Vom Lehn, D., Heath, C., and Hindmarsh, J., 2001. Exhibiting interaction: Conduct and collaboration in museums and galleries. *Symbolic Interaction*, 24(2), 189–216.

Yeoman, P. and Carvalho, L., 2014. Material entanglement in a primary school learning network. In: S. Bayne, C. Jones, M. de Laat, T. Ryberg, and C. Sinclair, eds., *Proceedings of the Ninth Networked Learning Conference*. April 7–9, 2014, Edinburgh. Edinburgh: Networked Learning Conference Organiser.

12

PRACTICALITIES OF DEVELOPING AND DEPLOYING A HANDHELD MULTIMEDIA GUIDE FOR MUSEUM VISITORS

Nigel Linge, Kate Booth, and David Parsons

Introduction

Museums and galleries provide a context for people's lives regardless of the nature of their collections, subject coverage, size, or location. Collectively they offer an enormous educational resource and are increasingly repositioning themselves as both formal and informal learning environments. However, a limitation in physical space inevitably creates a conflict between displaying artifacts in an appealing manner and providing sufficient supporting material to stimulate learning. Equally, the collections which museums and galleries hold are generally much larger than can be put on public display, resulting in a significant amount of this valuable resource remaining hidden from view. Consequently, museums and galleries have been turning to technology to enhance the visitor experience, whether for education or pleasure. In this chapter we discuss some of the challenges museums and galleries face when designing handheld technologies with learning purposes, such as museum guides.

Museums and galleries promote rich connections (e.g. between visitors and artifacts, or between visitors and the views of an art curator or an artist, and sometimes even amongst the visitors, see Carvalho Chapter 11) in order to convey information, knowledge, and experiences between the artifacts and the audience. These relationships can be interpreted as learning relationships (Haythornthwaite and De Laat 2012) and, as such, museums and galleries make good examples of place-based spaces for networked learning (Goodyear 2005). This chapter brings a brief overview of museum guides, discussing some of the different types of devices and technologies museums and galleries have adopted since the 1950s. The chapter also discusses practicalities in the development and deployment of multimedia guides through the case study of mi-Guide (Bates et al. 2007; Linge et al. 2007, 2012), as well as other examples of handheld devices. Designing for networked learning in a museum or gallery setting requires that educational designers and museum staff consider the effects of adopting handheld devices on the activity of museum audiences, the ways different technologies may mediate visitors' interaction with exhibits, with knowledge, and with other museum visitors/staff, as well as broader spatial and technical issues (e.g. a strategic location for making guides available to visitors, recharging requirements for mobile devices, and others). When designing for networked learning it is important to consider the practicalities of what works and what does not work in the development and deployment of mobile technologies in a museum context.

An Overview of the Introduction of Guides in Museums

In the 1950s radio technology was used to provide an early form of audio guide. For example, the National Gallery of Art (2010) in the United States launched their LecTour in which a radio commentary was transmitted to small portable radio receivers which visitors could carry with them as they walked around the gallery. Providing this additional audio stimulus enhanced the visitor experience by offering new insights into the works of art being viewed and opened up a new channel of communication which is consistent with cognitive learning theories which suggest that humans are limited in the amount of information they can process through a given input channel (Mayer 2005). Whilst these early guides forced visitors to follow the same commentary at the same time and offered no opportunities for personalization, they did nevertheless exploit both auditory/ verbal and visual/pictorial channels allowing people to concentrate on looking at an artifact whilst at the same time hearing additional information about it.

The adoption of the audio cassette in the 1970s was the first step in moving onward toward offering a more tailored or personalized visitor experience. Different audio commentaries could be offered to cater for a variety of age groups and languages. However, the cassette tape was still a linear medium that restricted the ease with which a visitor could move from one audio clip to another.

The move to digital technology took the visitor guide to the next level of development. Whilst digital technology offers enhanced control over the quality of the audio and greatly simplifies the navigation from one audio clip to another, the inclusion of a display screen allows the visitor guide to migrate into a fully functioning multimedia handheld device. An early example of this new generation of guide was the Tate Modern multimedia tour developed by Antenna Audio which was launched in 2002 in the UK. Here visitors were able to use a Personal Digital Assistant (PDA) handheld device, through which a multimedia tour offered new insights into each piece of art work through, for example, videos of experts discussing the finer points or the artists themselves explaining their motivation and techniques used for creating the work. This multimedia tour, however, was preloaded onto each device and was in effect static content.

Integrating the digital multimedia visitor guide with the Web has opened up even more opportunities and provided new ways of visitors interacting with museum and gallery collections. For example, the Los Angeles Zoo "Weird and Wonderful" series of tours combined an on-site visitor guide with an online version accessible through their website and an MP3 download. In this way, the same digital content is being made available in three different formats, each meeting the needs of a different type of user including those who would only ever visit the Zoo from cyberspace. This in turn greatly extends the reach of a museum or gallery's learning environment. As identified by Barry (2006) a virtuous circle needs to exist between online and physical spaces with the user experiencing a continuous and seamless journey from the website to the physical gallery, through the multimedia guide and back to the website.

The multimedia guide therefore allows museums and galleries to enhance the learning experience they offer by enabling visitors to discover more about each exhibit through audio commentary, video presentation, and animations, to receive a personalized tour that reflects who they are and what interests they have and to make accessible a far greater amount of their collections because the multimedia guide in effect offers unlimited storage and display options compared to the physical space constraints of a conventional gallery.

Naturally the smartphone has further transformed how museums and galleries can engage and interact with their visitors. The visitor guide now combines the potential of Internet access with a camera, a Global Positioning Satellite (GPS) location detection system, and an open interface for downloading and running specialist applications or apps. It also frees up the organization from having to supply technology, for now visitors bring their own device with them.

The smartphone also opens up opportunities to engage visitors via social media which offers a better understanding of their behavior and provides a route via which visitors can contribute their own content and make comments, thereby creating a more dynamic interaction. A user profile can also be exploited to tailor content to a specific individual to create a far stronger bond between visitor and gallery; a process termed "embodied interaction" by Wakkary et al. (2008). This flexibility in terms of personalizing digital content is a growing trend exemplified by the European funded CHESS project (Cultural Heritage Experiences through Socio-personal interactions and Storytelling) which uses an augmented reality approach to personalize a user's visit as an interactive storytelling experience and is currently being trialed in museums in Athens and Toulouse (CHESS 2014).

With visitors to museums and galleries becoming increasingly technologically aware, there is real potential to develop and exploit the handheld multimedia guide as the basis of a learning environment. Therefore museums and galleries should not fear the multimedia guide but, rather, embrace it as a tool for enhancing learning and interaction. As museums and galleries embrace new digital technologies to enhance the physical experience of visiting a museum, new opportunities for networked learning also emerge, encouraging connections not only between visitors and artifacts (e.g. making available different learning resources about a particular art work), but also amongst visitors (e.g. encouraging visitors to share their views) and visitors and staff (e.g. allowing staff collection of audience data). However, making that move can be challenging for some organizations and despite the huge potential, there are several important technical infrastructure and non-technical staffing issues that need to be fully understood to ensure an effective and productive deployment of a mobile multimedia visitor guide. The next section explores those issues through the experience gained in launching a multimedia visitor guide called mi-Guide (Bates et al. 2007; Linge et al. 2007, 2012) for the Museum of Science and Industry in Manchester, UK.

Introduction to mi-Guide

The Museum of Science and Industry in Manchester, UK, is a large museum that takes as its focus the development of science, technology, and industry with a particular emphasis on the role played by Manchester and the North West in developing the modern industrial age. The museum is part of the Science Museum Group, a non-departmental public body of the Department for Culture, Media and Sport, having merged with the National Science Museum in 2012. It is situated on the site of the world's oldest surviving mainline railway station, Manchester Liverpool Road railway station, which opened as part of the Liverpool and Manchester Railway in September 1830. In addition to the original station building, the museum is also home to the world's oldest railway warehouse, the so-named 1830 warehouse. Within this building is located the Connecting Manchester gallery which aims to tell the story of how communications evolved from early forms of writing to today's mobile phones.

The Connecting Manchester gallery (officially opened in October 2007) occupies three bays on the first floor of the warehouse building and is organized into four zones called: *Face to Face Communications*; *Recorded Information*; *Broadcasting*; and *The Digital Future*. The focus is respectively on human communication and early writing, the printed word and mass communications, the evolution of electrical communications, and, finally, convergence and the digital world. It is well populated with physical artifacts in cases, supplementary and contextual information on printed display panels, and a small number of interactive exhibits.

Development of the gallery began in 2006 and the overall design brief developed by the Museum identified a requirement for a multimedia visitor guide to enhance the visitor experience; the philosophy being to showcase the latest in communications systems within a gallery that celebrated the evolution of that very technology. Consequently this meant that the multimedia visitor guide would form the prime means of visitor engagement and therefore it was decided that the gallery itself would incorporate fewer conventional audio, visual displays, and graphics panels.

The Museum's design brief for the gallery in turn led to the formation of a partnership with the University of Salford which at that time had an active research program examining context-driven information systems, the results of which could be used to design a new multimedia visitor guide. One of the main themes of context research is personalization of computing services, being a part of the wider research area of ubiquitous computing which seeks to establish a network of interconnected objects that seamlessly and transparently form part of our everyday environment. Placed within the museum setting, the multimedia visitor guide, which became known as mi-Guide, consequently had personalization of the museum experience at its heart.

Whilst several museums and galleries had already adopted and had experience of multimedia guides, it was decided not to use an existing system but to develop mi-Guide ourselves so that it could be tailored to the specific requirements of the Connecting Manchester gallery. The main reasons for this were to permit full control over the content structure, organization, and layout design and to allow the system to incorporate ideas that had emerged from Salford's research program. However, mi-Guide did use commercial hardware and its software was written in a manner that would allow it to be adapted to other environments.

The Design of the mi-Guide System

The initial design philosophy of mi-Guide called for a handheld visitor guide that could locate where the visitor was within the Connecting Manchester gallery, deliver relevant multimedia content to the visitor about the artifacts at their location, and provide an easy to navigate and engaging user interface. The curators at the Museum concentrated on content authorship and selection, whilst the University team focused on the technical design and implementation.

mi-Guide (Networked) Learning Design Principles

Networked learning oriented design principles are about promoting collaboration, participation, and connections amongst people. Such principles guide design decisions in the development of elements that encourage people to take an active learning role, offering opportunities for construction and reflection on a learning experience. Most museum guiding systems, at a minimum, promote (virtual) connections between visitors and knowledge resources, and these in turn have often been specially curated and prepared by museum staff. In the case of mi-Guide, participation is encouraged by inviting visitors to extend a museum visit into an enriched learning experience. mi-Guide supports learning through displaying text, audio commentaries, and other media, in relation to an object in the gallery. After sensing the location of a visitor, the device displays topic choices for an object, and the visitor then selects what they want to learn about. These choices often include information curated and delivered under five different categories (described below), where visitors may be scaffolded in considering, for example, how does an object work, or its impact on communications. Visitors exercise autonomy in accessing information according to their interest and at their own pace, and so mi-Guide allows visitors to take an active role, in relation to their learning experience. Moreover, mi-Guide also enables visitors to be tracked, allowing museum staff to collect information and learn about visitors' needs and interests.

mi-Guide System Design

The final mi-Guide system design deployed within the Connecting Manchester gallery used a Dell Axim PDA as the visitor handheld device. Each guide was issued by museum staff as visitors entered the 1830 warehouse and recovered from them when they exited. Within the gallery, display cases and large exhibits for which mi-Guide content was available were identified by a mi-Guide symbol. Behind these symbols was placed a small electronic device known as a Radio Frequency IDentification (RFID) tag. Each mi-Guide handheld PDA was fitted with a RFID reader which, when placed close to a mi-Guide symbol, could read the tag that was placed behind it and obtain an object identifier which in turn allowed the handheld device to know where it was within the gallery. Having determined its location, the handheld device communicates via a WiFi network with a local server and requests multimedia information pertaining to the mi-Guide symbol that has just been scanned. Real-time content such as video and audio is then streamed to the PDA. Once an exhibit's mi-Guide symbol has been scanned, the visitor is free to walk away from it whilst still being able to access all of the information about that exhibit.

mi-Guide Assisted (Networked) Learning

From the visitor's point of view, when an exhibit is first scanned that exhibit's home page is displayed as shown in Figure 12.1. It comprises an image of the exhibit itself and five section titles: *Overview, Who's Who?, The Manchester Story, How Does It Work?,* and *Impact on Communications.* Naturally, not every section needs to be populated with content where none exists. On selecting

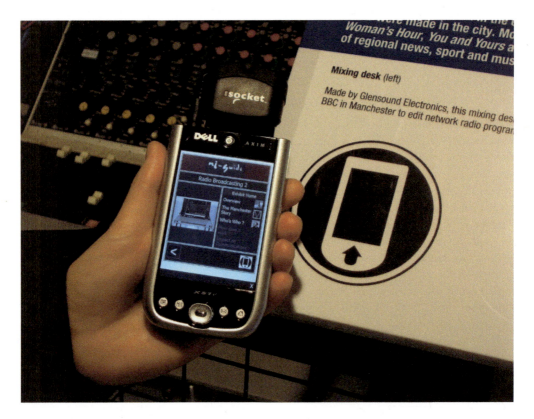

FIGURE 12.1 mi-Guide Exhibit Home Page for Radio Broadcasting

one of the titles the visitor is taken to the section page. At this point an audio commentary is played and, providing there is extra media content associated with this exhibit, the user can then explore further. Extra media content includes video on subjects related to telecommunications, clips from television programs, oral histories, and images. If a given media type is unavailable for that section then the associated audio and image icons are still shown but are grayed out. In total there are 55 mi-Guide object scan points distributed throughout the Connecting Manchester gallery.

Visitor guides can, however, only reach their full potential if the guide is designed, deployed, and managed effectively and sustainably. Through the rest of this chapter we wish to share the experience we gained in developing mi-Guide and use the lessons learned to highlight what museums and galleries need to appreciate when deploying multimedia technologies to aid the visitor experience.

Practicalities of Deploying Multimedia Guides and the Lessons Learnt from mi-Guide

Development work on mi-Guide began in 2006 which, from a technological point of view, was a very different world than 2016. In 2006 the smartphone "revolution" and its associated apps had not begun and whilst mobile phone ownership within the UK was high, mobile phones themselves still had a limited capability for accessing the Web. Inevitably, had mi-Guide been developed today, different technological decisions would probably have been taken. Nevertheless, we believe that the lessons we learnt and the experience we gained continue to have relevance in the context of today's smartphone technology and downloaded apps. In the following sections we will highlight those key points of generic relevance.

Engagement, Presentation, and Interface Design

Visitors to museums and galleries are increasingly digital savvy but with that comes heightened expectations of presentation quality, interactivity, and ease of use. Failure to recognize this and keep up with the pace of change will ultimately have a detrimental effect. However, the skill and role of museum curators in preserving, organizing, and displaying physical artifacts within a coherent gallery space remains a unique selling point of traditional museums. Today, multimedia allows for a much wider range of approaches to exhibition design, which in turn have the potential to broaden visitors' engagement but, from our experience, not all visitors wish to engage with digital media, and for those who don't the physical environment must continue to offer levels of engagement that satisfy them.

There is therefore a fine line to be drawn between an exhibition design that encourages engagement through a multimedia visitor guide and, at the same time, provides sufficient standalone information within the gallery itself. Striking this balance is clearly a key challenge but whatever decision is arrived at, it is absolutely essential to ensure that the multimedia guide enhances, rather than dominates or distracts, the visitor experience (Petrelli and Not 2005). Of course, it can be argued (Tallon and Walker 2008) that an exhibit label or display panel also distracts a visitor from the exhibit whilst they are reading. It is of paramount importance to remember that the primary function of a multimedia guide is to provide a mechanism to deliver content to a visitor, and so this content that is being delivered is what matters most and not the technology of the guide itself; a point that was reflected in the findings of the Museum Handheld Survey (Tallon 2009). It is also important that visitors' expectations of what a guide can offer them are met: visitors need clear direction on what exhibits have additional content via a guide, where/how to find them, and what that extra content is (Helal, Ancelet, and Maxson 2013). In general, it is important that guides are as easy as possible to use and have a very recognizable link to the physical space occupied by the exhibits (Rung and Laursen 2012).

Given the importance and familiarity of the Web, it was decided to design each mi-Guide screen to follow a typical web page arrangement with forward, back, and home buttons and the concept of clicking an icon for moving to the next section. Throughout the user interface development several focus group sessions were organized and generated invaluable feedback that influenced the design. For example, a desire to fully control streamed audio and video led to the inclusion of a media player panel at the bottom of the screen. Similarly, confusion over navigation between pages and access to the exhibit scan function led to the inclusion of icons at fixed points on the screen. The key points raised during these sessions led to a number of changes to the interface design and these are summarized in Table 12.1.

A further challenge is to make effective use of a handheld device's screen size. Our initial investigations suggested that for mi-Guide we would need a reasonably powerful portable device with a large touch screen, in order to both deliver a multimedia experience and enable visitors to easily interact with it whilst navigating the physical space of the gallery. At that time, the most prevalent handheld device with a suitably large touch screen was the PDA which was already being used as a multimedia guide in other museums and galleries, most notably at Tate Modern in London. At the time of development, the Dell Axim PDAs offered the largest screen size. Even with this, a major challenge that remained was how to make effective use of the screen. As a general principle it is recognized that visitors to museums and galleries prefer to look and listen rather than look and read. Therefore, it was decided to maximize the use of audio commentary and to prioritize the screen for providing navigation through the content and the display of images and videos.

TABLE 12.1 Focus Group Feedback on the mi-Guide User Interface Design

Summary of comments gathered in focus group	User interface design implication
There is a need to control the audio streams with pause, replay, and fast forward controls. A volume control is also desirable in addition to some form of display to show the length of each audio or video clip.	These were important design considerations. They included considerations of features that would allow users to be able to fully control the audio playback and to know in advance how long a piece of media would take to play, implying that in some cases they may choose to ignore a long piece. This feedback led to the inclusion of a media control bar shown at the bottom of the mi-Guide screen.
A "home" button is needed in case you press another button by mistake and need to return to a known start point.	Navigation is essential and, clearly, an easy way of returning to a fixed starting point is critical. Equally, there was confusion between the concept of home and back, and the need to be consistent with the adoption of a paradigm based on the design of a web browser.
Confusion over whether you click text or an icon to enter a section page.	This is another important consideration to address. The decision in mi-Guide's case was to make the icon only active and this was emphasized by placing a border around the icon.
It was not obvious that you had to go back to the scan page in order to access the next exhibit.	All of the scan points within the gallery are indicated by a special symbol. Therefore, this same symbol appears on relevant mi-Guide screens as a reminder to return to the scan page when changing exhibits.

Today's smartphones are generally of a size similar to or larger than the older PDAs we used and, of course, the growth in the usage of tablet devices offers an even larger screen size over these, thereby providing a greater display area. Developing mi-Guide for use on a single device brought significant benefits in that all of the content could be authored and designed in a way that optimized a single screen size. The situation today is, however, far more complex. Should one develop content for deployment on smartphones and tablets? Within these broader categories there is significant variation in screen size with smartphones having screens ranging from 4 to 6 inches and tablets extending this up to 11 inches. Larger screens do offer many benefits, not least of which is the fact that it is easier to physically touch active areas with a finger. The mi-Guide PDA screen, although large for its time, did work best when the visitor used a stylus to click on the touch sensitive active areas.

When considering a range of portable devices, predominantly comprising smartphones and tablets, there is no guarantee that the same content will be displayed in an identical manner. What fills and maximizes the screen of one of the smaller smartphones might look distorted on a larger screen, and content optimized for a tablet can be too small on a smartphone. Hence, a one size fits all, common denominator approach simply will not work and so intelligence needs to be built into systems to automatically detect the type of device being used and to adjust the presentation of the content to match the display properties appropriately. The broader the range of devices on offer, the greater the range of adjustment needed; an issue that intensifies when visitors are encouraged to bring their own device. A compromise may be the best, or indeed only, approach whereby a published list of supported devices is made available to the visitors.

Smartphones and tablets also have limited processing power and memory capacity compared to laptops and personal computers. This in turn means that they have cut-down versions of familiar software, such as web browsers. Our Dell Axim PDAs were no exception with a cut-down version of the Internet Explorer browser called Pocket Internet Explorer and a limitation that all streamed media files could only be played if they were in Microsoft .wma or .wmv formats. As mentioned earlier, the mi-Guide content was designed as a set of web pages that were displayed to the visitor through the Pocket Internet Explorer web browser. However, today's handheld technology supports several browsers and these in turn render the same webpage content in noticeably different ways. Equally, smartphones and tablets offer the added complication of using different operating systems, including Apple iOS, Android, and Windows Phone. Even within each of these operating systems, new versions are released on a regular basis and at any one time several different incarnations can co-exist. The impact of limitations in the browser and differences in operating system is that an apparently same software or content behaves differently across a range of devices. A way to address this issue is to ensure that any multimedia guide being developed is fully tested on a representative set of smartphones and tablets, on each commonly used operating system, and within all popular browsers and versions thereof.

With multimedia and audio guides it is important to consider how the audio will be played. Using a handheld device's speaker can be very disruptive to other visitors, especially if visitors keep the volume turned up. Naturally, the device can be held against your ear but that does require the visitor to keep hold of the device with one hand. Many visitors prefer to keep their hands free whilst walking around museums and galleries, which in turn necessitates the multimedia guide being supported by a neck strap. That implies the use of ear phones. However, a full headphone covering both ears has further implications for visitors who may not hear alarms or other visitor announcements made via public address systems. Consequently, each mi-Guide was fitted with only a single earpiece: as a result, even on maximum volume some visitors found it hard to hear the audio, especially as the quality of the earpieces varied.

Orientation is a key factor with all multimedia guides. This not only relates to visitors' understanding where they are within the navigation system of the guide itself (in the digital space) but also where and when to use the guide within the gallery (in the physical space). For mi-Guide every object scan point was clearly identified by a standard symbol thereby clearly indicating that mi-Guide content is available at that point. Once a symbol is scanned, the visitor is shown an image of the exhibit thereby confirming that the scan has been successful.

For mi-Guide the design and authorship of the content was the responsibility of the curatorial staff at the Museum of Science and Industry. Whilst developing their overall interpretation strategy for the Connecting Manchester gallery, a series of informal discussion sessions were held with their visitors. These identified the key areas of interest that artifacts stimulate and led to the adoption of five content categories per exhibit for mi-Guide. As mentioned previously, these became: *Overview*, *Who's Who?*, *The Manchester Story*, *How Does It Work?*, and *Impact on Communications*.

Creating the content for mi-Guide proved to be far more time-consuming than originally anticipated and allowances were needed for designing the overall interpretation strategy, authoring the content, translating the content into digital form, and testing it before launch. Within the Connecting Manchester gallery there are 55 mi-Guide scan symbols with most requiring unique content for five distinct sections, all of which had to be authored and then recorded. When authoring content it is also important to be fully aware of copyright restrictions in that some material may be approved for use within the confines of a given gallery or museum but not for use on the Web. This could even impact content being delivered to visitors physically present within the gallery, if it is in effect being delivered over the Internet to reach them.

Finally, no matter how digitally savvy visitors are, everybody needs to learn or be shown how to use a multimedia guide. Naturally this further reinforces the need for an intuitive and simple interface but it also requires sufficient signage or guidance from staff to show how to initiate the guide. Because mi-Guide was a bespoke system that had to be physically given to visitors, an orientation display case was located near to the Issue Desk which was fitted with a mi-Guide scan symbol. This allowed museum staff to use this case to demonstrate mi-Guide as each handheld device was handed out.

Technology Issues

In order for a multimedia guide to present a visitor with pertinent and relevant information, the guide must first "know" where it is within the gallery and, hence, which exhibit the visitor is examining. By far the most common method by which visitor guides determine location is by requiring visitors to input a unique reference number that is displayed alongside each exhibit. Whilst this is a simple process it does nevertheless require that visitors are able to find and read the number, to then physically enter the number into the guide, and for the gallery to ensure the correct number is located alongside the appropriate artifact.

For mi-Guide the goal was to automate this process as much as possible and consequently eliminate the need for any user input. This in turn required the multimedia guide to determine its location within the gallery. One obvious candidate was to use GPS as used within vehicle and smartphone navigation systems. However, GPS signals are rarely able to penetrate building structures with sufficient quality, and in that respect may not be reliable, especially in buildings with substantial metal content. Whilst the 1830 warehouse is mainly of brick and wooden construction, our tests showed that GPS was generally unreliable within the Connecting Manchester gallery which drove our decision to consider other location detection technologies.

One alternative technology is active tags. These are small electronic devices, often battery powered, that emit radio signals containing the identity of the tag which can be received and read by the approaching multimedia guide. To be effective within the Connecting Manchester gallery, the multimedia guide had to work accurately down to a granularity of one meter which was the average spacing between most of the display cases and exhibits. However, the read range of an active tag is usually so great that it is difficult to differentiate one exhibit from another when signals are simultaneously received from more than one tag. Some high-end production active tag systems on the market were considered, for example the Ekahau positioning engine. This system uses the WiFi network to determine the user's location, and at the time of the implementation it was only reportedly accurate to within a 3–5 meter range. An alternative was the Guide ID system which employs infra-red tags, requiring a line of sight. This system was previously used successfully in the Museum Boijmans van Beuningen in Rotterdam and in the Natural History Museum in London. Interestingly the Royal Institution in London also has an active tag solution for their eGuide (Tellis 2004), but in their case the visitor has to actively press a button on the guide in order for it to read the tag as opposed to using automatic location detection.

In our experience, it seemed that the best way to meet the granularity requirement in the mi-Guide implementation was to compromise and introduce the concept of the scan point. This involved using passive RFID electronic tags located at each exhibit where additional multimedia content was available. A passive RFID tag is a piece of technology that requires no power and can store information within non-volatile memory. Today, RFID is in widespread use in public transport such as the Oyster travel card used on London Transport, building access control, and package tracking. The contents of a RFID tag are read by an external reader, which emits a radio signal, providing sufficient energy that both powers the tag and communicates with it. This in turn necessitated the attachment of a RFID reader unit to the mi-Guide handheld unit as shown in Figure 12.2.

FIGURE 12.2 mi-Guide RFID Reader

Within the gallery each RFID tag was programmed with a unique identity, which can be easily changed in situ using a standard RFID reader and running specialist software. In order to activate each tag, the visitor simply places their multimedia guide next to the scan point at which point it is automatically read.

The limitation of this approach is the fact that RFID as a technology has not found widespread adoption within mobile technology. Several mobile phones do indeed now support what has become known as Near Field Communication (NFC) but these still remain in the minority. However, a more common form of input device available on smartphones is the in-built digital camera which can be used to access Quick Response (QR) codes. These are graphical symbols that provide a means of encoding information which can be read by simply taking a picture of them. Japan was an early adopter of QR codes but their popularity has grown considerably in recent years and QR codes are now readily seen in magazines, on websites, and on advertising and consumer products (Roulliard 2008). Typical QR code reader apps are freely available for all major brands of smartphone. Within a museum or gallery application, QR codes could be displayed alongside every exhibit for which additional content is available. A visitor would then simply take a picture of the QR code using a reader app to access this additional content.

Another important design consideration is to determine where the multimedia content should be stored. For example, should it be preloaded or downloaded onto the multimedia guide before use or transmitted to the guide as and when required? Where a museum issues guides to visitors, then these can be preloaded with content. However, that in turn brings with it an added maintenance overhead whenever content is revised or updated. On the other hand, downloading of content, for example where a visitor may be using their own device, also raises two key issues. First, when should one be downloading, and, second, how long will it take? If a museum decides to package their content within a mobile app, then the visitors will need to download that app to their smartphones before they are able to use the multimedia guide. The time taken to complete this task is directly related to the quantity and type of digital content and the quality of the visitor's network connection. If a visitor chose to download the app whilst within a gallery, and mobile signal strength at that point was poor, then the download time could increase considerably. Depending upon the terms of the visitor's mobile contract, such a download could also incur a charge. A potential solution to tackle these issues would be to offer public WiFi access. However, that would still require information and guidance to be provided on how to attach to the network.

For mi-Guide a decision was taken to transmit content to each multimedia guide as and when it was required. This necessitated loading content onto a central server and providing a communications network to connect this server to each mi-Guide handheld device. In this way, there were no concerns about software installation on the PDAs nor was there any need to update several copies when the content was changed. Centralizing the content was easier for maintenance purposes, at the expense of having to provide a communications network over which to deliver content.

Installing a dedicated wireless network to support the mi-Guide system was not without its problems. Prior to installation, a wireless survey of the gallery space revealed areas of poor coverage, especially in the areas between rooms where signals were obscured by the metal lift shafts. Even when the mobile network is being used to deliver content, a similar survey should be carried out to ascertain mobile phone coverage and ensure it is adequate. The most significant issue, however, was that the mi-Guide handheld devices needed to be stored and issued by staff on the ground floor of the 1830 warehouse, whereas the gallery is located on the first floor which required the WiFi network to be significantly extended to cover both of these areas.

A wireless network is constructed as a series of overlapping WiFi areas, each controlled by a single WiFi access point. For mi-Guide two such areas were needed; one covering the ground floor and the stairs and lift to the first floor and the second covering the Connecting Manchester gallery itself. A mobile device attaches to the wireless network by first detecting a WiFi access point and then connecting to it. Where more than one wireless area is used, a point is reached where the mobile needs to change its connection from one WiFi access point to another. This process is known as handover. Ideally, the multimedia guide should work like a mobile phone and always seek out the strongest signal for its particular location, then automatically and seamlessly handover to that access point. However, in practice the Dell Axim PDA used in the mi-Guide system had a tendency to hold on to the WiFi signal for as long as possible until it was simply too poor to be usable. Only then would it disconnect and start searching for a stronger signal. During this time, the PDA was in effect disconnected from the network and therefore unable to receive the mi-Guide service. Therefore, although when operating within either of the two WiFi areas performance of the mi-Guide service was good, visitors did experience this handover phenomenon and its apparent loss of service. As one focus group member commented:

> we immediately thought that the screen had frozen and it wasn't scanning. It slowly began to work again but I think it would be a really good idea to warn users about the delay. I don't think people would mind a delay if they were told about it, but could quickly become frustrated if not.
>
> (Focus group participant)

Experience gained from mi-Guide indicated that the worst case was that the handover delay could extend to a minute. In reality, in most cases the handover occurred without the visitor actually realizing it, but that result could never be guaranteed. Our experience is that once we explained, visitors had no problem accepting the handover delay, and performance of the WiFi delivery method has been good. Similar problems may occur in any WiFi installation where more than one access point is needed to cover a given physical space. For mi-Guide the problem arose because the Issue Desk was on a different floor to the gallery itself. Our view is that had it been possible to issue the mi-Guide devices within the main gallery space, then the problem would have been less likely to have arisen, because only one WiFi access point would provide all the necessary network coverage.

The capabilities and ownership of smartphones within the UK have increased significantly since mi-Guide was developed. That in turn opens up the possibilities of visitors using their own device. On the one hand, this is a very attractive option for it eliminates the need for a museum or gallery to maintain and support its own devices and associated infrastructure, but on the other hand, there are several points that need to be considered. As previously mentioned, there are no common standards across the diverse range of devices, operating systems, and software. This means that to ensure that a multimedia guide will work for the majority of visitors, the guide needs to be tested on the broadest range of devices possible. In addition, a decision has to be made concerning the delivery of content to the visitor's device. If this is to be done via a mobile phone network, then considerations about whether coverage is adequate within the gallery space become crucial. Many tablets are WiFi only and cannot connect to a mobile network. These issues may ultimately lead to a requirement to install public WiFi within the spaces where visitors are likely to use the multimedia guide.

In early 2014, the Victoria and Albert Museum in London carried out research into what it is like for museum visitors to connect to WiFi on a mobile phone (Lewis 2014). Their research identified that attention was required to the human computer interface (HCI) aspects to make content clear and welcoming. They also identified the need to clearly distinguish the type of commitment the user was entering, with regard to costs of using their own devices.

Finally, provision of "in-house" devices by museums and galleries remains important as not all visitors possess a suitable mobile device, and even those that do may not wish or be able to use it.

In a survey by Rung and Laursen (2012) on the attitudes of visitors to the National Museum of Denmark, users chose not to use a smartphone application for reasons ranging from not wanting to wait for the app to download, through to not having any earphones to use with the device, to having left the device in a storage locker elsewhere in the museum.

Deploying a multimedia guide within a museum brings enormous benefits, not only in terms of being able to provide visitors with more information and an enhanced experience but also by offering feedback, giving museum staff opportunities to learn about their museum audience. It is possible to determine which exhibits are the most popular, what information or type of information is accessed most often, and the order in which exhibits are viewed, hence revealing the routes taken by visitors through a gallery. This does mean that visitors' actions and behavior are being monitored and tracked. Where a museum chooses to issue its own multimedia guides, as was the case with mi-Guide, then there is no linkage between the visitor as an individual and the device they are using. However, when a visitor uses their own device then it is clearly possible to extract personal information from their devices. Whilst this may not be happening, the visitor may be suspicious that personal data is indeed being collected. Therefore it is essential to ensure that clear statements are given to the visitor about what information, if any, is being collected by the multimedia guide.

One of the most difficult and challenging aspects of multimedia guides is ensuring that the system is future proof. When we started our work the PDA was more powerful than the mobile phone; now the smartphone has overtaken the PDA. Technology obsolescence militates against a museum or gallery opting for a solution that requires dedicated hardware to be provided to the visitor. Developing content for delivery on a visitor's own technology alleviates some of these issues and allows museums to focus on their key skills of interpretation. However, with new models of device being released each month it is a never-ending challenge to ensure that multimedia content and apps continue to function on new devices whilst ensuring that older devices continue to be supported.

All mobile technology is battery powered and despite the obvious advances in capability, the battery remains a limitation. For mi-Guide all handheld devices were stored on their charging cradles when not in use and one full battery charge could support up to two average trips around the gallery. The two major factors in draining battery power were the RFID reader and WiFi network. Whilst the system was designed to minimize the time when the RFID reader was energized, the WiFi network had to remain on all of the time. Even with a modern smartphone, its WiFi and mobile phone interfaces are two of the largest consumers of battery power. Therefore a visitor with a low battery on their smartphone may be reluctant to use a multimedia guide in case they run the risk of running out of power. Visitors therefore need to be made aware of all the implications of using their own device.

Non-Technical Operational and Managerial Issues

Introducing new technology into museums also brings management and staff training considerations. Staff may not be equally keen to adopt and promote new technology; much depends on their own technical competences.

Where a museum or gallery chooses to provide its own guides, schemes need to be put in place for the storage, issue, and recovery of these devices. For mi-Guide staff had to be trained in the operation of the guide to ensure that they themselves felt comfortable and confident about handling the technology and answering visitors' queries. An early problem that emerged with mi-Guide was that technologically aware visitors were able to manipulate the mi-Guide PDA and change its settings. This meant that the visitor services staff had to be able to cope with what were in effect non-operational mi-Guide units and quickly reconfigure them. Whilst some staff were able to cope, recognize the problem, and understand what to do, others were less confident and consequently problems of this type fueled their fears of and natural reticence in using technology. Staff must also be generally confident in helping visitors to use the device and not just the application: a study by Gansemer et al. (2008) showed that over a quarter of visitors had handling problems when using a provided PDA, and Rung and Laursen (2012) found that around 50 percent of visitors who borrowed the iPod provided by the museum had never used one before.

Where a multimedia guide relates to a specific gallery, the careful selection of a location for issuing the guide will have great impact, which would preferably be within that gallery. Unfortunately, the organization of the building that hosts the Connecting Manchester gallery did not permit this and we faced the problem of trying to issue a mi-Guide before the visitor had reached the gallery. Once in the gallery, then it is too late and inconvenient for the visitor to backtrack and collect a mi-Guide. Under these circumstances, visitor services had to work much harder to both promote and encourage the uptake of mi-Guide. These difficulties are echoed by the work of Rung and Laursen (2012) in which it was found that take-up of guides depends critically on branding, exposure, and guidance, and a major reason for visitors not using a guide was because they "did not know it was there."

A strategy was also needed to ensure that a mi-Guide PDA could be issued to a visitor without too much inconvenience on their part, yet ensuring that sufficient incentives were in place to guarantee that each PDA would be returned at the end of the visit.

The enthusiasm of visitor services staff and the buy-in to mi-Guide is critical. These people are at the coal face of visitor interaction, yet this presents an additional workload for museum staff (European Union 2006). Recent Danish research (Laursen 2013) examined staff-visitor encounters in relation to using new technologies, and concluded that museums are faced with both challenges and opportunities in supporting visitors when adopting new technologies. In our experience, staff engagement inevitably varied from the technology enthusiasts who were keen to experience new developments, to those who were less comfortable with technology. An essential part of the mi-Guide deployment was to devise and deliver a staff training program, not only prior to the gallery launch, but also on an ongoing basis, because of staff turnover and the culture of employing short-term part-time contract staff. A key part of this initiative involved ensuring the support of senior management for the adoption of new technology and adoption of corporate strategies that communicated its importance to the organization.

Holding small training groups helped enormously in familiarizing staff with the mi-Guide system but so too did the production of a simple to follow, printed mi-Guide Quick Start Guide. A key feature was to devise a procedure whereby a mi-Guide PDA could be taken in any state and configured to run mi-Guide with absolute certainty that the system would work. In contrast, whilst it may be assumed that if visitors bring their own devices then staff are not required to help users having problems using their own devices, this is not necessarily correct: in a study by Gansemer et al. (2008) it was found that over a fifth of visitors using their own PDAs experienced device handling problems. Helping visitors in such a scenario may prove even harder to achieve, given the vast range and diversity in devices that visitors may have.

The development and deployment of mi-Guide was a standalone externally funded project led by the University of Salford, which highlights issues of integration associated with the Museum of Science and Industry's digital strategy. To be truly effective, multimedia guides must be fully integrated within an organization's core interpretation and outreach strategies with a seamless transition between the gallery, the website, and the multimedia guide. A multimedia guide should be viewed as an opportunity to do more, to engage a wider audience, and to offer an enhanced visitor experience, and not be seen as an alternative or threat to the traditional visit. Ultimately this would be tailored to the individual visitor, and data from visit patterns could be used to inform further gallery and/or guide development. Staff may also benefit from learning about what appeals to visitors. However, this would require due care and attention to be paid to privacy and security, so that an individual cannot be identified either intentionally or unintentionally from the data that is collected about them (Emmanouilidis, Koutsiamanis, and Tasidou 2013).

Conclusion

Handheld guides have been enhancing the experience of visitors to museums and galleries for many years. Advancements in technology have allowed the handheld guide to evolve into the multimedia guide and these in turn continue to define new paradigms not only in terms of access but also in terms of how information can be organized to exploit context. Multimedia guides provide access to a much richer experience, opening up collections to a far greater extent than is possible within the confines of a physical space and enhancing the museum's educational potential.

Research carried out by Fusion Research and Analytics members of the American Alliance of Museums (US) and the Museums Association (UK) identified several important trends and developments which will influence significantly the development of handheld museum guides (Fusion 2012–2013). These include the fact that museums which offer mobile guides are increasingly requiring visitors to use their own devices and QR codes are becoming the most common feature followed by audio tours and smartphone apps. However, they also found that half of their respondents cited a lack of budgets, limited resources, and lack of knowledge as reasons for not offering mobile features.

The European funded Learning Museum Network Project (LEM) has also identified important trends and developments (Learning Museum 2012), noting that museum visitors using the Internet are now of the same relevance to museums as physical visitors. Whilst the most conservative visitors will perhaps continue to prefer to use paper to communicate, communicating without technology will become more and more marginal for cultural institutions. Finally, they concluded that virtual museum content delivered over the Internet can reach a vast worldwide audience with only a fraction of this being also a physical audience.

In contrast to a growth in the use of technology, it was also observed that the area showing the greatest level of decline was conducted tours and talks, due to lack of funding and staff reductions. Audio tours were identified by 94 percent of those responding as being no longer used; however, use of iPads and other interactive mobile devices was increasing and the use of social media showed the greatest increase and largest growth in popularity.

Multimedia guides have the potential to greatly enhance the education and learning offered by museums and galleries by providing deeper levels of interpretation, whilst allowing the visitor a greater freedom to tailor the experience to his or her own specific needs and interests. However, technology in itself offers nothing. What matters is what is wrapped around the technology: the multimedia content being delivered to the visitor. Technology facilitates new and exciting ways of presenting and delivering multimedia but deploying such technology, including the provision of services to a visitor's own device, brings with it several technical and non-technical challenges that need to be both fully understood and properly managed to maximize potential. Transforming museums and galleries into effective networked learning environments through the use of multimedia guides therefore requires that "the entire technological system must be taken into account" (Reynolds, Walker, and Speight 2010).

References

Barry A., 2006. Creating a virtuous circle between a museum's on-line and physical spaces. In: J. Trant and D. Bearman, eds., *Museums and the Web 2006* (pp. 22–25). Toronto, CA: Archives & Museum Informatics.

Bates, D., Linge N., Parsons D., Holgate, R., Webb, P., Hay, D., Wynn-Jones, S., Newson, A., and Ward, D., 2007. Building context into a museum information guide. In: *Proceedings of the IASTED Conference Communication Systems, Networks and Applications* (pp. 235–241). October 8–10, 2007, Beijing. Beijing: ACATA Press.

CHESS, 2014. *Making museums a mobile, personalised and interactive experience*, European Union. [online]. Available from: http://ec.europa.eu/programmes/horizon2020/en/news/making-museums-mobile-personalised-and-interactive-experience [Accessed October 30, 2015].

Emmanouilidis, C., Koutsiamanis, R-K., and Tasidou, A., 2013. Mobile guides: Taxonomy of architectures, context awareness, technologies and applications. *Journal of Network and Computer Applications*, 36(1), 103–125.

European Union, 2006. FREEDOM: Using digital information systems to develop smart, PDA-based guiding systems in a museum. In: *Examples of innovation projects, Programme for Innovative Actions 2002–2006*. [online]. Available from: http://ec.europa.eu/regional_policy/archive/cooperation/interregional/ecochange/doc/proj_samples.pdf [Accessed October 30, 2015].

Fusion, 2012–2013. Mobile survey with "Mobile Technology Trends" 2013. [online]. Available from: www.aam-us.org/resources/center-for-the-future-of-museums/mobile-technology [Accessed July 17, 2015].

Gansemer, S., Grossmann, U., Suttrop, O., and Dobblemann, H., 2008. Digital cultural heritage—essential for tourism. In: *Proceedings of the 2nd EVA 2008 Vienna Conference*, August 25–28, Vienna. Vienna: Austrian Computer Society.

Goodyear, P., 2005. Educational design and networked learning: patterns, pattern languages and design practice. *Australasian Journal of Educational Technology*, 21(1), 82–101. [online]. Available from: http://ajet.org.au/index.php/AJET/article/view/1344 [Accessed March 16, 2016].

Haythornthwaite, C and De Laat, M., 2012. Social network informed design for learning with educational technology. In A. Olofson and O. Lindberg, eds., *Informed design of educational technologies in higher education: Enhanced learning and teaching* (pp. 352–374). Hershey: IGI-Global.

Helal, D., Ancelet, J., and Maxson, H., 2013. Lessons learned: Evaluating the Whitney's Multimedia Guide. In: *The Annual Conference of Museums and the Web 2013*. [online]. Available from: http://mw2013.museumsandtheweb.com/paper/lessons-learned-evaluating-the-whitneys-multimedia-guide [Accessed July 17, 2015].

Laursen, D., 2013. Balancing accessibility and familiarity: Offering digital media loans at the museum front desk. *Museum Management and Curatorship*, 28(5), 508–526.

Learning Museum, 2012. LEM: The learning museum network. [online]. Available from: www.ne-mo.org/about-us/the-lem-network.html [Accessed September 29, 2014].

Lewis, A., 2014. What's it like for museum visitors to connect to Wi-Fi on a mobile phone? V&A Museum. [online]. Available from: www.vam.ac.uk/blog/digital-media/mobile-wifi-screens [Accessed October 30, 2015].

Linge, N., Bates, D., Booth, K., Parsons, D., Heatley, L., Webb, P., and Holgate, R., 2012. Realising the potential of multimedia visitor guides—practical experiences of developing mi-Guide. *Museum Management and Curatorship*, 27(1), 67–82.

Linge, N., Parsons, D., Bates, D., Holgate, R., Webb, P., Hay, D., Ward, D., 2007. mi-Guide: A wireless context driven information system for museum visitors. In: *Proceedings of the 1st International Joint Workshop on Wireless Ubiquitous Computing*, 2007 (pp. 43–53). June 2007, Funchal, Portugal.

Mayer, R. E., 2005. Cognitive theory of multimedia learning. In: R. E. Mayer, ed., *The Cambridge handbook of multimedia learning* (pp. 31–48). Cambridge: Cambridge University Press.

National Gallery of Art, 2010. Then and now: Celebrating 60 years of the National Gallery of Art West Building. National Gallery of Art, Washington, DC. [online]. Available from: www.nga.gov/feature/thenandnow/audio.shtm [Accessed September 30, 2014].

Petrelli, D. and Not, E., 2005. User-centred design of flexible hypermedia for a mobile guide: Reflections on the hyperaudio experience. *User Modeling and User-Adapted Interaction*, 15(3–4), 303–338.

Reynolds, R., Walker, K., and Speight, C., 2010. Web-based museum trails on PDAs for university-level design students: Design and evaluation. *Computers & Education*, 55(3), 994–1003.

Rouillard, J., 2008. Contextual QR codes. In: *The third international multi-conference on computing in the global information technology* (pp. 50–55). July 27–Aug. 1, Athens. Athens: IEEE Computer Society Press.

Rung, M. H. and Laursen D., 2012. Adding to the experience: Use of smartphone applications by museum visitors. In: *Proceedings of the Transformative Museum Conference*, May 23–25, Roskilde, Denmark. Roskilde: Roskilde University.

Tallon, L., 2009. The 2009 International handheld guide survey: The use, challenges and future of handheld guides in museums. [online]. Available from: www.slideshare.net/LoicT/use-challenges-future-of-hand-held-guides-in-museums-2009-2670381 [Accessed October 30, 2015].

Tallon, L. and Walker, K., 2008. *Digital technologies and the museum experience: Handheld guides and other media.* Lanham, MD: AltaMira Press.

Tellis, C., 2004. Multimedia handhelds: One device, many audiences. In: D. Bearman and J. Trant, eds., *Museums and the Web 2004.* Arlington, Virginia: Archives & Museum Informatics. [online]. Available from: www.museumsandtheweb.com/mw2004/papers/tellis/tellis.html [Accessed April 12, 2006].

Wakkary, R., Muise, K., Tanenbaum, K., Hatala, M., and Kornfeld, L., 2008. Situating approaches to interactive museum guides. *Museum Management and Curatorship,* 23(4), 367–383.

13

CITIZEN CARTOGRAPHER

Juliet Sprake and Peter Rogers

Vantage points today are used professionally in urban and landscape planning, archaeology, and the military to survey areas of land that are in the line of sight (commonly known as "viewsheds"). In more everyday contexts, trainspotters, birdwatchers, and spectators all use tops of buildings to get a closer or better view of their object of interest, whilst tourists and city dwellers use vantage points as places of meeting and reflection. Viewing the urban landscape by looking down or across a distance from a vantage point affects how we feel about place and offers opportunities for exploring the surrounding area.

As researchers of *located learning*, we are interested in the public use of vantage points to gain different perspectives and views that can be linked into a way of navigating an area of the city and comparing the distinctions of areas and specialized districts that both spatially and emotionally define our understanding of urban places. Specifically, we investigate how locating vantage points and viewing the city from above can be described as a wayfinding activity. The street with its buildings and infrastructure, green spaces, and private/public zones becomes a site for learning. Here, data such as longitude, latitude, and altitude points provide a more abstract plane for recording waymarks that can be utilized to make and share personal excursions. The point of our research is exploratory; to devise ways of finding and recording views of the city for pleasure—using user-generated data to plot new kinds of topographical map. In this chapter we describe the ideas behind a "height sensitive" project and investigate how an abstract system of referencing, geo-location, may contribute to learning through direct experience. We present the development of a service for mobile devices that begins to articulate what we have gained from making physical vantage points into recorded waymarks in excursions that involve users in mapping the urban environment.

Citizen Cartographer Project 1: *Seven Metres*

In 2007 we developed a project, *Seven Metres*, which involved people considering how climate change may affect London if the Thames rises to seven meters above sea level and how long-term planning can involve making adaptations that may reduce the effect of climate change. Participants watched a visualization of the seven-meter contour line, produced using three mini digital video (DV) recorders, mounted on the front of a tricycle, that captured the front, left, and right views of the route along the north and south banks of the river (Figure 13.1).

FIGURE 13.1 *Seven Metres*: Contour Line Visualization

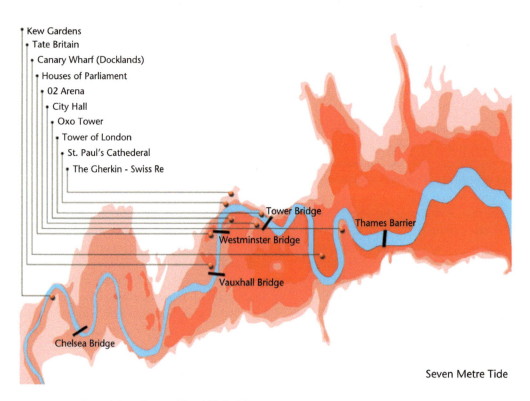

FIGURE 13.2 *Seven Metres*: Future Flood Plain Map

The concept for this project was to track the seven-meter-high contour on the north and south banks of the river (Figure 13.2) to visualize which locations would be flooded should the Thames rise to this level. Experimenting with alternative visualizations of contour lines allowed us to investigate direct experience of sea level change, a topic that is often associated with more abstract representations or frames of reference. For us as researchers, this involves mixing the physical and digital to explore mobile ways of knowing. Our design work involves creating situations that embrace the complexities of multiple actions people take in connection with the digital content we provide. In this project we did this by drawing, labeling, and reading the seven-meter contour using a tricycle and digital video, a method that was then adapted for public use.

The recorded route flowed clockwise with the right side generally showing the submerged area. The three synchronized DV camera recordings were displayed as a simultaneous three-way projection. Audio narrations from interviews with people along the way provided a GPS-tagged soundtrack for the contour line. This audio was then added to by delegates at a climate change event at the Greater London Authority (GLA) building in London, who recorded and plotted narrations at locations of significance to them. Here, viewers pedaled the tricycle and watched the three-view movie of the contour line. A smaller display tracked the aerial view map and the GPS plotted the route so that viewers could monitor the position of the route over time (Figure 13.3).

In this project we learned that orientation is about giving people opportunities to locate themselves using their experiences and knowledge about a place. *Seven Metres* illustrates how abstract topographical data can be actively explored and interrogated in creative and critical ways. Making the recordings for the projection, for example, involved plotting the route using Ordnance Survey (OS) data and then transferring this route to a street map in order to plan the actual roads to take.

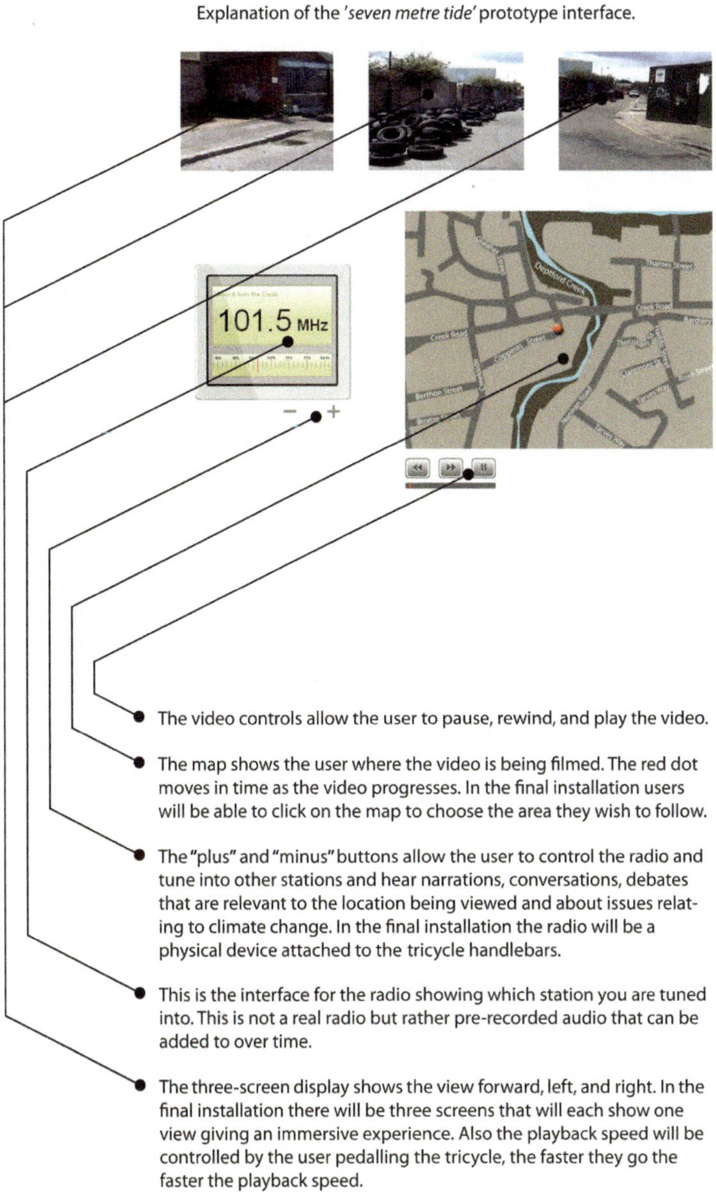

Explanation of the *'seven metre tide'* prototype interface.

The video controls allow the user to pause, rewind, and play the video.

The map shows the user where the video is being filmed. The red dot moves in time as the video progresses. In the final installation users will be able to click on the map to choose the area they wish to follow.

The "plus" and "minus" buttons allow the user to control the radio and tune into other stations and hear narrations, conversations, debates that are relevant to the location being viewed and about issues relating to climate change. In the final installation the radio will be a physical device attached to the tricycle handlebars.

This is the interface for the radio showing which station you are tuned into. This is not a real radio but rather pre-recorded audio that can be added to over time.

The three-screen display shows the view forward, left, and right. In the final installation there will be three screens that will each show one view giving an immersive experience. Also the playback speed will be controlled by the user pedalling the tricycle, the faster they go the faster the playback speed.

FIGURE 13.3 *Seven Metres*: User Interface Controls

This in itself required modifications as the OS map of London doesn't provide navigational information such as street names which are useful for following a linear route in a built-up area. The actual filming of the route required further physical activation of topographical data as the reality of cycling the streets is different from that represented on the maps (one-way streets, road works, etc.). The overarching aim of the project was to involve people in learning about changes in their working and living environment through making associations with significant buildings. They did this by following a topographical mapped feature of a contour line (more usually associated with locating elevation in rural areas). We then wanted to develop the concept of citizen cartography further for a new generation of geo-aware mobile adventurers who would focus on making personal topographical profiles from self-made elevation data.

Spatial Awareness and Tall Buildings

In the urban planning process, vantage points are used to create predominantly horizontal photographic montages of "objective" verifiable views concerning locations for tall buildings or structures. The parallacter system for making photomontages to protect views of St. Paul's Cathedral in the 1930s is still used in making contemporary planning applications based on sightlines and visibility of tall buildings and structures. In this way, elevation values of a specific vantage point can be assessed in terms of preserving historic or scenic value. In previous research projects, we have developed tools and methods to question these kinds of standardizing methods that claim accuracy in visualizing topographical views. "Ground Untruthing," for example, is a conceptual method for learning-through-touring based on the principle that "ground truth" is always open to subjective interpretation and contestation depending on the author and the frame through which the analysis has been set and who conducted it (Sprake 2012, Chapter 6). We now build on this critical practice to explore what kinds of altitude-sensitive methods or tools can heighten our spatial and emotional understanding of urban places by using vantage points to gain different perspectives and views.

Drawing on perception theory (e.g. Noë 2004) and Paul Rodaway's work on haptics in geography (Rodaway 1994), we understand haptic learning as a process in which people are simultaneously physical, cognitive, and emotional participants in developing a heightened sense of awareness. Specifically, they are reciprocally "in touch with" and "touched by" their physical environment (Rodaway 1994, p. 45). The work of Guliana Bruno (2002) and Tim Ingold (2000) is especially relevant in furthering understanding of movement in developing this sense of awareness through making voyages and journeys. Bruno describes "the haptic" in terms of the "motion of emotions" or the ways in which the body senses through movement (Sprake 2012). Ingold argues that:

> our perception of the environment as a whole, in short, is forged not in the ascent from a myopic, local perspective to a panoptic, global one, but in the passage from place to place, and in histories of movement and changing horizons along the way.
>
> (2000, p. 227)

He uses the official topographical map as a point of reference for critiquing scientific cartography (in its claim to accuracy and objectivity) and to contextualize his argument for "knowing as you go" in which people seamlessly integrate views from above and at ground level by moving "purposefully and attentively, from place to place." In this, "somewhere" is a position along a path and these paths of observation crisscross in a matrix-like way to form "regions" in our perception of the environment. Ingold's emphasis on lateral movement in "knowing as you go" resonates with our own explorations into mobilized learning and the emergence of localized networks.

What prompts learners to take action—by themselves or with others (Sprake and Rogers 2014a)? Working through this theoretical concept in practice, we have explored how the environment can be supplemented for learning to happen, particularly in the use of cues that can be designed to instigate or prompt movement and connections between places (Sprake and Rogers 2014b). The built environment offers us objects that cannot be "seen" as a whole from one viewpoint so movement around buildings is therefore important in developing our spatial perception. An "enactive" approach to perception (Noë 2004) focuses on how we make sense of our environments through movement and tactility in which capacities for action and thought are understood through the sensing activity of the body. An enactive approach to perception goes beyond simply having sensations; it is about understanding those sensations so that "perceiving is a way of acting" (Noë 2004, p. 1). Noë argues that an understanding of sensations is gained through gradual exploration of the world rather than through a separation of perception and action. His work on "enacting content" is particularly relevant in understanding how our perceptual experience is enacted and understood through the spatial bodily movement of actors. According to Noë, exploration, enquiry, and curiosity are active ways in which we perceive three-dimensional objects. A reading of Noë's theory of "action in perception" provides an opportunity to explore how sensorimotor knowledge and skills may be relevant to better understanding relations between mobility, place, and learning.

The term "enactive" suggests that perceiving is a way of acting or, as Noë says, "something we do." He argues that bodily skills enable us to act out our perceptual experience and perception is therefore "touch-like." Noë describes the way in which we move to perceive an object as automatic and describes how this can be evidenced through the way in which we squint eyes, crane necks, peer around, move closer to get a better look, sniff, brush against, etc. He suggests that perceiving is a "kind of skilful bodily activity" and that "perception and perceptual consciousness are types of thoughtful, knowledgeable activity" (2004, pp. 1–2). There is another dimension to Noë's basic idea on enactive approaches to perception that should be considered here. That is his notion that "self-movement depends on perceptual modes of self-awareness, for example, proprioception and also 'perspectival self-consciousness' (i.e., the ability to keep track of one's relation to the world around one)" (2004, p. 2). In an enactive approach to perception, objects can be said to have "sensorimotor profiles" in that the appearance of the object changes as the perceiver moves in relation to it; sensorimotor profiles are thus dependent on spatial relations between objects and are modulated by movement of the subject. We would argue that tall buildings and structures offer a kind of *extreme object* in Noë's theory as the built environment doesn't invite perception from one viewpoint but through bodily, sensory experience. Touch is intrinsically active in physical space through movement of our bodies. As we move so we touch and this involves us exercising our sensorimotor skills or practical bodily knowledge: "It is because mobile perceivers gain access to variation in perspectival properties as they move about that the spatial properties of objects are made available to the subject for experience" (Noë 2004, p. 86).

Architect Juhani Pallasmaa, who also positions the body as the "locus of perception," suggests that architecture "articulates the experiences of being-in-the-world and strengthens our sense of reality and self" and therefore has an active part to play in projecting and mediating meanings (2005, p.11). Self-motivated activities such as bird watching, touring, spectating, train spotting, or protesting, in which people are physically advantaged by the height of a tall building or structure, provide distance from the ground level for all kinds of fulfilling experiences in being "up high" and surveying the surrounding landscape. Our perception may be shifted, or mediated in startlingly unfamiliar ways, but we still do this perceiving (actively) from/with/in the body. Roland Barthes describes structure as "a corpus of intelligent forms" and sees visitors to the Eiffel Tower in Paris as engaging in "decipherment," spotting known and separate points and linking them into an "overall view." In this way, we can understand a panorama as an "image we attempt to decipher" (Barthes

1979, pp. 9–10). Using Barthes' ideas on deciphering, we can propose that elevated distance from ground level results in some kind of perceptual change. Michel de Certeau also argues that the elevated observer has a "clarified and enhanced vision" (de Certeau 1984, Chapter 7). Looking down from the top of the World Trade Center in New York, de Certeau describes the spectator as a "voyeur" who is freed from being "possessed" by the city by a pleasurable, totalizing reading of the "text" below. John Urry highlights an important historical association with the word "landscape" that also connects height with a particular way of viewing:

> With *landscape* [as opposed to *land*] an intangible resource develops which is that of appearance or look. This notion developed in western Europe from the eighteenth century onwards, part of the more general emergence of a specialized *visual* sense separate from the other senses and based upon novel technologies.
>
> (Urry 2007, p. 256, original emphasis)

He also suggests that the pleasures of touring are heightened through the "distance between" leisure activities and everyday life (Urry 2002).

The vantage as a privileged, all encompassing view can be traced through prospecting or surveying land for value and acquisition. In seventeenth-century London, Christine Stevenson describes how the Monument in London was built as a "telescope" to view the rebuilt city after the Great Fire, and how John Denham's poem "On Cooper's Hill" in 1642 "defined a new kind of poetry of place" as the view "from Cooper's Hill was informed by that from St Paul's Tower" (Stevenson 2008, p. 218). She goes on to argue that the experiences of seventeenth-century observers from tall buildings, retold through words and images, allowed for "elision"—in the sense of merging or forming connections between things, especially abstract ideas. We suggest that buildings themselves are not quiet in this process of elision—marking "the transition to a knowledge" (Barthes 1979, p. 14)—if we consider how buildings function in providing for elevated experiences, both opportunistic and designed. Surveillance posts, landing pads, open-air cinemas, and sky bars all evidence utilization of the rooftop areas afforded by tall buildings and these are connected to ground level by other architectural infrastructure such as stairwell windows, lookouts, glass lifts, and circuitous stairs that inform the activity of climbing. It is perhaps useful to broadly think about networks of buildings as containers, platforms, outlooks, gateways, and observatories in their capacity to offer vantage points on the urban landscape. Multi-storey car parks, for example, offer common accessible vantage points for viewing the urban landscape. Low ceilings and painted arrows direct the pedestrian toward the potential for a view (Figures 13.4 and 13.5). With their distinctive odors, cast concrete, and pitted tarmac, these buildings provide opportunities for sensory multi-directional views of the surrounding environment from each floor. If we consider the human body as a compass that can climb to different levels, the multi-storey car park offers a structure for orientating oneself in relation to the surrounding infrastructure.

Thomas A. Markus suggests that people are shaped by, and shape, buildings. Buildings have codes of behavior generated by users, technology, and design in which the "social practice of use is 'inscribed' into the building" (1993, p. 9). His work is relevant to understanding how buildings may be considered as active in producing relations between people and their environments. Markus says there is a powerful "property" in buildings "containing people in space," and that buildings are unique as "containers which interface products with people" (1993, p. 247). He highlights how this may be analyzed from a contemporary, critical perspective, one concerned with understanding how buildings may be described as dynamic in affecting the nature of social relations. Alongside the "container" view there is a complementary understanding of how buildings relate to one another through the connections made by people moving between them. Ingold's work on

FIGURE 13.4 View Framing 1: Multi-Storey Car Park, Peckham

FIGURE 13.5 View Framing 2: Multi-Storey Car Park, Peckham

mapping as "ambulatory knowing" provides a useful description of paths in stage crafting activities that acknowledge the multiplicity of ways in which people gain knowledge by finding their way between and through buildings: "[Likewise] in wayfinding, the path is specified not as a sequence of point-indexical images, but as the coming-into-sight and passing-out-of-sight of variously contoured and textured surfaces" (Ingold 2000, pp. 238–239).

The focus on subjective experience is a way into learning about a building by moving through and around it—and is often the impetus for exploration in the first place (e.g. personal memories, associations, interests, etc.). It is in making the excursion that exploratory movement happens, and topographic knowledge of distance traveled and height gained is made.

Citizen Cartographer Project 2: *Tall Buildings*

Being able to describe the functionality of a tall building or structure in its capacity to provide a view has generated a lexicon of elevated words that have a specificity when reading the built environment from above: zone, node, landmark, corridor, roofscape, pattern, artery, cluster, pepper-potting, panorama, prospect, kinetic view, belvedere, orientation, density, topography, mass, vista, surroundings, skyline, overshadowing, typology, scale, foreground, obstruction, and so on. The permeability of the built environment is a term that describes the accessibility, opening, and closing of views "to improve the legibility of the city and the wider townscape" (CABE 2007, p. 6). Our next project explores a user definition of permeability that involves citizens in making physical and emotional connections about place, using tall buildings as viewfinders and waymarks.

As in previous projects (Sprake 2012, Chapter 4), we operated a live walk research method to sound out the potential of vantage points as a way of developing situational awareness, wayfinding, and orientating skills for finding and climbing tall buildings and structures in and around London. An excursion to find and photograph the Cleveland Street Workhouse in London, a socially-historic building that is largely inaccessible to the public, started our research into user-generated vantage points. Discovering an adjacent vantage point affected how we as researchers felt about this building in its surrounding location. The following is taken from Juliet Sprake's fieldwork notes, January 2013:

> There's a building covered in tarpaulin on my left that I know is very near the location of the workhouse because it's on the junction with Howland Street. For a moment I think the workhouse has had it. Then I spot the NCP sign a bit further on—a flag marking the spot—and head towards it. Stopping in front of the boarded up front wall to the workhouse I can't help but notice the "IN" and "OUT" signs on gateposts. I start thinking about inmates arriving and leaving the institution . . . As I peer through gaps in the boards to find the front door I note that this is marked as a "goods delivery" entrance. So where did the inmates go in? Or is this evidence of the building's subsequent occupiers? The NCP car park has a pedestrian entrance (mental tick) and following this, I walk alongside the part-tiled sidewall of the workhouse. Photographing this, I spot the BT Tower again. I speak to a friendly guy in the NCP car park reception booth and explain that I want to go up to see the building next door. He confirms that the car park only occupies the ground level (mental cross). Undeterred and perhaps even more determined, I continue walking down Cleveland Street until I can turn left. I do this and then take a 2nd left down a side alleyway that brings me close to the side elevation view of the workhouse again. I discover that there is a brick wall that encloses the workhouse on this side and that there is possible access through a locked gate. The wall has been recently repaired in places with concrete and there's a step-ladder leaning against it. I retrace to the road and turn left again and into Charlotte Street knowing that I'm walking parallel to the back of the workhouse now. I pass by an NHS building on my left—the Traumatic Stress and Family Planning Clinic—and walk on to see if there's a better way to get into this building for a view of what's behind. Partially obscured by temporary construction hoardings is the door to another NHS building. The building work makes me think this might be "lax" enough for me to get in—a builder might say yes

or no. The door requires buzzer entry though and there's a reception desk. I'm let in and note a woman in NHS uniform chatting to the receptionist. I explain that I want to take photos of the workhouse and they suggest that I might get a good view from the 2nd floor kitchens and indicate the way. I'm in! This is obviously housing for NHS staff or students and I'm free to walk the corridors to find the best vantage point. The kitchen areas, same location on each floor, do offer a good view but the windows only open a crack and with the sun reflecting off them, it's difficult to photo the workhouse yard below. I decide to go right to the top of the building. There's a door out on to a roof space—I try it, and it opens. I lean against the rail, enjoying the view of the workhouse but also of the great vantage point to watch another building being demolished next door to it—the tarpaulined one I had noticed earlier. A construction worker joins me on the rooftop balcony and asks me how long I'll be, as he needs to lock the door. I find out that he's there to get an overview of the demolition process—"it's the best place to gauge how it's going". Lucky that we coincided at the same time then . . . Returning to street level I turn left out of the NHS building and then left again down Howland Street and join the few demolition public spectators that have gathered there. The once private spaces are now exposed and I use my camera to focus on the wallpapers, utility fittings and pipes that are being smashed and ripped. A memorable last encounter on this mission.

The walk highlighted how buildings could be accessed and used as vantage points to view objects of interest and, in the guise of an adventurer, how it felt to experience the thrill of a new perspective gained in unexpected ways. From this, the context for our brief opened up to consider what promotes movement between ground level infrastructure (or indeed, underground) and the top of tall buildings, and how this experience may be captured and shared. Can we design an activity that prompts people into making and sharing vertical excursions across the city in ways that enhance their understanding of place? We have found that when a user really participates, it is the activity of discovery that propels them to do so; our tools and applications have to encourage active participants rather than passive interpreters. We would therefore focus on designing activities and tools that prompt, but do not prescribe, action. For these to truly work, we must encourage unexpected augmentation of the app, including encouraging alternative ways of collecting data and visualizing the results.

In *Tall Buildings* (Sprake and Rogers 2014a) we set out to design a geo-located activity that enables participants to see from one vantage point to another, to step in between to the next point, to look back and then to go beyond. In other words, the participant stands on top or near the top of one publicly accessible structure or natural feature, identifies the next vantage point, and navigates their way toward it. The aim of this project is to explore the possibilities of creating a user-generated map that shares accessible vantage points so that people can playfully move from one point to another to see how many alternative views of the city they can find—to move through the city with this high view in mind. We want to see whether viewing the city from different perspectives changes our perception of areas of the city and whether the perception of places changes when viewing from other high points. How concentrated and close together could this web of vantage points become? How do perceptions change from closer or higher proximity? Our project provides a focused activity for users to learn on the move by *sighting* tall structures, *navigating* a route or path from one vantage point to another, *mapping* altitude, time, and distance data, and *describing* personal opinions of what is being viewed.

The purpose of our geo-located physical activity is to provide participants with the means to make digital contour paths at different elevations and encourage them to record and share the main features that best describe the elements of the route traveled. We have designed an app in which users are prompted into making vertical excursions to experience the sense of freedom provided by "being on top and looking down" from a tall building. Mobile technologies are used to capture and map those experiences in a playful way that invites others to share through engaging in activities associated with wayfinding and orientating. The core service for this project is a map that offers a visualization of the height of buildings and the distance traveled between them. The intended use of this service involves users in finding and climbing up tall buildings or structures, entering their height data, and a photo of the view. They use the view from the building or structure to work out where to go next. Users are able to see all of the high points they have climbed on their journey on the map as a series of extruded points. The map can be added to over time or done as a one-off activity. It gives you a record of buildings climbed and the views from them. It's not just about finding buildings but getting into them. Issues around what constitutes public space at ground level and higher up, how you get into a building, awareness of surveillance, and costs attached to roof top locations are all part of the experience (Figure 13.6).

Factors affecting the challenge of a vertical excursion		
	Easy	**Challenging**
Access	Entry is welcomed	Have to blag your way in
	There are lots of public areas	There are lots of private areas
	You are free to roam	You are expected to follow set rules
Cost	Free or within budget	Low or no budget
Distance covered	Higher the building the bigger the area for spotting next vantage point	The lower the building the smaller the area for spotting next vantage point
	More stretched topographical profile	More squeezed topographical profile
Density of buildings	Low number of vantage points climbed	High number of vantage points climbed
	Occasional vantage point to head for	Multiple vantage points identified
Location	High number of publicly accessible buildings/structures	Low number of publicly accessible buildings/structures
	Good local knowledge of (or unlimited access to experts/reliable information) accessible tall buildings/structures	Poor local knowledge of (or limited access to experts/reliable information) accessible tall buildings/structures
Height of vantage points	No constraints	Constraints set – e.g. max./min. height range, most undulating/straight topographical profile
	Use mobile technologies to calculate building/structure height (e.g. theodolite app)	Work out height of buildings/structures "by hand"
Navigation	Use GPS-enabled map to find your way to the next vantage point	Use your vantage point views to predict a route onwards by spotting thoroughfares, railway lines, landmarks, etc.
	No constraints on method of travel	Constraints on methods of travel

FIGURE 13.6 *Tall Buildings:* Vertical Excursion Challenges

Users are free to participate in collecting data, but can also just use the data for their own purpose (for example, pick a tall building close by to watch a sunset). A graph visualizes the base assets of the data—the height and distance between tall buildings. We placed value on proximity and height; the higher the location and the closer the building, the better. This is visualized as a rocket symbol for each individual location. The graph is produced from data gathered by each individual user and there is also a shared graph produced by all users, to enable areas of a city to compete for the most accessible tall buildings as the number of located buildings grows. The graph acts as an illustrative tool to show the density of user input and the corresponding quality—in this case, height. It also gamifies the activity, encouraging an adventurous user or group of users of city space to fill in the gaps by drawing the points on the graph closer together.

The *Tall Buildings* app works by users planting a flag for a tall building on the map. The flag acts as a location marker but also provides information about the name of the building or structure

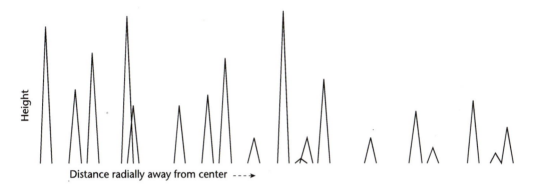

FIGURE 13.7 *Tall Buildings*: Height x Distance Graph

FIGURE 13.8 *Tall Buildings*: App Interface

and how to access it. Users are asked to write a "location name," then answer "How did you get in?" followed by "Enter the height in meters," before checking all is correct and planting their flag. The public map then represents the flag as an extruded building and also as a rocket ("tooth") on a height-distance graph. By clicking on the extruded building, users can access this metadata to find out the nearest tall buildings in their current location. And the settings function allows them to switch between two kinds of map view (roads and buildings or satellite view) as well as giving them the choice to add an identity if they want to "show off how many places you've explored."

FIGURE 13.9 View Framing 3: KölnTriangle, Cologne

In making and testing the service, we have identified several kinds of ways in which experiencing the pleasure of an elevated view has advantaged the user. Specifically, they are able to: navigate at ground level by locating infrastructure; orientate themselves in relation to other significant buildings; reminisce on personal histories; locate other kinds of rooftop activities; and identify differences in areas of an urban landscape. The challenge in finding and accessing tall buildings and structures is starting to populate the map with multi-authored data that opens up questions around user identity and reliability in interesting ways. For example, the planted flag tags clearly show there are many ways to estimate the height of a building—the dome of St. Paul's Cathedral has several different "official" heights in guidebooks, alongside overheard conjecture from visitors whilst climbing the stairs, as well as making comparisons with neighboring buildings. We have also found that a tall landmark building or structure can be used to find other vantage points that *radiate* from it. Nelson's Column in Trafalgar Square, London, for example, was the center point for several excursions that involved viewing it from other surrounding vantage points (Trafalgar Hotel, the National Portrait Gallery, Charing Cross Station, and so on). A few users have started to plant flags in geographically-distant locations. On a trip to Cologne, one user actively looked for tall buildings and surprisingly found an office tower block, the KölnTriangle, open to the public for taking in a 360-degree view of the city (Figure 13.9). And further afield, a user in Jodphur made a connection with the caste system in India and the blue painted Brahmin dwellings from their elevated position at the fort.

There are specific types of public building that are popular vantage points. These include: car parks, cathedral/church towers, rooftop bars/restaurants, art galleries and museums, and shopping centers. The Tate Modern art gallery in London, for example, has photographic multi-directional views recorded from the different floor levels that show how these can be used to panoramically-orientate oneself whilst finding a way to the top. The Westgate Museum in Winchester is tagged as a free vantage point alternative to the tower tour at the cathedral. The One New Change shopping center, adjacent to St. Paul's Cathedral, offered a free picnic lunch spot for one user and that has since been tagged by other users in the area for lunch. The notion of taking in a view as a temporal activity is also evidenced in a one-hour tour of Peckham. This user set a time limit to find their way round Peckham, starting by finding a rooftop cinema. By climbing the Bussey Building to the highest vantage point accessible during the day, they navigated to, and went up, a car park and then a library using the railway line as an orientating feature. Using a similar wayfinding method, another user went to the Whitgift Shopping Centre in Croydon with the intention of photographing it prior to redevelopment. Having accessed the open-air rooftop level, this user took photographs of material decay and reflected on childhood shopping trips, before making their way to another car park they had spotted from the top.

Conclusion

Overall, this project has expanded our concept of the citizen cartographer as a producer of topographical data. It has opened up our thinking about emotional responses to place in the design of geo-located services, particularly for mobile learning that involves making unexpected discoveries. Our focus for the citizen cartographer has been on the reading of civic text by user production of contours and elevation data made whilst on the move. As researchers, we understand that learning is an embodied, situated experience. Unexpectedly finding a vantage point that resulted in witnessing the demolition of a building illustrates a memorable kind of knowledge gained through movement between ground level and above. Or mobilized learning.

We have experimented in using abstract data to plot an excursion using vantage points as way-marks. These are integrated into a mapping process that is designed to facilitate semi-structured movement through the city. We have found that users who attempted to plan a route in advance inevitably went "off track" and this led to on-the-move modifications, unplanned stops, and negotiations that contributed to a richer mix of waypoint types (and entry information).

The authority of the topographic map lies with the users who locate and access vertical vantage points in relation to horizontal movement, define their own paths, and choose how to record and "tell the story" of the vistas collected along the way. Positioning the official topographic map in a vertical hierarchy has prompted us to use authoritative and abstract data in alternative ways that encourage people to make personal excursions and plot their own data.

Knowledge produced in making these vertical excursions is, of course, part of the wider histories of urban vantage points and cultures of viewing for pleasure. We have taken the idea of using vantage points as a method for making a route through an urban environment that draws on an innate physical and cultural pleasure in viewing from an elevated position. Regions of the city are made identifiable through moving up, down, and along physical paths that are marked by interactions with buildings and multi-dimensional vistas—created by moving and looking forwards, backwards, upwards, and downwards.

Tim Ingold uses a lovely phrase that encapsulates what underpins our work—the "attunement" of people to their surroundings (2000, p. 242). As researchers in this project, we have operated as mapmakers to develop ways in which this process of "attunement" happens through movement between one vantage point, and then the next . . .

References

Barthes, R., 1979. *The Eiffel Tower and other mythologies*. Berkeley: University of California Press.

Bruno, G., 2002. *Atlas of emotion*. London: Verso.

CABE, 2007. Guidance on tall buildings. [online]. Available from: www.english-heritage.org.uk/publications/guidance-on-tall-buildings-2007 [Accessed October 30, 2015].

de Certeau, M., 1984. *The practice of everyday life*. Berkeley, CA: University of California Press.

Ingold, T., 2000. *The perception of the environment: Essays in livelihood, dwelling and skill*. New York: Routledge.

Markus, T. A., 1993. *Buildings and power: Freedom and control in the origin of modern building types*. London: Routledge.

Noë, A., 2004. *Action in perception*. Cambridge, MA: MIT Press.

Pallasmaa, J., 2005. *The eyes of the skin: Architecture and the senses*. Chichester, UK: John Wiley & Sons.

Rodaway, P., 1994. *Sensuous geographies: Body, sense and place*. London: Routledge.

Sprake, J., 2012. *Learning through touring*. London: Sense.

Sprake, J. and Rogers, P., 2014a. Crowds, citizens and sensors: Process and practice for mobilising learning. *Personal and Ubiquitous Computing*, 18(3), 753–764.

Sprake, J. and Rogers, P., 2014b. Transecting the strand union workhouse: An excursion into social history along digital geo-located paths. In: O. Rhys and Z. Baveystock, eds., *Collecting the contemporary*. Boston: MuseumsEtc.

Stevenson, C., 2008. Vantage points in the seventeenth-century city. *The London Journal*, 33 (3), 217–232.

Urry, J., 2002. *The tourist gaze*. London: Sage.

Urry, J., 2007. *Mobilities*. Malden, MA: Polity Press.

14

DESIGNING HUBS FOR CONNECTED LEARNING

Social, Spatial, and Technological Insights from Coworking Spaces, Hackerspaces, and Meetup Groups

Mark Bilandzic and Marcus Foth

Introduction

In the knowledge economy of the twenty-first century, where disruptive innovation and creativity is increasingly based at the intersection of fields, disciplines, and cultures (Johansson 2004), locales for meeting and interacting with people from diverse backgrounds, cultures, and areas of expertise become more and more significant. Human need and desire to interact, work, and learn in socially diverse, real-world environments are illustrated by globally emerging trends of local, bottom-up, grassroots community initiatives such as Jelly coworking spaces (workatjelly.com 2012), hackerspaces (Borland 2007; Tweney 2009; Altman 2012) or meetup groups (Sander 2005; Edgerly 2010). These groups function as popular locales, where participants can engage in intrinsically-motivated activities whilst being co-present in a shared space with other likeminded people from different backgrounds, industry sectors, disciplines, fields, and organizations. Such communities where people are bound, come together, and seek participation based on what they do, share, and learn from each other have been defined as "Communities of Practice" (Wenger 1998, 1999). A crucial by-product (Schugurensky 2000; Bennett 2012) of participation in such communities of practice is social learning, a learning experience that Bingham and Conner define as:

> [the] result [of] people becoming more informed, gaining a wider perspective, and being able to make better decisions by engaging with others. [Social learning] acknowledges that learning happens with and through other people, as a matter of participating in a community, not just by acquiring knowledge.
>
> (2010, p. 7)

Thomas and Seely-Brown analyze how local communities of practice interconnect globally across geographical boundaries forming what they refer to as collectives (Thomas and Seely-Brown 2011, p. 52), i.e. networks of likeminded people that leverage online tools, platforms, and services in order to engage in their peer-culture and areas of passion as well as to share, collaborate, teach, and learn from each other.

Despite the new opportunities and benefits of online spaces, there is still a need for local hubs that facilitate social learning in physical places for communities of practice. This evident desire to mingle with likeminded peers, as well as members of other communities of practice—with their idiosyncratic backgrounds, cultures, and areas of expertise—has triggered a number of trends across different spaces over the past decade. Public libraries—as traditional facilitators of information, knowledge, and life-long learning—have been decreasing the number of bookshelves in order to provide more floorspace for infrastructure and interior design elements that invite coworking, peer-to-peer learning, and collaboration (Shill and Tonner 2003; Martin and Kenney 2004; LaPointe 2006; McDonald 2006), as well as serendipitous encounters amongst people of different ages, classes, cultures, religions, and ethnicities (Leckie and Hopkins 2002; Audunson 2005; Aabo, Audunson, and Varheim 2010; Aabo and Audunson 2012). Innovative organizations and office space proprietors experiment with different configurations of recreation, entertainment, and hospitality facilities, blended with professional office equipment and resources, aiming to not only make employees feel at ease, comfortable, and more productive, but also to increase opportunities for networking and serendipitous cross-fertilization of knowledge and ideas amongst colleagues. Coworking spaces started to gain global popularity in 2006 and have been experiencing exponential growth (Deskmag 2011)—providing similar, carefully curated, shared workspaces that facilitate networking and interaction opportunities across organizational and disciplinary boundaries.

A common feature in all these recent trends is a version of what has recently been promoted as connected learning (Ito et al. 2013)—a model that regards effective learning primarily as interest-driven and socially embedded experiences made in and across a variety of social networks and institutions (e.g. schools, libraries, museums). Rather than representing a learning theory per se, connected learning, as recently formulated by Ito et al., is an approach to education that is realized

> when a young person is able to pursue a personal interest or passion with the support of friends and caring adults, and is in turn able to link this learning and interest to academic achievement, career success or civic engagement.
>
> (2013, p. 4)

The connected learning research agenda focuses on mechanisms to intertwine and cross-fertilize learning made across the domains of personal interest and passion, peer culture, as well as academic and career life. This agenda covers design questions related to opportunities in physical, digital, as well as embodied hybrid spaces (Bilandzic and Johnson 2013), aiming to nourish the evolution of local and global supportive social networks for learning. Networked learning (Carvalho and Goodyear 2014) has had a similar agenda, based on learning as a social phenomenon; however, with a specific focus on how information and communications technology is used to facilitate connections to relevant learning networks and resources. As such, networked learning overlaps with connected learning. In fact, they share very similar design goals and methodological approaches: researchers and practitioners in both use phenomenological approaches in describing, analyzing, and understanding common practices and experiences of people who engage in connected/networked learning environments, in order to inform the future design of spaces that support respective forms of learning (De Laat and Jones 2016). Connected learning primarily addresses the gap between in-school and out-of-school learning and presents a useful theoretical position for understanding learning in coworking spaces.

This chapter contributes to the connected (and networked) learning research agenda by investigating three types of organically grown communities of practice (coworking spaces, hackerspaces, and meetup groups) where people meet in order to work together and share connected learning experiences. In particular, the chapter focuses on the following:

- *discourse and interactions:* What do people do when they meet for connected learning purposes? What structures and formats do their meetings and interactions follow?

- *location and infrastructure*: Where do they meet, and why do they meet where they meet?
- *intervention and facilitation*: What (social, spatial, technological) interventions do they employ to facilitate their connected learning experiences?

By means of understanding how such organically grown groups select, manage, curate, and coordinate their interactions and environments, this study aims to shed light on relevant socio-spatial aspects to inform the design of future spaces that support connected learning.

Investigating the Socio-Spatial Context of Meetup Groups, Hackerspaces, and Coworking Spaces

Meetup groups, hackerspaces, and coworking spaces were selected as instances of modern communities of practice where people regularly meet at local physical places, but also use digital tools and platforms to engage, learn, and connect with their community. This makes them timely and suitable case study subjects for the goals of this research.

We interviewed 13 organizers of meetup groups from Meetup.com in Brisbane, Australia. Prior to the interviews, we participated in seven of these meetup groups—for one or two of their sessions—in order to make observations and notes that would eventually inform the interview questions. In order to get broad insights from the meetup culture, we selected small non-profit, amateur meetups of up to 20 people (e.g. on filmmaking, photography, or writing; all free to attend or charging a nominal attendance fee of AUD \$2 to 5 to cover their basic costs), as well as meetups that regularly attract 200+ people for their events, e.g. focusing on creative thinking (Pecha Kucha), science education (BrisScience), or professional education in web design and digital marketing.

The first author has been an active member of Hackerspace Brisbane (HSBNE) and participated in their weekly meetups, making observations for six months prior to the interviews on hackerspace culture. We then interviewed the founding members or acting presidents of five hackerspaces across Australia (hackerspaces.org/wiki/Australia), i.e. HSBNE, Hackerspace Sydney (Robots and Dinosaurs), Hackerspace Adelaide, Gold Coast Techspace (GCTS), and Hackerspace Melbourne (CCHS—Connected Community HackerSpace).

To investigate the coworking space culture, we spent one week making observations at Hub Melbourne (hubmelbourne.com). Based on these observations, we conducted in-depth interviews with the general manager of Hub Melbourne as well as the general managers of three other coworking spaces in Australia. Thought Fort (thoughtfort.com.au) and Salt House (salthouse.bris.biz) have about 20 permanent coworkers each, whilst River City Labs (rivercitylabs.net) and Hub Melbourne represent bigger coworking spaces with a few hundred members each who come in more or less frequently, depending on their membership plan (ranging from every day to a few hours a month).

All interviews were conducted in face-to-face settings or via phone, according to each interviewee's availability and preference. The interviews were semi-structured and audio-recorded for follow-up transcription purposes. For the data analysis we followed a grounded theory approach (Strauss and Corbin 1997) and mapped (re-)emerging patterns as presented and discussed below.

Findings

Discourse and Interactions

The different communities of practice in this study follow different formats (structured, semi-structured, unstructured), have different levels of interaction between participants, and consequently

TABLE 14.1 The different groups in this study differ in the structure of interaction between participants, and learning experiences they provide.

	Group Interactions		
	Structured	*Semi-structured*	*Unstructured*
Format	strictly structured and fixed	semi-structured with room for co-curation by participants	unstructured, self-directed
Participation	passive	active or passive	active
Learning experience	curated, predictable	semi-curated, unpredictable	not curated, self-driven, social, serendipitous, unpredictable
Significance of interactivity with co-located participants	low	medium to high	high
Example	Pecha Kucha, BrisScience	Barcamp, Unconferences	coworking spaces, hackerspaces, small meetup groups

provide different learning experiences. An overview of the nature of group interactions that were found in the studied groups is presented in Table 14.1.

The smaller *meetup groups* in this study (Jelly, Games Engines, SNAP, Shut Up and Write) and hackerspaces mostly have no pre-structured elements that guide interactions and learning experiences amongst peers; group activities are often defined spontaneously, or are self-initiated and driven as individual projects, whilst co-present group members function as facilitators of each other's individual progress and learning experience. The learning outcome of these unstructured "hangouts" with the group is unpredictable and serendipitous. However, as Hackerspace Melbourne reports, the success of having a collaborative culture in the space depends on having

> a few key personalities who are actually doing a couple of things: drive enthusiasm, be willing and open to share their time and skill, to get other people involved or help them with their projects and so on . . . You kind of need almost these catalysing elements that will help it become a vibrant community, and partly there is leading by example.
>
> (Member, Hackerspace Melbourne)

In *hackerspaces*, this is usually the role of the president; however, this common ethos is also understood and promoted amongst all hackerspace members. The learning experience is heavily based on one's individual level of activity and openness to engage in interactions. More passive users usually have no or very poor (social) learning experiences (Figure 14.1).

Bigger group gatherings (Pecha Kucha, BrisScience) provide fixed timeslots for talks or presentations by pre-defined and promoted speakers. As such, the participation level of the audience is rather passive, and the learning experience quite predictable. (In other words, the range of learning opportunities is quite constrained.) The collective intelligence of participants is not leveraged as a learning resource during the talks; however, the social gatherings, conversations, and discussions around drinks and snacks after the talks provide a forum for richer social learning experiences. Barcamp, in contrast, is set up as an *unconference*, i.e. organized, curated, and driven by the

FIGURE 14.1 Hackerspace meetings usually do not have a learning agenda. Learning experiences are serendipitous and unpredictable, and based on active participation and self-driven interactions with other members.

participants themselves, rather than an official host. There are "no spectators—only participants," as our interviewee reported. All attendees are encouraged to contribute to the conference; either as a presenter or facilitator, e.g. through documenting the event via blog posts and sharing comments, pictures, links, and other relevant content via social media. The format of the event is semi-structured. It leaves plenty of opportunities for serendipitous encounters, conversations, discussions, and unpredictable (social) learning experiences, and provides a rough framework for particular user-driven activities. These include short "lightning talks" for attendees to share their projects, ideas, products, or any themes that they find interesting, and "show and tell" sessions to present work in progress or prototypes of current projects to inspire, discuss, and gather feedback from others. These elements are not only perceived as the core attraction of the event, but also as a means to spark interest and provide ice-breakers for follow-up conversations and connections amongst participants.

Coworking spaces mostly aim at providing unstructured environments, with respect to the kinds of activity in which people engage, though the material environment and the modes in which it may be used are more structured. Similar to the behavioral norm in hackerspaces, people in coworking spaces are focused on their individual, self-directed activities, but seek to gain social learning experiences as a result of sharing the same physical space with other coworkers.

A core aspect across all meetup groups, hackerspaces, and coworking spaces in this study is that their members perceive them as *social environments*, rather than purely *physical destinations*. The groups are founded and maintained as forums for social gathering, collaboration, and knowledge sharing with likeminded others. As such, they are different from the traditional notion of communities, as they are generally not based on a sense of *belonging* to a geographic location (Gusfield 1975; Foth et al. 2008) or to a group of people with close emotional ties. Rather, they have a sense of working convivially with others.

The meetup groups and hackerspaces in this study illustrate examples of communities of practice that regularly meet in physical environments where knowledge is being created and shared in a peer-to-peer and face-to-face fashion. People become part of these communities to feed their need for learning, progressing as well as expanding their skills, knowledge, and expertise in particular domains. The organizer of the local IxDA Brisbane group, for example, reports that the goal was to establish a platform for professional "User Interface and User Experience Designers" to network and connect with each other across organizational boundaries.

> [T]he core motivation of running a local IxDA group is to provide a space for interaction design and user experience design professionals in Brisbane to get together, share and learn from each other, giving professionals the opportunity to have contact with other likeminded and similarly skilled people outside of their workplace.

Other groups are formed based on their desire to connect with similar people within a larger subculture. Women who work in IT, for example, share the same interest, but—as a minority in the industry—struggle with particular issues. Girl Geek was formed as a meetup group for women who are interested in IT to support and help each other, share tips and experiences, and build networks. As one interviewee explains "you want to connect to someone who has not only the same interest to you, but also is similar to you; being a girl in this [IT] industry can be quite hard."

People's participation and learning is not reinforced or directed by a third party, such as a teacher or instructor, nor is it rewarded with a certificate, diploma, or degree. Participation in these communities is intrinsically motivated by personal interest and curiosity. Learning happens as a result of a more or less unstructured social gathering of people in a shared physical space, and of interactions that take place at those gatherings. As the founder of Hackerspace Adelaide reports:

> Something magic happens just by getting people together. When they are all together in one room, you work on your thing and just mention your idea or problem and someone else randomly picks up on that idea and comments on it and all of a sudden you have these ideas coming from different people. That's something bigger than everyone working on individual stuff.

Unlike in *formal* (schools, universities) and many *informal* learning environments (workshops, driving lessons, cooking classes), there tend to be no set agendas or learning goals. Rather, peer-to-peer learning and the exchange of experiences and knowledge are practiced through informal conversations and interactions with others. As a member from Hackerspace Melbourne puts it:

> turning up at a Hackerspace meeting, you never quite know who is gonna be there on a given night. Some nights there are people just doing research on their project, but you know, you'll turn up another night and some dude who has never turned up before has arrived with some bizarre thing they've created. It's fun to just go and hear these stories and see what they've built.

As such, the hackerspace and meetup groups provide an environment for intrinsically motivated, self-directed activities. At the same time, sharing the same space with a community of likeminded, creative other users, individuals are exposed to what Schugurensky (2000) refers to as incidental learning and learning through socialization. The function of the actual space is important (as described in the next section). Similarly, the philosophy of coworking spaces is to create benefit through knowledge spillovers and inspirations amongst coworkers. As one of the coworking space managers summarizes it: "The real asset, I suppose, is not the lease or the desks or any of that stuff, it's the relationships of people within the space. And I mean that's why people come back. That's why people work here."

Location and Infrastructure

Space is *built*, *selected*, or *organically re-appropriated* according to the group's needs and activities. The hackerspaces in this study all started as meetups of interested enthusiasts without having their own dedicated spaces. Hackerspace Sydney was started at a random public cafe in Sydney, which soon became overcrowded by more than a hundred participants. As the group became too big, they had to leave the cafe and continue their meeting on a close-by parking lot. One participant offered his vacant house as a gathering place, where soon after, people started bringing along tools and equipment to work with and share with the community. A couple of years later, the community became big enough, and financially strong enough, to afford and rent out a proper hackerspace. A similar evolution is reported by the founders of Hackerspace Brisbane, Adelaide, and Melbourne.

Other meetup groups, who are not yet large enough and do not have their own fixed community spaces yet, gather in public places in the city, such as bars, cafes, or restaurants. Such places have usually not been designed with collaborative or creative activities in mind, but rather as places for socialization or consumption. The groups carefully select their meetup place based on particular criteria, and apply tactical practices to re-appropriate such spaces according to their needs.

They tend to gravitate toward places that are easily accessible (central location in the city, close-by public transport, etc.), provide the required infrastructure for their group-specific activities (e.g. desks for work on laptops, projectors for presentations, WiFi, etc.), and have a social environment that suits their needs. The Games Engines and IxDA group, for example, seek quiet environments to film their presentations or work on collaborative tasks with minimal external disruptions. The Silicon Beach meetup, on the other hand, aims to facilitate initial connections between people who have mutual or complementary interests (technology developers/entrepreneurs, entrepreneurs/investors). They hold their meetups in local bars or restaurants to facilitate sociality whilst having food and drinks; work spaces are not required.

Meetups continuously evaluate and renegotiate their meetup space as their groups evolve. The Brisbane Jelly coworking group, for example, started as a meetup in the public library, but was not happy with the "no food" and "no backpacks" policy. They migrated to a close-by community center, which allowed food and backpacks; however, as their work was mainly laptop based and involved intense Internet usage, they found the lounge areas with no desks uncomfortable to work from, and the WiFi too slow for their purposes. Eventually, group members started to move desks from adjacent rooms to the communal lounge areas, and set up private 4G WiFi routers to create their own wireless Internet networks, which provided faster Internet access than the public one shared by all other visitors.

Other meetups, after realizing that they cannot appropriate public third spaces according to their needs, escape to private homes or office spaces that group participants volunteer for the group after work hours. The Brisbane IxDA meetup group, for example, started their meetings at a local Brisbane bar, but soon moved to an office space of the group organizer's employer, where they could use office facilities, the stationary cupboard, projector, and speakers to engage in collaborative workshop activities, or participate in interactive online workshops together. The office also provides a controlled, closed environment in the Central Business District (CBD), so the group does not have to worry about external interruptions.

However, a space that only provides optimal work conditions is often not sufficient. The SNAP architects meetup group, for example, is familiar with the recently launched local library space that provides dedicated meeting spaces and cutting edge technology infrastructure. However, the group does not use it for their meetings, because it does not cater for the social needs of the group very well. As the founder of SNAP architects reported:

> you can't get a glass of wine there or a beer [laughs]. Which I think, you know, you're asking people to come along after a full day's work and you're trying to create a setting that's overlapping, you wanna feel like you're going to something relaxing with friends yet at the same time you're really having like a meeting. So I don't know, being able to get a drink there is really one of the prerequisites I think.

On the other hand, if the atmosphere at a place is too social, the group does not feel comfortable with engaging in activities that are obviously work related.

> If you went to a lot of bars and you had, you know, several people there with like you know notepads and drawings, in most bars you'd probably feel like an idiot I think [laughing]. You've got all these people partying and yelling, and you know you'd feel a bit silly.
>
> (Founder, SNAP architects)

As a trade-off, the group specifically seeks places with an atmosphere that provides a healthy balance between formal work and sociality. An optimal place should accommodate what the interviewee refers to as "half-social, half-information meeting type situations." SNAP found two spots that cater for these specific needs, a cafe close to the library and a restaurant bar in the CBD. The founder describes the social atmosphere at these places as follows:

> [The cafe] at the State Library, there is WiFi and there are people there who you're competing for tables with, who have their laptop and they're skyping someone, they're drinking their coffee or having their wine. It's got that sort of overlap from the social and the sort of information transfer. And the same with [the restaurant bar] in the city, because it's like a bar in the city, business people would go there and meet there and it's open enough; it's not so noisy, so it's always people who've come down from the offices around "cause you know it's in the base, the podium around this office tower. . . . so there is always those sort of people having little business meetings.

A member of Hackerspace Melbourne reports that when they were looking for a space, it was important that it not only allowed "noisy, dirty and smelly activities without the fear of damaging good flooring," but could also host separate soft work areas (software programming and laptop activities) and social areas (kitchen, couches, TV, and game console area for chilling out, chatting, and relaxing). Such a mix between soft work areas and social areas was also a key selection criterion for Hackerspace Brisbane, when they were searching for their new premises.

The bigger meetup groups in our study recognized this need and provide catering service ranging from finger food and drinks to organized dinners. The BrisScience group—organized by the University of Queensland—invites a guest speaker for each of their monthly events, who gives a talk on science and technology related topics. The popularity of the gatherings is significantly based on the fact that it is perceived as a social outing that is fun, enjoyable, and informative, rather than a traditional science lecture.

You know, you would go and watch the ballet, or go to an art gallery and you would get enjoyment out of watching those things. I don't think there is any . . . shouldn't be any difference between those sorts of leisure pursuits and going to see a really stimulating science talk. The only difference is that you don't usually go to a science lecture and sip your wine while you discuss dinosaurs or cosmology.

(Organizer, BrisScience)

The organizers deliberately picked a venue off-campus in the city center, and close to the main train station. The meetup is easily accessible and attracts over 200 participants per event, mostly from the general public, not just academics. Similar setups and motivations were described by the organizers of Pecha Kucha Brisbane (a lightning talk series around design, arts, and other creative fields), Barcamp (an unconference around digital technology), and Silicon Beach (a meetup group for entrepreneurs, founders, and investors). In all these meetups, the actual core purpose of meeting up (e.g. peer-to-peer learning, inspiration, exchanging knowledge and experiences, discussion about latest developments in the field, networking, etc.) is embodied in practices of socialization, such as having drinks, snacks, and informal conversations. This fact is important to consider when designing spaces and making *places* that host such communities of practice. Professional coworking spaces embody some best practices for spatial facilitation in this regard, as described further below.

Intervention and Facilitation

Based on a comparison between coworking spaces, hackerspaces, and meetup groups in this study, we made the following observation: The bigger the group, the more opportunities for social learning there are; however, the more numerous and heterogeneous the people in the group are, the more facilitation is required to nurture connection, interaction, and social learning (Figure 14.2).

In the smaller coworking spaces in this study (Thought Fort and Salt House) with around 20 mid- to long-term members who work in the same or related industries (online marketing, web development, graphic design, etc.), social interaction between coworkers occurs almost naturally as a result of a small number frequently sharing the same physical space and interests. According to the Thought Fort manager "there is surely ways that we can make it better . . . , but I guess we just don't have such a big necessity for that."

At bigger coworking spaces (Hub Melbourne, River City Labs), on the other hand, a few hundred members regularly go in and out. In addition, they work across a wider variety of industry sectors (government, corporate businesses, small to medium enterprises, non-profits, social enterprises, academia) and disciplines (sustainability, technology and web, change management, organization development, arts and entertainment, innovation processes, journalism). As a consequence, there is no obvious connection between two random coworkers, and the space being regularly traversed by hundreds of people counteracts the natural bonding of small place-based communities. Therefore, bigger coworking spaces tend to invest more effort and resources in facilitating social learning experiences amongst their coworkers. We identified three major types of interventions: social, technological, and spatial facilitation.

Social Facilitation

Hub Melbourne hired a full-time person to catalyze connections between members—the "Space Host."

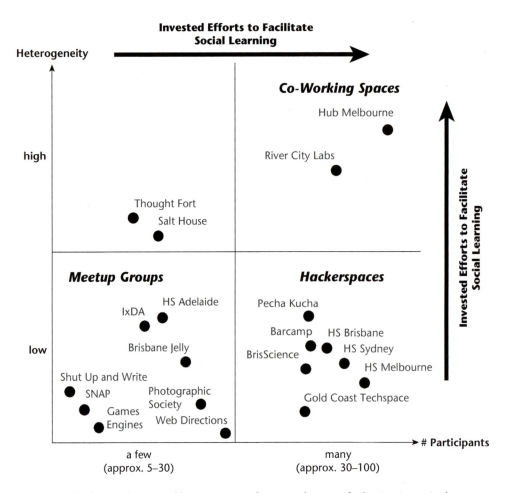

FIGURE 14.2 The bigger the size and heterogeneity of a group, the more facilitation is required to nurture connection, interaction, and social learning.

> Her role, full time, is to connect people. Which means that every single person who walks into Hub Melbourne knows her. She is everyone's friend, and it is through that friend, the Host, who will introduce you to someone else, that trust is built. We trust our peers, so she is now your peer and is able to build a connection with you, and that's how collaboration happens.
>
> (Member, Hub Melbourne)

The Space Host is carefully recruited as a person who understands work across different sectors, industries, disciplines, and cultures; she is a generalist, rather than a specialist, being able to understand the value of each individual member and their background, profession, and areas of expertise, to catalyze connections where there is a potential for collaboration. The Host also needs to have a "social touch" that allows her to not only match people based on their passion and skillsets, but also their personalities, attitudes, and beliefs—crucial factors for fruitful collaboration. Due to exponentially growing memberships, Hub Melbourne makes an active effort to crowd-source the role of the Host by encouraging all coworkers to catalyze connections, and reinforce a culture of networking and collaboration:

We often also make it very, very clear and obvious to everyone that you have the permission and you should connect people and be the Host yourself. . . . we think it's very natural for people to do certain things, but a lot of times even ourselves, we often need permission before we do anything . . . So we always make it very clear, and always tell people you have the permission to be the Host and you should be the Host as well.

(Member, Hub Melbourne)

Furthermore, established members can volunteer for a buddy system that helps new members to feel welcome, get connected, and settle in the space during the first three months of their membership. Hub Melbourne supports their members to initiate or join what are called "Hub Clubs"—member-driven groups that gather around a particular interest or passion (e.g. the "runners club" meets every Tuesday for a run through the city, and the "business club" forms around the exchange of ideas and concepts to improve businesses). This initiative nourishes little, tightly knit sub-communities within its larger community of coworkers. Informal social events such as brown bag lunches, shared dinners, or "Social Beer Fridays," also forge new cross-links between coworkers, creating a more and more connected, and tightly knit community. River City Labs as well as Hub Melbourne regularly invite industry experts to give a talk or workshop about a topic relevant to the coworkers' businesses. This provides another opportunity for likeminded coworkers to meet and "rub shoulders" before, in, and after such events.

Technological Facilitation

The different groups in this study, in particular the bigger meetup groups, hackerspaces, and coworking spaces, apply various technologies to connect and stay connected with other group members.

Hackerspace members are connected via IRC (an instant messaging system) and different email mailing lists (which connect each hackerspace locally as well as all hackerspaces across Australia)—all of which are logged, openly accessible, and browsable in history. The number of subscribers to the email lists are often ten times the number of active members (e.g. Hackerspace Adelaide has 10 to 12 members and approximately 150 mailing list subscribers, Hackerspace Sydney has 30 to 40 members and over 400 mailing list subscribers), which suggests that the conversational topics within the spaces are of interest to a broader community, of which the majority appear to be "lurkers" (Ebner, Holzinger, and Catarci 2005). In addition, many hackerspaces have websites or wikis listing tutorials of previous projects, instructions for particular tools and machinery, or lists of members with their particular areas of expertise. Such digital sources make it easy for members to identify other members with complementary skills and experiences.

Coworking spaces use various social media platforms to provide a virtual backchannel for their members. River City Labs has a Facebook group, Google Plus, and Google Groups. At Hub Melbourne, every member is automatically given a Yammer account, which is used as a continuous backchannel to share news, seek collaborators, ask for tips and recommendations, and announce or organize social after-work events. Recording and analyzing the number of visits and amount of Yammer messages per day over a period of one year, Hub Melbourne found that the amount of Yammer messages significantly correlates with the number of people who visit the space per day. These use patterns underscore the significance of Yammer as a simultaneous background channel between co-present coworkers. At the same time, members who do not work in situ regularly participate in such conversations. In addition, Hub Melbourne manually selects the core discussion themes and topics from members across different social media networks (Yammer, Facebook, and Twitter) and cross-pollinates the conversations by aggregating content into their weekly email newsletter.

Spatial Facilitation

The spatial infrastructure and interior design of all coworking spaces were designed with collaboration and social interaction in mind. For example, an active effort is made to keep the space open and the furniture is mostly arranged in a way that does not obstruct sightlines, but rather facilitates mutual awareness amongst coworkers. The Thought Fort manager reports that they:

> managed to find quite unusual desks, almost like triangle desks but with a curve edge, so three of those would fit together to form like a circle of desks . . . , so people weren't looking into the wall, but you could see sort of half the room. Not looking directly at anyone, but you're in an easy talking range.

Different *zones* are created to accommodate different types of work, activities, and moods. The main coworking area at Hub Melbourne, for example, provides different styles and sizes of desks (round, rectangle, small, large) to accommodate individual as well as team work (Figure 14.3). The interior is purposefully separated into meeting areas with whiteboards, a boardroom with video conferencing and presentation facilities, an idea room for brainstorming, silent areas for individual focused tasks, couches for informal conversations, a relaxation area with beach chairs and a hammock, and a large kitchen to prepare coffee and meals.

All coworking spaces in this study have a kitchen that allows members to store and prepare their own drinks and food. In the interviews, the kitchen was often described as a place where conversations between random individuals are easily initiated, as there is a mutual understanding that the other person is not being interrupted at work. Kitchens are perceived as what Goffman refers to as "open regions" (1966, p. 132), i.e. environments where it is socially acceptable to initiate a face-to-face conversation with a stranger. They are also designed as what our earlier meetup group interviewee referred to as "half-social, half-information meeting type situations." Hub Melbourne has a large dining table, a small library, and comfortable chairs, which invite activities in the kitchen that blend socialization and work. In fact, in the six days of observations, the kitchen at Hub Melbourne was almost continuously populated with people having breakfast, preparing lunch, or brewing tea or coffee whilst discussing work-related matters.

FIGURE 14.3 Coworking space at Hub Melbourne. The interior suits individual as well as collaborative work, and accommodates different activities and moods of work.

Source: Screenshot from http://hubmelbourne.com/coworking-space

Implications for the Design of Connected Learning Spaces

Meetup groups, hackerspaces, and coworking spaces represent grassroots initiatives to provide local forums for social interaction, collaboration, and encounters with other people around a shared interest. In contrast to traditional, fairly isolated organizational workspaces, they are based on open locales that continuously attract new people from various backgrounds, fields, disciplines, and interests. In doing so, they take better leverage of the social pluralism and diversity of urban environments. The exposure to people from other backgrounds, interests, and professional domains, as well as the opportunity to collaborate and interact on shared interests, were perceived as the main benefits by their members in this study. It appears that meetup groups, hackerspaces, and coworking spaces form a new type of work and learning configuration, but, more significantly, provide precious locales for social capital to evolve across disciplinary boundaries—an increasingly important function in today's globalized and networked society.

Coming back to the initial aim of this study, what implications for the design of connected learning spaces can we deduce from the socio-spatial practices in the groups revealed in this study? The study's insights indicate that there is no "one size fits all" solution. Each of the communities of practice has its own spatial requirements and employs group interaction formats (structured, semi-structured, unstructured) according to the group's evolving needs and motivations. Space proprietors need to do research about their target knowledge community, and shape their space and infrastructure to accommodate their particular activities, practices, and spatial needs, rather than adopting generic solutions. In fact, the evolution of meetup groups and hackerspaces shows that their communities of practice evolve even before there is a dedicated space that facilitates their interactions. Space is built and continuously shaped, or selected and continuously evaluated and renegotiated according to the group's activities and evolving needs—not the other way around. Space proprietors need to be sensitive to this, and afford organic, bottom-up appropriation of space. The community should be embraced as co-creators, co-designers, and co-owners of the space, rather than just "tenants" or "users." They need to be able to take partial ownership and continuously adjust and re-appropriate spatial arrangements according to their needs. However, such user-led spaces can cause tensions with traditionally imposed top-down regulations, such as health and safety policies or the requirements of facilities management. Those need to be re-evaluated to allow more flexibility, whilst, at the same time, keeping order.

Spatial arrangements, such as a central location in the city or accessibility through public transport, ergonomic desk spaces, and supportive infrastructure for individual and collaborative work are crucial elements to attract users. At the same time, different communities of practice and coworkers might have contradicting or competing motivations and spatial requirements. Space proprietors need to think about the core target groups that they are trying to attract and how the space can accommodate all their activities. Different zones can be dedicated to different activities (meetings and discussions, silent laptop work, socialization, etc.). Further, varying the purpose of space zones at different times for particular activities could increase the number of activities that a space can accommodate.

Creating what Goffman refers to as "open regions" (1966, p. 132), i.e. physically bounded places where initiating face-to-face contacts with unacquainted others is socially acceptable, e.g. a shared kitchen, provides opportunities for coworkers to initiate face-to-face conversations without the fear of interrupting the other person in a work-related activity. Previous initiatives have developed design concepts for creating dedicated open sub-regions in public transport (Trinh 2011) or urban public places (Pope 2012) to encourage interactions between random strangers. Further research needs to investigate how such design concepts could be adapted to collaborative work and learning environments.

The findings also suggest that the design and planning of successful collaboration spaces should not only be concerned with spatial and architectural arrangements, but more so with *social facilitation* and community building. Meetup groups, hackerspaces, and coworking spaces are usually not only perceived as physical destinations, but, more importantly, as places to meet new people, network, as well as engage in connected learning and collaborative activities. However, a community of knowledge sharing, collaboration, and learning does not always come about naturally but needs to be facilitated. Space proprietors need to think how they can attract "key personalities" as they exist in hackerspaces and meetup groups, and encourage them to share their enthusiasm and passion with other users. Mechanisms such as reward, reciprocity, or reputation are often applied to motivate people to share knowledge and contribute to online platforms (forums, wikis, content sharing, etc.). Further research needs to investigate how equivalent programs can increase user engagement in physical spaces that host communities of practice, and, possibly, how they can be linked back to, and cross-pollinated with, equivalent online spaces. Further, just as public libraries employ librarians to catalyze connections between people and information resources (books, collections, digital archives, etc.), evolving communities of practice need someone to catalyze connections between people with similar or complementary skills. This is particularly important for bigger groups, as with increasing size it gets harder to maintain an open and social atmosphere. Insights from Hub Melbourne (hiring a "space host," initiation of social clubs and events, etc.) provide a good example of how community building and creation of strong ties can be facilitated even in relatively large communities (600+ members in this case). Whilst it might be counterintuitive for institutionalized learning environments such as public libraries to get a license for serving beverages, in meetup groups, hackerspaces, and coworking spaces it appears to be a crucial ingredient for facilitating social interactions, discussions, and thus, ultimately, the co-creation of knowledge.

Technology can be applied to complement the physical space with digital backchannels that make invisible social aspects of space visible, thus enabling users to better identify likeminded others. As Bullinger et al. (1998, pp. 17–18) found, the lack of awareness that one's skills might be useful for someone else, and the lack of awareness which skills are in demand, are the main barriers of knowledge transfer between colleagues in organizational settings. Yet, most organizational systems are based on groupware, i.e. systems that assume that participants know each other (email, teleconferencing systems, etc.). In this context, Wellman suggests we should think of technology as "networkware," i.e. systems that facilitate connections with new people through "search for information and the selective disclosure of one's own information" (2002, p. 8). Elsewhere, we provide an overview of locative and mobile media (Bilandzic and Foth 2012) and ambient media architecture (Caldwell, Bilandzic, and Foth 2012) that facilitate such connections between physically co-located people. Space proprietors need to think about how such technologies can be applied to facilitate social interaction and contribute to community building within the space.

Conclusion

This chapter presents socio-spatial insights from meetup groups, hackerspaces, and coworking spaces. The findings show that their communities of practice serve as successful and—in the context of today's knowledge economy—increasingly important venues to meet and interact with likeminded people. They embrace the pluralism and diversity of society by providing open and inviting locales for networked individuals to meet around their work, interests, and passion—outside of the isolated barriers of formal employment and home. The tactical practices applied by the groups to find and reappropriate public places to suit their interactions and practices underscore their need for dedicated spaces that support their activities. The chapter explores and discusses a number of organically established patterns and best practices found in meetup groups, hackerspaces, and coworking spaces that not only contribute to accommodate spatial arrangements, but also to shape, nourish, and maintain a supportive community. These facilitations embrace spatial, social, and technological interventions, and are relevant considerations for designers, managers, and decision makers who have an interest in nourishing a place-based knowledge community, e.g. libraries, corporate office buildings, research laboratories, coworking spaces, etc.

References

Aabo, S. and Audunson, R., 2012. Use of library space and the library as place. *Library & Information Science Research*, 34(2), 138–149.

Aabo, S., Audunson, R., and Varheim, A., 2010. How do public libraries function as meeting places? *Library & Information Science Research*, 32(1), 16–26.

Altman, M., 2012. The hackerspace movement. [online]. Available from: https://www.youtube.com/watch?v=WkiX7R1-kaY [Accessed October 30, 2015].

Audunson, R., 2005. The public library as a meeting-place in a multicultural and digital context: The necessity of low-intensive meeting-places. *Journal of Documentation*, 61(3), 429–441.

Bennett, E., 2012. A four-part model of informal learning: Extending Schugurensky's conceptual model. In: *The proceedings of the Adult Education Research Conference,* May 31–June 3, 2012, Saratoga Springs. Saratoga Springs, NY: AERC.

Bilandzic, M. and Foth, M., 2012. A review of locative media, mobile and embodied spatial interaction. *International Journal of Human-Computer Studies*, 70(1), 66–71.

Bilandzic, M. and Johnson, D., 2013. Hybrid placemaking in the library: Designing digital technology to enhance users' on-site experience. *Australian Library Journal,* 62(4), 258–271.

Bingham, T. and Conner, M., 2010. *The new social learning.* San Francisco: Berrett-Koehler Publishers Inc.

Borland, J., 2007. "Hacker space" movement sought for U.S. [online]. Available from: www.wired.com/threatlevel/2007/08/us-hackers-moun [Accessed October 30, 2015].

Bullinger, H.-J., Warschat, J., Prieto, J., and Wörner, K., 1998. Wissensmanagement und wirklichkeit: Ergebnisse einer unternehmensstudie in Deutschland. *Information Management*, 1(98), 7–23.

Caldwell, G., Bilandzic, M., and Foth, M., 2012. Towards visualising people's ecology of hybrid personal learning environments. In: *The 4th Media Architecture Biennale Conference*, November 15–17, Aarhus, Denmark. Aarhus: MAB.

Carvalho, L. and Goodyear, P., eds., 2014. *The architecture of productive learning networks.* New York: Taylor & Francis.

De Laat, M. and Jones, C., 2016. Networked learning. In: C. Haythornwaite, R. Andrews, J. Fransman, and M. Kazmer, eds., *The Sage handbook of e-learning research.* London: Sage

Deskmag, 2011. The birth of coworking spaces. [online]. Available from: www.deskmag.com/en/the-birth-of-coworking-spaces-global-survey-176 [Accessed October 30, 2015].

Ebner, M., Holzinger, A., and Catarci, T., 2005. Lurking: An underestimated human-computer phenomenon. *Multimedia, IEEE*, 12(4), 70–75.

Edgerly, P.M., 2010. *Using the internet as an access to leisure: A study of Meetup.* Sacramento: California State University.

Foth, M., Choi, J. H., Bilandzic, M., and Satchell, C., 2008. Collective and network sociality in an urban village. In: *Proceedings MindTrek: 12ᵗʰ International Conference on Entertainment and Media in the Ubiquitous Era*, October 7–9, Tampere, Finland. Tampere: MindTrek08.

Goffman, E., 1966. *Behavior in public places: Notes on the social organization of gatherings.* New York: Free Press.

Gusfield, J. R., 1975. *The community: A critical response.* New York: Harper Colophon.

Ito, M., Gutiérrez, K., Livingstone, S., Penuel, B., Rhodes, J., Salen, K., Schor, J., Sefton-Green, J., and Watkins, S. C., 2013. Connected learning: An agenda for research and design. [online]. Available from: http://dml-hub.net/publications/connected-learning-agenda-for-research-and-design/ [Accessed October 30, 2015].

Johansson, F., 2004. *The Medici effect: Breakthrough insights at the intersection of ideas, concepts, and cultures.* Boston: Harvard Business Press.

LaPointe, L. M., 2006. Coffee anyone? *College & research libraries news*, 67(2), 97–99.

Leckie, G. J. and Hopkins, J., 2002. The public place of central libraries: Findings from Toronto and Vancouver. *The Library Quarterly*, 72(3), 326–372.

Martin, E. and Kenney, B., 2004. Great libraries in the making: A new generation of innovative public libraries is on the boards. *Library Journal*, 129(20), 70–73.

McDonald, A., 2006. The ten commandments revisited: The qualities of good library space. *LIBER Quarterly*, 16(2), 104–119.

Pope, C., 2012. The lonely battle of the chatty yellow bench. *Irish Times*. [online]. Available from: www.irishtimes.com/life-and-style/people/the-lonely-battle-of-the-chatty-yellow-bench-1.538258 [Accessed October 30, 2015].

Sander, T. H., 2005. E-associations? Using technology to connect citizens: The case of meetup.com. Paper presented at the annual meeting of the American Political Science Association, August 31–September 3, 2005, Washington, DC. [online]. Available from: www.hks.harvard.edu/saguaro/pdfs/e-associations.pdf [Accessed July 17, 2015].

Schugurensky, D., 2000. The forms of informal learning: Towards a conceptualization of the field. NALL Working Paper No.19. [online]. Available from: https://tspace.library.utoronto.ca/bitstream/1807/2733/2/19formsofinformal.pdf [Accessed July 17, 2015].

Shill, H. B. and Tonner, S., 2003. Creating a better place: Physical improvements in academic libraries, 1995–2002. *College & Research Libraries*, 64(6), 431–466.

Strauss, A. L. and Corbin, J. M., 1997. *Grounded theory in practice*. Thousand Oaks, CA: Sage Publications.

Thomas, D. and Seely-Brown, J., 2011. *A new culture of learning: Cultivating the imagination for a world of constant change*. Lexington, KY: CreateSpace.

Trinh, Y., 2011. Priority seating for people who want conversation. [online]. Available from: http://priorityseat.wordpress.com [Accessed October 30, 2015].

Tweney, D., 2009. DIY freaks flock to "hacker spaces" worldwide. [online]. Available from: www.wired.com/gadgetlab/2009/03/hackerspaces [Accessed October 30, 2015].

Wellman, B., 2002. Little boxes, glocalization, and networked individualism. In: M. Tanabe, P. van den Besselaar, and T. Ishida, eds., *Digital Cities*, Vol. LNCS 2362. Heidelberg, Germany: Springer.

Wenger, E., 1998. Communities of practice: Learning as a social system. *Systems Thinker*, 9(5), 2–3.

Wenger, E., 1999. *Communities of practice: Learning, meaning, and identity*. Cambridge: Cambridge University Press.

workatjelly.com, 2012. What is Jelly? [online]. Available from: http://wiki.workatjelly.com [Accessed October 30, 2015].

15

SPACES ENABLING CHANGE

X-Lab and Science Education 2020

Tina Hinton, Pippa Yeoman, Leslie Ashor, and Philip Poronnik

Introduction

Undergraduate science students learn science by "doing science" in the teaching laboratory. Laboratory-based learning provides the setting for tasks and the instructional approaches that facilitate practical application and consolidation of theoretical concepts and key principles in a discipline. Laboratories create opportunities for students to apply knowledge in "real world" and experimental contexts and to engage in the valued practices of scientists (DeHaan 2005). Traditionally, laboratory-based learning has been understood as the acquisition and application of discipline-specific knowledge, alongside valued practices in sciences such as interdisciplinary approaches to problem and solution generation, experimental design and analysis, quantitative competencies and manual research skills used in field or laboratory settings. Laboratory-based learning is also seen to foster the so-called generic, or transferable, skills such as communication and collaboration, the ability to act with autonomy and initiative and in an ethical and professional manner. In this chapter, we argue that laboratory-based learning involves "apprenticeship, authentic engagement in practice, legitimate peripheral participation, experiential learning, etc." (Goodyear and Carvalho 2013, p. 50); it is about "learning by doing," in a way that brings a learner closer to "learning to be" (Brown 2006). Hence we view students' participation in (and engagement with) learning activities, in a setting that offers continuous exposure to valued practices of scientists, as key factors in facilitating students' learning. We take a networked learning perspective to understand the connections between tools, tasks, and people (Goodyear 2005) within a teaching laboratory. The approach focuses on activity, asserting that there are some things that can be designed (e.g. tools and equipment in the physical or digital spaces, tasks proposed to students, social arrangements for groups in the lab), but the activity of students cannot be entirely predicted (Goodyear and Carvalho 2014a, 2014b). We argue that this networked learning perspective provides a fruitful basis to understand how the space, and its digital and material elements, may influence students' activity, as they learn discipline knowledge, and develop competencies and skills within science education. Social structures enabled by the physical/digital space set-up and the activities that occur within the space support the development of learning networks.

In contrast to traditional laboratory-based learning, current trends seem to place an emphasis on participatory learning. As a result, newly designed teaching laboratories and their environs now accommodate place-based access to an extended social network, which aims at facilitating and fostering the learning of science through on- and off-site connections, in which students work in teams on common problems toward shared outcomes. These teams develop the social, intellectual, and human capital to create problems, solutions, and outcomes in research-like settings that cannot be achieved by individuals working alone. In these respects learning activity in and around teaching laboratories is both physically and socially situated (Lave and Wenger 1991) and can be likened to learning studios, which promote collaboration in learning, with students and staff learning skills from one another and from each other's mistakes (Brown 2006). In this way students become creators and constructors of their own knowledge using the means by which scientific knowledge is created and constructed in practice; through open-ended scientific enquiry, exploration, and discovery within a curriculum that facilitates and enables research-like experiences (McWilliam, Poronnik, and Taylor 2008). The undergraduate teaching laboratory therefore provides an ideal setting to observe and evaluate student participation in learning activities and scientific practices, the influence of space and task design on learner activity, and the development of learning networks. In this chapter we describe an evaluation study of the X-Lab, a large, open-plan "wet" teaching laboratory housed in the Charles Perkins Centre, The University of Sydney (CPC), intended for multidisciplinary and interdisciplinary learning and teaching of the biomedical sciences. Our focus is on how the physical and virtual spaces of the X-Lab, within a multi- and interdisciplinary context, may influence learning and teaching activities.

The use of both physical and virtual space in curriculum design and the impact of this use on learning and teaching practices is gaining increasing attention in the higher education sector. The ways instructors and students use space, how they orientate themselves in space, the tools and instrumentation used for instruction and learning, and how these can be arranged and manipulated in the spaces, all influence learning and teaching activities. Space can therefore be seen as an enabler of change. Design decisions made in the creation of new learning spaces can partially shape how one learns and teaches (Kolb and Kolb 2005; Oblinger 2006; Boys 2011).

Many higher education institutions in Australia are investing in the design and redesign of buildings and grounds in acknowledgment of the necessity to refocus on the campus experience and needs of both students and staff (Lippincott 2009; Radcliffe 2009). Such "macro" level design processes can have a powerful influence on what happens at the "meso" level—the design of tasks that occur in spaces—as well as the "micro" level, for example choosing which pipettes to use (Goodyear and Carvalho 2013). The influence of space and the physical setting (digital and material) on learning activity is important, but under-researched (Goodyear, Carvalho, and Dohn 2014). Moreover, little evidence exists in the literature for research linking space design and learning outcomes, with much of the literature making unsupported or anecdotal claims about the benefits of changes to space design or configurations (Temple 2008). According to Lippincott (2009), considering the interrelationships between curriculum, pedagogical style, spaces (physical and virtual), and goals for student learning in the design process can yield major dividends. However, there is little work to demonstrate what these major dividends include, and how these improvements are measured.

In the next section, we offer a brief overview of traditional and current teaching trends in laboratory settings, followed by an introduction to the X-Lab facilities. We then present the evaluation tool used in our study, and discuss our findings, including the notion of the X-Lab as a place-based space for networked learning and how space can be seen as an enabler of change in science education.

Traditional and Current Teaching Laboratory Trends and the X-lab

In traditional teaching laboratory design, rooms are usually designed and furnished based on student count, anticipated learning activities, and factors relating to discipline or institutional goals. Group size is often based on subsets of the cohort, for example a 240-student cohort may be subdivided into two groups of 120 or four groups of 60 and these decisions will be guided by the number of students an instructor or institution believes they can manage, as well as access to assistants, teaching resources, and physical space. Some instructors prefer smaller laboratory sections due to perceived hazards, a desire to provide a more intimate and or interactive learning experience, concerns about levels of noise, as well as the challenges associated with the setting up and taking down of materials at student stations.

Arrangements of teaching laboratories have evolved from early single sided benches with "all eyes forward" facing the instructor, to more collaborative arrangements, which support students working in teams in active learning models, with less emphasis on what is occurring at the "front" of the laboratory. A significant decrease in the costs associated with computing technologies has replaced limited access to shared resources housed around a "dry" perimeter, with one-to-one access to smaller, multimedia-enabled machines equipped with specialized scientific applications at student workstations to be used during hands-on practical activities.

The shortcomings of historical teaching laboratories include the duplication of equipment and instrumentation, overscheduling of spaces where they support too many sections, and underutilization of spaces where they are designed to accommodate specialists. Further issues include a lack of flexibility to accommodate different physical working configurations of students, individually or in groups, and the inability to design tasks which require access to physical and digital materials from a single workspace.

Current learning theory challenges old paradigms in which learners were less physically active in their environments. Learning spaces must now support a pedagogical style that emphasizes interaction and engagement between staff and students, students and other students, and within teams of staff. Recommendations for planning such environments include generous margins for anticipating all manner of learning scenarios, including learning that is collaborative, active, blended, technology-enabled, mobile, integrated, multidisciplinary, simulated or real-world, hybrid, and augmented (Dugdale 2009; Wilson and Randall 2012).

The X-Lab in the Charles Perkins Centre at the University of Sydney not only meets the requirements for engaged and participatory learning but departs from the historical teaching model in respect of the desire to embody the paradigm of interdisciplinary and transdisciplinary learning akin to modern research environments. To enable this educational model, the laboratory was designed as a large, open space accommodating multiple disciplines and multiple techniques (molecular biology, cell culture, chemical synthesis, isolated tissue preparations, microbiology, biotechnology, etc.), across multiple degree programs, with different cohorts of various sizes engaged in different activities at the same time—all in a single teaching facility. In this way transparency in learning and teaching is facilitated, so that students can learn from other students and instructors are also able to learn and share practices. This departure would seem to be a natural evolution that has influenced research laboratories for the last 20–30 years; indeed the current focus on undergraduate research, as promoted by the American Council on Undergraduate Research (www.cur.org), is addressed in the design of the X-Lab. Most new research laboratories are built for flexibility, adaptability, enhanced collaboration, and sharing of costly equipment or specialty spaces, and the X-Lab has adopted these principles for the same reasons. Furnished with state-of-the-art instrumentation that is shared by all users, with an optimal student to equipment ratio, and through sophisticated information communications technology (ICT) solutions, the X-Lab is considered to facilitate research-like and hybrid learning in ways previously not able to be achieved. The affordances of the space are intended to prompt curriculum transformation to bring students closer to authentic learning of sciences in ways that model research and applications of science.

An Introduction to the X-Lab

The Charles Perkins Centre is the first example of the University of Sydney's commitment to creating environments that facilitate the emergence of new models of interdisciplinary engagement. It serves as a multi-faculty, cross-disciplinary research and education hub in which academic, technical, and support staff are co-located. Following its first year of occupancy, the Centre currently accommodates over 500 researchers, research students, and laboratory staff across four dedicated research levels, and the learning spaces, housed across two levels, were utilized by 7,450 students, 155 academic teaching staff, and 11 technical support staff for 782 classes in 84 units of study.

Learning and teaching spaces in the Centre have been designed with collaboration and flexibility in mind, to accommodate large student groups along with academic, technical, and support staff from different cohorts and disciplines (including biomedical, veterinary, health sciences, and molecular biosciences), years of candidature, units of study, and degree programs. Emerging from the design process are seven large, specialized learning spaces intended to accommodate a broad range of learning activities and extensive array of physical and virtual resources for learning. These spaces include: a 240-seat "wet" teaching laboratory—the X-Lab; three 60-seat "flexible dry" teaching laboratories containing lightweight, reconfigurable desks and chairs and 1:1 laptop computing solutions—two of these spaces can be opened up to accommodate up to 120 students at one time; two 60-seat microscope laboratories with 1:1 microscope and desktop computing solutions, which can be opened up to accommodate up to 120 students at one time; and a 20-seat exercise laboratory containing movable exercise equipment.

The X-Lab was designed as a research-enriched, technology-enabled, physical containment level 1 (PC1) learning environment for the biomedical and health sciences (human and animal), by a collaborative community of representatives from numerous stakeholder and services groups across campus. These included academic and technical staff from multiple disciplines, schools, and faculties (e.g. science, medicine, veterinary sciences), administrators, ICT and audio visual (AV) services, Student Centre Timetable Unit, and Sydney eLearning. Additionally, discipline and school representatives were involved in the selection of instrumentation, hardware, and software solutions and consumables suitable for their discipline needs, prototyping of laboratory benches and workstation set-ups, familiarization with ICT and AV solutions and innovations, and consideration of other design aspects such as layout, flexibility, furniture, lighting, etc. This process succeeded in delivering and sustaining a state-of-the-art teaching laboratory that is used by multiple disciplines across multiple faculties whose cohorts must achieve different learning outcomes.

As mentioned, the X-Lab is an open plan teaching laboratory (see Figure 15.1) and is equipped with highly sophisticated technologies, instrumentation, and facilities. These include research grade instrumentation, laminar flow fumehoods, and biosafety cabinets. Adjacent to the PC1 facility is a dedicated 12-seat physical containment level 2 (PC2) laboratory for the handling of genetically modified materials and group 2 microbiological organisms.

Innovative use of technology was required to enable multiple classes to operate concurrently in the same large space with ease. The solution included directional speakers, 1:1 computing, and the capacity to selectively stream live video demonstrations to each workstation. This AV/ICT solution was deliberately configured to facilitate multiple modes of communication including: multiple concurrent high definition digital video inputs to each student computer from the instructor's computer, a face camera and a digital visualizer located above the instructor's work area, access to digital and online resources, as well as customized software for experimentation and analysis. Figures 15.2 and 15.3 show instructor and student workstations, respectively, with adequate preparation, demonstration, and working areas along with the AV/ICT solutions as described.

FIGURE 15.1 Concept map of the Charles Perkins Centre X-Lab showing the 240-seat open plan design. Laminar flow fumehoods are indicated in dark green. Biosafety cabinets are indicated in yellow. Wash stations are indicated in pink. Instructor workstations occur at the end of every third bench. Instrumentation lines the perimeter of the laboratory.

FIGURE 15.2 Instructor workstation permitting control of audio and information technologies to dedicated student workstations via high definition video inputs from the computer, face camera, and a digital visualizer.

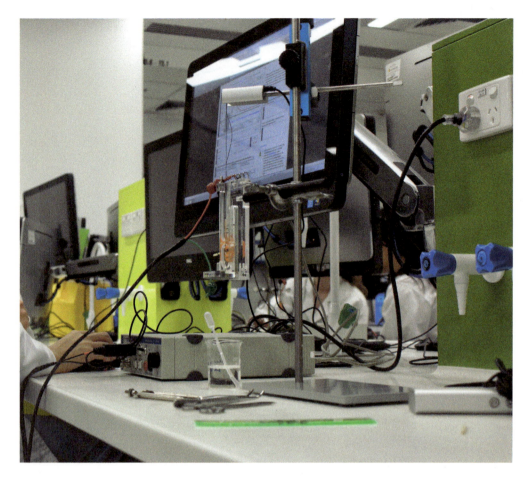

FIGURE 15.3 Student workstations providing adequate room for experimental preparations and 1:1 mounted, movable desktop computers which allow access to multiple modes of communication from the instructor workstations, alongside access to digital and online resources and customized software for experimentation and analysis.

Access to equipment and instrumentation in the X-Lab is not limited by walls, but is readily available on shared perimeter benches. Shared fumehoods and biosafety cabinets are also located around the perimeter, allowing students to perform advanced level techniques with materials that could not previously be handled in teaching laboratories. The increased equipment to student ratio means that students can work in smaller groups, compared to a standard teaching laboratory, which may have only had one or two of these provisions for several dozen students to share. Combining these assets in one large space results in greater access for all.

The aisles between benches in the X-Lab were designed to be wide enough to accommodate disabled students or instructors, and to maximize safety. Consequently students work alongside one another or back-to-back, with adequate space between to allow instructors to circulate, assisting their student groups with ease. The additional benefit of this is that groups expand and contract within this space when the results or methods of a particular group generate high levels of interest amongst the cohort.

Benches in the X-Lab have been designed to maintain line of sight, with minimal visual disruption, throughout the laboratory. The presences of windows along one full side and at the end of the central aisle allow daylight to filter deep into the laboratory. Wall and floor finishes are light and neutral with a mix of bright and pale furnishings, all of which helps to play the light within the space, creating a bright and pleasing environment.

Perimeter storage is provided within the X-Lab for laboratory materials, microscopes, and student kits. Direct access to the contained PC2 facility, specialty support spaces, and preparation rooms is available from one end of the X-Lab. Additional safety features include a demarcated entry area containing lockers for the storage of students' bags and personal materials, as well as washbasins for students to use upon completion of tasks. This separation of the X-Lab from the informal spaces outside delineates the laboratory zone, maximizing safety and providing a containment area for the handling of materials.

Whilst evaluation of flexible and collaborative learning spaces has previously been undertaken (e.g. Roberts and Weaver 2006; Cox, Harrison, and Hoadley 2009; Cennamo and Brandt 2012; Wilson and Randall 2012; Harrop and Turpin 2013), spaces for multi-faculty and interdisciplinary learning and teaching such as the X-Lab are relatively new, and evaluation of the way in which the affordances of such spaces influence learning and inform curriculum design and instructional decisions is rare. Through participant observation and description of learner activity, and semi-structured interviews, we sought to evaluate whether the X-Lab (the digital and material space and how this is used) is fostering networks in which science is learnt, prompting a move from single to inter- and transdisciplinary curricula, and facilitating the types of activity necessary for learning valued practices in science.

The Development of an Evaluation Tool for Learning Science in the X-Lab

We have developed and piloted an evaluation tool comprising participant observation and semi-structured interviews in order to explore the influence of design elements (physical/virtual, instructional, and social) and their interrelationships on networked learning. Specifically, our interest was in *the changing ways* these combined design elements support learning activities, and in student participation in practices valued in the sciences. The tool has its conceptual basis in Goodyear and Carvalho's (2013, 2014b) analysis of complex learning environments and the focus of analysis is learner activity, the doing of *tasks*, situated in physical and digital *settings*, within specific *social arrangements* (Figure 15.4). The *tasks*, or *epistemic design*, include the way in which learning and knowledge are structured and the activities learners are expected to engage in. *Epistemic design* may

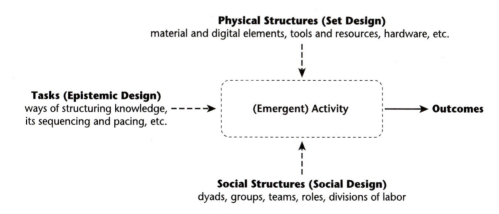

FIGURE 15.4 Key Elements of Complex Learning Environments

Source: Adapted from Goodyear and Carvalho 2014, p. 59

also reflect the way that knowledge is structured in the discipline/profession concerned and by its characteristic working practices. The *setting* includes material (tangible), digital, and hybrid spaces, tools, equipment, and other materials or resources for learning. *Set design* includes the configurations of physical resources and elements of the space aligned to structure and support the students' anticipated activities. The *social design* comprises social arrangements, inter-personal working relationships, social organization, divisions of labor, allocation of roles, etc. Thus changes in the design of the tasks, setting, and social arrangements may alter learner activities in ways that facilitate or impede learning. The different design elements do not exist independently, but interrelate and converge in complex ways (Goodyear and Carvalho 2013, 2014b), and the relationship between these elements and the learners' activities that emerge as a consequence can lead to outcomes not previously intended or anticipated.

Development of the evaluation tool has also taken into account a number of recommendations from the literature on the evaluation of learning spaces. In particular, we took into account aspects of the design—for example size of space, ambience, ergonomics, flexibility of use of space, resources and instrumentation available, and use of technologies (Dugdale 2009; Radcliffe 2009; Wilson and Randall 2012). We considered patterns of interactions occurring within the spaces (Temple 2008; Cox et al. 2009; Dugdale 2009), as well as how learners and instructors reconfigured and co-configured their environments (Hunley and Schaller 2009; Wilson and Randall 2012). Methods of evaluation were also taken into consideration. Goodyear and Carvalho (2014a) point out that learning can arise as the intended result of participation in learning activities, as the by-product of participation in learning activities, or incidentally from activities outside of deliberate engagement in learning activities. As such it was necessary to use methods that captured activity both inside and outside the X-Lab and perceptions that related to its use. Therefore we undertook direct (e.g. tracking student activity) and indirect (e.g. whiteboard content, computer screen content) (Hunley and Schaller 2009; Powell 2009) participant observation and open-ended survey questions (Powell 2009) to uncover the unanticipated. Interview questions were guided in part by a number of published studies (Temple 2008; Hunley and Schaller 2009; Long and Holeton 2009; Radcliffe 2009; Wilson and Randall 2012). Taken together these methods are considered appropriate for capturing the organic and emergent nature of practices in the teaching laboratory, and tracking how key elements of design influence and change the activities of students and instructors over time.

Participant Observations

Participant observations were undertaken across multiple spaces and cohorts. Rather than determining observational focus in advance, emergent activity was evaluated in situ, yielding ecologically valid determinants of learning through changes in activities, interactions, and manipulation of the physical environment. Observations were anchored in the framework developed by Goodyear and Carvalho (2013) for the analysis of complex learning environments (Carvalho and Goodyear 2014). Furthermore, observations were informed by theories of materiality (Sørensen 2009), material ecology (Ingold 2011), and practice (Shove 2012), and resulted in thick description (Geertz 1977) with both breadth and depth. In tracing the movement of people and things, consideration was given to pedagogy and place with the intention of describing how materials participate in practice and the ways in which the material and the digital suggest valued activity. The materials described included "the networks of interacting people, objects, activities, texts etc. that shape learning activities and outcomes" (Goodyear and Carvalho 2013, p. 54). The data recorded consisted of field notes, sketches, and photographs.

Interviews

Semi-structured interviews with open-ended questions were designed to probe and capture student and instructor perceptions and experiences of the learning spaces and their influence on practices. More specifically, interview questions and questionnaire items considered the influence of:

- *physical/space aspects* such as physical size, cohort size, noise levels, flow of movement in the space, access to resources, communication, individual workspace and comfort, as well as practical support
- *pedagogical aspects* such as existing and changing learning practices, for example collaborative practices, flexibility in learning options, curriculum renewal to accommodate cross-disciplinary learning and teaching, overall influences of space on curriculum design and enactment, influence and inclusion of new equipment and technologies into curriculum etc.
- *social aspects* such as working with other cohorts, communication, interaction with peers and staff within and outside the learning space, etc.

Semi-structured interviews were conducted individually and in groups of two participants. Digital audio recordings were made for subsequent transcription, and notes were collected. Data were analyzed for content through highlighting emerging recurring themes from participant responses and reporting their frequency (Hsieh and Shannon 2005; Starks and Trinidad 2007).

Participants

Participants in the evaluation described here were male and female students of the University of Sydney, aged 18–30, and fluent in English as a first or second language. Participants were sampled from a broad range of disciplines including cell pathology, histology, immunology and infectious diseases, pharmacology, physiology, and virology. These medical sciences disciplines carry out undergraduate training at the second and third year levels as well as graduate training in medicine and master's programs in the Charles Perkins Centre learning spaces. Students were recruited from discipline-specific and integrated units of study taught by these disciplines. The aim was to capture as broadly as possible the different activities taught across the X-Lab. Ethics approval for this study was provided by the University of Sydney Human Research Ethics Committee (approval number 2013/877). A total of 12 students (6 male, 6 female) studying across 16 units of study from the disciplines described above have so far been interviewed. Approximately 30 hours of observations have been conducted in the X-Lab thus far, on cohorts of students from units of study in the disciplines described above. Class sizes varied from ~20 to 100, whilst cohort sizes varied from ~60 to 250. This is a small but representative sample, which provides the basis for the early findings described here.

Findings and Implications from Our Learning Space Evaluation of the X-Lab

During observations, most tasks in which students participated were hands-on "wet pracs" involving the manipulation of observable phenomena and the collection of data. Objects of study ranged from DNA to proteins to cells and tissues. Of the tasks observed most were similar in design, starting with an introduction by the head instructor (length was determined by the quantity of theoretical material to be covered) followed by an orientation to the laboratory (location of materials, if not already at the workstations, and which pieces of equipment to use, etc.). Sometimes the introduction included a slide presentation mirrored on student's computers. The introduction and orientation were generally followed by a demonstration, via video or live feed to student computers. In some cases step-by-step instructions for students to set up their own preparations were given, whilst in other cases the preparations were set up and methods were demonstrated. Where this was the case, instructors made use of the digital visualizer to live stream their demonstrations to the bench-mounted student computer monitors, enabling them to follow from their workstations. Rarely were large groups of students observed clustering around single instructors to be shown these methods. Instructors used roving microphones connected via their workstations to directional speakers mounted above the benches allocated to their students, allowing seamless coupling of their spoken voice with the actions of their hands, visible on each student computer monitor. Furthermore, when instructors were speaking as they moved around the students at their benches, this system conveyed both location and directionality of sound, making it possible to track the path of the instructor through the space and to anticipate their arrival at a particular location, via auditory cues alone. During our observations of students' and instructors' activities, we noticed the ways they manipulated materials, how they moved around the space and completed assigned tasks, and were left with a sense of goodness of fit between tools, notably the set-up and sophistication of the technologies, and tasks.

Armed with theory and process, when given the green light, students were observed to work quickly and autonomously on their tasks. Students quickly assembled into small groups (usually no more than four per group), and arranged themselves in space to coincide with the divisions of labor for each task. Divisions of labor occurred naturally, students either assumed distinct roles or they shared roles. Intermittently the head instructor would interrupt students to give them some information or guide them to some phenomenon; however, instructors mostly worked side-by-side with students to troubleshoot or answer questions and facilitate procedures. It was evident that some sessions were stand-alone, that the entire experiment needed to be completed within the timeframe of the practical, whilst other sessions were clearly a continuation of previous weeks' experiments. Where this continuation occurred, students were observed to exhibit greater initiative in task commencement and much greater autonomy in the manipulation of instrumentation. The role of the head instructor also appeared to diminish in these cases, as less immediate and lengthy instruction, orientation, or demonstration was required.

Four major themes emerged from our analysis of learner activity and interview content and they will be described and discussed in detail. These related to: (1) aspects of open plan space associated with transparency, light, noise, and other ambient features; (2) the affordances of new technologies including state-of-the-art instrumentation and equipment; (3) the facilitation of interactions within the X-Lab and the broader community housed within the multidisciplinary Charles Perkins Centre precinct; and (4) the salience attributed to aspects of the space and the valued practices it accommodated.

(1) Aspects of Open Plan Space Associated with Transparency, Light, Noise, and Other Ambient Features

Our observations captured a light, bright, open plan laboratory, which was expansive without being impersonal, equipped with up-to-date laboratory equipment (Figure 15.5). Views out included trees, other buildings, and the sky and were visible from most workstations owing to the large floor- or bench-to-ceiling windows along two sides of the laboratory. When questioned about the general feeling of the X-Lab and the effect of the learning space (in general) on learning, student participants referred to a number of aspects of the space that they appreciated or felt influenced their learning. Specifically, two respondents recognized the brightness of the space facilitated focus and drive for their learning, whilst three others described their appreciation of the color and brightness as well as ambience with respect to temperature control, which made the environment amenable to carrying out various procedures in comfort. Seven interviewees commented on the spaciousness of the X-Lab

FIGURE 15.5   The X-Lab, a collaborative, multidisciplinary learning space in the Charles Perkins Centre Research and Education Precinct at the University of Sydney, demonstrating the open plan design, lines of sight, aisle width and degree of natural light.

permitting improved work practices, with more space to conduct experiments at their workbenches and at the same time feeling less crowded. Three participants highlighted that the layout of the laboratory facilitated social interaction, and five indicated that the size of the space gave more room to move around, with abundant space between benches, making the environment safer to work in, and permitting increased access by instructors to student workstations. Words used to describe the space included: "empowering," "amazing," "stimulating," "refreshed," "formal," "innovative," "professional," "newness," "modern/forward science," "more positive," "comfortable," and "exciting."

Our findings that the X-Lab space itself encourages a positive attitude toward learning echo previous studies which revealed that students preferred comfortable seating, convenient furniture layouts, temperature control, and pleasant outside views (Douglas and Gifford 2001), and that engagement was encouraged by learning spaces that were deemed to be open, flexible, comfortable, and appealing to the emotions (Hunley and Schaller 2009; Lee and Tan 2011).

(2) The Affordances of New Technologies Including State-of-the-Art Instrumentation and Equipment

Our observational findings were closely mirrored in the descriptions of student's experiences captured during the interviews. Where practical demonstrations were projected in real time or through pre-recorded videos onto student computer monitors, communication of task requirements was embodied in the concurrent movement of the instructor's hands, narration of the task, and facial expressions. This tight coupling, in real time, which included unexpected outcomes or the successful completion of a series of movements after repeated failure, served to communicate the everyday reality of "doing science." Furthermore, students would then work on their own experimental preparation with lab notes, pre-recorded demonstrations, and a view of the lecturer's current set-up visible on their computer monitor. The precise configuration of each was open to personalization in terms of number, type, and size of visible window. In many respects the technology facilitated a feeling that a small group had formed, the students at their workbench with the instructor/narrator on his or her computer.

From our observations, the configuration of student computer monitors to accommodate streaming of tasks alongside pre-recorded material, online notes, additional sources of information, and customized software to collect and analyze data seemed to permit the blending of the physical and the digital in ways that were not previously feasible nor even imagined. The physical preparation being worked on was but one of the elements within the experiment, not different—or any more or less real when considered alongside the digital resources—simply part of the assemblage.

Interview responses relating to the new teaching technologies were predominantly positive and are captured eloquently in the following passage from a student:

> The fact that I may be at a distance from the demonstrator but I can still see exactly what is going on in front of them, I can hear them from my computer and I can see what they are seeing, it essentially feels as if I am really close to them. The technology has a seamless way of making the large space seem rather cozy.

Ten of the twelve interviewees commented on how the innovative computing technology *facilitated engagement in tasks*; making practical activities and instructions, provided in live or video format, easier to follow when projected on to the students' individual computer monitors at their workstations. These respondents suggested the efficiency in using live or video projected feed meant no crowding around a demonstrator, allowing everyone to watch and follow demonstrations so that everyone could engage.

The state-of-the-art AV and ICT solutions in the X-Lab were designed to facilitate communication with cohorts of students in a space where multiple classes operate simultaneously. Based on user feedback and the observations described above, it is apparent that these unique solutions personalize learning and enhance participation in practice. What became apparent from observations of learner activity in the X-Lab was the ability for students to work in small groups, and maneuver to tasks readily with limited waiting time. The 1:1 or 1:2 ratio of equipment to students imbued a sense of ownership by students of their work and their set-ups. It was also evident that all students in a small group could participate in the experiment, that all had some role and/or responsibility in ensuring the task was completed. As described previously (Hinton et al. 2014), it appeared that students were not simply "repeaters" or "replicators" of tasks, but proceeded with their own versions of what had been demonstrated, showing an increased willingness to reconfigure their environment and experiment and communicate about similarities and differences. In such exchanges, it seemed the materials were waiting and the students were active, not the reverse. Access to materials no longer determined pace and progress and as such collegial groups of working apprentices emerged during lab time.

Eleven of the twelve interviewees indicated that the affordances of the new technologies and availability of equipment in the X-Lab *permitted more efficient and effective practices*, allowing all students to: have a go, multitask, take less time to complete tasks, access results faster, and permit numerous activities at once in the same laboratory session. As one participant stated:

> I think the fact that we have so many resources in the one room where before we may have had to separate practicals or learning outcomes, we can now achieve the same amount of learning in the one room in lesser time.

Another explicated the impact of the new technologies and equipment on student learning as follows, "So the whole thing cognitively, you understand each step, you don't forget the step before, and you can place the bigger picture together of what the whole experiment was actually about and the conclusions come much faster."

Three students identified that the new equipment and technologies were conducive to learning new laboratory techniques, increasing learning, and exposing students to greater options, "There is equipment I might not use but is there and if you ask you can get exposed to different techniques because it is so open." Three students also noted that the provision of new equipment and technologies had, from their perspective, clearly prompted changes to curriculum in their units of study.

> I knew the course had been changed for the CPC, and I appreciated that. And this should occur everywhere, change the courses to reflect the new resources, change the learning outcomes to replace outdated techniques. Techniques that are common practice in labs around the world can and should become common practice in our learning.

The X-Lab was designed by the discipline academics, the future users of the space, from the perspective of how it would be used. Decisions around physical and virtual (set) design were made according to practices current to spaces utilized prior to the X-Lab, whilst aiming to improve and extend the physical and digital resources available. This approach to design is anticipated to stimulate learning of discipline knowledge, as well as the development of students' competencies and skills (Lippincott 2009). Taken together, our findings suggest that the increased use and specifications of technology and instrumentation in the X-Lab provides opportunities for students to utilize a broader range of instruments without being limited by availability of individual resources, permitting learning of a greater number of techniques, more effectively, whilst retaining the ability to remain focused on task. Through improved participation in learning activities students more readily learn the science. It is also apparent that the technologies and instrumentation in the X-Lab permit designers of curriculum and instructors to modify tasks, capitalizing on physical and social design elements, and unencumbered by resource limitations, to bring learners closer to valued practices.

(3) The Facilitation of Interactions within the X-Lab and the Broader Community Housed within the Multidisciplinary Charles Perkins Centre Precinct

Interview questions about interaction with students and staff revolved around influences of the size of the X-lab, its multidisciplinary use, as well as exchanges within cohorts and with other cohorts in different units of study working in the laboratory at the same time. The majority of participants indicated that working in the X-Lab either made no difference to the way they interacted with peers and staff, or had limited influence on contact with other units of study working at the same time as they were, in the laboratory. Where interactions did occur with other cohorts, they were predominantly limited, unrelated to learning material, and mainly occurred with peers they knew and maintained ongoing contact with outside the space. The reticence to interact with other cohorts was often attributed to the fact that students were too focused on their own work, or that tasks were designed for students to work on their own material, which was not relevant to other units of study. To this end, three participants suggested that putting two cohorts together in the X-Lab was not likely to increase interdisciplinary collaboration, and that this sort of interaction needed to be designed through cross-disciplinary tasks to be carried out in the space.

This reporting by students is reinforced by observations of multiple cohorts from different units of study working concurrently in the X-Lab. A single empty bench commonly demarcated each unit of study group, so that the different cohorts were adjacent but not abutting. Students from different cohorts did not appear to comingle readily. In addition, instructors of distinct cohorts were identified by differently colored laboratory coats. Commonly, equipment and preparations for each cohort were set up in discrete areas. However, when blended use of space was required, for example when students from one cohort needed to populate spaces around another cohort (dependent upon fumehood and instrumentation location), students within the stationary cohort did not appear to respond to the movement of students from the second cohort into the proximal space. In fact they seemed accustomed to it. Students appeared to lack a sense of ownership of space.

On the other hand, some interviewees could give examples of where communications related to learning across disciplines had occurred, such as helping students in other disciplines with material (two of twelve), and communication around different methods with other cohorts (another two of twelve). Seven participants acknowledged that some aspects of working in the X-Lab had in fact increased interaction with students from other units of study, owing to the increased size with multiple cohorts working together, and sharing of resources, "the good thing is you learn to collaborate in terms of sharing equipment on a time schedule ... At one point I did have to share a fumehood with another discipline so that was cool to see what they were doing."

Another aspect of interaction highlighted by five respondents was that the X-Lab provided greater opportunity to interact with students in their own cohort. This was attributed to the openness and size of the space as well as the layout, permitting greater collaboration and communication and increasing the likelihood of sharing dialogue. Indeed, observations of learner activity reiterate these interview findings. In general, students were observed to work in small groups and interact continuously about what they needed to do, step by step, and when they anticipated transitions to occur. What was striking was how readily students assumed their roles and undertook tasks with minimal scaffolding. Students utilized each other first for answering questions, clarifying procedures, and ordering the sequencing of steps, and only called upon the instructors when they had exhausted their own resources.

An interesting finding from the interviews was that whilst the majority of participants did not tend to interact more with students from other cohorts working in the X-Lab, all participants indicated that they interacted much more with students from other disciplines and units of study, in and around the Charles Perkins Centre precinct, in the social and informal spaces, rather than formal learning spaces. This was attributed to the multidisciplinary nature of the precinct itself, increasing contact with students in the one environment, and reducing time spent in transit between other areas of campus whilst increasing time spent in and around the building. It was suggested this facilitated time spent in discussion with peers over matters relating to their learning, around career goals and "multidisciplinary conversations" about their studies. As one student pointed out, "You get to interact with students from other disciplines and that's a benefit, it bolsters cross-disciplinary friendship that may in future produce something academically useful. It's great in terms of collaborative science."

What was intriguing from the responses was the language of networks and social capital, such as: "It's a nice community that has developed"; "It's created a more closer-knit environment ... we are still part of, still sort of a big group"; and, "We interact a lot and see each others' faces and it builds a positive interaction. We tend to help each other and you want to return the favor."

The divisions of labor and complexity of tasks undertaken in the X-Lab seemed to encourage the development of learning networks, as students connected to other students and to learning resources, learning from each other and working together to achieve common goals in understanding and task completion. Just as learner activity in formal learning spaces is emergent and cannot be designed, so too are the networks that develop in spaces designed to facilitate interdisciplinary learning. Our early evaluation findings from the X-Lab echo prior studies of learning spaces which showed that flexible, collaborative, and technology-enhanced learning spaces increase interaction and engagement between students in tandem by enabling diverse learning activities and interpersonal interactions (Hunley and Schaller 2009; Wilson and Randall 2012). Collaborative learning spaces that increase transparency of learning enable students to learn from each other and from each other's successes and failures (Brown 2006; Wilson and Randall 2012).

Whilst the increased space size, cohort size, and openness of the X-Lab seemed to foster within-cohort interactions, we found that simply transplanting multiple discipline cohorts into one large space to continue discipline-specific work does not naturally lead to cross-disciplinary collaboration, though it is evident that it does increase the opportunity for students to learn from others in different disciplines. Increased interaction, over time, may evolve to greater cross-disciplinary exchanges, which may foster interdisciplinary learning. Thus, the learning networks that develop in a multidisciplinary space do not occur by virtue of set design elements alone. Clearly task and social design aspects are required. That tasks need to be designed for interdisciplinary learning is something that designers of curriculum should consider.

Whilst our early findings suggest that networks of learners do not just form in the formal learning spaces in which increased interaction occurs, we identified networks of learners in the informal spaces around the Charles Perkins Centre precinct, where learners across multiple disciplines interact. This finding is supported by previous research into informal learning spaces which shows that use of these spaces fosters engagement in learning and peer interaction (Kuh 1995; Matthews, Adams, and Gannaway 2009; Matthews, Andrews, and Adams 2011). It is in these spaces that students perceive the value of a sense of community and the reciprocal exchanges that occur within it. Indeed the learning networks that develop in shared learning spaces (formal and informal) may arise more readily by virtue of having multiple disciplines in one precinct. As suggested in reviews of learning space, physical environment may help to create "more effective social grouping (which we might think of in terms of social capital formation)" (Temple 2008, p. 233), social interactions, interpersonal relations, and communication with others, all of which strengthen learning (Brown 2005; Temple 2008). The concept that student learning may be facilitated by involvement in the creation and use of social capital requires further exploration (Temple 2008). We surmise that the development of social capital underpins the development of productive learning networks, the possibility of which is enhanced in shared learning spaces, to facilitate learning.

(4) The Salience Attributed to Aspects of the Space and the Valued Practices It Accommodated

The fourth major theme arising from our early findings was that of the salience attributed to aspects of the space and the valued practices that occur within it. Seven of the twelve respondents offered perceptions of the X-Lab as a "serious work environment," where "serious science" occurs, much like a research environment. The structured, clean working environment, the increased use of technology and up-to-date instrumentation, as well as adequate resourcing for all students irrespective of group size or shared space, the ability to undertake multiple tasks with multiple instruments in one space, and the increased interaction with multiple disciplines in the one space were all offered as reasons for this increased sense of the X-Lab being a serious science environment where particular modes of activity are valued. One interviewee pointed out that the X-Lab provides as close an experience as possible to a research environment for students, whilst another participant stated, "it actually does make you feel like 'hang on this is real science' . . . I actually do think that it propels you to act in a certain way, to do your work." Indeed, as affirmed by another student, "[I]f we cannot place emphasis on becoming more attuned with the frontline of research now, having a state-of-the-art facility, then there will never be a time."

What is apparent from our early evaluation of the X-Lab is that students identify the valued practices in science through the salience attributed to appropriate behaviors, tools, methods, and technologies used within the teaching laboratory. Our findings echo those of Hunley and Schaller (2009), who found that students and instructors engage in a full range of learning behaviors when the atmosphere encourages students and instructors to behave as if "serious work" is taking place. Students interpret the cues provided by instructors and the physical and digital setting to guide activities for their learning (Goodyear and Carvalho 2013). Indeed "our material environment visualizes as signs and meanings, pointing at our own physical presence and above all indicating our possibilities for performance, creativity and productive activity" (Osterberg 1993, cited in Wiers-Jenssen, Stenkaser, and Grogaard 2002). Thus, learning spaces designed to augment behaviors, tools, methods, and technologies that signify valued practices in science may facilitate learning of science.

Spaces Enabling Change: The X-Lab and Science Education

Our research is based on the assumption that undergraduate students learn science in teaching laboratories through participation in tasks designed to make use of tools and technologies appropriate for the manipulation of observable phenomena relevant to the discipline being learnt. It is also understood that students develop mastery of these tools and technologies through hands-on experimentation (Goodyear et al. 2014). Activity emerges, shaped by the physical and social context—what people learn is as a consequence of their activity, and only indirectly a result of the tasks set for them (Goodyear et al. 2014). Tasks designed for learning in teaching laboratories such as the X-Lab require students to exercise autonomy and creativity and student activity is best understood as emergent, rather than pre-determined (Carvalho and Goodyear 2014; Goodyear et al. 2014). As Radcliffe states, "a learning space *irrespective of its intended use* will tend to shape what people do in it and hence the patterns of teaching and learning" (2009, p. 14; emphasis added). This makes identification of the physical and social context and elements that foster learner activity and learning networks highly merited.

We have demonstrated how learner activity is influenced by elements of the environment and how the presence of networked technologies plays a role in enriching and extending place-based activities and experiences. Our findings from an evaluation of the X-Lab learning space revealed four dominant themes arising from observations of the early use of the space and feedback from students occupying the space in the first year of use. First, the space itself encourages a positive attitude toward learning by virtue of its size, ambience, spaciousness, and layout. Second, the new technologies and equipment designed to accommodate a diversity of disciplines, tasks, and objects of study facilitate participation and have prompted curriculum renewal. Third, the multidisciplinary and transparent nature of the X-Lab does not always encourage cross-disciplinary interaction, although the multidisciplinary characteristic of the Charles Perkins Centre precinct does encourage social interaction and cross-disciplinary networking. Finally, aspects of the X-Lab such as availability of resources and instrumentation, cleanliness, and its modern aspect imbue the space with a professional air, whilst attributing salience to valued practices by enabling students to "do science" like scientists do.

The design of laboratories that account for "active, social, contextual" learning can "connect students to knowledge-making activities and to one another" (Brown 2005; Long and Holeton 2009). Physical design is inextricably linked with the design of tasks to be undertaken in the learning space. Our preliminary evaluation of the influence of set, task, and social design elements on learner activity in the X-Lab shows that places can enhance participation in valued practices, they can stimulate connections between learners, learners and instructors, and with learning resources in evolving learning networks. Thus, the technology-enabled, research-like, and multidisciplinary aspects of the Charles Perkins Centre X-Lab combine to achieve this. These early findings form the beginning of an ongoing evaluation, which will help inform design decisions for learning spaces intending to achieve similar outcomes in science education.

References

Boys, J., 2011. *Towards creative learning spaces: Re-thinking the architecture of post-compulsory education*. New York: Routledge.

Brown, J. S., 2006. New learning environments for the 21st century: Exploring the edge. *Change*, September/October edition. [online]. Available from: www.johnseelybrown.com/Change%20article.pdf [Accessed October 30, 2015].

Brown, M., 2005. Learning spaces. In: D. G. Oblinger and J. L Oblinger, eds., *Educating the net generation*. [online]. Available from: www.educause.edu/educatingthenetgen [Accessed October 30, 2015].

Carvalho, L. and Goodyear, P., eds., 2014. *The architecture of productive learning networks*. London: Routledge.

Cennamo, K. and Brandt, C., 2012. The "right kind of telling": Knowledge building in the academic design studio. *Educational Technology Research and Development*, 60(5), 839–858.

Cox, C., Harrison, S., and Hoadley, C., 2009. Applying the "studio model" to learning technology design. In: C. DiGiano, S. Goldman, and M. Chorost, eds., *Educating learning technology designers* (pp. 145–164). New York: Routledge.

DeHaan, R. L., 2005. The impending revolution in undergraduate science education. *Journal of Science Education and Technology*, 14(2), 253–269.

Douglas, D. and Gifford, R., 2001. Evaluation of the physical classroom by students and professors: A lens model approach. *Educational Research*, 43(3), 295–309.

Dugdale, S., 2009. Space strategies for the new learning landscape. *Educause Review*, 44(2), 50–63.

Geertz, C., 1977. *The interpretation of cultures*. New York: Basic Books.

Goodyear, P., 2005. Educational design and networked learning: Patterns, pattern languages and design practice. *Australasian Journal of Educational Technology*, 21(1), 82–101.

Goodyear, P. and Carvalho, L., 2013. The analysis of complex learning environments. In: H. Beetham and R. Sharpe, eds., *Rethinking pedagogy for a digital age: Designing and delivering e-learning* (pp. 49–63). New York: Routledge.

Goodyear, P. and Carvalho, L., 2014a. Introduction: Networked learning and learning networks. In: L. Carvalho and P. Goodyear, eds., *The architecture of productive learning networks* (pp. 3–22). New York: Routledge.

Goodyear, P. and Carvalho, L., 2014b. Framing the analysis of learning network architectures. In: L. Carvalho and P. Goodyear, eds., *The architecture of productive learning networks* (pp. 48–70). New York: Routledge.

Goodyear, P., Carvalho, L., and Dohn, N., 2014. Design for networked learning: Framing relations between participants' activities and the physical setting. In: S. Bayne, C. Jones, M. de Laat, T. Ryberg, and C. Sinclair, eds., *Proceedings of the 9th International Conference on Networked Learning* (pp. 137–144). April 7–9, 2014. Edinburgh: Networked Learning Conference Organiser.

Harrop, D. and Turpin, B., 2013. A study exploring learners' informal learning space behaviors, attitudes, and preferences. *New Review of Academic Librarianship*, 19(1), 58–77.

Hinton, T., Yeoman, P., Carvalho, L., Parisio, M., Day, M., Byrne, S., Bell, A., Donohoe, K., Radford, J., Tregloan, P., Poronnik, P., and Goodyear, P., 2014. Participating in the communication of science: Identifying relationships between laboratory space designs and students' activities. *International Journal of Innovation in Science and Mathematics Education*, 22(5), 30–42.

Hsieh, H.-F. and Shannon, S. E., 2005. Three approaches to qualitative content analysis. *Qualitative Health Research*, 15(9), 1277–1288.

Hunley, S. and Schaller, M., 2009. Assessment: The key to creating spaces that promote learning. *Educause Review*, 44(2), 26–34.

Ingold, T., 2011. *Being alive: Essays on movement, knowledge and description.* Abingdon, UK: Routledge.

Kolb, A.Y. and Kolb, D.A., 2005. Learning styles and learning spaces: Enhancing experiential learning in higher education. *Academy of Management Learning & Education*, 4(2), 193–212.

Kuh, G. D., 1995. The other curriculum: Out-of-class experience associated with student learning and personal development. *Journal of Higher Education*, 66(2), 123–155.

Lave, J. and Wenger, E., 1991. *Situated learning: Legitimate peripheral participation.* Cambridge: Cambridge University Press.

Lee, N. and Tan, S., 2011. *A comprehensive learning space evaluation model: Final report.* Strawberry Hills: Australian Learning and Teaching Council.

Lippincott, J., 2009. Learning spaces: Involving faculty to improve pedagogy. *Educause Review*, 44(2), 16–25.

Long, P. D. and Holeton, R., 2009. Signposts of the revolution? What we talk about when we talk about learning spaces. *Educause Review*, 44(2), 36–49.

Matthews, K. E., Adams, P., and Gannaway, D., 2009. The impact of social learning spaces on student engagement. In: K. Nelson, ed., *Proceedings of the 12th Annual Pacific Rim First Year in Higher Education Conference* (pp. 1–10). June 29–July 1, 2009, Brisbane. Brisbane: QUT.

Matthews, K. E., Andrews, V., and Adams, P., 2011. Social learning spaces and student engagement. *Higher Education Research and Development*, 30(2), 105–120.

McWilliam, E., Poronnik, P., and Taylor, P., 2008. Re-designing science pedagogy: Reversing the flight from science. *Journal of Science Education and Technology*, 17(3), 226–235.

Oblinger, D., ed., 2006. *Learning spaces.* Washington, DC: Educause.

Powell, D., 2009. Evaluation and the pedagogy-space-technology framework. In: D. Radcliffe, H. Wilson, D. Powell, and B. Tibbetts, eds., *Proceedings of the Next Generation Learning Spaces 2008 Colloquium* (pp. 28–30). Brisbane: University of Queensland and the Australian Learning and Teaching Council.

Radcliffe, D., 2009. A pedagogy-space-technology (PST) framework for designing and evaluating learning places. In D. Radcliffe, H. Wilson, D. Powell, and B. Tibbetts, eds., *Designing next generation places of learning: collaboration at the pedagogy-space-technology nexus* (pp. 11–16). Brisbane: University of Queensland.

Roberts, S. and Weaver, M., 2006. Spaces for learners and learning: Evaluating the impact of technology-rich learning spaces. *New Review of Academic Librarianship*, 12(2), 95–107.

Shove, E., 2012. *The dynamics of social practice.* London: Sage.

Sørensen, E., 2009. *The materiality of learning: Technology and knowledge in educational practice.* Cambridge: Cambridge University Press.

Starks, H. and Trinidad, S., 2007. Choose your method: A comparison of phenomenology, discourse analysis, and grounded theory. *Qualitative Health Research*, 17(10), 1372–1380.

Temple, P., 2008. Learning spaces in higher education: An under-researched topic. *London Review of Education*, 6(3), 229–241.

Wiers-Jenssen, J., Stenkaser, B., and Grogaard, J. B., 2002. Student satisfaction: Towards an empirical deconstruction of the concept. *Quality in Higher Education*, 8(2), 183–195.

Wilson, G. and Randall, M., 2012. The implementation and evaluation of a new learning space: A pilot study. *Research in Learning Technology*, 20(2), 1–17.

16

TRANSLATING TRANSLATIONAL RESEARCH ON SPACE DESIGN FROM THE HEALTH SECTOR TO HIGHER EDUCATION

Lessons Learnt and Challenges Revealed

Robert A. Ellis and Kenn Fisher

Introduction

At first glance, universities and hospitals are very different kinds of institutions, with very different social roles. Yet closer inspection reveals a number of similarities. They are similar in scale and complexity and consequently share a number of management challenges. Moreover, many hospitals—and not just the formally designated "teaching hospitals"—are sites for training new healthcare professionals; networks of students learning to be doctors, nurses, radiologists, and paramedics straddle hospital and university sites, as do many of their teachers. Hospitals are also places for learning of other kinds. Patients have to learn how to be "good" patients by attending to medical advice and fitting in to the routines of life on the ward. Patients' families need to understand what is happening, so they can provide the right kinds of care and support. Effective care of patients depends on good communications to build shared understanding—amongst patients, nurses, specialist doctors (consultants), and surgeons, as well as other carers who are important to patient wellbeing and longer-term health outcomes. Much of the activity that goes on in hospitals has a "learning" quality to it—especially if one thinks about learning in an expansive way, so that it embraces such things as knowledge sharing, creating new forms of local knowledge, and learning how to interpret local practice. In short, healthcare places like hospitals are spaces within which learning and knowledge-sharing is vital.

Universities and hospitals also share some challenges and opportunities with respect to design of the spaces in which their activities unfold, and the place of new technologies in these activities. The healthcare sector is some way in advance of universities in one important respect: the *use of evidence* in space design. Approaches to the design, evaluation, and management of space in the healthcare sector have matured rapidly in the last ten years. This chapter reviews lessons learned, and challenges arising, with respect to these changes. In so doing, it pays particular attention to the implications for the university sector. In thinking about improvements to the planning and management of space in universities, one key insight we want to share concerns the need for a new professional role: the "translational developer" (Norman 2010). Crucially, people in this role enable two complementary processes to take place: they translate the challenges of learning space practice into useful questions for learning space research, and they translate the outcomes of learning space research into actionable ideas for learning space practice.

The first part of the chapter discusses the experience of the health sector over the last decade or so, focusing on the way the translational research agenda has expanded from evidence-based (EB) medicine to evidence-based healthcare space design (EBD). In the health sector's approach, the practice and experience of understanding and measuring how health practice works successfully is used as evidence for the design of new healthcare spaces, intended to support similar or different health outcomes. In the second part of the chapter, a series of observations, insights, and lessons learnt from health sector experience is considered. Here, our focus shifts to implications for the higher education sector's current design challenges in transforming university learning spaces. We make some explicit connections, in this part of the chapter, with recent research into learning networks (Carvalho and Goodyear 2014). The issues and trends considered in this chapter generally apply at the level of a whole sector, whether health or higher education, though we draw attention to exceptions where necessary. In discussing both sectors, common examples of hospitals and universities are used to conceptualize key elements of space design.

"Networking" in the health sector involves new and emerging assemblages of people and objects, both material and non-material (or virtual). Amongst these, technology-mediated healthcare processes (Chaudhry et al. 2006), including a growth in telemedicine, particularly over the last decade (Ekeland, Bowes, and Flottorp 2012), are helping to shape how these networks are developing. Technology-mediated activities have started to get systematic attention in the design processes for new hospital buildings (Li et al. 2006). Technology-mediated healthcare practices of various kinds are now generating much of the evidence used to inform the procurement and post-occupancy evaluation of the healthcare spaces, and this is being reflected in professional and procurement standards.

This is not yet the case in higher education. Whilst the integration of technology-mediated learning and virtual learning space is increasingly common in the higher education sector, this is yet to be reflected in sector-level awareness of evidence-based planning and design or of how to most effectively integrate technology-mediated learning and teaching into campus and precinct planning. In short, there is little evidence of evidence-based design for place-based learning networks. This is one of the main themes we pursue in the chapter.

The shape of the first part of the chapter has been influenced by the history of how spaces in the health sector have gradually introduced consideration of technology into the design process. Identifying evidence to inform *physical* healthcare space design constituted most of the early efforts in space design activity (Zimring et al. 2008). Digital technologies have played a significant and growing role in healthcare for some decades. That said, technology-enabled innovations in healthcare practices have had a particularly marked effect on space design in the last decade or so (Ekeland et al. 2012). Gradually, technology-based considerations are being integrated into physical healthcare space design. This typically starts with a policy-driven healthcare model. Then the *purpose* of the healthcare space is articulated: supporting the realization of the healthcare model. Finally, an understanding of on-the-ground healthcare activities drives the design. The next part of this chapter mirrors this trajectory, considering the lessons learnt from an end-to-end process of the design and development of institutional healthcare space through to its performance evaluation. In following this arc, we also consider how research has informed the design of physical healthcare space to improve the experience and effectiveness of stakeholders in that space.

Approaches to providing an evidence-base, including from user experiences, to inform healthcare space design, have involved changes in the typical membership of the teams doing the design work. The translational research philosophy now brings academic researchers into the design team: especially those who can translate research concepts and evidence into a form that the design team can make use of. Such teams now include at least a quadrumvirate of knowledge-holders and perspectives:

- clients or users of the space: in healthcare it is the doctors, nurses, and other health professionals, plus the patients; in higher education it is the students, teachers, program convenors, and educational leaders
- architects who are looking for a decision-making framework in which to apply their previous experience and knowledge to new designs
- technology providers: those charged with designing the information and communication technologies that are part of the networked physical space design
- academic researchers who are framing questions and investigating the key questions designed to move the field forward—developing knowledge of what works and why, building an evidence-based body of knowledge and a community of practice.

Whilst this is a potentially fruitful grouping of collaborators and perspectives with which to achieve outcomes, it has a number of potential disconnects that require some reflection. This is part of the motivation for this chapter. In a sense, a successful translational research approach to learning space design can be thought of as enabling the best understanding of these (often siloed) perspectives to intertwine without hindrance in a united purpose. If this is a valuable goal, then a key challenge is translating the most insightful observations of the users of the space into research questions, with the outcomes of research then being translated into design solutions for users. These design solutions also need to make sense to architects and technology providers who can then provide designs that meet the real needs of users. This is the goal and these are the aspirations we suggest for the much-needed role of "translational developer" in the learning space sector.

Stages in Healthcare Space Design and Development

In healthcare space design, there is rarely a fixed design template that can be implemented from project to project. This is because the outcomes of healthcare space projects must address the needs of different combinations of stakeholders who are involved in the different projects, including probable differences in healthcare models being implemented. Clearly there will be some transferability of a number of elements of the design solutions, but in terms of the detailed design required to meet the requirements of users, the variation reported in the literature is considerable. Furthermore, advances in technology and the opportunities to implement these in design occur more often than new major physical developments such as buildings, due in part to their contrasting life expectancies. Consequently, every healthcare space project, whether completely new or a refurbishment project, needs to consider the application of new and emerging technologies which may not even have been used and tested previously.

For this reason, the *method* underpinning the *process of design* for healthcare space has proven to be as important as the design *outcomes* from healthcare space projects. This primacy of design process has motivated the structure of this chapter.

The next part of this chapter presents the main ideas, based on stages in the development of healthcare space design programming. A review of the relevant studies shows that the healthcare space design process typically occurs within a fixed time period in which design decisions have to be made; that the design process is focused on a purpose, best informed by strategic healthcare activity, in which the activity of healthcare professionals is influenced by the physical and technological environments and the people around them.

The following stages have been identified during a process of reviewing the research studies which we summarize later in the chapter. In practice, there are many more stages involved; however, for the purposes of describing key parts of the sector's approach, the following structure serves to link the outcomes of the various studies reviewed:

Purpose of healthcare space development: This is intrinsic to design. Before any healthcare space development project is considered, there needs to be a purpose expressed in terms of the outcomes required. These outcomes are typically guided by a policy-informed, healthcare delivery model adopted within the institution concerned, and expressed at different levels of the institution and from different stakeholder perspectives.

a) *Patient experience*—improvements to the experience of the patient receiving care in the space.
b) *Professional caregiver*—improvements to the quality and efficacy of the process and experience of providing professional care to the patient(s), including technology-mediated processes that improve the experience of both the patient and the caregiver.
c) *Health management*—strategic and operational improvements to institutional-level health service provision. Strategic considerations may include being able to service a wider variety of patients because of the (evidence-based) improvements to the healthcare space. Operational considerations may include serving a greater number of people in the same category of care provision because of improved efficiencies and scale of processes.
d) *Health leadership*—improvements to the ability of health leaders to protect health standards and advocate for health improvements in the sector. Substantial healthcare space developments can achieve this.[1]

Preparatory research by the healthcare space design team: Each member of a healthcare space design team has their own cycle of professional research into healthcare space issues. This research considers such issues as known theories of EBD and the hypotheses they generate for effective design briefs; the challenges of capturing user requirements at project initiation stage, during detailed design and post-occupancy; variation in concepts and interpretations amongst the researchers, architects, technology providers, and users; principles for aligning space to purpose and the design approaches to improve the likelihood that the projects realize the desired outcomes. Such research draws on a body of evidence-based knowledge established over the past two decades or so.

User requirements specification: This happens throughout the life of healthcare space development projects, but particularly at a project's feasibility, procurement, and detailed design stages. The challenges of eliciting and articulating comprehensive requirements from all stakeholders is a significant issue for successful healthcare space design and development processes. The process typically involves the following stages:

a) At the feasibility stage, brainstorming, evaluating, and identifying are possible solutions, in collaboration with users.
b) At the commencement of the procurement stage, making sure these solutions are detailed sufficiently—increasingly in 3D and virtual formats—to ensure the users understand the solutions and how these correspond with documents provided, so that builders, architects, and technology providers can indicate the costs of meeting the design briefs.
c) At the detailed design stage, making sure the solutions are provided in visual and written forms in sufficient detail for the builders and technology providers to realize the final outcomes expected by the stakeholders.

Quality assurance: This takes place during and after the design and construction period, and involves testing, commissioning, and getting healthcare spaces ready for users.
Post-occupancy evaluation of healthcare spaces: This involves investigating performance of space and processes in the new space designs. This is an essential part of evidence-based design.

Purpose of Healthcare Space Development

Healthcare space research over the last decade or so has acknowledged that well-designed healthcare space, with a clear purpose, can enable institutional goals and improve the daily work of healthcare professionals—allowing them to achieve improved patient outcomes (Dijkstra, Pieterse, and Pruyn 2006; Joseph 2006; Henriksen et al. 2007; Vischer 2008; Zimring et al. 2008; Cesario 2009; Elf and Malmqvist 2009; Hignett and Lu 2010; Pati and Pati 2013; Sadatsafavi and Walewski 2013).

One of the difficulties health institutions experience in securing internal agreements on the purpose of healthcare space development is the tension that can arise between different levels of outcomes sought. For example, the health leadership goals of executives may be in tension with the sustainability of the daily activities of healthcare staff. Without careful consideration of how a high-level goal will impact on the daily practices of the healthcare workforce and on the quality of patient care, defining the purposes of healthcare space development can create unresolvable tensions in the design solution. For example, a high-level goal of assisting a wider section of the community with their health concerns, if not mediated with the reality of the daily professional practices of staff, may well lead to unsustainable workloads. This is particularly true when new designs incorporating technology affect everyday healthcare practice. If the purpose is not clear, unsustainable workloads can result (Leonard 2004).

One design strategy to address tensions in the purpose of healthcare space planning is to divide the space design into functional zones of healthcare activity which can then be aligned to different stakeholder interests (Al Zarooni, Abdou, and Lewis 2011). An example would be dividing hospital projects into nursing zones for patient care, clinical zones for diagnosis and treatment areas, administrative zones for management oversight of the healthcare activities, and other support zones (Dickerman 1992; Zilm and Spreckelmeyer 1995). This type of classification then offers design criteria for the different zones: criteria which should align to the high-level aspirations of management and the specific technology-mediated healthcare activity realized in each of the spaces. Using the previous example as context, if the vision of management is to treat a larger section of society through a redevelopment of the space and services offered by a hospital, then the workload and throughput of activities in the different zones need to be mapped to ensure that the hospital will be able to offer the range of support services necessary to sustain the increase in healthcare service provision.

Sometimes institutional healthcare space developments are shaped by strategic goals which require cultural change in the workforce. Healthcare space research has looked at the relationship between the quality of the built environment, organizational management practices such as human relations (HR) management, and the performance outcomes of healthcare workers (Sadatsafavi and Walewski 2013). Derived from the theoretical work of Wicker (1992), the purpose of this type of healthcare space development is to leverage positive associations between the quality of the built environment and experiences of the management and other staff. Sadatsafavi and Walewski (2013) identified links between the perception of the quality of the built environment by healthcare workers and their job satisfaction. They found that the two were related to the organizational commitment of staff and to patient safety, patient outcomes, and organizational efficiency. Such models are setting up the research agenda for healthcare space design for the next decade: they are still in their early stages of hypothesis testing and model development.

The Challenges of Evidence-Based Research and Design-Brief Development for Healthcare Space Projects

One of the main themes in healthcare space design research over the last decade is the role and use of evidence during the planning process. There has been much discussion about the meaning of "evidence-based planning" (EBP) and it remains a contested area amongst members of design teams and within the sector. Nevertheless, it has been a galvanizing force across the sector, raising the importance of linking healthcare practice to space design research and vice versa. It is in this context that the role of *translational development* is crystallized.

One of the challenges for evidence-based planning is agreeing on what counts as evidence. When design teams include architects, technology providers, researchers, and clients, the different values and perspectives they bring can make it very hard to agree on what constitutes reasonable evidence (Hamilton 2013). To overcome this, a number of studies have recommended post-positivist research approaches, which embrace an epistemology acknowledging that there is more than one truth or perspective on key issues and that, when combined, these perspectives offer a more complete understanding of the phenomenon under consideration than accepting only the latest view on what counts as useful evidence. This observation is consistent with recent research into learning networks which recognizes that new paradigms often displace all aspects of old paradigms, rather than building on them to create a more holistic understanding (Carvalho and Goodyear 2014, p. 27). This angle on evidence gathering encourages a combination of qualitative and quantitative data and a much wider range of investigative methods to provide evidence to inform key design issues—thus more readily covering the individual perspectives of each of the stakeholders.

Another challenge for a translational approach to evidence-based planning is deciding when and how to draw on evidence in the design process. Our review of the research has suggested that the effective integration of evidence into the design process is not necessarily linear or ordered, but rather creative and spontaneous, shaped by the issues raised and ideas offered by design team members in relation to different aspects of space development through perspectives drawn from their respective disciplines. This approach suggests that it is the combination of the innovative idea, any emerging evidence of its appropriateness for the space development under consideration, and how well it is understood by the stakeholders that shapes at what stage of the design process it should be considered. Having a translational developer coordinating this process is one way of ensuring that the right type of evidence is drawn on at the right stages of the process. For example, evidence coming from the environmental sciences is best considered when the design process is dealing with the engineering detail of the environmental design aspects of areas, as well as during the detailed design stage involving considerations such as ergonomics, lighting, and noise and their links with the recuperation time of patients (Zimring et al. 2008). Similarly, evidence from the social sciences on the links between factors such as stress and anxiety and physical space design (Joseph 2006; Hignett and Lu 2010) plays a part in design decisions when overlaying the healthcare activity onto the emerging physical space floorplans. Whilst individual examples such as these are relatively clear, the design process for large healthcare space projects can involve hundreds of such instances which need an informed and coherent view about how they all piece together. This is the type of role that a translational developer can play.

A distinct area of technology-mediated healthcare processes and practices is telemedicine, the purpose of which can be described at a high level as the remote diagnosis and treatment of patients by means of information and communication technologies (Sood et al. 2007). With the introduction of telemedicine solutions into hospital design processes, part of the difficulty in evidence-based planning is that the evidence for what works well may not have been captured prior to the project.

This occurs in part because innovation with technology in the healthcare sector usually outstrips the rigorous scholarly evaluation of that activity. Consequently, effective healthcare space design processes involving telemedicine need to incorporate processes within each project for identifying how technology-enabled health practice can inform the design of physical healthcare space. (See Ekeland et al. 2012; Fitzpatrick and Ellingsen 2013 for useful overviews of telemedicine.) Here we review examples of how technology-mediated healthcare processes, including telemedicine, have elaborated the physical, social, and technological dimensions of space design.

Telemedicine Practice Shaping Networked Space within a Health Institution

One of the areas where telemedicine has influenced hospital space design is intensive care. Changes in the model of care delivery in intensive care units (ICUs), brought about by the availability of new technologies, are reshaping the physical and functional design of such units. Technology-enabled workflow (observation, diagnosis, treatment, documentation), patient confidentiality and safety (identifying patients, medication and blood product administration), monitoring and communication for both emergency and non-emergency reasons (automatically monitoring patients' vital signs, paging doctors) are just some of the requirements enabled by technology which are reshaping the layout of the ICU design (Thompson et al. 2012). This can be as involved as improving bandwidth, capture, and display technologies for the transfer of large chunks of medical diagnostic data between departments, or as simple as integrating emergency monitoring signals with paging and communication systems.

Telemedicine Practice Shaping Networked Space between Two Health Institutions

Some approaches to telemedicine design involve creating two-way diagnostic and communication facilities amongst doctors and patients across two hospitals. In this type of approach, the design for the telemedicine function needs to suit a number of disciplinary requirements and is often provided through a stand-alone medical video-conferencing room in which there are facilities for observation of patients and the transmission of images (Major 2005). Design considerations that take account of the healthcare activity in the room can be quite detailed and involve both material and non-material considerations. For example, effective diagnosis of skin-related issues for patients over video-conferencing requires consideration of the wall colors at the patient's site: light blue is preferred over yellow-orange tones because these distort skin color and make diagnosis more difficult. As a further example, research into patient experiences in such facilities has found that the background image being projected at a distance to the patient from the specialist through the video-conferencing should not include doors in the line of sight of the patient. Patients have reported feeling that their privacy may be compromised during the observation stage of treatment over the video-conferencing connection because they feel the unlocked door represents a possibility that someone may walk in uninvited. This distraction in the communication between the doctor and patient at a distance compromises the quality of the diagnostic process.

Telemedicine Practice Shaping a "Hub and Spoke" Networked Space amongst Health Institutions

Some approaches to telemedicine design in hospitals are determined more precisely by the nature of the medical activities being provided in the healthcare space. When a medical speciality is in short supply in a region of a country, a "hub and spoke" design can be used to manage both the medical activity and the risks involved in patient care. One example of this approach is in the field of stroke prevention. The "hub" hospital is funded to provide stroke prevention specialists who work with non-specialist doctors and patients at a number of "spoke" hospitals. The medical activity across the rooms in the hub and spoke hospitals needs to take account of the following design considerations:

- Patients presenting with possible strokes at the spoke hospital are required to undergo a number of medical procedures. Results need to be captured and transferred to the specialist doctor at the hub hospital (for example blood samples, CAT scan images). The specialist doctor (a neurologist in this example) requires high definition live images of the patient from cameras in the room at the spoke hospital and high definition monitors in the room at the hub hospital.
- The room at the spoke hospital needs to be able to cater for video-communication between the patient, family members, the doctor, and the neurologist at the hub hospital.
- The emergency department at the spoke hospital needs to be included in the video communication, to help the neurologist at the hub hospital with the examination and laboratory results.
- The neurologist requires real-time observation of instruments attached to the patient in the room at the spoke hospital and may need to zoom in on the cardiac monitor during the video consultation.

Once the purpose of the healthcare space development project has been articulated, and the team has completed sufficient background research into issues related to the purpose of the project, the next challenge in the design process is the development of healthcare space design briefs.

Developing Healthcare Space Design Briefs

In the healthcare space design process, the articulation of user requirements to inform the design brief that will shape the final outcome is one of the most important stages in the whole design process. It is at this stage that the greatest influence on the likely outcomes of the process can be affected through careful attention (Hansen and Vanegas 2003; Lindahl and Ryd 2007).

Given that most healthcare space development projects are meant to improve patient outcomes as one of their key goals, it is unfortunate that healthcare space research has so far identified little evidence of patient feedback in healthcare space design briefs, in contrast to relatively significant feedback from healthcare professionals in design briefs (Elf and Malmqvist 2009). This is part of a broader concern about the quality of design briefs in the healthcare sector which has identified a lack of sufficient detail and structure in design briefs. The 2009 study investigated the content and quality of design briefs for multiple healthcare space projects and found little direct feedback from patients, despite most of the projects claiming to seek improvements to patient experience of healthcare. This is the type of oversight that can lead to misalignment in the briefing process between the purpose of the project and the final outcome (Vischer 2008; Cesario 2009).

To avoid gaps in the briefing stage of the design process, some recommended strategies are:

- providing sufficient room in the project to collect evidence of medical activities that will occur in the space, such as the technology-mediated issues raised earlier in this chapter (Leonard 2004; Li et al. 2006; Thompson et al. 2012)
- adopting standardized instruments for collecting user feedback as a key part of documentation processes (Barrett and Baldry 2009). Even so, care needs to be taken with the use of such instruments, as some dimensions necessary for the development of holistic design briefs can be overlooked when the same instrument is transferred between projects (Ryd 2004)
- ensuring that perspectives of all legitimate stakeholders are included: patients, their families, professional caregivers, management, leadership (Elf, Engström, and Wijk 2012).

Documenting user requirements in the design and development process for healthcare space research remains an ongoing challenge.

Testing, Commissioning, and Healthcare Space Readiness

Toward the end of the healthcare space development process, a key stage is the commissioning and testing of the space—in terms of the extent to which it supports the healthcare activities destined to operate there. Whilst this stage occurs toward the end of the build process, the integration of the principles of testing and commissioning begins well before, at least at the outset of healthcare space project specification, described above on p. 228. It is at this stage that those members of the design and development team who will oversee the testing and commissioning phase agree upon and establish the best available measurable project performance requirements (Henriksen et al. 2007). Apart from ensuring that compliance and operational processes aimed at improving efficiency have been achieved and that those responsible for their operations have been trained, the less easily measurable and more intangible aspects of the project outcomes need some consideration at this stage. This can be achieved by having the healthcare workers who will work in the space once it is commissioned engage in trials of the space and facilities as part of the commissioning process in order to provide advice on usability. Their feedback can provide the advice necessary to correct often simple but fundamental aspects of the outcomes of the build process.

A noticeable change in commissioning practice over the last decade in healthcare space development has arisen because of a greater use of technology to achieve health outcomes. With the increase of technology-mediated healthcare practice shaping the design of physical healthcare space, there is a greater imperative in the healthcare space commissioning phase to test the appropriateness of the design solutions for the healthcare professionals and patients. This has meant that the evaluative criteria for commissioning technology-mediated medical activity have moved from questions such as "Does the technology function?" to "To what extent does the design of the technology-mediated activity achieve the medical purpose for which it has been designed?" The latter evaluation question has superseded the former as the outcomes mediated by the technology have become more integrated and important in the healthcare processes. This shift in the emphasis of commissioning technology in healthcare space design has meant a greater attention to input from healthcare professionals at this stage of the design process than was the case in the past (Li et al. 2006). These staff are best placed to assess whether the technology is enabling the care processes in ways that will improve outcomes.

Post-Occupancy Evaluation of Healthcare Spaces

Post-occupancy evaluations that focus on holistic assessment of healthcare activity are not only an essential part of recognizing if the healthcare space project has met its goals, but can also be used as input into similar projects as one source of evidence. However, when considering their potential contribution to design decisions for subsequent builds, care is needed (Pati and Pati 2013). One of the common mistakes in claiming post-occupancy evaluations as evidence for ensuing design processes is that all such evaluations are not equal. They are typically designed for specific audiences. Consequently, if the purpose of the evaluation does not relate to the design issue under consideration, then it is unlikely to be of help in the decision-making framework.

One reason that post-occupancy evaluations may not be suitable for subsequent builds lies in the difference between physical and functional evaluations. The former focuses on the technical performance of the tangible and observable built environment. The latter focuses on the workplace processes that are enabled by the physical. In general, reviews of post-occupancy evaluations have found that very few focus on both the physical and functional, and consequently often only offer half the picture of the contribution of the design to the outcomes sought by stakeholders (Zimring and Rosenheck 2001).

Functional evaluations of healthcare space are where the benefits of designs informed by technology-mediated healthcare processes are likely to come to light. The methodology of post-occupancy evaluation in the health sector has become sufficiently developed to consider how effective the use of technology is in the practice of healthcare in new space developments (Chiu et al. 2014). Adopting a socio-technical approach, renewed post-occupancy evaluation methodologies can include measuring the interaction and adoption by healthcare workers of technology-enabled processes to yield insights into the effectiveness of the technology for the outcomes sought, as well as raising any ongoing issues for management and/or policy implications. Such approaches tend to measure the digital footprint left by healthcare workers on the space, and then use the context of the healthcare activity to judge to what extent the design of the process is meeting outcomes.

Lessons Learnt—Considering Health Sector Space Planning Practice in Relation to the Higher Education Sector

The overview of health sector planning and design practice in the first part of this chapter has described how an evidence-informed approach has shaped space development at the level of the sector. In doing so, it has begun to flesh out the remit a translational developer for learning space might have: one that can help promote greater use of evidence in design and a deeper understanding of the practice of learning and teaching for learning space research. In the following, we observe that the approaches to evidenced-based planning found in the health sector are rare in the higher education sector and we offer some explanations as to why this is so. We discuss a number of disciplinary and socio-cultural factors which may be shaping current approaches in both sectors.

In this section of the chapter we use three questions as a reflective framework in which to consider the issues:

- Why does sector-level planning for space design seem to be more developed in the health sector than the higher education sector?
- Why has the systematic integration of technology in health space planning in the health sector not been reflected in campus planning in the higher education sector?
- What lessons from space design in the health sector can improve approaches to learning space design in the higher education sector?

Before addressing these questions, reviewing some of the key concepts from related research will help to frame how our observations are made. In order to understand how networked learning occurs when considered in the healthcare space in which it is placed, the ideas of "set design," "social design," and "epistemic design" are useful (Carvalho and Goodyear 2014). These three ideas are relevant to the design and evaluation of healthcare space.

Set design of healthcare space: The description of how new physical designs and telemedicine are being integrated into healthcare building design can be understood as a type of "set design," or preparing of the space in which healthcare activity is to take place. From a stakeholder's point of view, the design of a modern hospital can be viewed as a bringing together of the very latest thinking about how to arrange specialist facilities, fixtures, fittings, and technologies to promote healthcare across physical and virtual space, recalling also that much of the activity in hospitals has a "learning" and "knowledge-sharing" quality to it. From the description in the first part of this chapter, we learn that if the design process is to be effective and well-informed, it should be centered on a socially orientated interpretation of the space—which has at its heart the needs of patients, healthcare workers, and healthcare leaders.

Social design of healthcare space: Putting the needs of stakeholders at the center of healthcare space design can be understood as privileging the "social design" of the space where "social" refers to the interaction of healthcare workers with patients and their families and leaders engaged in healthcare activity: all aimed at particular outcomes.

Epistemic design of healthcare space: The purpose of healthcare space development is to enable healthcare tasks and activities and is best informed if the design team understands the "epistemic design" requirements of the space, how it shapes the sequence of activities, and how it situates the participants within those sequences. Such design can be enriched by taking into account the learning and knowledge-sharing activities required for effective healthcare activity.

The following is not an exhaustive application of these ideas to space development in the higher education sector as there is insufficient room to give it due justice. Rather it is an opening of the discussion, framing developments in space design which may be applicable to more than one sector. Drawing some parallels between the set, social, and epistemic dimensions of (learning) space between the health and higher education sectors will help to clarify differences between the two.

Why Does Sector-Level Planning for Space Design Seem to be More Developed in the Health Sector than the Higher Education Sector?

The higher education sector as a whole has not seen an equivalent of the evidence-based movement that has informed space planning in the health sector. (See Rycroft-Malone and Bucknall 2013 for a wide range of outcomes from the health sector in evidence-based practice.) Some of the reasons why the health sector seems to be in advance of the higher education sector in space design may be related to differences in the interplay amongst epistemic and social relations in the sectors (Maton 2013). In the health sector, relatively greater sector-level advances in space development may be for one or more of the following reasons:

- the contestability of what constitutes good health outcomes in the health sector has not impeded the development of a sector-level awareness of how health outcomes can inform the design of healthcare spaces
- the contestability around learning outcomes in higher education has created some barriers to similar progress in learning space design
- knowledge about epistemic design of healthcare activity has been made relatively more explicit in the health sector than is the case with learning activity in the higher education sector
- evidence-based design as a sector-level approach has existed in health for at least two decades: the sector has had a "head start."

The remainder of this chapter examines these issues in more detail.

Learning Outcomes and Healthcare Outcomes

In higher education, learning outcomes can be difficult to define and even more difficult to measure. They are sometimes quite specific; their attainment may depend on the full awareness of the student (Marton and Booth 1997; Prosser and Trigwell 1999) and they can also be realized as the incidental by-products of study and other working activities and absorbed unwittingly by students (Goodyear and Carvalho 2014). They are subject to ceaseless contestation: within and between disciplines; between teaching staff, university managers, and external accreditation agencies; and between teaching staff and educational researchers.

Some degree of contestation is healthy. However, the downside of a ceaseless debate surrounding learning outcomes, we argue, is that it can paralyze activity at the level of the sector or of the university—activity that is necessary for the development of learning space. Defining health outcomes can be at least as difficult as defining learning outcomes, but across the health sector, contestation is not a permanent state of affairs. Rather, healthcare leaders and others periodically review "best available evidence" and agree protocols capable of informing design. There then follows a period of stability in which design can draw on best available evidence, without the distraction and paralysis that plagues professions in which no such consensus is obtainable. For example, when engaging in design of hospital space to enable diagnosis, treatment, and cure, the health sector has translated sufficient knowledge about practice to establish an understanding that informs some of the basics of healthcare space design. In contrast, such a sector-level agreement about the basics of learning space design is yet to be established in higher education. In relational terms, the difference in use of evidence across the two sectors could be described as the health sector providing a "knowledge code" of what constitutes health outcomes, sufficient for design, in contrast to the higher education sector treating an understanding of learning outcomes as a "knower code" (Maton 2013). Contestation amongst "knowers" means architects, designers, technology providers, and others do not know whose opinion to trust.

Lack of Systematic Evaluation of Learning Space at the Level of the Higher Education Sector

With a relatively greater contestability of what counts as legitimate outcomes in the higher education sector compared with the health sector, it is perhaps not surprising that there are significant differences in sector-level evaluation systems.

Internationally in the health sector, advocacy work for the development of evidence and evaluation for healthcare space is coordinated by EDAC (Evidence-based Design Accreditation and Certification)[2] and its accompanying journal *HERD* (*Health Environments Research and* Design).[3]

In the higher education sector, apart from SCUP (Society for College and University Planning)[4] and CEFPI (Council of Educational Facility Planners International),[5] there is no equivalent and those organizations are yet to have the same penetration as EDAC. Nor do they yet constitute a community of practice in evidence-based design.

There have been some significant efforts at the level of the higher education sector with respect to learning space research. Internationally, two bodies that have a prime focus on the use of technology in learning—Educause in the United States of America and the Joint Information Services Committee in the United Kingdom—became interested in learning spaces some ten years ago. (See, for example, JISC 2006; Oblinger 2006.) But funding has become more scarce since the global financial crisis and there are now only occasional projects—such as a recent attempt at codifying what constitutes a "good" learning environment—with a "learning space rating system" (Felix and Brown 2011). In Australia, the Office for Learning and Teaching has funded some studies of learning spaces (see, for example, Radcliffe et al. 2008; Mitchell et al. 2010; Lee, Dixon, and Andrews 2011; De la Harpe et al. 2014). These have been very valuable in raising the issue at the national level, but the complexity of understanding how integrated learning space is related to learning outcomes has meant that these studies have only just scratched the surface.

In the higher education sector internationally, an emphasis on discipline-based research activity rather than on teaching and learning tends to reduce the impetus for systematic learning space research. To reveal the benefits of translational development as a key activity for the higher education sector, and to bring about a sector-wide change in evaluation of learning space within countries, the development of a case for evidence-based learning space planning should be renewed and emphasized with the relevant governing bodies in the higher education sector, bodies such as the Higher Education Funding Council in the United Kingdom, Educause in the United States of America, Universities Australia, and the University Grants Committee in Hong Kong. Such a case, informed by some of the ideas of evidence-based space planning and design in the health sector, may be able to address the gap in the higher education sector. Any such strategy should include ways of helping the links between learning outcomes and space design to move increasingly toward a "knowledge code" in order to increase its chances of establishing sector-level awareness of the issues and complexities.

Why has the Systematic Integration of Technology in Health Space Planning to Enable Health Outcomes not been Reflected in Campus Planning in the Higher Education Sector?

Technology planning for learning is often best guided by starting from the learning outcomes sought from planned student experiences. By seeking an alignment running from intended learning outcomes to assessment to learning activities to technologies chosen to enable the activities, the likelihood of the technologies supporting the achievement of outcomes is increased (Laurillard 2002; Biggs and Tang 2007).

In healthcare space development, agreement about how technology enables health outcomes at the sector level has developed sufficiently to infuse knowledge about the integration of technology into precinct design (O'Hare 2011). There has been sufficient understanding at an individual task level for the knowledge to be aggregated into solutions that can shape building-level designs for technology to achieve health outcomes. As a consequence, many design approaches now work toward a holistic conception of the physical and virtual environment provided by buildings, and the alignment of building qualities with valued health outcomes (Gregory, Hopwood, and Boud 2014).

In contrast, there is no such "working consensus" in higher education about how technology enables the achievement of valued learning outcomes. So the research that does exist cannot be used to underpin evidence-based planning of how technology integration at the level of buildings and campuses can enable learning outcomes. This is impeding the realization of an "integrated learning space" approach to university campus design.

What Lessons from Healthcare Space Design in the Health Sector Can Inform the Approach to Learning Space Design in the Higher Education Sector?

One of the most galvanizing aspects of space design activity in the health sector over the last decade has been the recognition of the challenges and benefits of translating the practice of healthcare into healthcare space design research and the translation of the outcomes of healthcare space design research into realizations for healthcare practice. To facilitate a symbiotic translation, the emergence of the discipline and professional role of "translational developers" in the healthcare sector is key (Norman 2010). In the context of the forms of knowledge in the sector that we refer to above, these roles have helped to translate ideas about space design and health outcomes from being a "knower code" to a "knowledge code" (Maton 2013).

Evidence of the intent to develop a sector-level "knowledge code" in health can be seen in the publishing profile of professional journals focusing on space. The *Health Environments Research & Design Journal* focuses on providing peer reviewed evidence-based research on the benefits of physical healthcare space design for health outcomes. There are similar journals in the higher education sector, but none have yet committed to systematically publishing evidence of the links between physical learning space and learning outcomes. This is not to say that there are no publications on this matter, but rather that at the level of the sector, there is yet to be a systematic body of evidence and a publishing vehicle on the associations between learning outcomes and learning space, particularly models and knowledge that can help to explain the complex and indirect nature of associations between the two. Similarly, the idea of a role for translational developers in the higher education sector is yet to take hold.

A professional role of this kind would involve translating the practices and problems of education into research questions—generating answers that could guide learning space planning. If such a role existed in the higher education sector, disciplinary accreditation bodies would be able to call on the expertise of these translational developers who could play a part in more precisely describing the links between curriculum needs, building design, and campus planning for the purposes of learning.

The absence of this type of knowledge is evident in some of the key instruments in the higher education sector. The risks and interdependency between the provision of degree programs and learning space is yet to be reflected in the threshold standards for higher education award provision (for the Australian case, see TEQSA 2011). Similarly instruments used to evaluate the student experience, such as the University Experience Survey, the Graduate Destinations Survey, and the International Student Barometer, do not recognize the interdependencies between space and learning. Reading the items in these surveys suggests that the conceptual link between learning and teaching space and learning outcomes has progressed little further than recognizing that an absence of "access" to quality learning and teaching space will impede aspects of the learning experience.

The idea of a new professional category of "translational developers" as a discipline and legitimate role for the higher education sector will help to demystify the challenges in space design. It will help overcome the difficulty in translating into research questions the needs stemming from a deep understanding of what it takes in the practice of education to improve desired outcomes. Without sustained and systematic attention to this part of the learning space design process, progress in the field will be much slower across the sector.

If the higher education sector embraces the idea of "translational developers"—those whose role is to help to develop a sector-level knowledge code for the design of campuses as places of learning—new forms of knowledge will help to bridge the divide between research and practice in learning space development. Such knowledge can be referred to as "translational science," "translational engineering," or "translational design": "design is still an art, taught by apprenticeship, with many myths and strong beliefs, but incredibly little evidence. We do not know the best way to design something" (Norman 2010, p. 10).

Endnotes

1. A recent example of such a development is the Charles Perkins Centre "hub" at the University of Sydney. This aims to facilitate new approaches to problem-solving health issues through the combined efforts of specialists across the medical sciences, engineering, IT, arts, and humanities. Such developments are intended to create and foster an inter-disciplinary problem-solving culture of specialists who both advance their own disciplines and progress our understanding of how to deal with major societal issues, such as obesity, diabetes, and cardio-vascular disease. See Chapter 15 for more information on this subject.
2. www.healthdesign.org/edac/about
3. https://www.herdjournal.com
4. www.scup.org/page/index
5. www.cefpi.org/i4a/pages/index.cfm?pageid=3277

References

Al Zarooni, S., Abdou, A., and Lewis, J., 2011. Improving the client briefing for UAE public healthcare projects: Space programming guidelines. *Architectural Engineering and Design Management,* 7(4), 251–265.

Barrett, P. and Baldry, D., 2009. *Facilities management: Towards best practice.* Oxford: John Wiley & Sons.

Biggs, J. and Tang, C., 2007. *Teaching for quality learning at university: What the student does.* Buckingham, UK: Open University Press.

Carvalho, L. and Goodyear, P., eds., 2014. *The architecture of productive learning networks.* New York: Routledge.

Cesario, S. K., 2009. Designing health care environments: Part I. Basic concepts, principles, and issues related to evidence-based design. *Journal of Continuing Education in Nursing,* 40(6), 280–288.

Chaudhry, B., Wang, J., Wu, S., Maglione, M., Mojica, W., Roth, E., Morton S. C., and Shekelle, P. G., 2006. Systematic review: Impact of health information technology on quality, efficiency, and costs of medical care. *Annals of Internal Medicine,* 144(10), 742–752.

Chiu, L. F., Lowe, R., Raslan, R., Altamirano-Medina, H., and Wingfield, J., 2014. A socio-technical approach to post-occupancy evaluation: Interactive adaptability in domestic retrofit. *Building Research & Information,* 42(5), 574–590.

De la Harpe, B., Mason, T., McPherson, M., Fisher, K., and Imms, W., 2014. *Not a waste of space—professional development for staff teaching in New Generation Learning Spaces.* Sydney: Australian Learning and Teaching Council.

Dickerman, K., 1992. *Hospital space programming: Guidelines for departmental space requirements.* Jacksonville, FL: Health Facility Publishers.

Dijkstra, K., Pieterse, M., and Pruyn, A., 2006. Physical environmental stimuli that turn healthcare facilities into healing environments through psychologically mediated effects: Systematic review. *Journal of Advanced Nursing,* 56(2), 166–181.

Ekeland, A. G., Bowes, A., and Flottorp, S., 2012. Methodologies for assessing telemedicine: A systematic review of reviews. *International journal of medical informatics,* 81(1), 1–11.

Elf, M. and Malmqvist, I., 2009. Content and quality in briefs for healthcare spaces in Sweden. *Journal of Facility Management,* 7(3), 198–211.

Elf, M., Engström, M., and Wijk, H., 2012. Development of the content and quality in briefs instrument. *Health Environments Research & Design Journal,* 5(3), 74–88.

Felix, E. and Brown, M., 2011. The case for a learning space performance rating system. *Journal of Learning Spaces,* 1(1). [online]. Available from: http://libjournal.uncg.edu/index.php/jls/article/viewArticle/287/154 [Accessed October 30, 2015].

Fitzpatrick, G. and Ellingsen, G., 2013. A review of 25 years of CSCW research in healthcare: Contributions, challenges and future agendas. *Computer Supported Cooperative Work,* 22(4–6), 609–665.

Goodyear, P. and Carvalho, L., 2014. Introduction: Networked learning and learning networks. In: L. Carvalho and P. Goodyear, eds., *The architecture of productive networks* (pp. 3– 22). London: Routledge.

Gregory, L. R., Hopwood, N., and Boud, D., 2014. Interprofessional learning at work: What spatial theory can tell us about workplace learning in an acute care ward. *Journal of Interprofessional Care,* 28(3), 200–205.

Hamilton, D., 2013. Design collaboration: Practice and academic perspectives. *Health Environments Research & Design Journal,* 6(3), 120–125.

Hansen, L. K. and Vanegas, A. J., 2003. Improving design quality through briefing automation. *Building Research & Information,* 31(5), 379–386.

Henriksen, K., Isaacson., S., Sadler, L. B., and Zimring, M. C., 2007. The role of the physical environment in crossing the quality chasm. *Joint Commission Journal on Quality and Patient Safety,* 33(11), 68–80.

Hignett, S. and Lu, J., 2010. Space to care and treat safely in acute care hospitals: Recommendations from 1866 to 2008. *Applied Ergonomics,* 41(5), 666–673.

Joint Information Systems Committee (JISC), 2006. *Designing spaces for effective learning: A guide to 21st century learning space design.* Bristol: JISC. [online]. Available from: www.webarchive.org.uk/wayback/archive/20140616001949/http://www.jisc.ac.uk/media/documents/publications/learningspaces.pdf [Accessed October 30, 2015].

Joseph, A., 2006. *The role of the physical environment and social environment in promoting health, safety, and effectiveness in the healthcare workplace.* Concord, CA: Center for Health Design.

Laurillard, D., 2002. *Rethinking university education: A conversational framework for the effective use of learning technologies.* London: RoutledgeFalmer.

Lee, N., Dixon, J., and Andrews, T., 2011. *A comprehensive evaluation model for learning space—final report.* Sydney: Australian Learning and Teaching Council.

Leonard, K. J., 2004. Critical success factors relating to healthcare's adoption of new technology: A guide to increasing the likelihood of successful implementation. *Electronic Healthcare,* 2(4), 72–81.

Li, J., Wilson, L., Stapleton, S., and Cregan, P., 2006. Design of an advanced telemedicine system for emergency care. In: *Proceedings of Australian Computer-Human Interaction Special Interest Group, Design, Activities, Artefacts, Environments* (pp. 413–416). November 20–24, Sydney, Australia.

Lindahl, G. and Ryd, N., 2007. Clients' goals and the construction project management process. *Facilities,* 25(3–4), 147–156.

Major, J., 2005. Telemedicine room design. *Journal of Telemedicine and Telecare,* 11(1), 1–14.

Marton, F. and Booth, S., 1997. *Learning and awareness.* Mahwah, NJ: Lawrence Erlbaum Associates.

Maton, K., 2013. *Knowledge & knowers: Towards a realist sociology of education.* London: Routledge.

Mitchell, G., White, B., White, M. B., Pospisil, M. R., Killey, S., Liu, C. J., and Matthews, G., 2010. *Retrofitting university learning spaces—final report.* Sydney: Australian Learning and Teaching Council.

Norman D. A., 2010. The research-practice gap: The need for translational developers. *Interactions,* 17(4), 9–12.

Oblinger, D., 2006. *Learning spaces.* Washington, DC: Educause.

O'Hare, D., 2011. The development of knowledge nodes and health hubs as key structuring elements of the sustainable city region. Paper presented at the 17th Annual Pacific Rim Real Estate Society Conference (PRRES). Bond University, Gold Coast, Australia, January 16–19, 2011. [online]. Available from: www.prres.net/papers/OHare_The_development_of_knowledge_nodes.pdf [Accessed March 12, 2016].

Pati, D. and Pati, S., 2013. Methodological issues in conducting post-occupancy evaluations to support design decisions. *Health Environments Research & Design Journal,* 6(3), 157–163.

Prosser, M. and Trigwell, K., 1999. *Understanding learning and teaching: The experience in higher education.* Buckingham, UK: SRHE/Open University Press.

Radcliffe, D., Wilson, H., Powell, D., and Tibbetts, B., 2008. *Designing next generation places of learning: Collaboration at the pedagogy-space-technology nexus.* The University of Queensland. Available from: www.uq.edu.au/next-generationlearningspace/designing-next-generation-places-of-learning [Accessed October 30, 2015].

Rycroft-Malone, J. and Bucknall, T. eds., 2013. *Models and frameworks for implementing evidence-based practice: Linking evidence to action.* Oxford: John Wiley & Sons.

Ryd, N., 2004. The design brief as carrier of client information during the construction process. *Design Studies,* 25, 231–249.

Sadatsafavi, H. and Walewski, J., 2013. Corporate sustainability: The environmental design and human resource management interface in healthcare settings. *Health Environments Research & Design Journal,* 6(2), 98–118.

Sood, S., Mbarika, V., Jugoo, S., Dookhy, R., Doarn, C. R., Prakash, N., and Merrell, R. C., 2007. What is telemedicine? A collection of 104 peer-reviewed perspectives and theoretical underpinnings. *Telemedicine and e-Health,* 13(5), 573–590.

TEQSA., 2011. Higher education standards framework (Threshold Standards). [online]. Available from: www.comlaw.gov.au/Details/F2013C00169 [Accessed October 30, 2015].

Thompson, D., Hamilton, K., Cadenhead, C., and Swoboda, S., 2012. Guidelines for intensive care unit design. *Critical Care Medicine,* 40(5), 1586–1600.

Vischer, J., 2008. Towards a user-centered theory of built environment. *Building Research and Information,* 36(3), 231–240.

Wicker, A., 1992. Making sense of environments. In: K. C. W. Walsh and R. Price, eds., *Person-environment psychology: Models and perspectives* (pp. 187–192). Hillsdale, NJ: Lawrence Erlbaum Associates.

Zilm, F. and Spreckelmeyer, K., 1995. *Space planner toolkit: Hospital edition.* Chicago, IL: The American Society for Healthcare Engineering of the American Hospital Association.

Zimring, C., and Rosenheck, T., 2001. Post-occupancy evaluation and organizational learning. In: *Learning from our buildings: A state-of-the-practice summary of post-occupancy evaluation* (pp. 42–53). Washington, DC: National Academy Press.

Zimring, C., Ulrich, R., Zhu, X., DuBose, J., Seo, H., Choi, Y., Quan, X., and Joseph, A., 2008. A review of the research literature on evidence-based healthcare design. *Health Environments Research & Design Journal,* 1(3), 61–125.

17

CONCLUSION—PLACE-BASED SPACES FOR NETWORKED LEARNING

Emerging Themes and Issues

Peter Goodyear, Lucila Carvalho, Vivien Hodgson, and Maarten de Laat

Today, we are located in the midst of a complex ecosystem of old and new technologies and materials, where "the actual is porous with the virtual" (Kozel 2013, p. 339). Brick-and-mortar architectures are being adapted and reconfigured, their tangible surfaces and substrates pierced and breached by invisible networks smuggling in new software architectures and places. Via this hard, knock-on-wood realm, the soft digital world is reaching through and drawing itself ever closer to us, palpating and recording, following and cataloguing, calculating and conditioning our movements with algorithmic precision. We are being coaxed and carried (with invisible hands) preperceptually but swiftly along new avenues, corridors, and pathways, and into a wholly synthetic landscape with its own curricula and outcomes.

(Adams 2014, p. 4)

Introduction

The opening chapter of this book sketched a number of ideas that help understand some complex sets of evolving relations: between the activities of networked learning and the physical, digital, social, and epistemic contexts which both frame and are reshaped by those activities. We offered that introductory account to help new readers approach the subsequent chapters with a stronger sense of the focus and logic of the book. In this final chapter, we want to revisit some of these ideas, and extend them through reference to themes and issues we see emerging in the body of the book, as well as by making firmer connections to some areas of related literature.

The chapter focuses on the following five topics, each of which is treated in a separate section:

- The growing entanglement of the physical and digital—how best can we conceptualize the issues that arise, for the purposes of analysis and design?
- Network, spatial, semiotic, and materials-based forms of explanation—which works well for what kinds of issues?
- A richer conception of the human being in networked learning—how can ideas from phenomenology and embodied and grounded cognition help us make more sense of the relations between people, places, things, etc.?

- Understanding the relations between places and spaces for networked learning; exploring and pushing at the boundaries of what is deemed normal and possible, to open up further learning opportunities.
- Understanding approaches to analysis and design for networked learning.

It is the last of these—analysis and design—that helps define what is most crucial amongst the issues explored in the other sections. We can say this because of our pragmatic concern for usable knowledge: we have a strong commitment to helping the work of people who are themselves committed to helping other people learn. In short, our primary interest in achieving better ways of thinking about learning networks is to help improve opportunities for networked learning. But this should not be mistaken for a simple instrumentalism. Looking deeply into the arrangements and experiences of networked learning can provide valuable knowledge that may disturb, disrupt, unsettle, confront, or dismay as well as endorse, guide, and inspire.

The Growing Entanglement of the Physical and Digital

As we explained in *The Architecture of Productive Learning Networks* (Carvalho and Goodyear 2014), the early years of networked learning were characterized by people interacting with one another through terminals or desktop computers. It was a static or even sessile practice. In the discourse of the 1980s and 1990s, networked learners peered through their computer screens into an imagined virtual world or "cyberspace."

> Because the Internet was mostly accessed through fixed interfaces (e.g. personal computers) that were physically attached to a home or office space, physical spaces were perceived as independent from digital spaces. Accordingly, digital worlds, such as chat rooms and multiuser environments, were considered "virtual" because they allowed people to meet in nonphysical, simulated spaces.
>
> (de Souza e Silva and Sutko 2011, p. 25)

The narrowing of interaction to eyes on screen and fingers on keyboard misled some otherwise savvy commentators into what Ray Land has called the "incorporeal fallacy" (Land 2005)—that networked learning is essentially disembodied (Dreyfus 2009). We will return to the question of embodiment shortly, but for now we want to make the point that the increasing use of mobile networked devices and the growth of so-called ubiquitous or "ambient" computing are bringing the physicality of place and embodiment back to center stage (McCulloch 2005, 2013; Dourish and Bell 2011; Shepard 2011; Farman 2012). The more portable and pervasive that technology becomes, the more—as designers and analysts—we need to pay attention to relations between the digital and physical. Digital technologies can change the way we experience physical space, and the physical properties of the spaces in which we find ourselves have implications for how—and even whether—we make use of digital devices.

The interplay between the physical and digital is becoming more complicated, and some might wonder how much longer it will be possible, or useful, to unpick the two (Hafermalz and Riemer 2015). At a minimum, we might say that it no longer makes much sense to see the physical and digital as oppositional or *alternatives*—to perpetuate a competition between them as notional settings for learning activity ("online," "face-to-face," or "blended"). Rather, we need to be able to work with complex entanglements of physical, digital, and hybrid tools and artifacts in physically anchored places. As Jason Farman notes, the "real/virtual" opposition emerges from a misconception of the "virtual" (2012, p. 22). Farman argues that we see more clearly if we understand the virtual as a layering, or multiplicity: "the constant interplay that bonds the virtual and the actual together is the pleasure of virtuality" (2012, p. 38). "The move from personal computing to pervasive computing, a shift characterized by the move from immobility to mobility, has allowed for online space to interact with material space in unprecedented ways" (2012, p. 39).

Richard Coyne frames the way in which digital technologies are used to modify what we do in, and how we experience, physical spaces as a process of "tuning," or rather, a set of practices involved in the modification of place-based relationships:

> Tuning-in is an interpretive and relational process concerned with contingent human interactions and participation in human solidarity. My use of tuning in this book is intended to embrace tuning-in and attunement, opening up an examination of the micropractices by which designers and users engage with the materiality of pervasive digital media and devices, including the inexorable accumulation of small changes, divisions, and ticks of such devices . . . *The tuning of place is a set of practices by which people use devices, willfully or unwittingly, to influence their interactions with one another in places.*
>
> (Coyne 2010, pp. xv–xvi, emphasis added)

A number of chapters in this book illustrate new ways in which digital devices are used to change the experience of place—for oneself and for others. An example of how complex this can quickly become is provided in Chapter 2 (Ashe and Dohn). They introduce the example of the Place-AR system—which can be used to read and create digital, textual annotations that are "overlaid on the physical world" when that world is viewed through a mobile device like a smartphone. Their example also involves, in this scenario, using the Place-AR system whilst visiting the Sculpture by the Sea exhibition. This outdoor exhibition is itself designed—taking advantage of a location which is both urban and coastal. In their day-to-day actions, creators of the art pieces, and the curators of the exhibition, are influenced by imagined and experienced relationships between the objects and the places in which they (will) sit. What is seen—or noticed—by visitors to the exhibition depends intimately on "the kind of beings we are (humans) and the lives we live (human lives)." Objects become significant by virtue of "the kind of body we have and the ways in which we have learned to use this body in the socio-cultural settings in which we partake" (Ashe and Dohn, pp. 14–15). Design relies on a (partly tacit) appreciation of the relations between objects, places, bodies, and culture. This appreciation allows sculptors and curators to work in ways that make sense to and of people, places, and things. The Place-AR system—with its overlay of the digital, its two-way relationship between digital display and physical location, and its capacity to influence how people look, where they walk, what is in focus, what is figure and what is ground—adds extra layers to both the human experience of the exhibition and the complexity of the (distributed) design activities that converge on the exhibition. (The designers of Place-AR will doubtless be coming to a more elaborate understanding of the relations between people, tools, texts, and places as their work continues.)

As a further example, the children in Yeoman's study (Chapter 4) move smoothly and skillfully in physical space, shifting from physical tools to digital tools and back again. They pause from time to time, wondering about how to deal with a new task or a "media break"—moving information from the physical to the digital to the physical—and improvising working methods, spatial arrangements, and divisions of labor as they go.

> For in a world-already-in-motion, the skilled are those who can match their movements to the perturbations in the environment without interrupting the flow of their actions. So defined, skill is not an attribute to be acquired once, but something that grows in the doer as

he or she develops through active engagement with his or her environment (Ingold 2011). And within this framing, the role of things becomes increasingly important to understand—in learning, as in life.

(Yeoman, p. 51)

Of course, design choices that push things between physical and digital can't just be seen neutrally or as matters to be judged solely by canons of efficiency. As Jos Boys puts it (Chapter 5):

> I would argue that acts of delegation (say from physical places to online networks) are not only about effectiveness, but also concern existing patterns of power and differentiation, already inscribed with assumptions about what is *normal* or *should be normal*. Human and non-human assemblages, then, are not just exchanges of agency evaluated against some abstract concept of durability, but include a tendency to delegate *toward* or *away from* particular bodies, technologies, spaces, functions, etc.

(Boys, p. 62, original emphasis)

This engagement in the normative is normal in education, where more or less informal contracts exist—obliging and allowing teachers and designers to provide structures for the taught. For example, in Chapter 8, De Laat and Dawson describe an app (NetMap) that provides a bridging function—bridging between students with complementary interests or skills and bridging across digital and physical spaces. Outside education, the use of such bridging or matching and locating apps entails complex questions of privacy, safety, choice, and power. Within education, and especially in the context of supporting "open educational practices" their use takes on a different character. This does not mean, of course, that questions of who is looking for whom (and why) in physical, digital, social, or epistemic spaces can be ignored; but the broader educational purposes give these a different character.

Some of the cases described by Bilandzic and Foth, in Chapter 14, also show how digital social media can be used to make it easier for people to find others in their group or physical space who have complementary interests and skills. They also describe how social media tools provide a "virtual backchannel" complementing interaction in the physical hacker, coworking, and meetup spaces. This "digital augmentation" of possibilities for face-to-face interaction in physical places now seems quite normal in many areas of working life, though it still feels somewhat edgy and risky in, and on the margins of, formal education.

Separate treatments of the digital and the physical, in the past, have meant that the former tends to be analyzed from a network perspective (setting distance on one side) whilst the latter tends to be analyzed—more or less explicitly—in spatial terms (focusing on what is co-present). In the next section, we look more closely at these modes of explanation, not least because entanglements of the digital and physical need both network and spatial treatments.

Network, Spatial, Semiotic, and Materials-Based Forms of Explanation

If we want to understand how a place-based learning network is functioning—how people work together, how they appropriate tools and other artifacts and develop new skills and understandings, how all the elements of the network fit together—then we need forms of explanation that can deal with both networked and spatially related phenomena. Put another way, neither network-based nor place-based modes of analysis or explanation are likely to be sufficient on their own. A number of the chapters in this book draw upon additional forms of analysis and explanation—drawing, for example, on theory and constructs from social semiotics (e.g. Chapters 9 and 10) and sociomateriality (e.g. Chapters 4, 6, 7, 13, and 15). In this section we can only provide brief summaries of the main lines of approach to understanding learning networks—using ideas from network research, studies of space and place, and research inspired by (social) semiotics and socio-materiality. Our main goal is to alert the reader to these sources of explanatory ideas, and to begin to sketch the analytic tasks for which each approach is particularly appropriate.

Network Explanations

Understanding from a network perspective is probably the most familiar mode to readers of this book. On one level, it is not specially complicated: "to explain is not a mysterious cognitive feat, but a very practical world-building enterprise that consists in connecting entities with other entities, that is, in tracing a network" (Latour 2005, p. 103).

But there is more to "tracing a network" than might be assumed. One of the chief problems is knowing how to find boundaries; another is determining what constitutes a node in a network and what constitutes a link. One must also make an ontological commitment—deciding whether networks exist as networks, or whether (as a researcher or analyst) one is summoning a network into being (Jones 2004). That said, once one has decided to view something in network terms, a discipline of network analysis can be used to avoid the doubt that all one's attributions of network characteristics are arbitrary.

Amongst the strengths of network explanations are the following:

- an ability to "span and articulate different scales of analysis, from micro to global" (Knappett 2013, p. 4)
- an ability to integrate treatment of both people and things, the social, and the physical/digital
- encouraging relational modes of thought: looking for explanations in connections rather than in independent properties of the things connected.

Søren Sindbœk puts it thus:

> network-based methodologies provide [us] with potential insight into local and global properties of systems of interconnected objects, which can neither be discovered by studying the interacting agents individually or in pairs, nor by studying the average properties of the system as a whole.
>
> (2013, p. 72)

Research on Space and Place as Sources of Explanatory Ideas

Fenwick, Edwards, and Sawchuk (2011, Chapters 8 and 9) offer a useful summary of the implications of the "spatial turn" in social science for educational research.

> Spatiality, the socio-material effects and relations of space-time is, more critically, a tool for analysis. Issues for education and work include how spaces become specifically educational or learning spaces; how they are constituted in ways that enable or inhibit learning, create inequalities or exclusions, open or limit possibilities for new practices and knowledge; and how space is represented in the artefacts we use in educational practices . . .
>
> (Fenwick et al. 2011, p. 129)

Within the field of research on social networks, there has been a recent *rapprochement* between network-based and spatially based forms of analysis. In general, studies which combine network and spatial analyses are combining measures of topology (connectivity, centrality, etc.) with measures of relative location. For instance, social networks are both a motivation for and a means of making decisions about which house to buy—deciding where in a city to live, for example (Adams, Faust, and Lovasi 2012).

This needs to be distinguished carefully from place-based analyses, which are focused on the specific qualities of particular place(s), rather than relative locations in more abstract kinds of space. Many of the studies in this book tell us a great deal about what is present and possible in a particular place. For example, in Chapter 14 (on hackerspaces, coworking spaces, and meetup groups) Bilandzic and Foth discuss the various functional spaces used by groups of people meeting and working together—kitchen spaces, spaces for messy jobs, spaces that are not too noisy, and so on. As a second example, Hinton et al. (Chapter 15) show how the physical arrangements of different kinds of laboratory space generate particular kinds of problems and opportunities for the students and staff using them.

So a key point in considering combinations of network and spatial analyses is to be careful in distinguishing place from space.[1] It is one thing to focus on identifying the educational affordances of a particular place (digitally networked or otherwise) and quite another thing to examine the spatial extent of a learning network. We return to this theme shortly.

Semiotic Explanations

Social semiotics focuses on the communicative potential of situations and materials, taking a view that any type of physical activity or material resource can be deemed to be a possible semiotic resource—something that has potential for making meaning. This theoretical perspective assumes that it is not only linguistic structures that incite specific interpretations of experience and forms of social interaction, but also visual structures may fulfill this role—e.g. colors may alert a driver to stop and wait or continue driving (Kress and Van Leeuwen 2006). Semiotic resources are usually studied within historical, cultural, and institutional contexts, with social semioticians paying special attention to how such resources have been, are, and could be used for communication (Van Leeuwen 2005; Kress and Van Leeuwen 2006). In Chapter 9 of this book, Ravelli and McMurtrie draw on social semiotics to analyze how the materials, humans, and virtual components come together in the learning space of a university library. Their analysis of the Menzies Library demonstrates the application of three underlying functions of communication that are specified in a social-semiotic model (Kress and Van Leeuwen 2006). These functions refer to meanings that are (or can potentially be) made in a particular place, through: (i) interactional relations (the types of potential relationships between users, and users and the institution); (ii) representational meanings (what are the activities and roles about); and (iii) organizational meanings (how all the components fit together).

Ravelli and McMurtrie claim that networked learning places can be seen as communicative resources, because these are:

> spaces that "make meaning" in terms of potential uses, the kinds of relationships that can be enabled by participation in a networked place, and the different ways the component elements are integrated into a meaningful whole. At the same time, however it is that the spaces are designed, users might reconfigure them for their own purposes, and thus change their communicative potential.
>
> (Ravelli and McMurtrie, p. 111)

Stenglin, in Chapter 10, explores the connections between design and people's emotions. In using social semiotics to analyze how places make us feel, Stenglin introduces the ideas of Binding and Bonding, and links these to the powerful role of emotions in learning. Binding is about how secure one feels in a space: too tightly confined by place, and we feel suffocated or claustrophobic; too weakly/loosely restrained and we experience a sense of vertigo, or of being lost or overpowered by empty space. Bonding links ways of using space to establish or strengthen connections with community. As Stenglin suggests:

> Binding and Bonding are powerful tools. They can add a more nuanced perspective to our understanding of learning networks; how the complexities of what has been designed (set, epistemic, and social) may influence the activities of learners and how learning takes place in galleries/museums, schools/universities, and ICT.
>
> (Stenglin, p. 141)

The idea of design being about making things that are meaningful to others is also explored by Klaus Krippendorff (2006) in *The Semantic Turn*. People rely on their senses to attribute meanings to artifacts and to interact with them, and also on context and culture. People derive meaning through what they perceive they can do with artifacts, or how they see artifacts could affect them. Krippendorff (2006) explores the meaning of artifacts in a number of ways, for example, in relation to their use (through people's interactions with them), in language (how people speak about artifacts), in the lives of artifacts (the artifact's life cycle), and in an ecology of artifacts (how an artifact may possibly interact with other artifacts). From the insights derived by such analysis, he constructs a new framing of design: one that is less concerned about the surface qualities of designed artifacts and much more concerned about what designed things will *mean* in the lives of their users.

Explanations Grounded in Materials and Materiality

One response to the ambitions of semiotic analysis is to question the tacit privileging of language-based forms of explanation over explanations that refer to the material world. Pippa Yeoman (Chapter 4) quotes Karen Barad: "How did language come to be more trustworthy than matter? Why are language and culture granted their own agency and historicity while matter is figured as passive and immutable . . . ?" (2003, p. 801).

The "material(ist) turn" opens up questions about the connections between objects in the world and human action—and these questions are fundamental to understanding how to design. How can one try to influence the learning activity of others by shaping the digital and material qualities of the places in which their learning activity unfolds? For many designers and design researchers, the notion of "affordance" is key here. At a basic level, this term denotes nothing more specific than "what is offered (to x by y)." As Gibson (1977) said, an affordance is what the environment offers an animal. But as Ashe and Dohn (Chapter 2) point out, affordances are not simple, stable, universal properties of things or places. They are better conceived as relational.

> [G]iven the differences (personally, socio-culturally, and bodily) in the skills we have each developed, an object's affordance will vary between individuals and across cultures. Therefore, the affordance of an object is not held within the object alone, but is a *relationship* between object and individual.
>
> (Ashe and Dohn, p. 23, emphasis added)

We have argued elsewhere that "affordance" is a particularly useful *connecting construct* in situations where the "taking up" of the affordance does not depend on substantial interpretive work or complex decision-making (Goodyear and Carvalho 2013; Carvalho and Goodyear 2014). Affordance, on this view, is pre-reflective, and is more closely related to the "fast" system of thought identified by Kahneman (2011). That is, it relates to cognitive activity that seems automatic—such as when one encounters familiar things in familiar circumstances. "Interpretation" is another connecting construct (Goodyear and Carvalho 2013), but it relates to situations that demand greater mental energy: such as those where people need to stop and ponder, work things out more slowly—corresponding to Kahneman's "slow" system of thought (Kahneman 2011). One might say that "interpretation" is more of a semiotic construct and "affordance" more of a materialist construct; though both entail relationships between material properties, human perception, and sense-making. The ideas of affordance and interpretation both have a role to play in design for networked learning. Carefully designed learning situations will build on their distinct but complementary roles: nudging people this way rather than that, encouraging them to stop and ponder at certain points, helping them focus on what is core to the given learning task, and moving them along, quickly and smoothly, when less crucial secondary tasks are in play.

What things afford—the opportunities they offer—are not all to do with making human action smooth and easy, of course. As Cathy Adams points out:

> Things persist, but they also resist. Even in the transparency of our most skillful ready-to-hand apprehension, a thing must resist and stand firm in order to do its work for us. The guitarist, for example, relies on the sturdy neck of the instrument in his hand, the taut harmonic resonances of its strings against his fingertips, the warm hollow thump of a palm beat against its body. Indeed, the thing's chaffing resistance is what matters: it is in the bite of friction that significance, *différance*, and meaning is founded.
>
> (2014, p. 3)

On material forms of explanation, Carvalho (Chapter 11), drawing on Hodder (2012, 2014), explains that it is not (just) that the social and material constitutively entangle—relationality is not the main point. Rather, there are asymmetries between humans and things—things need to be cared for (as well as used) and humans can become dependent on things: "humans become entrapped in the lives and temporalities of things" (Carvalho, p. 153). Hodder's concepts of *dependence* and *dependency* help in probing these asymmetries in the relationships between humans and things. *Dependence* facilitates our understanding of people's reliance on things, through a productive and enabling framing. It suggests that the human use of things has allowed us to evolve—we see this when considering things and how they help people eat, interact socially, think, etc. (Hodder 2014). Conversely, the concept of *dependency* reflects constraints in the relations between humans and things. It expresses humans' excessive reliance on things, which limits the capacity to evolve as a society or as individuals. Another of Hodder's key concepts is *fittingness*. This refers to the qualities of humans or things, and how these qualities enable both—humans or things—to function and achieve a certain end. It is simultaneously about the "fit" or the coherence of the whole. *Fittingness* between humans and things may be disturbed by an occurrence—by something that may lead to problems or alterations of the overall entanglement. Hodder (2012) calls such an occurrence a *conjunctural event*: something that requires fixing and fitting solutions. The introduction of a new device—e.g. a mobile device like the "O" (Carvalho, Chapter 11)—creates a conjunctural event which means that fittingness is disturbed and (re)design has to be undertaken. It is then necessary to check through the network of connections between humans and things, till a new fittingness is established—a new entanglement. A similar lesson can be seen in Linge, Booth, and Parsons' chapter (Chapter 12) where the entire technological system needs to be taken into account whenever a change to one entity is needed. In short, the propagation of effects through networks of interconnected things (and people) makes piecemeal design and analysis highly problematic.

Spatial-Material Explanations

In paying attention to how things and humans fit together, we must not lose sight of the influence of the space and of others with whom we share our situated experience. For example, Carvalho's analysis of the O in MONA explores the role of ambient lighting, as it gently nudges visitors toward certain paths, helping them to see important things (e.g. the exhibits, the O screen). Carvalho combines a spatial-material explanation and the role of unknown others in the museum space—in a socio-spatial and sociomaterial view. These connections are further illustrated with Carvalho's example of the *Pulse Room*, an interactive installation by Rafael Lozano-Hemmer: where a computing device senses the pulse/heart rate of each visitor and the lighting in the room responds—showing, at any given time, flashing bulbs that mimic the heart beats of the hundred most recent visitors.

Spatial-material explanations are also offered by Linge et al. (Chapter 12) through the practical lessons they learned in the development and deployment of the mi-Guide. Some of these issues relate, for example, to the spatial resolution of devices that enable location-aware applications; others relate to equally critical material issues—battery life, WiFi access, limitations on RFID tags, etc. These are not *directly* related to meaning making or other aspects of the visitor experience, but their successful entanglement is a precondition for a successful visit.

In Chapter 14, Bilandzic and Foth contribute with a socio-spatial analysis of hackerspaces, coworking spaces, and meetup groups. The environments they study are not only seen as physical places/spaces. Their social role is also emphasized—in gathering people together, so that knowledge can be shared with likeminded peers: "their members perceive them as *social environments*, rather than purely *physical destinations*" (p. 195, original emphasis).

A Richer Conception of the Human Being in Networked Learning

In this section, we draw together a few ideas that provide some richer ways of thinking about the *people* involved in networked learning—ideas which help create an expanded conception of how human beings function in a material world. The ideas emanate from three main sources: (i) writing on the "extended mind," "person plus," and the cyborg (e.g. Haraway 1991; Clark 2003); (ii) theories of embodied and grounded cognition (e.g. Barsalou 2010; Hutchins 2010; Kirsh 2013); and (iii) phenomenology (e.g. Merleau-Ponty 1945/2014; Dohn 2009; Ingold 2011).

Close attention to the human—in or as part of the material world—came to the fore when the entanglements between the human–machine interface and what we experience as us and/or the machine became prominent in the early 1990s. This was as a result of the work of Suchman (1987), Haraway (1991), and others. Haraway (1991), for example, made the point that:

> The machine is not an it to be animated, worshipped, and dominated. The machine is us, our processes, an aspect of our embodiment. We can be responsible for machines: they do not dominate or threaten us. We are responsible for boundaries; we are they.
>
> (Haraway 1991, p. 180)

At that time, it felt as if our capacities to think and know were just beginning to be extended beyond our imagination, through the emerging digital apparatus of the World Wide Web and the technological tools and possibilities associated with ICT: "Our nearly seamless interfacing with this machined and algorithmed realm is not only interactive but also *interpassive*: we increasingly hand over (outsource) our human thinking and doing to the Digital to think and do for us" (Adams 2014, p. 2, emphasis added).

As discussed by Hodgson (1997), Lyotard claimed that technologies, with their electronically generated data-processing capacities, were "material extensions of our capacity to memorise." Similar to Haraway he wrote; "technologies show in their own way that there is no break between matter and mind" (Lyotard 1991, p. 43). Lyotard also foresaw the potential the new information and communication technology had, or could have, upon the cultural dimension of education—as a consequence of moving from an ethnocultural apparatus for memorizing information to a telegraphic apparatus which is no longer rooted in local culture but diffused across the surface of the globe (1991, p. 63). Arguably, the movement from the ethnocultural to the global is now being reconfigured in a more place-based experience and concept of networked learning and education.

On the other hand, our relationship to who we are and how we experience our embodied selves in the digitally pervasive and entangled world we inhabit is re-emerging as an area of interest within critical theory and in relation to the so-called "affective turn" (Clough 2007). For Clough, the human body is no longer a closed system seeking homeostasis and equilibrium but an open system stretching beyond the containment of the human organism. As Clough explains, the affective turn is a recent turn in critical theory, drawing on the ideas of Deleuze and Guattari, running back through to Bergson and Spinoza. There is, she claims, following Deleuzian biophilosophy, a move away from thinking of bodies only in terms of human organisms to rethinking the relationship of life, information, and technology. For Clough, no longer are bodily affects and relationships with specifically technology and information seen as discrete and separate entities but rather as part of a complex and interwoven affective economy, which Deleuze refers to in terms of "societies of control." Within the affective turn, technology is no longer simply the machine or digital apparatus that is us. It is, along with the human organism, part of the relationship with life, information, and technology: a relationship where affect has the possibility to augment or diminish the body's capacity to act, to engage, and to connect. These are all important ideas when considering the involvement and position of the "person" in networked learning

Similarly, for the past 10–15 years in the cognitive sciences, we have also seen a deep questioning of the notion that the mind is bounded by the skull. Theories of embodied and grounded cognition articulate connections between perception, memory, language, and thought (Clark 2008; Barsalou 2010; Kirsh 2013). According to these theories, cognition is usually grounded in our perceptual-action experiences with objects in the physical world, as cognitive processes related to language and memory are also seen as connected to systems related to perception and action (Borghi and Pecher 2012). On this view, "the more we have tool mediated experiences the more our understanding of the world is situated in the way we interact through tools" (Kirsh 2013, p. 3). The types of (place-based) activities in which we engage, and knowing by doing, can therefore be much more powerful than knowing by seeing (Kirsh 2013).

Another source of enriched conceptions of what it is to be human—and what this means for thinking about the analysis of places, things, networks, etc.—comes from phenomenology, especially through the use of ideas from Heidegger and Merleau-Ponty. In thinking about embodiment and the Internet, Hubert Dreyfus remarks: "[Th]e crucial question is whether our relation to the world is that of a disembodied, detached spectator or an involved, embodied agent" (Dreyfus 2009, p. 53).

Following Merleau-Ponty, Dreyfus is concerned that the disembodied spectator can't get an "optimal grip on the world"—they lose the sense of being in close touch with the world; the primordial belief in the reality of the world is shaken. In Chapter 2, Ashe and Dohn remind us that how place is seen, how objects in places are perceived, what comes into focus—all depend on our bodily being and the cultures in which we have grown.

In general, these two aspects—our bodily being and our socio-culturally developed expectations and practices—are not factors working independently of one another to determine focus. Rather, in most instances, they act in integration so that what stands out for us as the "naturally" given figure does so on the basis of our bodily being with all its socio-culturally acquired skills and understandings.

(Ashe and Dohn, p. 16)

In perceiving the qualities of place, humans are so constituted that they notice and feel drawn toward places that are welcoming—places that are "alive" and that exhibit that elusive "quality without a name." Drawing on Christopher Alexander, Ana Pinto (Chapter 3) remarks:

evolution has equipped human beings to appreciate subtle qualities in the environment, and people intuitively assign degrees of wholeness to both designed and natural worlds. Accordingly, people intuitively recognize that a place, a city, a building, a painting, a little artifact, etc. manifest life. Likewise, we intuitively realize if a river, a mountain, a beach, or even a person is more, or less, alive.

(Pinto, p. 28)

Boys (Chapter 5) also comments on this *sensing*:

the most immediately powerful impact on students' learning was in shifting their perceptions of *the role of the senses* in designing. The students all reported feeling themselves much more intensely *in* the material spaces around them; expanding their *awareness of their own bodily sensations* and taking notice of barriers in the built environment they had previously ignored. As one student commented: "I felt my space, because the disabled artists have helped put me in my space" (Student feedback May 11, 2007).

(Boys, p. 67, first and third emphases added)

Finally, Sprake and Rogers (Chapter 13) drawing on Noë and ideas of *enactive perception*—perception being something we do, rather than something that happens to us—underline the significance of embodiment in space for understanding the importance of movement in learning: coming to adopt new perspectives on familiar urban places, for example, or engagement in "haptic" learning: "a process in which people are simultaneously physical, cognitive, and emotional participants in developing a heightened sense of awareness. Specifically, they are reciprocally "in touch with" and "touched by" their physical environment" (Sprake and Rodgers, p. 180).

Relations between Places and Spaces for Networked Learning

The idea of connecting with other people and things via the Internet conjures up images of disembodiment and displacement. But only embodied humans use the Internet, and—of necessity—they do this from *somewhere*. Jason Farman uses Edward Casey's notion of "implacement" to help cut through the conceptual fog around interaction through mobile and ubiquitous technologies (Casey 2009).

[I]mplacement locates our situated nature and our sense of proprioception with others and with objects in a space. [It] gives us the sense of direction in a particular place—direction not only in movement but also in purpose. Implacement gives us a sense of embodied integrity in a particular locale . . . For emerging generations, such questions no longer prioritize between material space and digital space since these spaces simultaneously inform our experience of implacement. Our lived conception of space, especially the online realm, is very much a situated experience, always contextually informed.

(Farman 2012, pp. 40–42)

On the theme of place-based spaces for networked learning, we can now draw on a number of examples from the earlier chapters to explore and illustrate relations between place, space, and learning. Many of the chapters conjure up images of specific places in which the use of mobile devices creates new opportunities for learning. A space of learning opportunities thereby comes into being.

Place and Space

Some of our contributors talk about space where others might prefer to use the term "place." Because the word "place" doesn't have an adjectival form, and because insisting on "place" can sometimes produce very ugly English, we have been quite relaxed on this terminological matter. The important point is a more fundamental conceptual one, and the contributors are in broad agreement about the need to avoid conjuring up images of space (or place) as a pre-existing "container" for human activity. As Boys says in Chapter 5, it is important to challenge

> the basic assumption that space and occupants exist as pre-existing entities that then have "relationships" with each other. This means refusing to accept the assumed "logic" of, say, behavioral cause/effect, function, or meaning. Rather, spaces, objects, our bodies, and our encounters are utterly intermeshed, and need to be analyzed instead as *dynamic practices*.
>
> (Boys, p. 59, original emphasis)

Or as Gourlay and Oliver (Chapter 6) put it:

> Space cannot be understood simply as a kind of container, a backcloth, or something that just forms a neutral, given context in which studying happens. Instead, it is contingent, emergent. and endlessly constituted through the networked unfolding of socialmaterial, posthuman, and textual practices—practices that cannot be neatly bundled together as "studying," but instead consist of countless acts of reading, writing, noting, curating, speaking, and so on. Space is constantly enacted through, and entangled in, these complex day-to-day practices that make up students' studying.
>
> (Gourlay and Oliver, p. 84)

Places (inhabited spaces) are not abstract coordinates that specify where life happens, they arise through the interweaving of human and other streams of activity. Drawing on the work of Christopher Alexander, Ana Pinto (Chapter 3) puts it thus:

> For Alexander, spaces and structures acquire their characters according to certain patterns of events that happen in combination. These patterns of events involve both human and non-human phenomena. For instance, natural phenomena such as "the sunshine shining on the windowsill, the wind blowing in the grass" affect people just as much as social events do (1979, p. 64). A "quality without a name" manifests itself when the patterns of events happening in a space allow a person to feel most alive and whole (1979, p. 41).
>
> (Pinto, p. 26)

Networked Learning and Spaces of Possibility

Now that we have a shared sense of places (inhabited spaces) as concrete, experienced, and performed, and have made allowance for the confusion that can emerge if conflating realized place with abstract space, it is time to say that "abstract space" can be a useful construct. For one thing, we might say that spaces for networked learning are *spaces of possibility*. They are constituted by, and offer some structure for, an array of affordances—perceptual, conceptual, social, epistemic, and more. Once a person acts to take up what is on offer, the nature of their place changes.

This notion of creating, sharing, and defending spaces of opportunity for learning is a strong theme in the literature of networked learning. For example, a brief survey identifies interest in:

- *spaces for dialogue*: safe spaces for learning with and from others, through discourse and dialogue, through articulating what might otherwise remain tacit, contrasting and contesting interpretations of the world, etc.
- *spaces for critical reflection*: where unexamined assumptions, beliefs, and experiences, or otherwise tacit knowledge, can be thought about and subjected to critique—either personally or with others (Jandric and Boras 2015; Jones 2015)
- *spaces for shared experience/narration or for information flows/bonds*: Wittel (2001) has suggested that social relations are becoming increasingly instrumental and functional, based on informational rather than narrational bonds. That is, they are based on just-in-time exchange of data, rather than shared experiences and common histories. This is not inevitable. Valuable spaces can be made that function to reinforce community and shared identity, and to document shared experience. But this is not a trivial task. As Adams suggests:

> Our long history of trying to engineer closeness and nearness through media, communication, and transportation technologies has indeed conquered all distance. Yet these techniques have not given rise to genuine nearness at all, but ironically, to its short-circuiting, dispersal, and shallow imitation.
>
> (2014, p. 1)

- *spaces for surveillance*: what people choose to bring into the open becomes visible to all, including to those who would use what they then see to buttress their power
- *bounded spaces*: without bounding, the sense of direction can be weak or anomie can set in; too tightly bound, and scope for exploration may be endangered; tight bounding can manifest itself in a number of ways—a strictly circumscribed curriculum, tight limits on what is permitted and valued, etc.

In sum, we can think of desirable and undesirable qualities of spaces of possibility, within which—for whatever reason—dialogue may co-exist with surveillance, or freedom with anomie. Understanding how such spaces evolve, and may be reconfigured, is part of understanding how to enable networked learning.

Approaches to Analysis and Design for Networked Learning

As we mentioned at the start of this chapter, the main reason we think it is important to have a richer repertoire of constructs for understanding learning networks and networked learning is so that we can do a better job of analyzing what is occurring, so that we can design enhancements. As Jos Boys (Chapter 5) puts it, we need to:

> move beyond simplistic understandings about how to improve learning as just a case of implementing better technologies or innovative learning spaces. By getting under the surface of the multiple spaces of different participants (both human and non-human) as they

enact the everyday social and material practices of learning and subject, I suggest that we can produce much more detailed and sophisticated understandings of how we learn, and that we can take better account of the complexities of our everyday entanglements across both conceptual spaces and actual—situated—places.

(Boys, p. 70)

In this section, we tackle this topic at two levels. The first level concerns ways of understanding the relationships between things that can be designed and the activities in which people ("learners") engage. The second level is perhaps a meta-level: it is concerned with ways of integrating processes of analysis and design. On both levels, various alternative approaches exist and many have merits. But we will focus on two examples: the ACAD framework and design anthropology.

We should note that not all approaches to networked learning give a serious place to design. In the early days of networked learning, when most interaction was through text-based group discussions, design did not feature very strongly. Instead, the focus was on pedagogy. What students experienced depended quite closely on how their teachers enacted their role, how they said what they said, what they encouraged students to do, and so on. Suggestions about tasks to tackle, or how to divide work up so that different groups tackled different tasks, could be made "on-the-fly." The complex mixtures of places, things, and human activity now constituting networked learning make design essential—though we might argue that the need for design has simply become more obvious as more aspects of networked learning have become visible. What students did at home or at work was not always so salient in the past.

Activity-Centered Analysis and Design (ACAD)

As we explained in Chapter 1, ACAD gives a central place to *activity*—what the participants in a learning network are actually doing. This is not to say that activity is easy to observe, capture, or understand. But each person in a network is doing stuff, is experiencing, is seeing, hearing, thinking, talking, reflecting, and so on. This activity is causally related to what they learn—again, not in any straightforwardly observable or predictable way, but (we assert) learning emerges in and from activity. This activity is situated, by which we mean that "every course of action depends in essential ways on its material and social circumstances" (Suchman 2007, p. 70). What is done and what is learned are influenced in sometimes subtle and sometimes powerful ways by qualities of place, tools, and other artifacts that come to hand, layouts of buildings—or screens—that nudge movement or suggest appropriate actions, and by the presence, availability, and actions of other people. To say that human activity is materially and socially situated is to say more than this, but the key point is to warn against an overly mentalistic or rational account that sees action as, essentially, the execution of pre-formed plans, hatched in the mind of the actor.

Ashe and Dohn (Chapter 2) put it nicely:

designed elements in [places or] spaces for networked learning do not, of themselves, ensure certain activities will (or will not) occur; rather, designed elements can contribute to the likelihood of a particular activity taking place. The activity is not determined by the designed objects or by the learners, but becomes a relationship between both.

So what designers can do is design for the complexity and dynamicity of the way focus is placed, *taking into account the way context develops in interaction between learners and artifacts*, whilst accepting that whatever features they design may be taken up in different ways by the learners—or not taken up at all.

(Ashe and Dohn, p. 23, emphasis added)

Design for networked learning has to be seen as an indirect process (Goodyear 1997, 2000; Jones, Dirckinck-Homfeld, and Lindstrom 2006; Jones 2015), though it sometimes has elements that work quite directly. This is particularly the case with what we have called "epistemic design" or "task design" (Carvalho and Goodyear 2014; and see Chapter 1). Tasks—which are ways of proposing good things to do—can sometimes be seen as imperatives and sometimes as subtle hints. "Get this essay in by Friday" is quite direct. "Spend some time exploring these exhibits and reflect on what they might have meant to their creators" is less directly shaping of action. And sometimes, designed tasks can only be uncovered by analyzing action: a way of working out the meaning of what people are doing together is to infer some implied task.

So design for networked learning is forward-oriented, but it is also informed by analysis of what exists and what has happened. When a learning network has taken on a life of its own, analysis and design circle around—temporally structured by periods when some significant redesign is possible (Dimitriadis and Goodyear 2013; Goodyear and Dimitriadis 2013). Design is also distributed. Typically, all the people in a learning network will contribute in some way to design—whether customizing their own set of tools and resources or shaping what is available to others. That said, it is common to have a small group of people who have some responsibility for the life of the network, and who can play a more substantial role in (re)design. And then, many of the elements that come together in a learning network are assembled from what already exists—things designed and created by others who are distant in time and space, and who may have no knowledge of how their creations are taken up, reconfigured, or repurposed by others. (For example, mobile phones and tablets are not designed specifically for networked learning. The same may be true of many other artifacts that become enrolled in a learning network.)

Analysis for the purposes of informing design for networked learning can then be seen as a process concerned with describing how the network functions, and—because we are choosing to analyze in network terms—how diverse elements are connected together, how they are produced and used, what flows through the network, and how capabilities and activities emerge in and from these patterns of connection.

People learning in place-based networked spaces are affected by their relationships with things. People think *through* things, even if they are often unaware of how things shape their minds; things influence emotions and the enactment and formation of human cognition (Malafouris and Renfrew 2010).

For example, in Chapter 6, Gourlay and Oliver's analysis of personal study spaces focuses on discovering where, when, and with what students studied. One of these personalized study spaces is captured in Yuki's image of an iPad on the edge of a bath, accompanied by her description of the bath as a good place to read. In looking at the image, one can easily empathize with Yuki's description of this as a peaceful place to focus on reading, and one cannot help but wonder how being in a bath—surrounded by the warm water, the feeling of containment—whilst holding an iPad (with the plastic enveloping the device) may affect Yuki's studying and cognitive processes. How do the qualities of this place, so configured, affect thought and feeling? How might they be said to help shape the mind? Similarly, the work of Gallagher, Lamb, and Bayne (Chapter 7) sets out to investigate the personal study spaces of "distance online" students, through use of the students' constructed representations of their spaces. We see a range of spaces negotiated from within domestic settings, with couches, beds, and cushions salient: "the construction of study space is a complex negotiation between the private and the shared, the sounded and the silent, the bounded and the fluid" (Gallagher et al., p. 97).

How should we draw connections between the qualities of the materials in these places and the students' thinking and learning? In ACAD, we talk about students (re)configuring tasks, toolsets, and environments. Gourlay and Oliver (Chapter 6) provide some good examples of this—not just the reconfiguration of things in one place, but also connecting places in sequence, to map onto phases of an activity.

> What also became apparent was the way in which movement between these spaces formed part of the rhythm of studying; certain spaces were strung together in sequences (e.g. reading on the bus, accessing files on a computer in the library, searching for books on the library shelves, etc.), and these were often associated with specific phases of studying (e.g. working in the library when looking for resources at an early stage of writing an essay, visiting a field site when undertaking empirical studies, etc.).
>
> (Gourlay and Oliver, p. 80)

Ravelli and McMurtrie (Chapter 9) also refer to these regularities in their analysis of a university library—distinguishing between the staccato rhythms of activity in a conventional library and the gentler waves/flows in new learning spaces (p. 128).

Another form of (re)configuring space/place is singled out in Gallagher et al. (Chapter 7)—"spatial-acoustic self-determination"—there are times when one needs to be able to defend against "sonic trespass" in order to focus on study. But also, especially with increasing use of such things as Khan Academy videoclips, video-recorded lectures, and so on, in domestic and public spaces, one develops a "hyper-awareness of oneself as audible" (p. 91).

Part of the point of the ACAD framework is to encourage exploration of relations that constitute the physically situated character of learning activity: relations between things and people, broadly conceived. It therefore sits comfortably alongside ideas in the emerging field of *design anthropology*.

Design Anthropology

Design anthropology involves a distinctive style of knowing: one that sees the production of knowledge as going beyond thinking and reasoning—to also include practices of acting on the world (Otto and Smith 2013). In combining two different traditions—design *and* anthropology— different objectives and methods are also blended. On the one hand, *design* involves the creation of contextual knowledge to address specific problems; it is both solution-oriented and practical; and, on the other hand, *anthropology* is concerned with theorization about the context of usage and the cultural meaning of things (Gunn, Otto, and Smith 2013). In bringing these two traditions together, design anthropologists strive to find ways of theorizing and understanding a given phenomenon, but within a forward oriented perspective that works to move concepts beyond analysis and description only, toward generating design concepts (Otto and Smith 2013). This is one of the ways in which we imagine that the role of "translational designer" or "translational developer" could be approached (see Ellis and Fisher, Chapter 16).

Design involves transforming knowledge and ideas into a (material/digital) product or situation in a process that engages both an "intellectual component" but with also a "mechanical or bodily component" of execution (Gatt and Ingold 2013; Simonsen et al. 2014). Schön (1983, 1992) refers to designing as a reflective conversation with materials, or as knowing-in-action, a process that involves combining reflection and experimentation, connecting thought and action in the moment. Design ideas rarely spring fully formed into a designer's mind. Ideas are more likely to build on other ideas, with designers drawing upon "a repertoire of precedents, of remembered images and recollections of other objects" as they work to shape a "coherent, practicable and attractive form to the concept" (Cross 2010, p. 19).

Anthropologists remind us that the properties of materials, however, are not fixed but instead they are processual and relational (Ingold 2011). Things around us change, as the substances of which they are formed mix and react to life; for example, a line of ink that fades from a piece of paper as time goes by, wood that degenerates and decomposes, and so on. It is not really possible to objectively determine or describe the properties of objects, instead Ingold advises us that the properties of objects are to be practically experienced—"what happens to them as they flow, mix and mutate" (2011, p. 30). Thus, designers design in a *world in motion*, and they need to be aware of the constantly evolving nature of things, using their creative abilities to respond "to the ever-changing circumstances in their lives" (Gatt and Ingold 2013, p. 145). This necessarily involves "finding the grain of the world's becoming—the way it wants to go—but also in bending it to an evolving purpose . . . giving direction rather than specifying end points" (Gatt and Ingold 2013, p. 144).

Endnote

1. One of the difficulties involved in making and sustaining distinctions between "place" and "space" is that there is no "place" equivalent of the adjective "spatial."

References

Adams, C., 2014. *In search of the secret body of the digital.* Keynote address at the International Human Sciences Research Conference, St. Francis Xavier University, Antigonish, Nova Scotia.

Adams, J., Faust, K., and Lovasi, G. S., 2012. Capturing context: Integrating spatial and social network analyses. *Social Networks,* 34(1), 1–5. (Introduction to special issue). doi:http://dx.doi.org/10.1016/j.socnet.2011.10.007

Alexander, C., 1979. *The timeless way of building.* New York: Oxford University Press.

Barad, K., 2003. Posthumanist performativity: Toward an understanding of how matter comes to matter. *Signs: Journal of Women in Culture and Society,* 28(3), 801–831.

Barsalou, L. W., 2010. Grounded cognition: Past, present, and future. *Topics in Cognitive Science,* 2(4), 716–724.

Borghi, A. M. and Pecher, D., 2012. Introduction to the special topic embodied and grounded cognition. *Embodied and grounded cognition,* ebook: Frontiers Media SA. [online]. Available from: www.frontiersin.org/books/Embodied_and_grounded_cognition/52 [Accessed November 14, 2015].

Carvalho, L. and Goodyear, P., eds., 2014. *The architecture of productive learning networks.* New York: Routledge.

Casey, E., 2009. *Getting back into place: Toward a new understanding of the place-world.* Bloomington: Indiana University Press.

Clark, A., 2003. *Natural-born cyborgs: Minds, technologies, and the future of human intelligence.* Oxford: Oxford University Press.

Clark, A., 2008. *Supersizing the mind: Embodiment, action, and cognitive extension.* Oxford: Oxford University Press.

Clough, T., 2007. Introduction. In T. Clough and J. Halley, eds., *The affective turn: Theorizing the social* (pp. 1–33). Durham, NC: Duke University Press.

Coyne, R., 2010. *The tuning of place: Sociable spaces and pervasive digital media.* Cambridge, MA: MIT Press.

Cross, N., 2010. *Design thinking: Understanding how designers think and work.* Oxford: Berg.

de Souza e Silva, A. and Sutko, D., 2011. Theorizing locative technologies through philosophies of the virtual. *Communication Theory,* 21, 23–42.

Dimitriadis, Y. and Goodyear, P., 2013. Forward-oriented design for learning: Illustrating the approach. *Research in Learning Technology,* 21. doi: http://dx.doi.org/10.3402/rlt.v21i0.20290 [online]. Available from: www.researchinlearningtechnology.net/index.php/rlt/article/view/20290 [Accessed November 17, 2015].

Dohn, N., 2009. Affordances revisited: Articulating a Merleau-Pontian view. *International Journal of Computer-Supported Collaborative Learning,* 4(2), 151–170. doi:10.1007/s11412-009-9062-z

Dourish, P. and Bell, G., 2011. *Divining a digital future: Mess and mythology in ubiquitous computing.* Cambridge, MA: MIT Press.

Dreyfus, H. L., 2009. *On the Internet,* 2nd edition. London: Routledge.

Farman, J., 2012. *Mobile interface theory: Embodied space and locative media.* London: Routledge.

Fenwick, T., Edwards, R., and Sawchuk, P., 2011. *Emerging approaches to educational research: tracing the sociomaterial.* Abingdon, UK: Routledge.

Gatt, C. and Ingold, T., 2013. From description to correspondence: Anthropology in real time. In: W. Gunn, T. Otto, and R. C. Smith, eds., *Design anthropology: Theory and practice* (pp. 139–158). London: Bloomsbury Academic.

Gibson, J., 1977. The theory of affordances. In: R. Shaw and J. Bransford, eds., *Perceiving, acting, and knowing: Toward an ecological psychology* (pp. 67–82). Hillsdale, NJ: Lawrence Erlbaum.

Goodyear, P., 1997. The ergonomics of learning environments: Learner-managed learning and new technology. *Creacion de materiales para la innovacion educativas con nuevas tecnologias* (pp. 7–17). Malaga: Instituto de Ciencias de la Educacion. Universidad de Malaga.

Goodyear, P., 2000. Environments for lifelong learning: Ergonomics, architecture and educational design. In: J. M. Spector and T. Anderson, eds., *Integrated and holistic perspectives on learning. Instruction & technology: Understanding complexity* (pp. 1–18). Dordrecht, The Netherlands: Kluwer Academic Publishers.

Goodyear, P. and Carvalho, L., 2013. The analysis of complex learning environments. In: H. Beetham and R. Sharpe, eds., *Rethinking pedagogy for a digital age: Designing and delivering e-learning* (pp. 49–63). New York: RoutledgeFalmer.

Goodyear, P. and Dimitriadis, Y., 2013. *In medias res*: Reframing design for learning. *Research in Learning Technology*, 21. doi:http://dx.doi.org/10.3402/rlt.v21i0.19909 [online]. Available from: www.researchin learningtechnology.net/index.php/rlt/article/view/19909 [Accessed November 17, 2015].

Gunn, W., Otto, T., and Smith, R. C., 2013. *Design anthropology: Theory and practice.* London: Bloomsbury Academic.

Hafermalz, E., and Riemer, K., 2015. *The question of materiality: Mattering in the network society.* Paper presented at the 23rd European Conference on Information Systems, May 26–29, Munster.

Haraway, D., 1991. *Simians, cyborgs, and women: The reinvention of nature.* London: Free Association Books.

Hodder, I., 2012. *Entangled: An archaeology of the relationships between humans and things.* Chichester: Wiley-Blackwell.

Hodder, I., 2014. The entanglements of humans and things: A long-term view. *New Literary History*, 45(1), 19–36.

Hodgson, V., 1997. New technology and learning: Accepting the challenge. In: R. Burgoyne and M. Reynolds, eds., *Management learning: Integrating perspectives in theory and practice* (pp. 215–225). London: Sage.

Hutchins, E., 2010. Cognitive ecology. *Topics in Cognitive Science*, 2, 705–715.

Ingold, T., 2011. *Being alive: Essays on movement, knowledge and description.* Abingdon, UK: Routledge.

Jandric, P. and Boras, D., 2015. *Critical learning in digital networks.* Dordrecht, The Netherlands: Springer.

Jones, C., 2004. Networks and learning: Communities, practices and the metaphor of networks. *ALT-J: Journal of the Association for Learning Technology*, 12(1), 81–93.

Jones, C., 2015. *Networked learning: An educational paradigm for the age of digital networks.* Dordrecht, The Netherlands: Springer.

Jones, C., Dirckinck-Homfeld, L., and Lindstrom, B., 2006. A relational, indirect, meso-level approach to CSCL design in the next decade. *International Journal of Computer-Supported Collaborative Learning*, 1(1), 35–56.

Kahneman, D., 2011. *Thinking, fast and slow.* New York: Farrar, Straus and Giroux.

Kirsh, D., 2013. Embodied cognition and the magical future of interaction design. *ACM Transactions on Computer-Human Interaction*, 20(1), 1–30. doi:10.1145/2442106.2442109

Knappett, C., ed., 2013. *Network analysis in archaeology: New approaches to regional interaction.* Oxford: Oxford University Press.

Kozel, S., 2013. Sinews of ubiquity: A corporeal ethics for ubiquitous computing. In: U. Ekman, ed., *Throughout: Art and culture emerging with ubiquitous computing* (pp. 337–350). Cambridge, MA: MIT Press.

Kress, G. and Van Leeuwen, T., 2006. *Reading images: The grammar of visual design*, 2nd edition. New York: Routledge.

Krippendorff, K., 2006. *The semantic turn: A new foundation for design.* Boca Raton. FL: CRC Press.

Land, R., 2005. Embodiment and risk in cyberspace education. In: R. Land and S. Bayne, eds., *Education in cyberspace* (pp. 149–164). London: Routledge.

Latour, B., 2005. *Reassembling the social: An introduction to actor-network-theory.* Oxford: Oxford University Press.

Lyotard, J. F., 1991. *The inhuman: Reflections on time.* Cambridge: Polity Press.

Malafouris, L. and Renfrew, C., 2010. The cognitive life of things: Archaeology, material engagement and the extended mind. In L. Malafouris and C. Renfrew, eds., *The cognitive life of things: Recasting the boundaries of the mind* (pp. 1–12). Cambridge: McDonald Institute for Archaeological Research.

McCullough, M., 2005. *Digital ground: Architecture, pervasive computing, and environmental knowing.* Cambridge, MA: MIT Press.

McCullough, M., 2013. *Ambient commons: Attention in the age of embodied information.* Cambridge, MA: MIT Press.

Merleau-Ponty, M., 1945/2014. *Phenomenology of perception* (D. Landes, trans.). Abingdon, UK: Routledge.

Otto, T. and Smith, R. C., 2013, Design anthropology: A distinct style of knowing. In: W. Gunn, T. Otto, and R. C. Smith, eds., *Design anthropology: Theory and practice* (pp. 1–32). London: Bloomsbury Academic.

Schön, D., 1983. *The reflective practitioner: How professionals think in action.* London: Temple Smith.

Schön, D., 1992. Design as reflective conversation with the materials of a design situation. *Research in Engineering Design,* 3, 131–147.

Shepard, M., ed., 2011. *Sentient city: Ubiquitous computing, architecture, and the future of urban space.* Cambridge, MA: MIT Press.

Simonsen, J., Svabo, C., Strandvad, S., Samson, K., Hertzum, M., and Hansen, O., 2014. *Situated design methods.* Cambridge, MA: MIT Press.

Sindbœk, S., 2013. Broken links and black boxes: Material affiliations and contextual network synthesis in the Viking world. In: C. Knappett, ed., *Network analysis in archaeology: New approaches to regional interaction* (pp. 71–94). Oxford: Oxford University Press.

Suchman, L., 1987. *Plans and situated actions: The problem of human-machine communication.* Cambridge: Cambridge University Press.

Suchman, L., 2007. *Human-machine reconfigurations: Plans and situated actions,* 2nd edition. Cambridge: Cambridge University Press.

Van Leeuwen, T., 2005. *Introducing social semiotics.* New York: Routledge.

Wittel, A., 2001, Towards a network sociality. *Theory, Culture and Society,* 18(6), 51–76.

AUTHOR BIOGRAPHIES

David Ashe is a Postdoctoral Research Associate at the Centre for Research on Learning and Innovation at the University of Sydney, Australia. He is a member of Peter Goodyear's ARC Laureate Project team (Learning, Technology and Design: Architectures for Productive Networked Learning) and works with the university's STEM Teacher Enrichment Academy. David's Ph.D. research explored school students' thinking when faced with "sustainability" issues and investigated the interface between school students' everyday and scientific reasoning. He holds a degree in Agricultural Engineering, is a qualified Mathematics and Science teacher, and has spent many years in the information technology industry. David is currently investigating pre-service teachers' understanding and implementation of "inquiry science"; observing epistemic barriers between teachers' intentions and practice.

Leslie Ashor is a San Diego, California based architect who has focused exclusively on laboratory design for over 15 years. The previous 15 years encompassed a wide variety of commercial architecture project types. Her passion is creating world-class, highly sustainable, innovative, flexible, and adaptable laboratory solutions for teaching, research, and industry clients. After designing multiple, large-scale teaching laboratories, she has been conducting research on the "Super Lab" notion, design, and effectiveness. Leslie led the laboratory design efforts for the recently completed South Australia Health and Medical Research Institute (SAHMRI) in Adelaide, which has received the highest honors in the global Lab of the Year awards.

Sian Bayne is Professor of Digital Education in the School of Education at the University of Edinburgh. She convenes the Digital Cultures and Education research group, and teaches on the M.Sc. in Digital Education. Her research interests revolve around educational change and teaching practice as digital cultures become pervasive. Current particular interests are around critical post-humanism and online education, and multimodal academic literacies.

Mark Bilandzic has a Media Computer Science and Technology Management background, and specialized in User Experience (UX) and Design Research. He studied at Ludwig-Maximilians-Universität München, Technische Universität München, and University of California, Berkeley, and completed a Ph.D. at the Urban Informatics Research Lab at Queensland University of Technology, Brisbane. He has worked on digital product development projects in academic, freelance, and organizational settings, including Siemens/Croatia, Infosys Technologies/India, Computershare/ Germany, State Library of Queensland/Australia, and Allianz Deutschland AG/Germany. Mark's work focuses on user-centered research to inform the design and development of innovative digital products that augment social interactions and experiences in the physical world. His Ph.D. thesis, in particular, presents a new approach and prototype system to enhance connected learning amongst users in public libraries and collaboration spaces. Mark's research has been published in conference proceedings, journals, and book chapters across various disciplines, including Human–Computer Interaction, Community Informatics, Library Studies, Learning Environments, and Technology Management. Find a full list of publications at https://kavasmlikon.wordpress.com/publications

Nina Bonderup Dohn is an Associate Professor in Humanistic Information Science at the Department of Design and Communication, University of Southern Denmark. She holds an M.A. in Philosophy and Physics from Aarhus University and a Ph.D. in Learning Theory from Aalborg University. In 2013 she was a Visiting Scholar for six months at the Centre for Research on Computer Supported Learning and Cognition, The University of Sydney. Before that, she has twice been a Visiting Scholar for seven months at the Department of Philosophy, University of California, Berkeley, in 2000–2001 and again in 2009–2010. Her main research areas integrate epistemology, learning sciences, web communication, and technology-mediated learning with a focus on the role of tacit knowledge. She has published extensively in Danish and English on philosophical and pedagogical issues within knowledge theory, web 2.0, ICT-mediated learning, and teaching and learning in higher education. Nina's webpage is available at www.sdu.dk/staff/nina

Kate Booth is a Senior Lecturer in Computer Network Systems at the University of Salford. She has over 25 years' experience in education, mostly as a member of academic staff, having started off as a physicist and then moving into the area of computer networking approximately 15 years ago. She has a particular interest in network security and public engagement and has developed activities combining the two to help students and the general public understand the concepts and context of security. She takes an active interest in the increased participation of women and people from a Black and Minority Ethnic background in Science and Engineering, and has conducted research in this area. Kate is a member of the Institution of Engineering and Technology, and the British Computer Society. She is also a member of the Institute for Scientific and Technical Communication.

Jos Boys is currently an Academic Developer at the University of New South Wales, Sydney. With a background in architecture she has taught at various universities globally, and also worked as a researcher and community-based design activist. Dr. Boys is author of *Building Better Universities; Strategies, Spaces, Technologies* (Routledge 2014) and *Towards Creative Learning Spaces: Re-Thinking the Architecture of Post-Compulsory Education* (Routledge 2010), and has contributed to many other volumes. Her main interests are in the interconnections between space, learning, and social and material practices.

Lucila Carvalho is a Research Fellow in the Centre for Research on Learning and Innovation at the University of Sydney. She is a member of Peter Goodyear's ARC Laureate Project team, within which she leads the research on analyzing learning networks. Her Ph.D. research investigated the sociology of learning in/about design and ways of practically implementing principles from the sociology of knowledge in e-learning design. She has studied and carried out research in Australia, New Zealand, the UK, and Brazil. She has presented her work at various international conferences in the fields of education, sociology, systemic functional linguistics, design, and software engineering. She is the Co-Editor (with Peter Goodyear) of *The Architecture of Productive Learning Networks* (Routledge 2014).

Shane Dawson is a Professor of Learning Analytics and Director of the Teaching Innovation Unit at the University of South Australia. His primary research area centers on the analysis of learner trace data derived from user engagements with various educational and social technologies. Shane is a Co-Editor of the *International Journal for Learning Analytics* and a founding executive member of the Society for Learning Analytics Research.

Maarten de Laat is Professor of Professional Development in Social Networks at the Welten Institute of the Open University of the Netherlands. He coordinates research on Networked Learning Practices. He has published and presented his research extensively in international research journals, books, and conferences. He has given several invited keynotes at international conferences. He has been appointed a Visiting Professor at the University of South Australia in Adelaide. He is Co-Chair of the International Networked Learning Conference (NLC) as well as Co-Chair of the minitrack Social Media & Learning at HICSS (Hawaiian International Conference on System Sciences). He is Co-Editor (with Vivien Hodgson, David McConnell, and Thomas Ryberg) of *Design, Experience and Practice of Networked Learning* (Springer 2014).

Robert A. Ellis is an Associate Professor at the University of Sydney, where he is a member of the Centre for Research on Learning and Innovation. Robert has extensive professional experience of the management of physical learning spaces and e-learning systems in higher education. He has also been a chief investigator on four major research projects funded by the Australian Research Council. He currently leads a large ARC project on *Modelling Complex Learning Spaces*. He is the author of *Students' Experiences of e-Learning in Higher Education: The Ecology of Sustainable Innovation* (Routledge 2010, with Peter Goodyear) and is also editor of Springer's new book series on Understanding Teaching-Learning Practice.

Kenn Fisher is Associate Professor in the Faculty of Architecture, Building and Planning at the University of Melbourne in Australia. Kenn is recognized as one of the leading learning environment specialists practicing internationally. As a consultant to the OECD and UNESCO he has practiced in Australia, Asia, the Middle East, and Europe. He is multi-skilled in a range of disciplines having practiced in all education sectors as a teacher and academic, a strategic facility and campus planner, and as a project, facility, and design manager. Kenn is a Chief Investigator on the Australian Research Council funded project *Evaluating 21st Century Learning Environments* and a Partner Investigator on the *Modelling Complex Learning Spaces Project*—also funded by ARC.

Marcus Foth is Founder and Director of the Urban Informatics Research Lab, Research Leader of the School of Design, and Professor in Interactive & Visual Design, Creative Industries Faculty at Queensland University of Technology. Marcus' research focuses on the relationships between people, place, and technology. He leads a cross-disciplinary team that develops practical approaches to complex urban problems. He adopts human–computer interaction and design methodologies to build engagement around emerging issues facing our cities. Marcus has authored and co-authored over 130 publications in journals, edited books, and conference proceedings and received over AUS$4 million in national competitive grants and industry funding. He received a Queensland Young Tall Poppy Science Award 2013, and was inducted by the planning, design, and development site Planetizen to the world's top 25 leading thinkers and innovators in the field of urban planning and technology. He can be reached at m.foth@qut.edu.au as well as @sunday9pm on Twitter.

Michael Sean Gallagher is an Assistant Professor at Hankuk University of Foreign Studies in Seoul, South Korea. He is also currently a doctoral student at University College London and Director and Co-Founder of Panoply Digital, a consultancy firm specializing in mobile learning in developing nations. His research focus is on developing mobile environments and communities to support academic practice in the humanities in higher education. He is also researching new pedagogies and theoretical positions to support mobile learning, particularly how mobile technology both evidences and structures learning activity into learning trajectories. Aside from mobile learning, he is most interested in online learning, multimodality, and open learning.

Peter Goodyear is Professor of Education and Australian Laureate Fellow at the University of Sydney. He is the founding Co-Director of the university's Centre for Research on Learning and Innovation. He has been carrying out research in the field of learning and technology since the early 1980s and has published nine books and over 100 journal articles and book chapters. His most recent books are *The Architecture of Productive Learning Networks* (Routledge 2014, co-edited with Lucila Carvalho), *Handbook of Design in Educational Technology* (Routledge 2013, co-edited with Rose Luckin and colleagues), *Technology-Enhanced Learning: Design Patterns and Pattern Languages* (Sense 2013, co-edited with Simeon Retalis), and *Students' Experiences of e-Learning in Higher Education: The Ecology of Sustainable Innovation* (Routledge 2010, with Robert Ellis).

Lesley Gourlay is Head of the Department of Culture, Communication and Media, and Director of the Academic Writing Centre at UCL Institute of Education. Her background is in Applied Linguistics, and her current research interests include academic literacies, multimodality, and digital mediation in higher education, focusing on meaning making, textual practices, digital literacies, and multimodality. Dr. Gourlay's recent publications have focused on the relationships between sociomaterial perspectives and practices in higher education, with an emphasis on the role of textuality and meaning making. She is a member of the Executive Editorial Board of the journal *Teaching in Higher Education*.

Tina Hinton is a Senior Lecturer in Pharmacology at the University of Sydney. She teaches Pharmacology to Medical Science, Science, Pharmacy, and Medicine students across undergraduate and graduate programs, and is involved in biomedical sciences learning and teaching leadership and governance at discipline, school, and faculty levels. Dr. Hinton is also closely involved in the design of new learning spaces on campus. Dr. Hinton's primary research area is neuropharmacology. More recently, however, her research focuses on complex learning environments for biomedical sciences and the influences on learner experience and learner participation in valued practices and learning. Dr. Hinton achieved the Australasian Society of Clinical and Experimental Pharmacologists and Toxicologists Early Educator Award in 2012. In 2014 she successfully obtained the Sydney Medical School Academic Excellence Award for Systems that Achieve Collective Excellence for the work of the Charles Perkins Centre Learning and Teaching Team in the collaborative design of the Charles Perkins Centre learning spaces.

Vivien Hodgson is Professor of Networked Management Learning at Lancaster University Management School, UK, and guest Obel Chair at e-Learning Lab, University of Aalborg, Denmark. She is the Co-Editor of the Springer book series on Researching Networked Learning and recently stood down as one of the founding co-chairs of the international bi-annual conference series Networked Learning. She is currently leading a cross-faculty initiative supporting and encouraging staff to develop innovative pedagogical designs and online spaces that adopt and use digital learning resources and activities across a range of Management School programs at UG and PG level.

James Lamb is a Ph.D. student in the School of Education at the University of Edinburgh. His research interests include multimodal assessment and the learning environments of online students. He tutors on the M.Sc. in Digital Education, contributing to courses in online assessment and digital learning environments.

Nigel Linge is Professor of Telecommunications at the University of Salford with over 25 years' experience as a member of academic staff. He is an electronic engineer by profession who specializes in telecommunication networks and their applications and has research interests that cover location and context aware services, multimedia visitor guides, communication and routing protocols, ultra-high definition television, intelligent and adaptive networks, domestic energy monitoring, and network design. He also takes a keen interest in telecommunications heritage and is active in public and schools engagement. Nigel is a Chartered Engineer and Chartered IT Professional, a Fellow of both the Institution of Engineering and Technology and British Computer Society and a member of the Institute of Telecommunication Professionals. Nigel can be contacted at n.linge@salford.ac.uk or @nigellinge on Twitter.

Robert J. McMurtrie is a Ph.D. Graduate of the University of New South Wales, and was awarded the Faculty of Arts and Social Sciences Best Thesis Prize for 2013, as well as the University Medal for his Honors Degree in Linguistics (2008). He has an extensive teaching background in English Language, Academic and Business Literacy, Linguistics, and Multimodal Discourse Analysis. He now teaches Academic and Design Communication at the University of Technology, Sydney.

Martin Oliver is Professor of Education and Technology at the UCL Institute of Education. He is based in the London Knowledge Lab, a research center focused on the future of learning with digital technologies. His research focuses on the use of technology in higher education, including areas such as curriculum design and the student experience, and with a particular focus on theory and methodology.

David Parsons is a Royal Academy of Engineering Visiting Professor at the University of Salford where his practical experience informs both teaching and research. He retired from Barclays Bank in late 1993 as Group Director—Advanced Technology Research after a 35-year career in branch banking and computing. Since "early retirement" he has worked with many other universities and organizations including the European Commission, EPSRC, and the British Computer Society. His research interests include the practical application of high performance computing and networking. Public engagement activities focus on raising public, including schools', awareness of the history and potential of computational and communications technologies. David is a Fellow of the British Computer Society, Fellow of the Royal Geographical Society, Member of the Institution of Engineering and Technology, Professional Member of the ACM, IEEE, the Institute of Telecommunications Professionals, the World Future Society, and a Chartered IT Professional.

Ana Pinto is currently completing a Ph.D. at the Centre for Research on Learning and Innovation at the University of Sydney. Her research focuses on analysis of and design for digitally mediated networked learning. Ana's research interests include educational design, technology-enhanced learning, new literacies, and adult literacy education. Her long professional experience has revolved around literacy and designing, developing, and delivering training for teachers. Ana's academic background encompasses educational psychology, pedagogy, language and literacy, and computing studies. She received her M.A. in information technology in education from the University of Sydney in 2001.

Philip Poronnik is Professor of Biomedical Science in the School of Medical Science in the Sydney Medical School at the University of Sydney. He graduated from Sydney University with a Ph.D. in Electrophysiology, after which he worked as an ARC Research Fellow in Physiology and in the renal research laboratory at Royal North Shore Hospital. In 2003 he moved to the School of Biomedical Sciences at the University of Queensland where he was Professor of Physiology. In 2009 he moved to RMIT as head of the Pharmaceutical Sciences program, returning to Sydney in 2013. He was awarded the UQ Research Foundation Excellence award in 2005, and the Roberts award of the Australian Physiological Society for excellence in teaching in 2010. In addition to his basic research program, he is also very active in the tertiary science curriculum where he is the Head of the Biosciences Education Australia Network.

Louise J. Ravelli is Associate Professor of Communication in the School of the Arts and Media at the University of New South Wales. She researches communication in professional contexts, using social-semiotic approaches, including systemic functional linguistics and multimodal discourse analysis, to enhance communication outcomes. Her books include *Museum Texts: Communication Frameworks* (Routledge 2006) and *Doctoral Writing in the Creative and Performing Arts* (Libri 2014, with Brian Paltridge and Sue Starfield).

Juliet Sprake is a Senior Lecturer and **Peter Rogers** is the Senior Computing Tutor in the Design Department at Goldsmiths, University of London. Juliet and Peter teach on a range of programs and are members of the Prospect & Innovation Studio research unit. They have worked as creative partners since 2005 developing projects in geolocated learning, participatory sensing, and designing alternative methods for navigating the urban landscape. An important aspect of their work is using technologies to sense and record change in the material fabric of our built environment so that buildings can be described as "learning-enabled." Juliet has written about some of this in her book, *Learning-through-Touring* (Springer 2012). They enjoy dabbling in crowd theory and making interactive digital activities for finding ways into, up, and around the city.

Maree Stenglin is a Social Semiotician who has been theorizing 3D space since 1999. Her interest in this area was sparked by her first hand experience of working at the Australian Museum and Djamu Gallery, especially as a member of the project team developing the *Indigenous Australians* exhibition. Since the completion of her doctoral thesis on 3D space, she has analyzed a range of sites (exhibitions, homes, restaurants, a winery, universities), and has recently been theorizing hospital birth spaces. She has co-edited a volume on multimodality, *Semiotic Margins: Meaning in Multimodalities* (Continuum 2010, with Shooshana Dreyfus and Sue Hood), and is currently writing a book, *Meanings We Inhabit: A Social Semiotic Grammar of 3D Space* with Professor James Martin, The University of Sydney. Her research interests include multimodality, critical discourse analysis, and multiliteracies.

Pippa Yeoman is an Ethnographer with a particular interest in describing and theorizing the mutually shaping relations between learning activity and the learning environment. She is a Postdoctoral Research Associate on Peter Goodyear's ARC Laureate Project, based in the Centre for Research on Learning and Innovation at the University of Sydney. Pippa has presented her work at a number of international academic conferences, to professional audiences in Sydney, and acts as a juror for the annual Australasian CEFPI (Council of Educational Facility Planners International) awards.

INDEX